YOUNG
REFLECTIONS

ACKNOWLEDGEMENTS

The publishers and editors are grateful for the efforts of the following
individuals in making this anthology possible:

Natasha Jackson, Peter Jones,
Joanne Sydenham and Stephen Sydenham

YOUNG REFLECTIONS

An Anthology
of verse from the
younger generation

Vanessa Sydenham
Editor

Steve Sydenham
Publisher and Managing Editor

ISBN 0-9550329-2-X

Published by
Poetry In Print
PO Box 141
Paignton
TQ3 1YY

Printed In Scotland
by Bell & Bain Ltd., Glasgow

INTRODUCTION

Welcome to our twelfth anthology of verse specifically for children and young adults. This came about as a direct result of a competition open to schools and we sincerely thank teachers and parents for their enthusiasm and for helping to make the competition and the anthology such a success.

Congratulations to the winners of the competition and to all of our young contributors, well done, a superb effort by all concerned. Most of the poems that appear within these pages are from young poets whose work is appearing in print for the first time and for many we are sure it will not be the last.

The competition was open to all ages and abilities and for some of the contributors an extraordinary effort was required simply to submit an entry. To these children in particular the excitement of seeing their work published means so much and we sincerely hope this will help to encourage them to write even more in the future. The comments made by their teachers and parents has been most rewarding to all concerned at Poetry In Print.

Theories of what a poem should be are only of minor importance here. It is more important that the student has taken the time to write something, perhaps loosely poetic, but interesting and often unique. The editors have truly enjoyed putting this anthology together. The poems are written with such honesty and openness, coupled with a lively imagination and expression that can only come from young minds.

We wish all of our young contributors much success for the future and hope all of their dreams and aspirations come true and we thank them very sincerely for their efforts.

CONTENTS

Prizewinners
Open Poetry Competition for Schools

13-16 Years

1st: **Amy Tiri** / Worcester Park, Surrey   **(Nonsuch High School for Girls)**
2nd: **Lucy Brands** / Coppenhall, Staffordshire   **(Stafford Grammar School)**
3rd: **Joanna Alpern** / London   **(City of London School for Girls)**

Runners-up:

Alex Bailey-Smith (Westbourne School)
Olivia Codd (Hazelwood School)
Sophie Heuze (Sharples School)
Callum Hough (St Chads Catholic High School)
Jack Powell (Stafford Grammar School)

Kate Clarke (Henry Cort Community College)
Elizabeth Egan (Stafford Grammar School)
Sophie Holt (Brighton Hill Community College)
Harriet Phillips (Stafford Grammar School)
Linda Tran (St Monica's High School)

9-12 Years

1st: **Jordan Lloyd** / Ivybridge, Devon   **(Stowford Primary School)**
2nd: **Emily Gamble** / Kings Langley, Herts   **(Abbots Langley School)**
3rd: **Emily Ellett** / Budleigh Salterton, Devon   **(Exmouth Community College)**

Runners-up:

Caitlin Astley (Gresham Prep School)
Rajveer Chohan (Abbotsford School)
Elizabeth Cole (Nutfield Church Primary School)
Antonia Francis (Abbotsbury Primary School)
Patrick Rutter (Abbotsford School)

Lauren Carter (Sarum St Pauls School)
Tyne-Lexy Clarson (St Dominic's School)
Jack Eden (Abbotsbury Primary School)
James Ireland (Tiffin School)
Migena Sadikaj (Abbotsbury Primary School)

8 Years & Under

1st: **Shay Ralph**/ St Albans, Herts   **(Cunningham Hill Junior School)**
2nd: **Joshua Jones** /Ivybridge, Devon   **(Stowford Primary School)**
3rd: **Owen Jones** / Farnham, Surrey   **(Hale School)**

Runners-up:

Holly Allen (Sarum St Pauls School)
Toby Carless (Whittington Primary School)
Nicola Ingles (Danbury Park Primary School)
Jessica King (Stowford Primary School)
Billy Teather (St Andrew's Primary School)

Maxim Calver (Corton Primary School)
Samantha Hubbard (West Coker Primary School)
Syed Nazmul Islam (Cunningham Hill Junior School)
Rosie King (Cunningham Hill Junior School)
George S.K. Turner (Thurston Primary School)

Congratulations to <u>ALL</u> entrants for such a magnificent effort - Well Done

First Prize Winners

Time

A clock measures the device of time
Regulating the sandy grains,
As they slip through our open fingers
Despite all happiness and all pains,
Try to capture a moment
Try to grab a grain of sand,
Keep it preserved in a memory
Tight in the fist of your hand,
But for every grain that's kept
Another thousand fall,
Cascading down around your head
Lost for one and all,
It's the only lesson of time
The cosmic balances way,
To make past mistakes forgotten
To make us seize the day

Amy Tiri (Age 13)

Chased!

Running, running for my life,
Heart heavy, so heavy and thumping as if something is inside me
And it's trying to get out,
War all around me,
Shooting sounds everywhere,
Running without a care,
Breathing, breathing heavy and hard,
Darkness all around,
Finding myself inside a tomb,
I suddenly stop,
I have reached a massive dead end.
I look to my side and see a gigantic hole of spikes,
I also look to my other side and see an egyptian mummy,
A tremendous dose of fear filled me,
And then bang,
What a horrible sound.
Almost as if the Volcano Krakatoa had just exploded,
And as the bullet hit me I fell to the ground in an instant.

Jordan Lloyd (Age 9)

Tiger

Eye of the tiger burning bright
In the jungle of the night,
Creeping crawling on the ground
Stalking her prey not a sound,
The smallest movement makes her still
Getting ready to make her kill,
Her cubs need to eat meat to make them strong
To make them fast and their claws long,
She needs to survive
To keep herself and her cubs alive,
Eye of the tiger burning bright
In the jungle of the night.

Shay Ralph (Age 7)

Second Prize Winners

The Letter

You sealed my fate in the envelope,
And shook me with every pen stroke
Gripping the letter between clenched fists,
I spluttered and started to choke.

Letting that note become my downfall,
Letting your lies engulf me,
Not understanding a word you wrote,
Trapped, although I am free.

I glanced towards the corner,
Where I left my shattered ways,
Scattered over the clothes you wore,
On that tainted, tattered day.

Where I lie, is where you left me,
A shadow-shell of what I was,
Crippled by your poison pen,
Your reason - 'Just because'.

Lost so no one wants me,
Sprawled in the centre of your floor,
Your twisted tales fade into dust,
The reason - 'I can't bear anymore'.

Lucy Brands (Age 14)

Fire

Fire . . . An untamed hungry beast,
Swallowing down houses.
Reds, oranges and yellows,
Heating up the street.
Running down the alley way,
Trudging up the hill.
Blinding all the fire fighters,
Unpredictable and unbearable.
Evaporating the streams of water,
Squirting at the monster.
I sit here wondering will this ever end?

Fire . . . A never ending childs tantrum,
Natures worst enemy.
An indestructable wall of flame,
Angrily destroying peace.
Taking away laughter and happiness.
Bringing back sadness and grief.
And I sit here wondering what will happen next?
Suddenly there's nothing,
Everything is quiet.

Emily Gamble (Age 11)

Fear

Hear thumping, thumping like an elephant stomping through your chest.
Your hair's standing on end like a hedgehog in a ball.
The wolf was faster than me.
Eyes, eyes watering like a fast flowing river.
Dry mouth like hot sandy desert.
Stuck, stuck to the ground like someone trying to lift weights.
Then I open the door...

Joshua Jones (Age 8)

Third Prize Winners

If Your Life Ever Comes To A Halt

If your life ever comes to a halt -
Cry but realise it isn't your fault.
And whenever you're feeling totally alone -
Sigh but I'm serious - it's just your hormones.
And whilst dwelling in the shards of a broken heart -
Understand it wasn't you who made it fall apart.
And at the time when your soul shivers fast -
Wince, but I'll assure you the pain will not last.
And when drowning your miseries in alcohol -
Keep drinking but trust me, you don't need it at all.
And when your knife tells you it's the end -
Finger the knife, but first talk to a friend.
And whenever you're sad you should seek an antidote,
But no matter how down you are, don't create a scapegoat.

Joanna Alpern (Age 13)

The Untamed Element

As day fades into night,
The window panes begin to shatter like a tornado
Excavating into the earth's face.

A trident of immense brilliance rips out of the shadowy sky,
Leaving nothing but emptiness and fear.
The thunder breaks the silence!

On the midst of the horizon a worrying blur of velocity
Slices its path.
Trees splintering across the wind's turbulence
Hurling anything in its way to one side
Or the cyclone would convey its contents.

The wind whips up quagmire
With the sound of a blade squelching
Into living flesh.
As the baby wails we wonder if it will
EVER stop . . .

Emily Ellett (Age 12)

The Iron Man

Cold as ice,
In pitch black darkness,
I lie scattered,
What happened to me?

I can see only an array of rocks,
Hear only the stormy sea,
Will anyone
Ever find me?

I can only feel
Powdery, brown coloured chrome.
What will I eat?
What will I do?

Morning comes,
Still I lie,
What will happen
To me?

Owen Jones (Age 8)

War

There was death
Then I closed my eyes
There was killing
Then I closed my eyes
There were lies
Then I closed my eyes
There was no-one
Then I closed my eyes
There was terror
Then I closed my eyes
There was I
Then I closed my eyes
I was hurt
Then I closed my eyes
I was dead my eyes were closed

Harry Agombar (Age 13)

What Is Red?

What is red?
A rose is red
Growing in a garden shed.
What is green?
A leaf is green
The shiniest leaf I've ever seen.
What is gold?
A watch is gold
I found one which was very old.

Callum Arnold (Age 7)

The Count

One wobbly whale wiggling wildly.
Two tiny tigers towing towards town.
Three teddy bears running away.
Four funny frogs jumping in a lake.
Five fox fishing.
Six snacks wearing shoes.
Seven sausages smelling like a cherry.
Eight elephants riding a car.
Nine nice girls were called Nicole.
Ten teacups drinking tea.

Ammarah Adam (Age 6)

Ocean Travel

If I could travel
the oceans blue
these are the things
that I would do.

Go in the water
and find a potion.
Sit on a rock
at the bottom of the ocean.

Go on the beach
and find some joy.
Go on the rocks
and find a toy.

Go round the rocks
and find a boat.
go in the trees
and find a goat.

Holly Allen (Age 8)

The Circus

I am at the circus now,
A guys doing an act,
People are laughing their heads off,
At a funny fact!

I wonder what will happen next,
Perhaps there'll be a lion,
The lion might be well trained,
And it's name is Brian

Or they're be might someone on stilts,
He will be very tall,
Very funny, very happy,
And good at pool.

But no, it's acrobats,
The most boring thing of all,
So I'm abandoning the show,
And I'll give my friend a call!

Francesca Arnold (Age 8)

World

So much left unsaid,
So much undiscovered,
So many questions left unanswered,
A big blur in space.

So much water,
Little earth,
People, animals and things,
A big round thing in space.

It's big, it's round,
It's one of nine planets,
It's a world covered in mixed emotions,
But yet so many secrets.

It's kind of like this poem,
I'm afraid, so many questions left open.

Charlie Adey (Age 12)

Fox Hunting

I feel like fainting
I feel like dying
I feel like running
I feel like crying

Should I run?
Should I stay?
Should I hide?
Or should I pray?

Shawkat Al-Baghdadi (Age 11)

Santa, Oh, Santa

Santa, oh, Santa,
Here is my wish,
I'd like a white Christmas,
Oh please give me this.

I want the snow to come
Falling down,
And touch the floor
Everywhere and all around!

Down the chimney
You will come,
Eating your biscuit
And drinking your rum.

So come on Santa,
Don't be shy,
Deliver me this,
And I'll give you a mince pie!!!

Amy Bennett (Age 12)

Everyday Life

Rush hour in Constantinople has just started
Homes are empty everyone has departed
People commuting all over the place.
A business man is carrying a case!

Crowded trains pull into Southside station
Containing people from every nation
Busy people rush around town going to work
By bus, by train, by car and taxi they flirt!

Aeroplanes booked, buses packed, taxis full
Boats sailing all over the place including Hull!
Offices are emptying workers disappear
People drained of patience drive far and near

Matthew Allison (Age 10)

Christmas

When Christmas comes, decorations dance.
The snow falls and strikes the ground.
Shoppers trundle from shop to shop.
Wrapping paper squeaks as presents are wrapped.
Bags and presents lay on the floor.
The bells ring as they enjoy themselves.
As cards come zig zagging down
Snowflakes as they float, float, float.

Summer Aldred (Age 10)

The River

Spurting fountain out of the rock,
Hurrying and scurrying eager to awake,
Gushing and rushing past the sheep in a flock,
Where will the journey of the river take?

Faster and faster, the slope steepens again,
Rubble and trouble gather with speed
A sheer drop suddenly appears and then,
Falling out of the sky like a bird freed.

Hitting the ground beneath with force,
Dashing and dancing keen to be first,
The torrent passes a wild horse,
The slope starts to lessen and give up its thirst.

Now slowly meandering like a slithery snake,
The burbling waters wander on,
This strange journey where will it take?
Will it be the shimmering sea or will it be a glistening lake?

Lisa Antona (Age 11)

Christmas Time

At Christmas time we have trees.
Father Christmas has magic keys to get into halls.
Not far away a lovely meal of hay,
My pony will not stray.
On Christmas day, we feed my
Pony with a deal of hay.
My pony runs about.
At winter there is lots of snow,
My pony is covered in snow
We have to wash him off.
The snow is very windy.
It is very cold.

Jessica Alger (Age 6)

The Fish Smile

Children don't want to go home
Boats are travelling to meet us
The sun won't go to bed
People find their children and take them home
Fish smile at each other

Emma Aspray (Age 5)

A Rainforest Life

Frogs going hipperty hop,
Toucan high up in the treetop,
Indian elephants lumbering past,
Colourful tiger speeding so fast,
Screeching monkeys up in trees,
Down below are buzzing bees,
Here comes anaconda slithering by,
A herd of colours in the sky,
A spotty figure playing hide and seek,
An army of ants so tiny and weak,
A lush chamelon relaxing in the shade,
All the animals in the rainforest glade.

Louise Andersson (Age 10)

My Horse

He sleeps in a stable
He sleeps in the field
He trots
He bucks
He poos and wees
In his stable

Max Ashman (Age 6)

The Girl Who Never Stopped Talking

There once was a girl and her name was Pearl,
And she could never stop talking.
She was walking and walking and just started talking
And she's never stopped since

Pearl was a charming girl but the thing about her was . . .
That she would never shut up!

It got to the time,
When her parents died.
And there was a big funeral,
But then again it wasn't so good because she started talking.

People came over, with lots of giant clovers and wished dear Pearl good luck.
She talked and she cried deep, deep inside.
They asked if she was alright,
She said yes but she lied!

Later she felt a bit queasy inside,
At that moment she dropped down and died.
Now that she's dead she floats around talking,
Round the cemetery just talking and talking.

Gemma Amato (Age 10)

Anger

Anger is red like blazing hot fire,
It tastes like cold sharp pins scratching their way down my throat,
It smells burnt and smokey,
It looks like red hot fireworks firing into the sky,
It sounds like thunder loud and blaring,
It feels like walking across hot coal!!

Victoria Adams (Age 11)

Autumn

A utumn leaves are crunchy and noisy
U p on the horsechestnut tree conkers are ripening
T ea is lovely in the autumn because it keeps you warm
U nder the autumn leaves hedgehogs are hibernating
M ornings are colder and windscreens are covered with dew
N ight time in Autumn seems to come sooner

Hannah Jade Arnold (Age 9)

When Grandaughter

When she wake up in de mornin'
An' de only t'ing that's jealous
Be the sun
Everyt'ing be after her
When me grandaughter run.

Peter Allin (Age 9)

Colourful Butterfly

Butterfly, butterfly you look odd as a pupa
But when you are caterpillar
I don't mind how you look
When your wings come out
You look so pretty butterfly
Butterfly, beautiful butterfly

Ibukun-Oluwa Adeyemi (Age 9)

Pig

Mud roller
Messy eater
Soil jumper
Slow walker
Loud oinker

Ella Alexander (Age 8)

Footie Mad!

Footie is my favourite game, I play it every day,
It gets me off the settee where I sometimes like to lay.

Rain or shine, sun or snow you'll always find me there,
Running round, playing fast, wind rushing through my hair.

I love the feeling and the pride that footie gives to me,
Until my mum shouts out so loud "Come in now Ellis time for tea".

Ellis Allan (Age 7)

The Ballet Dancer

Head turner
Skirt twirler
Toe pointer
Graceful leaper
Delicate nimbler
Romantic mover
Story teller

Elizabeth Allin (Age 11)

Aliens

A ll the aliens up in their spaceship,
L ighting up their ugly heads,
I nvestigating what's going down on earth.
E vil is what humans think,
N osing around our planet,
S end them away!!!

Adam Aspden (Age 12)

Human Cinquain

Human
I'm a human
Could be danger to all
Maybe, alien I don't know
Human

Miriam Assoufi (Age 10)

The Girl Who Ate Nails

Little Emma Gales,
Was always eating nails,
Stop, her mum would always say,
She would twist and walk away.
She would always go and steal nails,
From really long rails.
Until one really scary night,
She gave her family quite a fright.
She said chewing nails is something I should not do,
I am really sorry I didn't listen to you.
And then a nail went through her heart,
Speeding fast like a dart,
And now there is no Emma Gales,
Who died because of eating nails.

Randolph Armah (Age 9)

Cats

All around are furry mounds,
Sleeping cats are what you've found,
On the sofa, on your bed
In the garage, in the shed,
On your car, the boot or bonnet,
A sunny spot, a cat is on it,
Flower beds, the rabbits hutch,
A day awake is far too much,
And at night you're squashed at the edge,
Whilst your cat enjoys your bed,
And you're feeling tired and groggy,
Because you love and adore your moggy,
And will you move this furry intruder,
Of yourse you won't, what could be ruder.

James Antoniou (Age 8)

The 5 Senses

At the beach . . .

Listen to the sound of the waves crashing on the sand,
Look at the horizon, maybe you can see France,
The sand why don't you try to touch it?
Do you know what it feels like?
Having a picnic are you?
What does your banana taste like?
Can you smell the salty sea?

On the eve of spring . . .

Oh can you see the buds on the tree?
Can you smell the flowers that are ready?
Can you hear the birds singing for you?
Yes I can hear them too!
Can you feel the flower's petal?
And can you taste the basil from your garden?

Rachel Azulay (Age 9)

Guess What I Am?

I am speedy when running
I leap, skip, hop and kick
Oh, when I chomp
My teeth chatter out that's very quick
A bushy tail round and fat like some candyfloss
Plump like a plum
Round like a big tyre but bouncy like a ball
Got it yet?
Come on guess . . . . .

I'm a rabbit.

Dominique Adams (Age 8)

Clocks

Tick tock goes the clock
Non stop all day and all night,
In the morning it wakes you up
But every other hour
It's just the same old tick tock,
Some people say it's annoying,
Some people say that it's peaceful,
Listening to the clock
But others just simply say
It's the same old boring repeated
Tick tock!

Amy Baron (Age 10)

Premier League

Football, football a great sport,
Never ever stuck in court.
Everyone likes to play,
And never takes a rest to lay.
Look at us football players,
All around seats of layers.

Smoothly rolling on the pitch,
Thank goodness there is no ditch.
See the ball flying near,
And there the goal keeper in fear.
Oh yeah! What a goal,
Fulham stood there in the cold.

Chelsea won,
Two nil,
Fulham done
Over bill.
What a shame never mind,
Maybe next time they will dine.

Raya-Tul-Islam Ahmed-Sakhi (Age 9)

My Magic Box

I will put in the box . . .

The crashing waves of the sparkling blue sea,
The glittering silver of the moonlight shining in the sky,
The scented breeze touching the shimmering river making it ripple,

I will put in the box . . .

The gorgeous sunset full with vibrant colours,
The natural milk from a huge coconut tasting so sweet,
The dust of a plane caught in the wind from a zebra's run,

I will put in the box . . .

A loud buzzing bee bringing all flowers to life,
The sound of the twittering birds in the morning light,
The fresh spring water rushing down from the icy mountain tops,

I will put in the box . . .

The gigantic palm tree's leaf so green and full of texture,
A handful of sand flying swiftly against the cool summer's breeze,
An orange and red autumn leaf falling elegantly of a magnificent tree,

I pass on this box to a friend and they will do the same as I.
They will place all of their magical memories, belongings and thoughts gracefully into it.
This way they will not be lost.
They will be kept safe and sound forever and ever.

Jai-Puneet Aulakh (Age 12)

Fear

Heart thumping, thumping as if it's beating in your head
Eyes watering, watering like they're Niagara falls.
Sweating, sweating as if you've been drenched in water
Glued to the spot, glued as if you've landed in sticky tar.
Screaming, screaming as if you've fallen out of a plane.
Dry mouth, dry as the air in the hottest dessert.
Running, running like a cheetah is chasing you
Teeth chattering, chattering like fresh diamond drills.

Then . . . . nothing

Matthew Atkins (Age 9)

Rainy Road

The water on the roof, pitter patter
The windscreen wipers going full blast
The heating blowing quickly
Seatbelts tightened securely
Eyes on the road
Red lights ahead
Car stops
But someone did not!
BANG!

Carly Abbs (Age 14)

Walking Through The Farmyard

Walking through the farmyard
What do you see?
I see a pig oinking at me

Walking through the farmyard
What do you see?
I see a horse looking at me

Lilly Alexander (Age 6)

Best Friends Forever

If I were lady of companionship
Friendship would be as solid as a rock
As important as life
Gazing at the picture the gentle graceful girls grin
They chuckle and rustle their yellow toys
Dressed almost identically in white frills
Preparing a tea party for the discarded dollies

The two girls each in their own worlds
Shoulder to shoulder.
Quiet as a mouse
I watch my mum
With her finger on the picture
A tear D
R
O
P
S
down her melancholy cheek

Caitlin Astley (Age 9)

Our Friendship

Jade, Laura. Kelsey are really good friends,
We play with each other everyday,
We play with each other no matter what
Because we are really good friends.
Everyday we go round each others houses,
People always spy on us,
Because we always break up.
We share beds but not heads,
We like books but not hooks,
We love Tracy Beaker but not Justine Little Wood,
We go to karate together,
And we will always be best friends for ever.

Jade Abbott (Age 9)

Summer Days

Sun hot
Rain cold
Summer's new
Winter's old

Flowers red
Grass green
Sea blue
Summer beam

Jamie Amor (Age 8)

I've Got Nothing To Write

You are late why?
Because well here it is Miss,
My dog fell down the stairs
My baby fell down the potty
My Nan fell down the side of the house
My mum kept going around the lamp
My dad kept tripping down on my Gran
My friend kept getting glued to the wall
My guineapig got stuck in the door
My sister got stuck on the roof
My brother got stuck on the chimney
Oh No! Just get on with your story,
Please Miss I've got nothing to write about!

Brooke Bailey (Age 7)

Ocean Travel

If I could travel
The oceans blue
These are the things
That I would do.

Swim like a dolphin
Up and down
Show me the things
That you have found.

Swim far and far
Like a shark
And get home fast
Because it's nearly dark.

Sam Blake (Age 8)

The Railway

It stretches on for miles and miles,
Further than the view from your window, but
No roads lie next to it or under it,
Only sand and dust. Plants only grow
When water falls off a passing train.

The tracks are old and rusted
Like unshaven stubble on an old man's cheek
They scrape at the bare wheels and scratch
At the train and sometimes cause a leak
Then, later, the train will keel and crash.

The rails have not been touched
By human hands since that day when they were laid.
Not much has touched them.
Apart from trains, the great iron snakes intimidate
Any animal that dares enter the desert.

Eventually the trains shall stop.
One by one disappearing into sand and dust.
Not coming back. And soon fewer and few
Till they stop. and for years they are left until found.
And hope could turn the track into something better and new.

William Arterton (Age 13)

Children Playing In The Sea

Children playing in the sea
Boats bobbing on the sea
The sun is bright yellow
People going in the sea
Fish swimming up and down

Phoebe Bohana (Age 6)

A Frosty Morning

The frost was the colour of crunchy white.
The frost looks like a birthday cake dusted with icing sugar.
The icy grass feels like worms under your hand.
It sounds like glass when it breaks.
It looks like little frills on ribbon.

Grace Beard (Age 7)

Creatures!

The sea is rough,
The sky is blue,
The sun is shining brightly,
The clouds look like splattered glue,
Because cows go moo.

I look in my cupboard
I think there's a monster,
I think it's a grizzly bear,
But it's just my jumper.

The forest looks like a giant,
He smiles with a grin,
He wants to eat my picnic,
Whilst I throw my rubbish in the bin.

Jake Blunden (Age 8)

On The Farm

There are horses in the paddock
Grey, brown, bay and black
Lots of lovely colours
All ready to run on the track.

There are sheep on the hills
Black, brown and white
Like big fluffy clouds
All woolly and bright.

There are cows in the field
Black, white and brown
They give lots of milk
And they act like a clown.

Ellie Brewer (Age 7)

Chased!

Being chased by aliens,
Running, thinking, it's going to get you!
Heart stomping like an elephant stomping through your chest.
Eyes watering like a waterfall,
Still running,
It's getting closer!
Found a place to hide now,
Stuck to the ground like super glue,
As cold as ice,
Looking for your hiding place
So close now,
About to kill you.

Christopher Arnold (Age 9)

Autumn

Cold, misty mornings
Golden sunshine glistening on the leaves
Scarves, mittens, hats and coats.
Jumping in mountains of raked up leaves
What a treat!
It's Autumn!

Elizabeth Aitken (Age 10)

The Cheetah

Quick as a lightning bolt
Coat like the golden sun with small black blots.
Claws like small horns on its paws
Teeth like sharp and dangerous knives
Eyes like binoculars and as big as green emeralds
A mouth as big as my hand
Tail like a snake always moving around
It roars like ten loud foghorns
It eats meat raw like chewy warthogs.

Tina Burdett (Age 8)

A Black Swinger

A black swinger
A loud ringer
A big personality
A lot of originality
A broad thinker
A tuneful singer
A smash-hit winner
Because being FUNKEY makes me a MONKEY!

Ellen Victoria Behan (Age 11)

Fire

Angry fire incandecent to
Get revenge.
The fire jumping in the air,
As it dares
To spread.
Fire roars as water comes to
Stop their plan
From working.
Fire threatens as it passes
In and out wet.
Passage ways.
Fire pouncing as it
Gets put out.

Talia Baldwin (Age 10)

Seagull

Flying high
Great eyes
Pinching food
People cry
Eating icecream
Also chips
All fish
Mostly treats!!!

Jessica Benney (Age 8)

Spring Days

Flowers bloom
Crowded streets
Sweeping broom
Fairground beats

Little chickens
Easter eggs
Little bunnies
Sleepy heads

Taylor Burridge (Age 9)

The Roaring Sea

The sea bashing the bay
The sea scratching the coast
The sea cleans your hands
The sea brings treasures
As it bashes on the rocks
The waves feed the fish
As they swim on their way.

Charlie Butler (Age 9)

Am I

I don't fit in
I feel like a black sheep
In a herd of white sheep
No-one knows I'm here
I just live in fear
Everyone walks right through me
I feel so empty
I feel so unwanted
So cold . . . . so haunted
They just walk past
Not even a glance
They act as if I'm dead
I'm full of dread
Thinking I'm dead
I'm just a wandering soul
On this earth with no purpose
I can't be . . . I can't be
Everyone's happy but me
I hide away from society
Am I really . . .

Bethney Brown (Age 13)

In A Castle

Frozen in the hallway at night
A hooting owl gave me a fright
I ran to a door
There were tacks on the floor

I ran too quick
I felt sick
I needed a map
I fell into a trap

Samuel Bristow (Age 10)

The Countryside

In the countryside
I can see a fat pig

In the countryside
I can hear a long tree rustling

In the countryside
I can smell fresh corn growing

In the countryside
I can touch a white owl tooting

In the countryside
I can taste a bit of corn waving

In the countryside
I feel excited and happy

Joshua Barton (Age 7)

Over The Woods And Fields

Over the woods and fields I run,
I leap, I bound,
Forests, farms and fens fly past,
Under sky, over ground.

I race; the forests seem to moan,
Emerald leaves, whispering grass,
Through Breck and Broad, under glistening sun,
I fly, I pass.

Free as the wind I bound along,
Birdsong, the whispering reeds,
My road goes ever on and on,
The forest breathes,
The forest bleeds.

I'll roam the wilds, proud and pure,
As the wind is free,
Until I find that special place
That's just for me.

James Baillie (Age 12)

Origami

A piece of paper flat and white,
I twist and turn it in the night.
From the ground I'll make you fly,
And make you a bird frog or butterfly

In the Japanese land today,
You'll see a crane fly past your way.
From a youthful kid short and spout,
Whose learnt origami without no doubt.

Sam Berwick (Age 11)

My Shadow

While I am writing poems on a plate,
My shadow draws on a plate.

While I am thinking what game we should play,
My shadow tells me what games to play.

While I am watching a Tweenies video,
My shadow watches something grown-up.

While I am eating crackers on a plate,
My shadow eats off the table.

While I am waiting in the queue,
My shadow pushes to the front.

While I am making a piggy bank,
My shadow makes some money.

Jessica Billington (Age 6)

Dreams!

When the house is quiet and all is still
And I have fallen asleep
My mind has lots of ideas and thoughts which I like to call dreams.
Last night I dreamed that I was swimming in chocolate
And I was eating custard creams.
Then a little person came along that was made out of sweets
He said to me this is my home and I've got a lot more treats.
He showed me around and I said, "Have you got my ice-cream?"
It's very hot around here, what a strange but nice dream!
He said yes of course and took me around to the back of his house
On the way we found a mouse.
The little man said, "Get away, I don't want you nibbling at my house!"
It was a lot cooler back there.
I said thank-you for the ice-cream and that I'd better be getting back now.
"Is there anything I could do for you, you have been so incredibly nice?"
"Yes you could cut me a slice."
"Of what?" I said
"Of cake if you please I am too small to reach."
"Here you go, goodbye and thank you for a fabulous night's dream!"

Hannah Bowen (Age 11)

Rock Band

N ever stop rocking
I rresistable music
R ock music
V ariation of sounds
A ll of the members are dead
N on stop guitar solos
A massive hit

Sam Broughton (Age 10)

Megalosaurus Kenning

Jurassic hunter
Thirty footer
Two tonner
Land dweller
Meat eater
Water drinker
Nest builder
Egg layer
Fern flattener
Tree breaker
Print maker
Prey stalker
Fear bringer
Teeth gnasher
Herbivore killer
Flesh ripper
Bone crusher
Skeleton leaver
Museum filler

Steven Ballard (Age 9)

Lucy Patches And Her Matches

This is the tale of Lucy Patches,
Who was always playing with matches.
Lucy found her matches then some itches,
What turned into stitches.
Lucy got her matches then she got some burns,
Her mother said "won't you ever learn."
She was in agony with her little cute head,
Hit the pillow then she was dead.

Lauren Baichoo-Hoskins (Age 8)

Layers Of Life

In the emergent layer where insects crawl,
And tree frogs jump.
Birds nest in the bright to see the beauty of the light.

High up in canopy,
The coati coming down to get bugs.
A few metres away,
The sloth will sway.

Lower to the ground,
The flying gecko glides.
As the jumping snake,
Snaps with its jaws,
The geckos lucky it doesn't have claws.

Right on the ground,
The Hercules beetle,
Sharp claws nip.
Approaching the saddleback
Feeding on a pip.

Theo Brown (Age 9)

Changes Of My Life

My life, it's a strange old thing, sad, happy who knows
It could be night or day, whatever the way,
For I am always here; Here that's me.
Cemented into the ground. For I can never come out.

The day, I am happy, not sad.
People rushing by late for work
They come sit on me, waiting for the bus
Hoping it won't be late.
But I know, yes I know;
I wish they could hear me,
Then they wouldn't be late,
"Hop on this bus".
But no, they just sit and wait.

Night, it's lonely and cold,
Drunks walk by with their jelly like legs
Tumbling and laughing
Chucking empty beer bottles at me,
It hurts, I shout but they can't hear me
They don't care, no, why should they.
They don't think I have a heart, I do, I do.

Tamsin Barber (Age 12)

Blue

Blue is the sky,
The slishy sloshy rain,
Blue is the sky,
You will see it over and over again.
The colour of the sea,
The fish's scales,
Over the boats go,
With their sails.
The Angel's shoes,
Shiny blue,
Blue Eeyore,
From Winnie the Pooh.
Blue velvet cloth,
Running over your face,
Blue velvet cloth,
Smoothing lots of space.
Blue wellington boots,
Splish, splosh, splash,
Blue puddles,
Bish, bosh, bash.

Mollie Brook (Age 7)

Big Shooting Star

Shooting star flying across the earth
Moving night and day
Shining like the sun at night
Flying up and down across the sky
Night and day it moves all over the world
Shooting star flying across the sky

Connor Brown (Age 9)

Tamagotchis

Tamagotchis playing
Games and shopping
You would really like one
Tamagotchi are cheerful
Tamagotchis are like people
You will like them!!!

Charlie Butler (Age 7)

My Multicoloured Hair

I slither through a weedy bog, trembling through the misty fog,
Beginning my journey on muddy ground, my long silky hair a murky brown.
I start my sprint in my gilded gown, running, running, gushing down,
My hair now dark, no longer bright, is now as black as a winter's night.
Shining eyes dart to and fro, search for a place that I can go,
My hair is now a beautiful blue, with a lustrous silvery hue.
I dive - jump off - cascading . . . somersault-plunge-parading . . .
CRASH! LUNGE! SPLASH! SPRAY! My energy is fading away.
Swirling, swirling, my hair is still blue, though now - I am no longer new,
I'm slowing down; I'm getting old, I used to be so uncontrolled!
Moving slower into a stroll, watching the waterweed gently roll,
Seagulls dive, snatch up their fish, swooping up with a gentle swish.
Emerald hair shines upon my head, I shuffle over the golden seabed,
I greet my close and long lost friends, this is where my journey ends . . .

Chloe Bramwell (Age 11)

To My Loving Mama . . .

To my loving Mama, up high in the air,
Watching down on me with your luscious curly hair.

It's different in London, I wish you could see,
The Grahams are lovely apart from Kevin.

I want to rewind, rewind to the start,
And listen to the rhythm, of my calm beating heart.

Femi is scared, but tries to be strong
I wish Papa would not be too long!

New clothes on our skins, shoes on our feet,
And cooking, their food could never beat,

Yours is the best,
Like you sparkling, fruit nest.

We're scared about Papa, and what he will do,
What if he's in heaven, along beside you?

So many questions, so many lies,
But there is still a sparkle in Femi's teary eyes.

Katy Barnes (Age 13)

It's Coming

When it's happened, it's happened,
When it's done, it's done,
You can't do anything, you're helpless,
So you hide, you're resisting.

You know it's coming,
So you try to stop it,
You panic, you don't know what to expect,
You wring your hands, you've got stressed.

It's in autumn, and in the New Year,
It's in our fashion, and in our friends,
It's in our streets, and in our shops,
It's got everywhere.

What is it?
It affects us all,
But no-one knows,
We have a vague idea.

It has a name,
They call it change.

Nick Baker (Age 13)

Autumn

A utumn is cold, wet and dull
U ntil the leaves start to fall, it's shivery quivery
T rails of leaves all around - oh, what's that a conker I've found
U ntil the day fades away, slippy time, hooray hooray
M ucky mud, under it slimy pink worms hibernating - sh, sh - they're asleep
N aughty hedgehogs snuffle snuffle, creeping in the night
　　　　What's that? It sees a fox - you're going in my tea . . .

Charlotte Bird (Age 7)

The Mad Welsh Dragon

Once said a scaly dragon on a day of March 1st
Please give me a drink or two or I would rather burst

To make sure I'm as good as gold I'd like a nice big cake,
But could you do it please, please, please
Because I cannot bake!

His name was smoky yes it was he flew off crazily,
He flew so far he caught a star and then he missed his tea!

His tail was like a great big spear that could bring down storms of hail.
He had sharp claws and almighty jaws and beautiful shiny scales.

Sarah Brice (Age 7)

25

Tension

The fire lights inside my head,
As the flames roar with anger.

The fire lights inside my head,
As my sweat continuously drips.

The doors slam inside my head,
As I run from my fear.

It burns and hurts inside my head,
Like a devil with a pitch fork.

The fire lights inside my head,
And I wish I'd never done it.

Zarthast Bajwa (Age 11)

My Three Numbers

Hup too hup too up to the top
I find number two in the tree top

Hup too hup too go to the middle
I find number one having a fiddle

Hup too hup too down to the bottom
I find zero at the bottom

Samuel Berryman (Age 7)

What Am I?

Fast Waddler
Slow runner
Speedy swimmer
Fish eater
Body heater
Ice slider
Snow slipper
Loud quacker
Ice cracker
Ground traveller
Wing haver
Non flyer
Water skier
Enemy fleer
Desperate survivor
Excellent diver
Predator escaper
Shelter maker
Massive power
Snow shower

Liam Bristow (Age 11)

Floating On Ice

My feet glide across the smooth untouched floor
Through our world and beyond
To a planet where only angels live.
My heart flies softly around me
In small serene strokes.
I twirl around and around
Like a delicate but beautiful creature
Trying to find its balance on the wet slippery floors
With a slight chill that flies within me
But I still stand up tall and dance like a fairy in the moonlight.
I am in my own unknown world
Full of pleasure
But still the floor is icy cold.

Lauren Billingham (Age 12)

The War

Bobby lived during the Second World War
He and his family were very poor
When the planes came and bombs showered down
Upon Bobby's beautiful town.
Bobby fled to the underground.
The enemies made friends on Christmas day
Got out a football and began to play
Now the war is at an end,
Germany and England are once again friends.

Daniel Biswas (Age 8)

The Joy Of Snow

Snow flutters down and we yell with glee!
Charging outside,
For a snowball fight,
To make snow angels, or even a snowman.
Even the tiniest shower,
Makes us shout out loud,
"Look everyone, it's snowing!"

As it floats down to earth, like the leaves of autumn,
Hands reach out to touch it,
Delighting in its sudden chill
Before it melts away
To nothing.
Scooping up handfuls
And packing it tight,
We throw it,
Enjoying the look of surprise on our target's face!

Then disappointment
As carefully made snowmen melt with the warmth of the sun.
Snow is just water,
So why don't we shout when it rains?

Matthew Barrett (Age 12)

The Smell Collector

A stranger barged in this morning
Dressed in purple and blue
Put the smells into a bag
And went into the bathroom to go and smell our loo

The smell of my coffee
The smell of apples fresh
The burping from my father and the dogs mess

The smell of cheesy milk
The pot of lumpy stew
The horrible smell in the room that is coming from you

The smell of red roses
The scent of mum's shampoo
Her most expensive perfume a bit strong but ooh ooh

The smell of fish
The smell of chips
And the most nicest smell of all mmmm her best food dish

A stranger came this morning
Hope he never comes again
Oh he caused some trouble
But most of all pain

Amy Beck (Age 9)

Raindrops

Onto your lip, lip,
The raindrops drip, drip,
Onto your face, face,
The raindrops race, race.

They make you wet, wet,
So you won't forget, forget,
That awful shower, shower,
Of maximum power, power.

They pour down like powder, powder,
Always getting louder, louder,
Through the mighty sky, sky,
They quickly, dribble by, by.

Down to earth they tumble, tumble,
Making the ground look humble, humble,
The treetops are drenched, drenched,
Their massive thirst quenched, quenched.

But after the sun comes out,
The children sing and shout,
The rain has finally gone,
But I wonder for how long?

William Barnes (Age 10)

Dogs

Some dogs are fat, more than a cat.
My dog is puffy and always fluffy.
My dog, is clever and will be fore ever.
My dog is funny and he looks like a bunny.

Nikita Barnes (Age 9)

Cinquain

Caring
And loving me
For ever and ever
My family is brilliant
To me

Jasmine Burton (Age 10)

Gassed

All exhausted, legs weak coughing from the exhaustion of war,
Longing for the safety of the trenches.
We trudge back from the lines, each step hurting, shivering from cold,
Backs to the trenches.
The men are tired, trudge through the sludge,
Half asleep. Feet are sore, cut and blistered.
They don't hear the gas shells falling.
"Gas! Masks on now!" I scream.
There is a scramble for masks, men hurriedly putting them on.
Tiredness forgotten
As the gas descends, everyone has their masks on except for one.
He is staggering around, crying.
The clouds are thick now; we stumble round, blind, waiting for it to clear.
The dying man comes flailing towards me. He coughs, water gargles in his throat.
We walk behind the cart, our comrade inside, spluttering, choking to death, mucus and water filling his lungs.
If it was your friend dying in such a way,
Would you still believe the liars that say it is glorious to die for your country?

Daniel Brooks (Age 12)

Girls And Boys

Girls and boys are very different
They both like varied things,
Girls like skirts, make-up and bags
And boys like bikes and bling.

Girls have brushes, straighteners, scrunches
They're admirers of their hair,
Boys don't own brushes only gel
And don't really seem to care.

Boys have skateboards, trainers, bikes
They're crash courses on scabby legs,
Girls are more petite and fragile
And scream at the sight of mouldy eggs.

Overall no-ones the same
Girls prefer playstations and football,
Some do not like skirts,
Or don't like either at all.

So even though they like the same
It doesn't mean they are,
They're all different shapes and sizes
And your best friend can't be far.

Sophie Butler (Age 12)

Spain

S unshine is in Spain
P laying is what to do
A time to do things like lullaby
I n Spain it is great
N ow it's time to say goodbye!

Alicia Baron (Age 8)

Four O'Clock Friday

On Monday at school we had R.E.,
Then when I got home I had my tea,

On Tuesday morning we did some maths,
On the afternoon we went to the swimming baths,

On Wednesday lunch time I had a grape,
Then I found a piece of tape,

On Thursday break I ate my snack,
Then I fell over and hurt my back,

Four o'clock Friday home at last,
Time to forget the week that's past.

Zoe Hannah Brown (Age 10)

The Bunk Barn

I am so bored,
Stuck in one place
My only visitors come,
In the summer holidays.

Outside of summer it always rains,
It is all cold and damp.
The wind is always blowing,
Like a constant fan blowing on me.

But summer is when all my fun happens
When the people come.
The constant buzz of conversation;
Makes me glow with warmth.

They play games on my table,
Laughter is all round.
And joy is found everywhere,
I learn all sorts of different games.

Oh and when they cook;
Lovely smells make my taste buds go crazy.
Their cooking is great,
I would love to taste but I am only a bunk barn.

Matthew Babai (Age 12)

Snow Poem

Snow falling like blossom from a tree
Birds calling wanting to be free
Soon I see a bird's footprints in the snow
Happily I prance along the snow
Now I see my footprints

Aimee Brooks (Age 8)

Autumn

Crunch as the people are walking,
The wind blows as they are talking,
Hurrying home on a cold autumn night,
Looking at the fallen leaves so colourful and bright

Their house is warm
They see a carpet of leaves on the front lawn,
Outside the fireworks explode
And they watch the reload

W
H
O
O
S
H

Georgia Boroda (Age 8)

Football

F is for the field where you play with all your mates
O oh is for excitement when you see your home match dates
O oh
T is for the tunnel where the professionals wait to play
B is for the ball kicked around on world cup day
A is for all the cheers when you score the winning goal
L is for the love of it you feel down into your soul
L is for the lines marking out the pitch on turf

Football is for sure the greatest game on planet earth

Jack Brownlow (Age 9)

Senses

As soft as a rhino's back,
As soft as a velvet lace.
The sweet smell of a cake,
The foul smell of diesel.
The gruesome sight of war,
And the fearsome sight of a boar.
The lovely taste of chocolate,
The strange taste of carrots.
The sound of a new car, lovely and soft,
The sound of road works hammering hard!

Robert Blanchard (Age 12)

Patrick's Pets

In his bedroom Patrick kept
TEN black cats with cute white paws,
NINE green toads who hopped around,
EIGHT small beetles under the bed,
SEVEN brown hamsters in their cage
SIX white mice with pointed ears
FIVE long pythons wrapped around his arm
FOUR cheeky monkeys swinging from the light
THREE dead spiders lying on the ground
TWO tall horses running like mad
and ONE . . . . . GUESS WHAT?

Hannah Beaumont (Age 9)

Bullying

I saw a cloud shaking in fear,
I saw a mountain towering near.
I saw the darkness gathering round,
I saw the lightning strike the ground.
I saw the rain melt the snow,
I saw no way out or a place to go.
I saw a tornado destroying all life,
I saw nothing there, only strife.
I saw no end to the vicious storm,
I saw the cloud beaten and torn.

Joshua Blake (Age 11)

Thoughts Of Death

Thoughts of death are plastered across our minds,
Haunting all thoughts and feelings
All we hear is the slice of gunfire whipping through the air.

We turn our backs to the explosions of the shells and begin to trudge to safety
The thought of shelter is of little comfort to the soldiers.
They have seen so much, nothing makes them happy,
Blinded by sadness and deafened by sorrow, they fail to hear the low hiss of gas.

"Quick Boys! Masks on"

In a frenzy we fumble to get on the heavy rubber masks
A thick green fog slowly creeps towards us, smothering us with a green blanket of death,
Huddling together, we try to find the path to shelter

As we stumble through the screen of gas a splutter erupts from behind.
Knowing what we'll see we turn round and find kneeling before us
A soldier with only his mouth to breathe through.
As he shudders and trembles in pain, I think what he will miss about life;
His family; friends; the chance of being a father.

As he is carted away I try not to watch him struggle to breath.
I think of how life was before the war and of my family.
My wife thinks I am in a glorious war saving the country.
But the truth is, there is no glory, there is no honour, never let them trick you in to that lie, never.

Alex Bailey-Smith (Age 13)

If I Had A Ship

If I had a ship then she would have at least a thousand sails,
With a million pirates with swords in their hands threatening you to walk my plank.

I'd be the captain of my ship with a compass in my hand,
Fighting serpents and dragons and eagles and myths in caves and seas alike.

If I had a ship it would be ready for battle even on the quietest days,
With cannons and guns and shields and swords I would never loose a fight.

There's no mercy allowed on my ship or your throat would be cut in two,
The treasure's ours and it's not yours and the booty is all mine.

Most ships are made of wood but mine are made of bones,
But the bones aren't white the bones are black for they have began to rot.

You can't see my ship well in the night,
So keep your eyes open or you are in for a fright.

My ship is known as the swift streamer,
So stay out of the way or you are in for a screamer.

Once we tried to steal some rum we thought it was alright,
But the victims caught us red handed and so we got into a fight.

If I had a ship then I would be known as almighty Black Eyed Joe,
With a captain headquaters made of gold I'll be the richest in the seas.

But I don't have a ship and I'm just a boy wishing that it would be real,
But I'm over it now and I gave it a thought and it is not a really big deal.

Joseph Brook (Age 10)

My Magic Box

I will put in my magic box,
The sound of the wild, whistling wind.

My box is styled from gold and glitter.
My lid is decorated with purple daisies and poppies
The hinges are fashioned from sparkles and silver

Sarah Beaumont (Age 7)

Scared

Scared is black like in a dark room.
It tastes like ice running down your spine.
It smells liken burning with no escape.
It looks like a mountain towering over you.
It sounds like a firework ready to jump out.
It feels like falling ready to . . . BANG.

Rebecca Burke (Age 9)

A Friend

A friend is like the sunshine, cheering you up,
If you're good friends, you might go to the world cup.

A friend can always help you,
They're like an object that's always around you.

A friend can always care,
A friend will always share.

When you are playing, you are a pair
A friend is always there . . .

Amy Brown (Age 11)

Water

Trickle trickle down and down,
See the world as it was found.

Swoosh swoosh the water falls,
The seaside animals call and call.

Wearing away what you can't see,
Making new land for you and me.

Be careful not to fall in
Try and look for a dolphin's fin.

Nassira Bash-Taqi (Age 9)

The Five Senses

Saxophones play outside in the street
Underground too, everywhere I hear music.
Now the music stops but I can still hear
Ding, ding, ding, ding.

Turkey tastes great, apples taste better,
Sausages are horrible,
Tomatoes have pips,
Eggs fill my belly for breakfast.

Socks smell really bad, monkeys smell like bananas,
Eels don't smell,
Leopards smell of blood,
Letters smell of the postman.

Sand on the beach looks lovely. in the mountains are lots of rocks.
Green hills are really lovely.
High in the sky it's really scary.
Thorpe Park's rollercoasters are really fun!

Teeth feel really hard. Ouch! I say my tooth is wobbly,
Up in the gum my tooth is bleeding.
Crunch! Oww! my tooth is out,
Hooray! no more pain to feel.

Daniel Bondatti (Age 10)

My Teacher

My teacher is a butterfly,
She helps me reach up to the sky
She guides me through the day with ease
Makes my school and life such a breeze

Alex Brierley (Age 7)

Volcano

The dragon that lives deep in the middle of the earth,
The dangerous dragon roars his mighty roar.
The earth rumbles,
The scarlet lava pours out of the stony surface.
The smoke fills the air.

Zoe Bartlett (Age 9)

I Spied A Stallion

A swish of a jet black tail,
The gleam of a shiny bronze coat,
A thudding of hooves,
On the dew sprinkled grass.

Through the trees he gallops,
Leading his herd,
I shrink into the depths of the shadows,
He skids to a halt in a cloud of dust.

He turns silently to face me,
I scarcely dare to breathe,
He looks at me with soft brown eyes,
And is gone with the wind.

And ever since that moment,
I knew that we were friends.

Jessica Bickers (Age 11)

Noise

I like noise . . .
The **BOOM** of a bomb
The **crunch** of crisps
The **THUD** of a hoof
The **slam** of a door
The **crash** of a glass
The **roar** of a train
The **rattle** of rain
The *crack* of a rifle
The **drip** of a leaking tap
The **cheer** of a winning team
The *growl* of a lion
The **slurp** of someone drinking through a straw
The **thwack** of a cricket ball battered by a bat
The **tick tock** of the clock
I like noise.

Jithin Bittu (Age 12)

31

My Pet

My cat is called Tuffy
She is really fluffy,
She's also really puffy,
She has green eyes,
I can hear her cries,
She never lies,
She's better than a bat
I love my cat,
Write a poem about that.

Jessica Bowden (Age 9)

My Snowman

I wish my snowman could come inside my warm bed
And cuddle me by the red firelight.
I wish my snowman could share my sweet berries
And listen to my scary stories.
I wish he could come and sit down at the table
To eat a crunchy apple.
But the next day the North wind blew him through the door,
And now there is nothing left of him but a puddle on the floor.

Amy Bradley (Age 8)

Sum Poem

10 ÷ 3 = smelly peas
2 - 2 = a clean shoe
1 ÷ 5 = a bee hive
7 + 7 = I will go to heaven
6 + 6 = six sticks
4 + 4 = a big door
9 - 9 = some wine
10 x 10 = a pen
3 + 3 = a bee
4 ÷ 4 = a dog's paw

Scott Brookes (Age 7)

Spring

Candyfloss is like a blossom tree all full of bright colours
As pink as a poodle
Neat and bright it reminds me of a night light
Donkeys run around the field with horses they will play
Young calves drink milk from their mummy
Frolicking animals come out to play
Laughing while they're on their way
Oh it's nearly gone
Summer is about to come
Oh summer's about to come

Liora Bean (Age 8)

Tiger

Tigers are sly,
cunning,
fierce,
clever,
sneaky,
brainy,
artful,
furry,
skillful,
intelligent,
talented
and very, very quiet. Sshhh!

Felix Beard (Age 7)

In The Magic Box

I will put in

The shining moonlight reflecting on the water
The rising sun of east Japan
The snow silently sprinkling slowly on the frozen grass
The glazing star from the dark night sky
The beautiful dress for a baby's first Christmas

I will put in

A paint pallet with all the colours of the rainbow

Amy Bentley (Age 9)

Rhino

R onny the rhino, rumbled through the rough road and round the roundabout two times
H arvey and Harry hid in the haunted house and helped Harriet up
I nside the indigo igloo there was ivy and a person called Ian
N ine naughty nits nibbled on Nicola's nice hair
O ne otter opened the orange door

Jake Bowman (Age 8)

The Magic Rocking Horse

There once was a magic rocking horse
Who flew away to space
You should have seen the shell shocked look
On Julie and Jamie's face
They snuggled in his acres of fur
And clung for dear life
The horse flew high and wide and strong
As straight as the edge of a knife

They cut through space
They flew through time
They spun around the globe
As their journey was nearing its end
They passed a martian probe
They landed in the nursery
The rocking horse stood still
The magic slept until next time
The three would need a thrill

Rachel Louise Ball (Age 8)

Old Mrs Smith

Old Mrs Smith lives on my street,
She is the nicest woman you'll ever meet,
She likes to dance, laugh and sing,
In fact she likes to do everything.

Mrs Smith wears a pale yellow skirt,
And a bright orange jacket over her shirt,
Her shoes are made out of pure snake skin,
And her head supports a hat that's incredibly thin.

If you walk past her house at night,
She will always invite you in for a bite,
She cooks roast beef for her supper,
And drizzles on it lemon sugar.

Even though she might be weird,
To insult Mrs Smith is unheard,
People love her for what she is,
She's like an actress in show biz.

Peter Beesley (Age 14)

Autumn

A utumn is a time when . . .
U mbrellas float in the air on a whistly day
T rees leaves go
U mber
M ornings are misty
N ights get longer

Hannah Baker (Age 6)

Walking Through The Farmyard

Walking through the farmyard
What do you see?
I see a cow mooing at me.

Walking through the farmyard
What do you see?
I see a dog barking at me.

Abigail Bowman (Age 5)

The Writer Of This Poem Is . . .

As glamorous as a glittering movie star,
As lively as an orchestra,
As energetic as a busy town,
As wacky as a funny clown.

As misunderstood as an erupting volcano
As moody as a rampaging rhino,
As chatty as a nutty chimp,
As mischievous as a naughty imp.

As jumpy as a jelly bean
As bright as the colour aquamarine
As petite as a mocking bird
As sweet as lemon curd

She's one in a million billion
Or so the poem says.

Lauren Bailey (Age 11)

Fun Land

If I were Lord of Funland I would see
The Gyrocopter, like a bee, taking people for a ride.
Happiness is humming in the bright sky.
Gazing at the picture, jolly Gyro gliding round
Whizzing,
It soared around the sky
Yellow and black
Full of tranquillity.

If I were Lord of Funland
I would get jolly Gyro to pick me up for a ride.
Sting.
An army of wasps invades,
He flung me down and went
Weaving through the wasps, shouting,
"Die! Die! Die!"
His voice faded . . .

Gregor Bailey (Age 9)

Untitled

One jumping frog jumping in the sea,
Two sparkling flowers reflecting on me.
Three flying butterflies waiting for their tea,
Four little girls looking at a bee.
Five little boys eating bread,
Six men in their bed.
Seven children having fun,
Eight boys having a run.
Nine children doing a rhyme,
Ten mummies having a good time.

Naomi Bynon (Age 6)

My Cat

My cat got fatter and fatter
I didn't know what was the matter.
Until one day she disappeared,
You can't imagine how much I feared.
Then one day I heard a noise,
And saw something that was turquoise.
I crept into the study,
And saw my cat was muddy.
She was also very thin,
With a great big grin.
That's when I noticed,
She had KITTENS!
1-2-3-4
I LOVE MY CATS.

Jack Barber (Age 9)

Spring

Spring, Spring
I love Spring
We can play outside again
Spring, Spring
Buds shoot out
Birds build nests with twigs and feathers
Spring, Spring
Winter's over
I like Spring

Georgia Baker (Age 7)

Friends

Friends are like super glue
They never leave you
They always stay with you
We are friends!

Friends are always there
They always care
They never swear
We are friends!

Friends never lie
Friendship never dies
When you cry
Friends never sigh
We are friends!

Kieran Bedford (Age 10)

I Am . . .

Sometimes, I wish I wasn't so lonely,
I wish, I could sing so well that it touched your heart,
I wish, I could explain my work of art, showing the true colours inside me,
I wish, I was good at something.

Why am I feeling like this?
Upset?

Well, stitch that, because you know why?
I am someone much better . . .

. . . I am who I am. And, you don't need to be hurt because,
You are who you are and, no-one can take that away from you.

So,
Embrace yourself,
You are not lonely,
That is your true identity . . .

. . . SHOW IT TO THE WORLD,

BE HAPPY!

Akash Bansal (Age 15)

Truck Poem

Air horns that toot
Up the motorway I shoot
I have a fifth wheel
My lovely engine you can reveal
I'm made of steel
I may jack-knife
That'll risk someone's life
I'm big and strong
And always long
I have a tacograph
When I stop people laugh
I'm heavy on the gas
Oh you let me pass

Ryan Brown (Age 10)

Soar Mill Cove On A Winter's Day

Wind rumbling
Rocks tumbling

Foam spraying
Seagulls playing

Breakers splashing
Pebbles crashing

Current rushing
Water gushing

Waves booming
High tide looming

Cliffs amazing
People gazing

Oliver Brouwer (Age 9)

Limericks

There was a chimney from North-Stoke,
Who loved to drink caffeine-free coke
His dad told him off,
Then started to cough,
As instead he had started to smoke!

There once was a man from Dundee,
Who loved to drink flavoured iced-tea.
He tried orange flavoured,
But lemon he favoured,
And drank four whole gallons did he!

Noah Bodinetz (Age 10)

Sonnet On Growing Up

Mewling Babe, newly born, first steps in life,
Unaware of happenings around you.
Not yet knowing feelings of joy or strife,
Talent inside you, waiting for its cue.
Older now, past put behind you, moving on.
New feelings hit your body, clouding your mind.
Baby-like fingers, toes and hands are gone,
Entering the world not knowing what to find.
Older still, finding your true calling,
A sense of knowledge and of belonging.
Last few years of life, you start wondering,
"What was life like before I was crawling?"
Then without warning comes the imminent death,
Re-living your life as you take your last breath.

Adam Brooks (Age 12)

Animals

There are dogs, there are cats
There are elephants, there are bats
They live in homes their own habitats
Some bite, some chew
Some are nice, some are new

Some are spoilt, some are smacked
They make us happy, some are attacked
They are cute, they are happy
Big, small, fat, thin
Animals can be anything

Different shapes different sizes
Sometimes they leave you surprises
Some good, some are bad
Who cares we love them all

Johanna Baker (Age 11)

Friends And Foe

My best friend is Katherine Madge,
She is funny and very mad.
She makes me giggle, laugh and wriggle.
My best friend is Katherine Madge,
She makes me feel like I've just won a badge.

My worst enemy is Lucy Ball,
She is strange and very tall.
She almost threw me down the pit,
I don't like her one bit.
My worst enemy is Lucy Ball,
No-one likes her at all.

Caitlin Bonning (Age 8)

The Night

Beautiful night, stars bright
Not a cloud in sight
Cats squealing, mice squeaking
What a beautiful night

Stars twinkling like glitter
Rabbits snuffling like hedgehogs
Badgers digging like shovels
What a beautiful night

Georgia Brewer (Age 9)

War Poem

We are the weary, the wet and the wounded,
Fighting for freedom, our country to save.
Obeying orders, even if stupid
Otherwise we die at the dawn.

The bodies they stink as they're rotting,
The rats have a feast on the dead where they lay.
The medics run ragged as they try to relax,
The wounded away to be treated today.

Jamie Bourke (Age 13)

Six Ways Of Looking At A Dog

My dog's teeth are like knives,
That cut meat into slices
My dogs claws are like spears,
That they use in movies
My dog's eyes are black,
Like the darkness outside
My dog's fluff is all spiked up,
Just like men do with their hair
My dog is a female dog
Just like ladies are females
My dog is cute
Just like babies

Jordan Baggott (Age 9)

The Joys Of Spring

Daffodils sprouting amongst the dew,
Crocuses, daisies and tulips too.
A newly born lamb just begins to walk
The flowers start to bloom as they rest on their stalks.
A small field mouse scurries along the ground,
Quickly but carefully, without a sound.
The eggs on the farm slowly turn to chicks,
The calves learn to moo and their tails start to flick
The bare trees steadily turn to green,
As the winter passes, spring is on the scene.

Gemma Boothroyd (Age 11)

Sun

A huge dot,
A fire pot,

A burning light,
A brilliant sight,

A great star,
Shines so far,

A sky clinger,
A light bringer,

A golden ray,
No word to explain,

Goes at night,
The moon in sight,

A catalogue to make me the

SUN

Alice Byrne (Age 10)

Tsunami

Towering . . .
And reaching miles up into the sky
Pushing . . .
And blowing down the rim of your face
Then suddenly . . .
Smash went the wave
Into a whirl pool of horror
The pushing and the force too
Unbearable to think of

Destroying . . .
And grabbing the air
Drowning everything in its path
Agitated squawking
As the birds get pulled down to extinction
Then suddenly . . .
Everything went silent
Everyone rose
Looked around
Everything was demolished

Matthew Bowden (Age 11)

Stressed Out Mum

Over the hills in the trees
Lives a stressed out mum
You see she screams and shouts
Kicks people out
And won't let you jump up and about
But one day this stressed out mum you see,
Who went for a walk
Where she found herself
She just didn't know
So she screamed and shouted
Jumped up and down
But then just fell down a hole.

Matthew Bailey (Age 11)

I Want A Cat

I want a cat,
Any sort of cat.
A big cat,
A small cat,
A fat cat,
A tall cat,
A crazy cat,
A lazy cat,
A furry cat,
A hairy cat,
A cruel cat,
A cool cat,
A sneaky cat,
A cheeky cat,

BUT I WANT A CAT!!!

Anna Blake (Age 7)

Away To War

Away to war on the wavy sea,
Where a blustery north wind blows.
France lay dead ahead of us . . .
What next nobody knows?
The clouds began to leak above,
Covering us in rain,
Suddenly ahead of us
We could see land again.

We docked and saw the cavalry,
Mounted on noble steeds
The landscape we were walking through
Was covered in dark green weeds
A messenger had seen the foes,
In a clearing miles ahead.
A question we needed the answer to
Are we going to be dead?

Bradley Bull (Age 10)

Spring Is Here

Spring is here. Spring is here.
Everything is turning greener.
All the world is looking cleaner.

Come out buds. Come out buds
All the daffodils are sprouting
Like a glorious yellow fountain.

Wonderful blossom. Wonderful blossom.
Like some fluffy candyfloss
Or like snow on the moss.
Spring makes me feel happy.

Maxim Calver (Age 6)

The Music Of The Spheres

The blissful music,
Flies around us.
And we realise,
We have committed sins.

The war
And fighting
Has settled down
Now.

We are all
A family,
Together
Forever.

Emily Botelle (Age 8)

The Lion In Africa

Hunting . . .
Carefully and slowly
Then suddenly pounces on her prey
Wisely . . .
Sleek and strong
Then she lay
Calmly . . .
Peaceful and playful
Playing with her young
Gently . . .
Cheerful and lazy
Tail swaying in the sun
Running . . .
Leaping and jumping
Through the bushes they run
Happy . . .
Excited and merry
Lion cubs are having fun!

Sophie Benjamin (Age 11)

Spring

Spring is coming
Dew drops dripping
Early sun singing
Church bells ringing
Lively lambs playing
Seeds are growing
Buds are shooting
Fluffy clouds soaring
Chicks are clucking
Easter bunny bouncing
Christ Jesus rising
Children happily skipping
Chocolate egg giving
Welcome Spring

Maddy Bullett (Age 8)

Dartmoor

If I were Lord of Dartmoor,
And my land was as yellow as the sun,
Happiness is everywhere there in my little land.
Gazing at the picture, I feel the green grass tickling my feet.
Whoosh! The wind through my hair.
Tweet! Go the birds up high.
The grass and trees would bow down to me,
All my world would come to meet me.
My world would be happy.

Staring through my window,
I see a mud track trailing off.
The hills, as beautiful as ever,
The sky is turquoise blue.
Every day the sun jumps out of bed,
And strokes my world, to raise its head.

Jack Barter (Age 10)

Untitled

Frogs jumping
Giraffes bumping
Dogs sleeping
Spiders creeping

Emilie Bell (Age 5)

Jake's Cakes

There was a man called Jake,
And he loved to eat cake,
He went to Reeves,
And saw some thieves,
So he thought, "Which one should I take?"

Freddie Boston (Age 10)

Brazil

B om dia!
R ain forest in Brazil!
A mazing costumes at carnival!
Z ooming fireworks on the streets!
I t's fun at the carnival!
L ove the action!

James Brennan (Age 7)

The Runner Bean Story

The stream is like a runner bean running away from town
The sound of a plop when the runner bean jumps into the stream
The sound of a splash when he's trying to get out
The sound of a whoosh as an owl grabs him
The owl looked like an old, old man
The sound of a gulp when the owl eats him up
The sound of a clonk when he hits the owls belly
The sound of a gurgle when he's saying the end

Paige Banks (Age 9)

The Tractor

A tractor is as red as blood
A tractor is enormous
A tractor is as noisy as a trumpet
A tractor is powerful
A tractor is a large engine
A tractor is a large tank
A tractor is like a transformer
A tractor is four wheels

Jake Bettinson (Age 8)

The Day The Zoo Escaped

The day the zoo escaped . . .
The tigers went out quickly
The snails went out slickly
The tortoises went out slowly
The eagles flew out lowly
The buzzard flew out ghastly
The wolves went out lastly
But the hippopotamus stubbornly, just stayed where it was

Paul Batty (Age 11)

Touch

Touch!
(What can you feel)
The silky spindly thread
Of a spider's web

Touch!
(What can you feel)
The sharp thin point
Of a pencil lead
The soft white pillow
Of a feather bed

Touch!
(What can you feel)
The soft stripy fur
Of a bumble bee
The rough brown bark
Of a sycamore tree

Rebecca Bainbridge (Age 7)

Brazil

B om dia!
R ainforest is amazing!
A stonishing Amazon!
Z oom go the animals!
I t is great!
L ove it!

Abigail Bishop (Age 8)

My Pets

My pets play with me anytime
They like me
My pets jump up

Katie Brooks (Age 6)

Untitled

Kangaroos hopping
Elephants munching
Snakes wriggling
Children giggling
Cats fetching
Dogs stretching
Whales swimming
Frogs leaping
Monkeys swinging
Worms slithering
Bees flying
Lions lying

Kieran Baumann (Age 6)

Tornado

Tornado . . .
Tearing through towns and cities
Ripping
Tornado . . .
Powerful as an untamed beast, it's coming, coming to find you
Tornado . . .
Hungry for more
As it sucks in roofs
Takes lives from people
Just wanting
More and more, it's coming, coming to find you
Tornado . . .
Ripping through your house
Tornado . . .
It's coming
Coming to find you

Abigail Buckingham (Age 11)

Sun Set

The sun is rising once again.
It is time for a brand new day.
My eyes are opening extremely slowly.
Now I'm fully awake.
It has been a great day.
But now it is time for the sun to go away.

Hailey Blaymire (Age 10)

My Poem

I love teacher
She is good at singing
She makes me feel happy

Andrew Bradshaw (Age 13)

The Tobacconists

An old man rocks back in his rickety chair
Puffing the sound of his dreams
Out through a half hung pipe,
Resting on his lip.
A beard hangs loose, as brown as the wonders,
Kept inside his tightly sealed jam jars.
In a dimly lit room, tucked away,
On the corner of an empty street.
Rarely ever visited
And stated in bold, dust coated letters above the shop.
'Tobacconists'

William Bowler (Age 12)

Spelling Test

As Miss handed out the homework books
I checkt my score 12/20
Did you learn you're your spelings Sophie it red
I fel orful my friends talkt about ther scors
Theres said 20/20 2 house points
Its not fair I told my mum about it
And the nex spelling test my mum made me leurn them 10 times
The nex spelling test I got 20/20 2 house points I was much happier
I told my mum what I scored and she took me to Macdonalds.
I loved it.

Sophie Beresford (Age 7)

Confused Lion

I'm yellow and orange,
I've got a big mane,
I'm ruler of the jungle
And the plain

Animals think I'm scary,
I don't know why,
But when they see me,
They only say "Goodbye!"

William Chandler (Age 10)

Beautiful Night

Beautiful night, the crystal moon
All stars in sight, owls sing their lovely tunes

Cats with their bright eyes, owls singing their song
People eating apple pies, as the train chugs along

Dark is fun, children playing games
Waiting for the sun, while parents shout names

Time to go to bed, so the night can come again
Come and rest your head, sleepy sleepy head

Abbie Brewer (Age 9)

Seven Colours In The Sky

The red of my blood
The orange of the sun,
The yellow of the daffodil
The green of nature,
The blue of the sky,
The indigo of your eyes,
The violet of the finishing day
Seven colours in the sky,
This can only be
The beautiful rainbow

Basile Cariou (Age 9)

The Funny Countryside

In the countryside I can see people playing
In the countryside I can hear aeroplanes flying
In the countryside I can smell animals eating
In the countryside I can touch bananas falling
In the countryside I can taste juicy red apples hanging
In the countryside I feel very happy

Jack Bartram (Age 6)

Autumn

A utmn is a time when . . .
U pside down leaves fall
T wirling left to right
U mbrellas up and down
M isty days are really
N asty and horrible

Cian Corrigan (Age 7)

The Farm

Walking through the farmyard what do you see?
I can see a galloping horse looking at me.
Running through the farmyard what do you see?
I can see a pink pig looking at me.
Skipping through the farmyard what do you see?
Skipping through the farmyard what do you see?
I can see a clucking chicken at me.

Summer Birchnall (Age 6)

Fire

Fire jumps like a lion,
It spreads it's arms,
To engulf all around.
The fire never gives up,
Until he's had his meal.
He rants and raves,
Till he gets what he wants.

Ryan Cloherty (Age 10)

What Is The Sun?

The sun is a toffee apple
Floating in the sky.
It is a golden bullet
Shot into space.

The sun is a glowing frisbee
Skimming on the clouds.
It is an orange basketball
Bouncing around the earth.

The sun is a golden gem
Spinning on the clouds.
It is a golden penny
Flicked up to space.

Josh Boon (Age 8)

Feelings

When I'm happy a collage smile is on my face,
When I'm sad a group of tears rush down my face,
When I'm lonely I sit on the bench all on my own,
When I'm worried I bite my nails,
When I'm nervous I don't stop blinking.

Dominique Backhouse (Age 9)

Chin Up

Keep your chin up high!,
Right into the sky!,
Like a bird, like a plane.
Everybody on your lane
Will say . . .
You have never been the same
Since you kept your chin up
HIGH!!

Thomas Bamforth (Age 9)

Monster

Mythical monsters munch marshmallows
O melets, oranges and oysters
N ectarines, nachos, nuggets and nuts
S oup, spaghetti and sausages
T eacakes, tomatoes, turkeys and treacle
E ven eggs and eccles cakes
R ock cakes, rice, rhubarb and raviolli

Rachel Bellamy (Age 12)

Discovery

Faraway places
So many faces
Interesting event go by
That makes you laugh or cry.

Cities never visited
Easy to see
Mysteries unravel
And I travel to be

In the world to be shared
Big event I have failed
In the pages I have read
And the seven oceans I have sailed

Stories in books
Pictures well
Mystical tales
Only books tell

Ray Bekoe (Age 10)

Family

Love filled family
Sharing memories good, bad
Together we're strong

Sarah Beswick (Age 11)

Untitled

Their hands are like crinckled leaves
Their faces are like wobbly jelly
Their eyes are eyeballs in pop guns
Their clothes are brand new
When they walk they look like dogs
They are thinking how to surprise me
I am thinking I like them

Jack Billington (Age 9)

Sadness

Sadness is the colour of black clouds
It tastes like brussel sprouts
It smells like mouldy socks
It looks like my sister's nappy
It sounds like my mum snoring at night
It feels like empty space

Joshua Briggs (Age 10)

The Writer Of This Poem

The writer of this poem
Is no ordinary boy
He is as sporty as a footballer
And as loud as a fire alarm
Or I guess you could say
As loud as all the animals on the farm
I'm as cheeky as a cheetah
And as slow as a snail
All the girls hate me
And that's my tale

Daniel Collins (Age 12)

Snow

The snow falls straight towards you,
You move out the way but there's no escape,
More and more but you can't get out.
The crystal snowflake hits your skin with a calming touch,
Soft on your skin, but it shouldn't it's solid ice,
But it's slowly heating, vanishing, going forever,
Never coming back. The taste on your tongue is delicate,
Even though there's no real taste as long as you believe
It's the best taste in the world.

Owen Carine (Age 10)

Boredom

A gigantic grey cloud
Abusing the dull space
Around it

Liam Bryant (Age 10)

Clear Water

Splash! go the waves as they hit the water
Whoosh! go the dolphins as they jump and swim
Bang! goes the stone as it touches the floor
Gulp! go the fish as they try to get away

Amber Cochrane (Age 9)

Spring

Spring means laughter
Spring means roses blossoming
Spring means peace and love
Spring means enjoyment and fun
Spring means baby chicks chirping

Daniel Caldicott (Age 9)

Spring

S pring is here, but it is cold
P lants and trees promise they will turn colourful
R eplacing snow is growing grass
I n the houses windows open as it gets warmer
N ourishing colours of the rainbow sometimes appear
G raceful butterflies battle to get to new bursting buttercups

Liam Cowing (Age 11)

A Roman Army Poem

The Roman Army were made up of strong men
Who wore red and shiny armour
They took prisoners chained at the neck
Led them away to begin a new life as slaves
Some down the mines
Some working the quarries
Some rowing the Roman navy's fighting ships
And some farming.
Then the slaves were sold to the highest bidder
And sent to school and trained to fight as gladiators
They would eat porridge and ash to give strength
No use trying to escape or they would be branded flogged or put in stocks or even a prison
So after training is over they would be taken to perform in the games.
There they would salute the emperor "Hail Caesar"
We who are about to die salute you!
They must be victorious winning is all that matters
If you lose you die
So, be brave, fight, conquer . . . and live!

Toby Carless (Age 8)

Countryside

C orn is like golden grass swaying in the wind.
O wls hooting in the dark woods at night
U nderneath the ground there are moles digging lots of holes
N ettles growing in the ditches
T he peaceful scene will soon make you relax
R abbits hopping freely over the fields
Y ellow buttercups attracting many insects with their bright petals
S mell the fragrance of the roses and the freshly cut grass
I can hear the birds singing in the trees
D ucks swimming on the lakes with the sun shining down
E ggs laid by the clucking chickens

Amy Chenery (Age 12)

Walking Through The Farmyard

Walking through the farmyard
What do you see?
I see a horse neighing at me

Walking through the farmyard
What do you see?
I see a chick cheeping at me

Walking through the farmyard
What do you see?
I see a donkey looking at me

Sophie Chapman (Age 5)

Haunted House

If you come to my house you are sure to get a fright
When the light flickers, the fangmangeler will strike!
I see shadows moving in the night . . .
It moves in a flash of black light.
No sweat, it's just the landing lights flickering
Oh no . . . it's the fangmangeler!

Matthew Cooper (Age 8)

Brazil

B om tarda!
R ain forests!
A mazoon rainforests!
Z ooming footballs on the pitch!
I t is so fun in Rio!
L ots of lovely dances, Like Samba!

Natalie Cording (Age 8)

The Sun

When the sun comes out each day it is a sign it's time to play
When the sun comes floating past you get a shiver of happiness
When the sun turns away none of the children want to play
So if the sun comes out to play all of the children shout HOORAY!

Sonny Casey (Age 7)

The True Meaning Of Easter

Far away in Bethlehem a Baby Boy was born;
Born with neither riches nor fame,
Yet wise men came from all around to bring their gifts,
And all who heard his name felt peace.

Angels watched Him as He slept, and gently rocked his manger,
Their voices sang softly in his ear;
His mother Mary and father Joseph both gave thanks to God above,
For the greatest gift of their son so dear.

They knew his life upon the earth would not be filled with wealth,
They also knew he would encounter strife;
But most of all, they knew that he would be a loving child,
And teach the love of God throughout his life.

At Easter as we celebrate the resurrection of Jesus Christ,
Lets keep in mind the true meaning of Easter,
For it's not the Easter egg wrappers, nor the egg that lies within,
But our gift of love to others in every way.

Charlotte Carvalho (Age 11)

The Racehorse

His coat gleamed in the sun
The race had only just begun
His ears were pricked tense and alert
For this race he was a cert
His muscles rippled he flicked his tail
Our hopes were up, he wouldn't fail
Jockey mounted, ready to race
They start off at a steady pace
Furlong after furlong, thundering over turf
This horse had meant to be a winner since birth
The winning post was in sight
The chance of him losing was very slight
At last he thundered in
Spread across the owner's face there was a grin
Cool water was splashed across his back the horse was thankful of that.

Roberta Coll (Age 11)

Spring

Spring is fun. Spring is fun.
Spring is when Easter comes.
Spring is fun. Spring is fun.
When Spring appears the sun comes.
Spring is coming. Spring is coming.
Children enjoy skipping and running.
Spring is here. Spring is here.
Spring is when baby animals are near.
So if, like me, you like the Spring,
Then come outside and go on the swing.

Annabel Canham (Age 7)

Winter

Children having snowball fights
Spheres of snow used in war
Troops of snowmen ready for battle
Round white and bare

Squirrels and hedgehogs go into hibernation
Full of food to keep them warm
Bare trees waving in the wind.
The dark sky becomes darker every day

Asher Cosgrove (Age 8)

The Hidden Troll

Be careful of the hidden troll,
You never know if he's there,
He can hear you almost everywhere,
So be careful if he's there,
Never take a stroll one day,
Far, far and away,
Because the troll is anywhere,
You could slip inside his lair.

Rebecca Clark (Age 9)

Bee In The Classroom

Bee in the classroom
Hovering over flowers
Children stop and point
At the bees super powers
As the bee flies across
The big wide sky
The scardy cat's jump
And begin to cry

Tomas Cornelly (Age 9)

The Railway Carriage

Patchwork meadows never stop
Bunnies and squirrels always hop
Smoke from chimneys join the air
Branches on trees, not yet bare
Eagles spread their mighty wings
To hear the sound of church bells ring
Clean white clouds float on by
Littered flowers there they lie

Megan Casey (Age 9)

The Dog Star

Up in the heavens, there is a star,
The star in the heaven,
That all dogs will love,
Cats to chase no owners who shout,
Just chewing their bones and running about,
Parks to run, balls to play,
Mud to roll in and no bath forever,
There is more in store so bark your way.

Zoe Chu (Age 10)

The Victim Of A Vampire

It was dark, the moon had arisen
I was late coming home from work
I heard a rustle in the bushes
I thought nothing of it
I took a shortcut through an alleyway
I heard a thump on top of one of the buildings next to me
I started to walk faster, my paces getting bigger
Then once I got out of the alleyway
I realised that I had taken a wrong turn
I was back on the path
I started walking again
I heard a rustle again in a bush
I went down the same alleyway again
I heard a thump on the rooftop
It was followed by a swoosh
There in front of me, was a tall figure
Wearing a black hooded cloak
Underneath the hood were two white fangs
Then the figure pounced!
Now I'm immortal

Steven Craig (Age 11)

Anger

Anger is dark red like blood on the floor,
It tastes like blood in your mouth,
It smells like the stench of rotting bodies,
It looks evil like fire,
It sounds like burning wood,
It feels like you want to kill someone.

Robert Challingsworth (Age 11)

The Walk

It was cold, damp, dark
I could hardly see anything
The fog was blinding
In the distance I could hear a rustling
I didn't know what it was but something was there

All of a sudden an icy hand grabbed my shoulder
It's touch was as cold as the snow queen's breath
I stopped, everything stopped
Nothing could be heard apart from
The occasional car passing by

I didn't want to look around and see what it was
But I could feel its heavy breath on my neck
As I took the first step round
The leaves crunched and a bright light shone in my eyes
A familiar face it wasn't a surprise to me.

Olivia Codd (Age 13)

Dancing

I love dancing
All week long
Keeps me fit
And I have fun

Tap is lively
Makes lots of noise
My feet are talking
And so are the boys!

Ballet is graceful
Stretch your feet
Your arms are elegant
Your hair is neat

Modern is jazzy
Flexible and quick
Splits and cartwheels
Make your fingers flick!

Alexandra Cook (Age 8)

Spring

S pring is lovely
P ips that are in the field
R ings of daisies are all around us
I n the field daffodils grow
N ature's animals come out
G o on and enjoy Spring

Sophie Cannon (Age 9)

Spring

Winter's gone spring is here,
The freezing cold there is no fear

Baby chicks sing away
March, april don't forget May

Little lambs just been born,
On the fields lots of corn

On the trees, blossom will grow,
The smell of cut grass when we mow

Lots of butterflies on the trees
Lots of insects, caterpillar and the bees

Little clouds in the sky
Relax now MY, MY

Ellen Lisa Craig (Age 10)

Big Cat Fred

"Run!" screams the skylark.
"Hide!" mutters the vole.
"Soar into the sky!"
"No! make for that hole."

"Flee!" says the flea.
"He's on the prowl."
"Who is?" enquires the dung beetle.
"Is it me? Do I smell foul?"

"No," whispers the roe deer.
"The cat's around,
Though I don't hear his footstep
On the ground."

"This is a stupid idea," ventures the possum.
"Why, the last time we did it, I got a sore bottom.
The easiest thing is to just act dead."
Then out of the bushes comes BIG CAT FRED.

There is a munch.
There is a rush.
There is a crunch.
There is a mush.

Laurence Childs (Age 9)

Music Of The Spheres

The peaceful music is calming me down,
It's lovely, it's peaceful
The music is magical,
You fall into a world of your own.

You can see a space-bat-angel-dragon,
It is like a black dot flying past the sun.
They've stopped making weapons,
Now it is a calm place.

Brandon Christian (Age 8)

My Family

I love my family and my family loves me,
We like to share our time together happy as can be,
We go to the pictures we go to the park,
We always have a jolly good lark,
We share good times we share bad,
Sometimes were happy sometimes were sad,
We like it best when we're together,
My family and me,
I love them and they love me.

Mark Chapman (Age 10)

Rapping

Rapping, rapping,
Can you, hear the, rapping.

If you listen close enough,
The band will play out loud,
And if you have an instrument,
Show that you're proud.

Rapping, rapping,
Can you, hear the, rapping.

If you have some money,
Come and watch us play,
We'll play for you all night,
And all of the next day,
If you feel miserable,
The band will make you right,
Come and enjoy yourself,
You won't get a fright!

Quick raps, slip slaps, dip daps, clip claps,
Listen to the rap!

Rapping, rapping,
Can you, hear the, rapping.

Laura Marie Clay (Age 9)

Dinosaurs

D inosaurs are big
I n the forest they eat leaves
N ever go near T-Rex
O h no he is coming to eat me
S it on a dinosaur if you dare
A nkylosaurus is coming for his dinner
U p in the sky flies a Pteradon
R un run a dinosaur is coming
S tegosaurus has long spikes

Finley Canniff (Age 6)

Steam Train

The sky is as dark as a black hole!
The moon is as light as a light bulb
The snow on the tree glistened like glitter
The coldness of the snow was very bitter
Now I see it coming closer and closer
It's just alike a long black poster
When I ride on it, it feels like a roller coaster
I hear an owl hooting
I see a baby shaking his bootie

Victoria Cocks (Age 8)

The Evacuee

I'm sitting on the station stair
No-one else is there
I'm feeling small and shy
I may be about to cry
A thick long tear runs down my cheek
And ends up at my feet
I have to be strong;
It's all gone wrong.
I'm sitting here in the street
I don't know who I will meet
It's hard to lose your hopes and dreams
It's sadder than it seems
When I get on the train
My life will never be the same
It's getting near sunrise
It's time for my goodbyes
Poor lonely child gets upon the train
It will never, be the same
Poor me - the evacuee

Elizabeth Cole (Age 9)

My Poems

Twinkle Twinkle

Twinkle, twinkle, little monkey,
Why are you so funky?

Five Little Monkeys

Five little monkeys standing in the bath,
One fell out and had a laugh.

Birds

Birds come out to sing and play,
They do it every day.

Jodie Cronin (Age 7)

What Is The Sun?

The sun is a toffee apple
Sparkling over the sea
It is a bright sweet orange
Floating over the horizon

The sun is a nut
Fading away behind the clouds
It is a powershot
Skimming through the air

The sun is a fine ball
Glowing through the window
It is a disco ball
Dancing in the sky

Billy Carter (Age 7)

The River

A corpse in the flowing river,
Steady as the beating drum,
Never pausing for a thought
Choices made at an instant
Alone but surrounded
I live this life
Crying out inside my mind
Piece by piece, I break
Falling,
        falling,
                falling
Someone catch me
Someone save me
Someone heal me
Understand me, for who I am
For I can't be anything else
To try will only crush me
I don't want to be
The corpse in the flowing river

Kate Clarke (Age 14)

Fish

Fish swim in the sea
They swim by the key
A fish is a creature
Some fish are a teacher
Some fish are a ray
And on the seabed they lay
A ray is a fish
As flat as a dish

A fish is a jelly fish
That goes swish, swish, swish
A jellyfish stings you on the shoe
Jellyfish stay together
With which one another

Victoria Chapman (Age 7)

The Countryside

In the countryside I can see
Green shiny grass waving

In the countryside I can smell
Shining black berries

In the countryside I can hear
A fat blackbird singing

In the countryside I can taste
A fresh strip of tasty corn and it is growing

In the countryside
I feel happy and excited.

Amber Circuit (Age 6)

Mystical River

Water trickles out of gaps between jagged rocks,
Slowly, it grows larger and larger,
Mystical river, oh - how it roars into life . . .
Nothing can stop it rampaging on!
Pulsating waves crash against each other,
You can hear the roaring from afar.

Sluggishly, the river slows down,
Bubbling water is crystal clear,
The river sparkles like gems in the sunlight,
It meanders and flows through tight and sharp bends,
Spitting and spouting water as it plunges drastically down a waterfall....

Now the river is calmer and frothy on the surface,
Lively and energetic is what it used to be,
The sapphire-blue river is radiant as ever,
As the magical river comes to its end,
It says its goodbyes and joins the rough sea.

Rajveer Chohan (Age 11)

What is . . . Autumn

Autumn is an amazing magic show
Making scarlet leaves appear out of nowhere

It is the tiny blackbirds
Having a conversation with the magpies

It is greeting winter
With news that summer is gone

Christopher Christophi (Age 10)

Animals

Tigers strike their prey
Using all their might
Pouncing heavily on their backs
Prey dies overnight

The giraffe stands tall and proud
Its patchwork shines in the sun
Watching the tigers from high above
They think it's a load of fun

Lois Collins (Age 11)

The Zumblies

The zumblies are little red things
And they have more money than kings
They eat smelly feet
And munch on stinky treats
In the land where the zumblies live

Their teeth are navy blue
And they drink a snooker cue
They smash cola glasses
And they play in the ashes
In the land where the zumblies live

Instead of football and tennis being played for fun
They play it for fame and for a jam bun
When they cry they create rivers
And then the snake god slithers
In the land where the zumblies live

Jack Conroy (Age 10)

Snake

The
Soft
Slimy
Slivery
Snake
Slivered
So quietly
Across
The
Snowy
Ground
So small
And
Silent
As a
Small
Snail

Sam Cornick (Age 9)

48

Animals

One orange orang-utan opened our oven
Two tiny toddlers touched our tea
Three terrific tigers fought ten t-rexes
Four fat frogs ate all the logs
Five furry ferrets fought all day long
Six sad snakes slithered into town
Seven stinky skunks smelt the sizzling sausages
Eight elephants drank eighty cups of water
Nine naughty nits fell on people's noses
Ten toads tooting to the tortoises

Chloe Craze (Age 9)

Buddy!

Buddy's here,
Buddy's there,
Buddy's everywhere,
He's my best friend you know,
One of the best I've ever had,
He's there to calm,
He's there to sooth,
There to make me happy when I'm in a mood,
And that's all I have to say,
Because that's the truth!

Rozella Challis (Age 11)

Riddle

My first is in saddle but not in ladle
My second is in strain but not in swan
My third is in rain but not in stain
My fourth is in ant and in apple
My fifth is in waddle and in wait
My sixth is in banana but not in an
My seventh is in cake but not cat
My eighth is in rasp but not in wasp
My ninth is in in rope but not in hope
My last is in yoghurt but not in hurdle

What am I?

Lauren Clarke (Age 12)

Max And Millie

My two best friends are Max and Millie
We're always mucking around and being silly

Playing games and running around
We make too much noise we make too much sound

We're always together day and night
We never let one another out of sight

My two dogs are my best friends
As long as we're together
Our friendship will never end

Jordan Camsey (Age 12)

The Lion The Witch And The Wardrobe

The Pevensie children, thanks to them
We won the war and lived in peace again

Peter the oldest went into battle to fight
He loves and takes care of his family and kisses them goodnight

Susan the gentle thinks she's so smart
But in the professor's house she got told off for touching the historical art

Edmund the just, he picks on Lucy because he thinks he's so bold
But most of the time Peter has to say, "When will you ever learn to do as you are told"

Lucy the youngest is honest and sweet
She was the one who stepped into Narnia first and saw snow at her feet

The wicked white witch lives in a castle of ice
She's mean and cruel and trust me she's not very nice

Aslan the lion killed the white witch
And the war we had won, but for the Pevensie children it had only just begun

Lucy Cottrell (Age 10)

Aeroplanes

Aeroplanes fly higher than the highest cloud
Their wings are wide and engines loud
They soar like birds of prey
Upon clouds do their weightless bodies lay
From windows the passengers see houses
They are so far down they look like louses
There will be no turbulence
For the plane has perfect balance
There is no limit to the sky
It can fly far and high
Sometimes the stewardess will speak
Her voice sharp and uniform sleek
Aeroplanes fly higher than the highest cloud
Their wings wide and engines loud

Dan Carpenter (Age 13)

Happiness

Happiness is skippy
He goes with a certain flow,
It's happy and it can show,
With a smile a skip and a kind hello.

He fights away your worry,
It runs away in a hurry,
Its face is a golden ball,
It's how I feel after school.
Its eyes are pieces of the sun,
When I'm with it I have lots of fun.

Happiness you want forever
But sometimes it won't stay,
Because it feels it's time to go time to go away.

Troy Clark (Age 12)

Farmer

Pig slaughterer
Mad driver
Animal carer
Hard worker
Corn thrower
Loud Shouter
Grows our food

Jordan Codling (Age 8)

Dinosaur Acrostic Poem

D inosaurs are friendly.
I n the forest they eat leaves.
N ever go near T-Rex.
O ver the sea they fly.
S harp teeth.
A nkylosaurus is coming for me.
U p in the sky flies a Pteradon.
R un run run a dinosaur is coming.
S tegosaurus had long spikes.

Lewis Darvill (Age 5)

The Seaside

Ice-cream dribbles as it starts to shrink in the heat of the sunrays
Beach balls jump up and down tapping the gentle sand
Deck chairs sun bathe, as they settle in a comfy position
The sea whistles a tuneful song, as it dances on the shore

Danielle Cowing (Age 9)

Graveyard

I am alone in the graveyard.
Apart from my slow breathing it is a deadly silence.
Did I really say I am alone?
A sharp shiver shoots down my spine, as an ice cold breath touches my skin.
I don't want to turn but I do.
As I turn it whispers "Nice night for dying."
I am standing here face to face with a blood sucking vampire!
As it lifts its arm I see shrivelled up skin.
I cry "please don't kill me"
As he reaches for me I pinch myself.
It isn't a dream.
It is real!

Chelsea Marie Charles (Age 11)

The Horse

I'm a horse
A horse I say
I love to gallop
And eat lots of hay

I love my grass
And all that
I love all food
And I'm very fat

I'm a horse a horse
And I'm very cool
I'm very clever
And I'm no fool

I have lots of friends
They're all cool like me
And you can tell
As they all live by the sea

Bobbie Caines (Age 10)

Friends

How can we explain friends?
Kind, happy funny, jolly
They are the people that pick us up when we're down
They make us laugh, they make us smile

They're always there for us when we're sad or upset
Always with a smile or a helping hand
Always talking, always giving good advice
They see you through the good times and the bad

Just think about your friends
What good things have they done for you?
Cheered you up? Made you laugh?
Whatever it was they did it for you

So the next time you take your friend for granted
Or you don't treat them that well
Just remember this
How many times have they been there for you?

Amy Chatten (Age 12)

Waterfalls Poem

Waterfalls crashing
Waterfalls smashing
Waterfalls bashing
Waterfalls roaring
Waterfalls clashing
Waterfalls trickling
Waterfalls dashing

Luke Jon Coombes (Age 9)

Love

Love is red like beautiful roses,
It tastes like sugared strawberries,
It smells like scented perfume,
It looks like two connected hearts,
It sounds like peaceful music,
It feels like being together.

Melissa Crouch (Age 11)

Imagine

Imagine a world where everything's numb,
Can't feel any pain, no hurt from your life
You'd take the chance to escape from reality.
Screaming for your life to be over, nothing's worth living for.
Lie alone in your realm and pray for someone
To save you from the darkness of your life
To show you the way and set your soul free,
Releasing your spirit, the person inside you is alive

Milly Chapman (Age 13)

A Tiger Attack

A volcano is like a tiger ready to catch its prey
A tiger is harmless when it's asleep
But when it is awake it causes everything to malfunction and disappear,
A tiger's temper will lash out on anything that gets in its path
A tiger sits there looking harmless
Until before you know it there is a stream of lava
Racing down the side of the volcano

Daniel Collyer (Age 10)

Other Side Of Truth

I stepped outside into the sun,
Played about and had some fun.
This is the city, in which I stayed, until only yesterday.
A bang and a thud was the only sound,
As my mam Adewell fell to the ground.
A car screeched away in a flurry of dust,
That was the person who made all the fuss.
Around my mama laid a puddle of blood,
I'm disappointed the gunmen felt good.
I packed my suitcase left the door,
Now I was worried even more.
I got in my car, and I set off far.
On the journey my uncle was funny,
As we paid the police some good money.
We stepped out the car and there she stood,
In a pile of wet soggy mud.
Talking to a pole,
Was Mrs Bankole.
Here the misery starts,
As papa and I part.

Laura Coathup (Age 12)

Ella

My kitten Ella was a wonderful sight,
She was a magnificent torte 'n' white.
Sadly I lost her three years ago,
When her pure white soul took to flight.

A moving experience one may say,
Because it happened suddenly one day.
On April the fifth two thousand and three,
Happened that terrible tragedy.

I will never get over it I'm sure,
It brings a large lump in my throat.
I'll always remember her good and pure,
Purer than a lily afloat.

Oh Ella, Oh Ella I miss you so,
Oh Ella, Oh Ella I think you should know
How much we miss you, your brother and I
But the way we feel can't be described.

Gabrielle Corry-Mead (Age 10)

I Should Like To . . . .

I should like to see the glamorous pot of gold at the end of a rainbow
The sun from Pluto on a fascinating, dark night
A rocket's flames bursting into the distance of the night sky
The future straight before my seeking eyes and nose

I should like to understand the properties of all the wonderful shapes there are
The thoughts of the animals in their cages travelling on a powerful lorry
Why the English had to attack the Zulus hundreds of years ago
And how the sun came to our fantastic universe

Joseph Caley (Age 9)

Harvest

The soft breeze tickles my face
In the blazing summer sunshine,
Clouds dance overhead, like new-born lambs playing in the spring.
As the monster, whirring loudly, approaches,
Startled rabbits dive for cover
The nettles swaying in the sudden gust of wind.
Dust flies through the air.
A black cloud casting shadows on the freshly cut stubble.
In the sheltered barn,
I watch as the monster roars past me,
Straw whirling around my feet like a small tornado.
And then it dies.
The sound is gone, only a distant echo lingers,
Birds begin to sing again.
Everything is still, peaceful.
And harvest is over for another year.

Lucy Chubbock (Age 12)

Easter

E aster bunny brings Easter eggs
A re you excited it's Easter?
S o many Easter eggs
T oo many eggs, eggs, eggs.
E aster is full of fun and laughter
R ip, rip, rip, it's all gone!

Paisley Carter (Age 9)

My Dog

He is black
He hangs out of the window
He jumps up at me
He jumps up to catch discs
He brings it back ready for another go

Freya Cooper (Age 6)

Mother's Day

Mother's Day is another chance for me to let you know,
The happiness we're sharing means more than words can show . . .
You're such a wonderful Mum that we know is true,
And I want you to know how much I really love you . . .
So enjoy your very special day, a day that is filled with love,
For the most very special woman who I think the whole world of,
You mean the world to me, you lifted me when I couldn't stand,
Your eyes sparkled when I was happy, you were beside me when I was afraid,
You comforted me when I was sad, you brought me strength when I was weak,
You gave me your wisdom when I was lost, Mummy, you loved me no matter what.

Matthew Coates (Age 10)

My Little Brother Robbie

My little brother Robbie, is as annoying as can be!
If you dare to read on you will see!

First thing in the morning, he's banging on the walls.
Then he's running down the stairs making prank calls!!

Screaming and shouting, slamming doors, rolling around on all fours.
Hallelujah as the sun goes down, my little brother Robbie calms down.

At last peace and quiet reigns over the house,
Nothing much moving except for a mouse.

Lauren Cully (Age 10)

Months Of The Year

January - New year begins with lots of cheers
February - whispers of love on Valentine
March - bunches of flowers for a Mother's Day love
April - Easter eggs and bunnies
May - new life begins for baby lambs
June - Father's Day love for my Dad
July - I'm too busy thinking of sun and sand
August - is when I'm just lazing around
September - school term begins
October - witches and wizards for Halloween
November - Guy Fawkes and fireworks for bonfire night
December - Christmas trees, presents and lots of fun for now we have done a twelve month run

Rosie Clarke (Age 11)

Snow Leopard

The Snow Leopard awakens Walks out of her den
And see prey . . . .
Hides and then
Dangerously pounces
And hit her prey
She drags her prey to her babies

But slip on the cliff
Down she goes
She tries to get up
But can't
Her leg is broken
Suddenly . . .
Rocks start to fall
The snow leopard is not fast enough to move
What will happen to the Snow Leopard

Reece Chick (Age 11)

Summer Time

Me sketching
Dog fetching

Zebra bumping
Elephant trumping

Children bumping
Me dumping

Fish splashing
Elephant mashing

Dad sun bathing
Me fun bathing

Mum washing
Me splashing

Phoebe Cole (Age 6)

Pat

There once was a boy called Pat,
Who was always dressed in a hat.
One day he was sat
On a big fluffy mat
Watching a cat that was chasing a rat.

Chloe Campling (Age 9)

Brazil

B om dia means 'good morning!'
R io de Janeiro! is a big city!
A ntelope zooming at speed!
Z ebras running about!
I am in Brazil!
L et's have fun!

Bethany Collins (Age 7)

Weird Day

On a very weird day
In a very weird town
Where the sky was green
And the grass was brown

There in the town
There lived just two
A cat and a dog
Who both played the digeridoo

They played all day
And they played all night
They played by themselves
But they did not fight

The cat and the dog
Best friends they were
"That's weird" I thought
But it was all a blur

Charlotte Cascarina (Age 10)

Screaming

Loud noises,
Cracking bangs,
Loads of screaming,
All over the lands.

Dogs growling,
People scowling,
Nobody sleeping,
Children weeping.

Fireworks displays,
Dramatic plays,
Screaming fans,
Of singing bands.

Load of screaming,
All over the lands.

Adam Cloney (Age 10)

Spring

I like Spring
Snow drops are lovely
Daffodils are nice
The grass is green
Flowers grow in the
Green grass
Spring is nice

Joshua Cresswell (Age 7)

The Sea

As the restless tide flows through the weeds
The gleaming shells crash against the rocks.
The silver pearls melt in the sea with their silver coat shining
And the crashing waves push against the jagged rocks.
And the glowing scales of the fish swimming in the sea!
The whooshing waves glide through the sea
And see the weeds flowing roughly in the sea.

Tyne-Lexy Clarson (Age 9)

School

S is for super work
C is for cool friends
H is for harmony at school
O is for outstanding teachers
O is for outstanding things
L is for a lovely place

Charlotte Chippendale (Age 8)

Books

I see books just lying there on the shelves
I hear them crying out for desperate help
I seem to be the only one who can hear them
Should I rescue them from their mansion of death
Or wait till I come back
Are you next?

Natalie Cain (Age 9)

Cheetah

I'm a cheetah, I am fast
If you race me you'll be last
I'll have you for my tea
You'll be crunchy as can be

Ben Cuss (Age 10)

Fireworks

Up, up and away
The fireworks launch from off the floor
They twizzle and turn as they get higher and higher
Then it explodes with a big *BANG*
The lots of colours spread all over the sky, yellow, red, green, purple.

Daniel Cook (Age 10)

Anger

It is like a devil
On your back
Biting you!

James Colbourne (Age 10)

The Man From Brazil

There once was a man from Brazil,
Who lived on a very big hill,
He thought he could fly,
So he gave it a try,
And was caught by his good friend Bill.

Alex Coull (Age 12)

River

Roaring loudly
Very cloudy
Extremely fast
Running past
Splashing wellies
Very fun
Can't stop
Every day

Hannah Coulton (Age 8)

Sister

S ophie snake silently slithered through the silky grass
I ndigo ivy is in an iglow in an ink pot
S melly sausages smile in a small silly stupid pan in sauce
T erry tiger tiptoed to Tipsy tiger with no thumb thinking of
Terry
E smerelda is an empty elephant inside an elephant
R orry rabbit runs rapidly round Rachele

Zoe Denly (Age 8)

What Is The Sun?

The sun is a golden frisbee
Soaring through the daylight clouds
It is a shining bronze penny
Flicked so high in the sky

The sun is a golden bullet
Shot up high straight to heaven
It is a beautiful glistening gem
Floating and shooting beams by magic

The sun is a glittery disco ball
Turning and swaying in the daylight
It is a hot air balloon
Shining and moving past the hills

The sun is a swirling boat
Paddled by the most amazing workers
It is a golden medal
Looking down on you from above

The sun is a delicate dandelion
Swaying in the morning time
It is a fiery ball
Shot by a magic wizard

Tom Crisp (Age 9)

A Renga: Two Cockatoo Haikus

My Reggie is dead.
Eyes still, claws stiff, feathers flat.
Maybe the bad cat.

My Ronnie is fine.
Flapping like mad, squawking.
Birthday tomorrow.

Michael Clare (Age 11)

Frog

Frog jumping and leaping
Laying frogspawn
Tiny balls of jelly
Eating their way out
Tadpoles swimming in your pond
Gills close up and grow back legs
Then they grow front legs
Tail goes and froglets emerge
Then they are a fully grown frog
Jumping about!
Strong leg muscles
Shoot out tongues to catch food
Rock sitter
Cannot breath under water
Starts again.

Thomas Carlton (Age 10)

Joey

His family think he's a nice kid
They say he is so quiet
They think he's very placid
But actually, he causes quite a riot

He curses and
He swears
He also says things to people
That most others wouldn't dare

He kicks and
He punches
He takes kids' school money
That's for their lunches

He wears his hoody
On the street corner
"Get off that bench!"
Shouts old Mr Lawner

His family think he's a nice kid
They say he is so quiet
They think he's very placid
But actually, he causes quite a riot

Jamie Dabrowiecki (Age 11)

Monkeys

Monkeys swing on the trees
And eat the leaves.
They munch and they crunch.

They are funny and they are sunny.
They make me giggle.
They make me laugh.

Imogen Cooper (Age 6)

Fairy Dancer

All is silent; all is still
Until the beautiful little fairy dancer starts to dance...
In the darkness, flowers sway and dew drops drip
As the fairy dancer does a flick, kick,click
As she quickly leaps across the ground,
Thunder rumbles all-around.
As lightning and rain starts lashing down
The fairy dancer stops and frowns,
But she carries on in a rage, twirling and swirling
Like she's in an iron cage.
Soaking wet she stomps her feet and storms off
To her warm bed to sleep,
Until the moon comes again
The fairy dancer sleeps contently in the rain.

Marni-Lee Clarson (Age 12)

Fear

Running, running as fast as a cheetah chasing its prey,
Away from the half-horse, half-dragon that is chasing me.
Feel cold like someone has poured ice all over me;
My heart is thumping like elephants stampeding all around my chest.
I can hear the monster smashing windows behind me.
Sweating like I have just run the marathon.
My mouth is as dry as a hot, sandy desert,
It's hard to breathe, as if a camel had got stuck in my throat.
I lock myself in a house but . . .

Elena Crowle (Age 8)

Swiss Alps

S now sets all over the peaks
When I climb I always bring the gear
I trek to the summit
S oon to find my goal
S o high I am I could touch the clouds

A hh the top, my destination
L ets go down now, to some warmth
P laying in the snow nice and fun
S oon I'm at the end just where I begun!

William Coombes (Age 10)

The Hairy Horis

The Hairy Horis is a beast with super sweaty hair
He has smelly spotted teeth brown as a bear
His feet are smooth slimy and bare
If you enter his hive he'll make it so bright
Do you want something to eat well I'll put out the light
And sing you some songs which will keep you in sight
Until well after midnight,
When he'll say with his friend Morris
"There's nothing in this world
Like the songs of a Hairy Horis"

Shannon Cavan (Age 9)

You Are Late

You are late!
Well my dad got stuck in the car.
My friend got stuck in the house.
My mum got stuck in the bedroom.
My hamster escaped from the cage.
My dog bit my mum.
My baby got stuck in the cot.
My nan, well she got stuck in the garden.
Please Miss, I have nothing to write about.

Lucy Connolly (Age 7)

Cats

In our home we have three cats
Millie, Molly and Charlie.
They get up to mischief all the time
This is why I am writing this rhyme.
They run in the woods and chase the birds
But are scared of dogs and things they hear.
They run like the wind all day long
But when they come in they just eat and sleep.

Christopher Dodd (Age 11)

Colours

What is yellow?
Yellow is a fresh lemon
Yellow is abright sunflower
Yellow is a fresh mellon

What is red?
Red is like a red rose
Red is like a red sharpener
Red is like red rose choices

Jamie Cook (Age 7)

On The Sea

The sea is as beautiful as a rose
When there is no wind the sea is beautiful and calm
As the waves dive up and down they pose

The sea is as powerful as lightning
There the sea can be stormy
When there is rain the sea keeps fighting
It can be warmy

Ellie Demetriou (Age 9)

Nitro

Nitro is soft and small
Nitro is one foot tall
Nitro likes to go all nutty
Especially when I play footy
Nitro is fun when he's around
Nitro is black with spots of brown
Nitro is cool and fun
Even when he's in the sun
Nitro cries when I am gone
Nitro is my number one
Nitro jumps when I come home
Even when I have his bone
Nitro barks when cars go by
He's a puppy, I guess that's why

Kira Cummins (Age 12)

My Rainforest Poem

There's no snowy winter
In the dense rainforest
Dense and warm and wet.

The poison-arrow frog creeps
In the dense rainforest
Dense and warm and wet.

The piranha is ready to shred
In the dense rainforest
Dense and warm and wet.

The sloth is somewhere so beware
In the dense rainforest
Dense and warm and wet.

Adam Dunbabin (Age 8)

Easter

I see the sight of holy blood
I taste the cold air
I smell the death of the holy man
I hear the scream of crucifixion
I touch the very edge of the wooden cross

Daniel Carpenter (Age 9)

Is It Real?

The winter rolls on like a blast from the north
Ice is faded like a layer of time soon to die
But the snow is silent . . . silent like troops on a battlefield
Given the order finally to slowly advance
It fills every corner, crevasse and hill and more it spread
Covering the land in a silent grace

Toby Dixon (Age 11)

Frost

A harsh bitter night unfolds the first winter frost
The lonely fox is snug in his lair.
His thick furry coat saves him from the raw winds.
His belly grumbling for food, but not daring to find it.
The trees look lifeless next to the immortal evergreens.
Cheerful children race down the white hill on their brand new sledges,
While black cat runs past the children putting the head on their large snowman.
Their breath hangs in the air.
Rosy cheeks and bright smiles on each and every face.
But then as the snow melts away.
They look forward to next year.

Matthew Cork (Age 12)

Nervousness

Nervousness tastes like bitter sea water slipping down your throat,
It looks like a lonely, long corridor with no one in with all my worries plastered on the wall,
It smells like a clogged up room with no windows or doors,
It sounds like people's shouts hollering from distant lands,
It feels like hands are tying knots in my tummy.

Lauren Carter (Age 10)

A to Z Poem Of The Rainforest

A nimals living freely
B irds eating fruit
C anopy is dropping fruit
D angers animals
E volving monkeys
F ish in the river
G rowing trees
H appy animals jumping around
I n eggs babies lie
J umping moonlight frogs
K icking praying mantises
L eopards stalking their prey
M onkeys leaping from tree to tree
N asty animals killing each other
O pen spaces for animals to hunt
P rancing cubs
Q uickly the lion stalks his prey
R apid rushing rivers
S melly animals picking each other
T oucan singing in the trees
U nder story crèches
V arious varieties of birds
W ater rapids crashing against the rocks
X mas is celebrated there as well as here
Y oung animals crawling to their mums
Z ipping sloth's

Daniel Dunbabin (Age 10)

Elementary

There was a tree, on a borderless frame,
There was a star, fifteen feet high,
There was a house, full of green liquid,
There was a vase, fluffy and wispy white,
There was a cloud, ill with the craters of time,
There was a moon, endless to the human eye,
There was a sky, smaller than the sands on the seashore,
There was a stone, twinkle in the starry night sky,
There was a fire, as loud as a supersonic boom,
There was a cry, chained by an ivy belt,
There is a world that carries the midst of life.

John Daniels (Age 13)

Walking Through The Farmyard

Walking through the farmyard
What do you see?
I can see a jumping horse looking at me

Skipping through the farmyard
What do you see?
I can see a pig oinking at me

Walking through the farmyard
What do you see
I can see sheep baaing at me

Sophie Drummond (Age 6)

The Green, The White And The Blue

You can always trust a country with a tricolour flag,
Better by far than some old, imperial rag,
Equality, fraternity and liberty,
The three old ideas that still sound right to me,
Home of the brave, land of the free.

What about the captive heart,
Pulled three ways and torn apart,
English home, Scot's blood, Irish soul,
In one boy, a thousand years,
Of history, joy and tears.

The mystery of three in one,
Like the spirit, the father and the son,
Who you are is hard to say,
When the question arises every day,
So you play it by ear, come what may.

A new nation beating in a single breast,
Not sure what to do, hoping for the best.

Christopher Devitt (Age 13)

Carrie's War

Bombs rained on London town,
Children were sent away,
Children had suitcases brown,
With the Evans they had to stay.

Mr Evans was strict,
Auntie Lou was kind,
Mr Evans hit Nick with a stick,
Mess, Auntie Lou didn't mind.

Nick was a greedy boy,
Carrie was alright,
Mr Evans saw him OI!
He was in the spot light.

Auntie Lou met a soldier,
Mr Evans looked after the shop,
Nick hurt his shoulder,
Carrie cleaned up with a mop

Georgia Duckworth (Age 10)

Olivia Jayne

My little sister's so much fun,
She loves to play out in the sun.

Olivia Jayne is so sweet,
But she cannot keep her things neat.

She loves to make all kinds of mess,
And get our mum into a stress.

Olivia Jayne is so sweet,
But she cannot keep her things neat.

She cheers you up when you are down,
She hates to see anyone frown.

Olivia Jayne is so sweet,
But she cannot keep her things neat.

Even though she's only just four,
Each day we love her more and more.

Olivia Jayne is so sweet,
But she cannot keep her things neat.

Toni Donnelly (Age 13)

Carrie's War

Bombs were falling on London town
Children were sent away
Carrie and Nick sat down on the train
With Auntie Lou they went to stay

Mr Evans was very strict
Auntie Lou was kind
Mr Evans hit you with a stick
And mess Auntie Lou didn't mind

In Wales they stayed
Picking berries all day long
While Mr Evans prayed
And auntie Lou sang a song

Nick went stealing biscuits
Mr Evans caught him
Nick was they greediest boy in the district
Mr Evans prayed with him

Mrs Gotobed was quite old
She died and left Carrie a ring
Auntie Lou promised to have and to hold
Left with her soldier and started to sing

Holly Dixon (Age 10)

School

Answering questions from
French and Maths I can tell you all the facts
English and Science I need a lot of guidance
Music and drama I may be a little calmer
Geography, DT, I will run away scarily
Art and PE the answer comes more easily
RE and History the answer is a mystery
But then comes Games, which will be fine with James.

James Deakin (Age 12)

Football

Score a goal - scream and shout
You get substituted - you're out

Score an own goal - lots of tears
Score a wicked volley - loads of cheers

Get a red card - three week ban
Get booed - by an angry fan

Dominic Davies (Age 10)

Magnificent Cat

My magnificent cat:
My cat has eyes that sparkle like stars in the midnight sky.
My cat's whiskers are thin, like the eye of a needle.
My cat's fur is snowy, like the white ground in winter.
My cat's nose is pink, like the fur of a new born piglet.
My cat's ears are velvety, like the inside of a chestnut shell.
My cat's purr is contented, like the humming of a baby.
Her tail is as delicate as a china mug.
Her head stands proud, like the morning sun.
She has claws as sharp as a pin.
Her legs are as dainty as a flower in the spring.
My cat's teeth are as sharp as a razor knife -
But her tongue is as smooth as a rabbit's skin.

Natasha Daniels (Age 11)

Horse

Loud neigher
Apple lover
Grass eater
Fast runner
Slow walker
Lovely creature
Great jumper
Cute and cuddly
Very big
Huge creature
Nice and lovely
Great swimmer
Slow eater
Great runner

Samantha Darling (Age 8)

Animals

Early in the morning as the sun begins to rise, the pigs are feeling hungry and they're snorting in their sties.
The rooster wakes the farm up with a cock-a-doodle-doo, the sheepdog won't stop barking the cows begin to moo.
There's a stomping in the stable there's a bleating in the barn, so let's climb aboard the tractor and explore the noisy farm.

Dog
I am the farmer's old sheepdog, his faithful and loyal best friend,
I've been by his side from the day I was born and I'll stay with him right till the end.

Horse
There's nothing like hay when you're hungry, it's lovely to munch a whole bale,
But sometimes I stop for a clippety clop, or to flick a few flies with my tail.

Cat
Hello, I am the fat farmyard kitty, I sleep in the shade of the house,
But I always keep one eye half open, to spot every passing plump mouse.

Turkey
I've got these funny floppy things that hang down from my neck,
They dangle when I gobble and they wobble when I peck.

Cow
I sometimes moo when I'm chewing, I hope you don't think it is rude,
But mooing and chewing are what I like doing, do you moo when you chew your food?

Piglets
I love looking after my piglets and watching them wriggle and squeal,
They clamber all over each other all day, to snuffle around for a meal.

Alexandra Davis (Age 9)

Anger

Anger is like a big raging ball of fire,
It feels like the sun is coming closer and closer,
It also feels like lava pouring on top of you,
You can't feel your flesh all you have left is skin and bones

Phillip Dauwalder (Age 11)

A Chick

A chick
Little, solemn
Exploring, protecting
Running to the dinner table
Baby finch

Bill de Witt (Age 9)

Roley My Dog!

Rampaging round the garden, we call it his 'mad half hour'
Obviously thinking he's in charge and has got all the power,
Lots and lots of energy that makes him want to bound,
Everybody loves him when he's asleep, sweet and sound.
You know you want to stroke him when he doesn't want to pound.

Isolated toys that have been rejected
Sugary foods fear him, as Roley has detected.

Munching, lunching, crunching through food
Imaginatively thinking of himself in a mood
Now and then he likes to cuddle
Even in the night he might not stop for a huddle.

Lydia Dyer (Age 10)

Don't Go Dad

Dad turned, closed the door,
Now I don't see him anymore,
Mum cried, I did too
We both didn't know what to do
A family of three turned to two
Now there's only me and you
I've turned so weak,
I cannot speak
We have to be strong
Or things will go wrong
Dad turned, closed the door
Now we don't see him anymore
This was the day my heart broke,
Since this day I have not spoke.

Katie Davenport (Age 10)

61

The Reason I Wet My Bed

What lies under my bed, what goes boo.
Is it a monster that's green, red, yellow, blue.
I don't know I never looked
Those horror books got me really hooked.

He has fangs, teeth, mean eyes and claws,
Flesh between his horrid jaws.
Furry, hairy, six feet tall
Suspends my night with it's mating calls.

My mate got one he told me so
He ate his brother in one go.
I wet my bed too scared to go pee
He is under there waiting for tea.

I'm sitting in my bed desperate now
My bowel and bladder having a row.
I'm going down to be lunch
Here it comes oh . . . . .no crunch!

Ashley Dale (Age 14)

Snowy Day

Winter weather morning glow
Snowflakes falling
Boots crunching crisp white snow
Golden sun rising
Birds all sitting in a row
Orange shadows crawling from the sun
Children playing in the snow
Sledges speeding
Slip sliding in the snow
Snowballs flying everyone having fun

Tace Day (Age 9)

School Bus

There was a boy on the bus,
He was going to school.
"I will not get off," he shouted.
His friends said, "Come on."
"I don't want to come off!"

"Yes, Ok I will come on.
Let's go to the classroom
I will get my books.
Oh look the teacher."

"What were you doing today?
Let's go to the hall children,
It's time for assembly.
After, you can go out.
Listen to the teacher.
Now, we will say the Lord's Prayer."

Luke Dodds (Age 10)

Demons

A demon is a creature,
Always there beside you
And never far away

You can hear its little voice
Inside of your head
If you don't know what to do
It can always tell you

All you have to do
Is ask it what to do
Because you can always hear its voice
Inside of your head

You know your demon
And you always will
Because your little demon
Is the conscience inside of you

Alastair Dobson (Age 12)

My Dad!!

My Dad is REALLY funny
He makes me laugh all the time!
He tickles me when I'm sad
And that makes me happy
But sometimes he gets grumpy
And that's not nice at all!
Sometimes he blows raspberries
And that's funny I'm sure you'd agree!
My Dad is kind as well
And that's fantastic!

Jonathan Philip Dyke (Age 8)

The River And I

I walk along the river bank.
The river is calm and settled.
I hear the spending of the stream,
Sometimes the river gleams.

My soul has grown deep like the river,
Sometimes it makes me quiver.
The river is tough and rough,
It flows rapidly and wildly,

I see the river crushing and crashing,
Rolling and twirling, WHOOSH!
It's come to an end.
It rushes away.

The river glitters in the sun.
Oh, what fun.

Cameron Davis (Age 10)

The Sea

I can see it moving,
A mass of dark and cold,
Tossing and turning as if disturbed,
Uncovering secrets from centuries old.

Pushing and pulling at the land,
Taking mercilessly, set out to kill,
Crying and roaring, out loud in the air,
It will take you, you know it will.

The monsters that are locked inside,
Are tearing up trees and plants,
The wreckages of fateful ships,
Doing their own crazy dance.

Huge whirlwinds of water,
Still pulling down and under,
You must have to be so careful,
Don't make even a blunder.

Beware the image of death,
At all times stay away,
Unless you have a death wish,
For today, please stay away.

Imogen Dunning (Age 13)

Summer Senses

The softness of the grass
That comes into your hands
The feeling of trees
That move with the breeze.

The sound of the singing
Of the little birds chirping
The sound of the air
That blows through my hair.

The smell of the roses
That wafts into our noses
The smell of a fire
That goes higher and higher.

The taste of strawberries
And the tasty fruit
That are found in the wild
Where it is always mild.

The view of the sea
And the flying bee,
The sight of the sun
And the people having fun.

Adriana de Zunzunegui Pinera (Age 11)

Dinosaurs

D inosaurs are massive
I like dinosaurs
N ever go near a dinosaur
O h no it is coming to eat me
S it on a dinosaur if you dare
A nkylosaurus is coming for his dinner
U p in the sky flies a Pteradon
R un run run away
S tegosaurus has long spikes

Liam Dale (Age 5)

My Mum

My mum is always saying
Change Gianni's nappy!
Have a shower!
Look after Gianni!
Brush your teeth!
Wash your face!
Come down for breakfast!
Put the apples in the bin!
Be quick!
Make me a cup of coffee now!

Dario Di-Francesco (Age 8)

Spectacular

The early morning sun is not far away and its fading yellow shines proudly across the land,
Dew glistens on the ground like a field of precious gems,
The trees wave magically as if dancing a secret dance that they have been rehearsing all year,
I walk along I hear the twisting and turning of the wind
It's like a wondrous symphony playing just for me,
Squeaks and rustling behind me tells me that the wildlife has finally risen from their slumber,
The bulbs of flowers are fiercly pushing their way through the earth
Desperately trying to show off their splendour and sophistication,
Spring has arrived and it is so pleasurable to be a part of it.

Stephanie Darlington (Age 13)

Colours

What is yellow?
Yellow is the sun
Yellow is fresh melon
Yellow is light lightning
Yellow is our school spelling book

What is Red?
Red is our school shirt
Red is a big balloon
Red is a red rose

What is green?
Green is a green crocodile
Green is a green snake
Green is green grass
Green is as green as a frog

Christian Dowen (Age 8)

Endless Blizzard

Flutter, the feathery flakes gently drift to the ground.
There is no other sound except the sound of silence.
The sharp, stinging, icy cold feeling
Send shivers down your spine
As one by one tiny fluffy snowflakes hit your face.
The ice-cold taste of water overwhelms your body
As the freezing flakes bounce off of your tongue.
The fresh smell of icy water drifts all around you.
The green grass begins to turn spotty
As though snow drops are sprouting from nowhere
Before the green completely disappears.
And all of time there is the gentle flutter, flutter, flutter.
Yet still the endless blizzard swirls and drifts around me.

Corinne Davis-Cooke (Age 11)

New Life

Jelly dots
Lumpy clump
Squidgy Squiggler
Back legs
Front legs
Loses tail
Fully grown
Starts again

Jasmin Dowen (Age 9)

Tiger

A volcano is like a tiger,
First having a long sleep then waking and feeling hungry
The tigers go out scaring deer
The tigers kill with their pointed teeth,
They eat their prey then go back to sleep,
Volcanoes do the same except they kill with their lava,
That's how they're the same.

Millie Dillon-Boylan (Age 9)

Rapping

Rapping rapping
Can you
Hear the
Rapping

Can you hear the footballs
Crashing in the net
If you get a red card
Don't be upset

The clashing of the hockey sticks
All day long
But after that
Have a game of ping-pong

Rapping rapping
Can you
Hear the
Rapping!

Bradley Dobson (Age 10)

Explore

So large a world, so small a place
Billions of people, of a different race.
Japanese, British, Asian too
A different language, I speak to you.

So many countries, so many nations
Travelling the world, you must have patience.
Different climates, a different home
From Africa to Italy, China to Rome.

So far to go, so much to see
Explore the world, you and me.
The Amazon Rainforest, the Niagara Falls
We will see everything, not just these four walls.

We'll fly, we'll drive, we'll run, we'll walk
And all the way, we'll laugh and talk.
So pack your bag, don't hesitate
For no longer we shall wait.

Saroop Dhesi (Age 12)

Holly

Holly is the family cat
And she loves the sun
She's not very fat
And she is a lot of fun
She walks around the bed
Asking for food
Mum makes sure she's fed
She's a cool dude!

Holly is the family cat
She is twenty-four years old
All she does is lie on a mat
And snuggles up so she doesn't get cold!
She's the Queen of the house
And as quiet as a mouse!

Laura Darlington (Age 10)

Exploding Computer!

Beep, beep, beep, BOOM!
That's my computer,
I'm facing my doom!
Dad will tell me off,
And send me to my room!
In comes my brother,
What a loon!
He scrambles upstairs,
Eating pizza with a spooon!
"You'll be in big trouble" he chirps,
He leans to my face,
And does a burp!

Emma Doyle (Age 10)

How Far To Go

Horses galloping through fields
Whizzing round the trees in a dusty cloud
The wind whistling . . .
As the powerful monsters
Thunder through the woods
Magical mysterious mammals
Glide gracefully round the greenery
Sleek as black cats
Pouncing on prey
As they stop to
Drink out of the cool pool

Emily Drake (Age 10)

Hi I'm Jet

Hi I'm Jet
And I'm here to say
I'm a super hero
And I was born in May!

Hi I'm Jet
And I'm here to say
I'll chase those villains
With my trusty gun Ray!

Hi I'm Jet
And I'm here to say
I can train dolphins
And I do it on Sunday

Harry Douglas (Age 8)

The Fog's Descending On Me

The fog's descending on me the ghosts are falling down
The leopard's got me in his grasp I feel I'm going to drown

The fog's descending on me the silence has grabbed my ears
This never-ending passage brings me all my fears

The fog's descending on me I'm lost in an eerie-place
I want to leave this bleak wonderland I want to be encased

The fog's descending on me it's charging down the light
I'm alone in a misty, wispy wilderness I'm full of tense fright

The fog's descending on me it's chasing me down the street
It's tapping at the window and growling at my feet

The fog's descending on me but it's stranded at the door
I'll hurry in front of the fireplace and flop down on the floor

Charlie Dowden (Age 11)

Volcano's Blast Off

The lion slept as quiet as a mouse until
the day
the thick
hot
burning
gooey
lava would burst and cover the land.

That day is today.
Rumbles as loud as thunder.
The lion's tremendous roar covers the earth with noise
then
silence!

Suddenly the solid, stoney rock begins to crack.
Lava as bright as the sun
runs swiftly down the walls of the lion.
The flamey lava covers the land as fast as a cheetah.

Finally the dull grey smoke fades away.
The ground is dry and thick
The lion is once more asleep.

Abbie Dayman-Johns (Age 10)

A Day At The Beach

Sight

When I get out of the car,
I can see so far.
I can see a boat,
I take off my coat.

Smell

You can smell the sea,
Luckily we brought tea.
I can smell the fresh air,
My skin needs care.

Sound

Hear the whale wailing,
Lots of people sailing.
Birds chirping along,
They sing a wonderful song.

Rebecca Evered (Age 11)

Dinosaur

On my way to school I saw a dinosaur
It was a brown dinosaur
It was a sharp-toothed, brown dinosaur
It was an ugly, sharp-toothed, brown dinosaur
It was a wild, ugly, sharp-toothed, brown dinosaur
It was an escaped, wild, ugly, sharp-toothed, brown dinosaur
And it is coming after me!

Jordan Darley (Age 6)

Seasons

Hot seasons, cold seasons,
Windy seasons, mild seasons.
Some are boring, some are great.
Summer's my favourite and I can't wait.
Winter's icy and there's frost about
So when it's winter you better watch out
Autumn's windy, leaves fall
But I like summer best of all.

Tony Dainteth (Age 12)

An Ocean's Enemy

L oudly, the ocean roars and rages against my unbreakable body,
I t tries to knock me down ,as though I am a pencil but I am
G igantic and strong and will not fall
H ungrily, the ferocious waves pound me over and over again, but I hold firm and will not fall
T ragically I have witnessed horrific deaths committed by this uncaring ocean

H elping is what I try to do, but it is hard when all the weather is against you
O ccasionally my help is fulfilled and I swell with well earned pride
U ndoing the knotted sea and its precious tide
S tanding tall I try to win the constant battle between me and the unforgiving ocean but,
E ventually I will fall to the sea, but I don't know how long until that will be.

Jasper Dymoke (Age 12)

The Magic Box

I will put in the box
Gold from a dragon's cave,
A flame from a bonfire
And a tractor from my farm.

I will put in the box
A dinosaur from the museum,
The magic from a witch's book
And my friend James.

I will put in the box
A Playstation 2 and a television,
The whole wide world,
And Spiderman.

I will put in my box,
Every gun in the world,
A surfboard
And a mummy from Ancient Egypt.

My box is fashioned from steel and iron,
With gold in the corners, its hinges are bits of reed.

I shall rally in my box
On a rally track and win the race.

Daniel Dapling (Age 10)

Easter

I can see the tears streaming down his face
I can taste the bread and wine from the last supper
I can smell Jesus slowly dying
I can hear everyone's hearts breaking in two
I can feel the nails ripping his skin

Erin Davis (Age 9)

You Are Late

You are late,
The class are doing their work and have done the register,
Why is that?
Well, my sister didn't wake up,
My dad was taking his time,
My mum sat and watched her programs,
My brother played on his Playstation 2
My dog ran away for a bone,
My auntie fell down the stairs,
My grandad got stuck in the shed,
My snake kept hissing,
My cat kept eating the fish,
My baby sister wet herself,
Ok, sit down and get on with your work
Please Miss I have nothing to write about!!

Laelle Disu (Age 7)

The Holy Man

Jesus was a holy man
A holy man was he,
He upset loads of people,
But he didn't upset me.

Jesus was a holy man
A holy man was he,
He healed loads of people,
But they didn't let him free.

Jesus was a holy man
A holy man was he,
He was mocked by loads of people,
But he didn't want to be.

Jesus was a holy man
A holy man was he,
He was put on the crucifix
But he was hurt, that you could see.

Jesus was a holy man
A holy man was he,
He was taken back to heaven
But he wasn't sad to be.

Charleigh Eley (Age 11)

Orkney Haiku

Grey blocks still and tall
The Standing Stones of Stenness
Giant stone fingers

Martina Doran (Age 10)

My Dog

My dog is black,
Her eyes are blue,
She makes me smile
I hope I can too.

She lies on her bed,
Her four legs in the air,
And she reminds me
Of my big black chair.

Until the food is on the table,
She jumps and scampers,
Until she's not able.
She knows our weaknesses
So she begs and begs,
Until we all admit that she wins,
But that's only until she goes to bed.

Henry Downing (Age 11)

Alone

I'm on my own,
All alone!
The clock strikes midnight,
I'm out of sight.
In my dream,
I hear someone scream!
The witches fly past on their brooms,
Behind me there are empty tombs!!!
It's pitch black,
I'm under attack,
Ghosts fly,
High up in the sky!
I am shocked,
The door gets knocked!!!

Elinor Dollery (Age 8)

Rabbit

Carrot eater
Fast hopper
Grass nibbler
Ear flopper
Sound scarer
Tail flasher
Timid runner

Molly Daynes (Age 7)

The Scorpion

The Scorpion is,
horrible,
tough,
scratchy,
angry,
hard,
spiky,
black,
sharp,
with claws.

Remi de Lausun (Age 7)

Kenning's Cat Is

Sun lover
Milk drinker
Toy player
Fish eater
Ball popper
Grass stamper
Skin scratcher
Small biter

Bethany Davey (Age 12)

My Shadow

While I am sleeping on the comfy sofa,
My shadow is watching the noisy television.

While I am fishing for tasty fish,
My shadow is eating the nasty fish.

While I am shopping for healthy food,
My shadow is eating chips and crisps.

While I am choosing a healthy drink,
My shadow is slamming the door.

While I am reading a scary book,
My shadow is snoring.

Cerys Dally (Age 6)

Monday's Child

Monday's child has no friends
Tuesday's child looks after hens
Wednesday's child fancies all the boys
Thursday's child likes to cuddle her toys
Friday's child thinks of her tum
Saturday's child loves her mum
But the child who was born on the Sabbath day
Never eats pancakes on Shrove Tuesday

Isabelle Derere (Age 8)

Monday's Child

Monday's child is a little bit dizzy
Tuesday's child has a friend called Izzy
Wednesday's child has a dog
Thursday's child does not like the fog
Friday's child loves P.E
Saturday's child has a wobbly knee
But the child who is born on the Sabbath day
Has a good looking horse that goes Neigh!!!!!

Jessica Dargue (Age 8)

Spring Is Coming

Spring is coming
And the flowers are growing
And the place is turning green
Baby animals play in the fields
Birds build nests out of sticks
I feel happy

Henry Dalton (Age 6)

The Iron Man

Why am I here?
What is that noise?
It is trying to wash me away?
I lay here.
My head as big as a bin.
My head whistling like a washing machine.
This tender bed so soft.
That water is softly sprinkling on to me
I can't move
I have rusted
What is that dazzling light on the hill?
I can see some folk fishing.
I still lay as still as a wall.
How did I get here?
I have nobody.
What shall I do?
I don't know.

George Dewey (Age 8)

Rapping Double

My name is Paul,
I am a fool,
I am also small
And my Dad is very tall,
I'm from Senegal,
I like football
I kick it against the wall
It's powerful,
I go to school,
It's not that cool,
I go to the mall
Which has a swimming pool,
I play pool
At the bar with all,

That is the end of my rap,
Now I need a nap.

Lewis Davies (Age 10)

Reflection

My reflection is a twin,
It copies me with everything,
My reflection is like a shadow

I can only see her in a mirror or water,
She can't talk to me,
Why does she copy me.

No-one has the same twin,
She can't come with me,
My twin stays in the mirror all the time.

Molly Delmar (Age 8)

One Two Three . . .

One orange owl opened an old object,
Two tough tigers tickling tortoises tummies,
Three ticklish turtles tickling their heads,
Four fat fishes fishing for fish,
Five famous frogs fighting fat foxes,
Six silly snakes smell like sausages,
Seven smelly sharks shaking socks,
Eight evil elephants eat eggs,
Nine nice newts need night,
Ten tortoises turtles flying in the air.

Rhiannon Dally (Age 8)

River

River rough
River smooth
River quick
River move
River cold
River hot
River splish
River drop
River splash
River splat
River wide
River tide
River side
River dip
River slip
River dive
River mined

Patrick Dawe (Age 8)

The Game

There was a game on Sunday morning
We were against the league champions
The whistle blew we were off
They scored first
They scored second
They scored third
Our heads were down
And then I thought how our manager
Would feel after training us, building us up
And then losing, so I said to the team
Let's do this for Stuart
We scored fourth
We scored fifth
We scored sixth and seventh
We won!!

Oliver Daw (Age 12)

Have You Seen My Metal Teddy Bear?

Have you seen my metal teddy bear?
I left him on my straw bed,
Maybe he's gone out for the day,
I lost him when I was eating my grass seeds,
My cat was looking out of the cardboard window,
Whilst drinking blueberry juice,
Maybe my metal teddy bear has been trying on my clothes,
Because when I went to put my p-jamas away,
My clothes were in a big messy heap,
I was mending my little brother's wooden slippers,
When my metal teddy bear disappeared!

Codie Downs (Age 10)

Silver

Silver for the tiny tooth hidden under the pillow
Silver for the shining knife
Silver leaf on the willow
Silver coin in puddings
Satin silver dish
Silver face of midnight moon
Silvery slippery fish
Silver sheen of trumpet
Silver fox at play
Silver threads in grandma's hair
At the ending of the day

Bronte Dixon (Age 8)

Winter Days

I can see the ice-cold snow falling down on me
I can feel the blizzard that falls on me at a very high speed,
But the snowdrops fall on me like a feather

The taste of ice-cold snowdrops that drop on my tongue
Make me giggle and laugh

The smell of the fresh green grass and snow flakes
Makes me notice that winter is here

But . . .
I can hear nothing but silence it's like
I'm the only person in the world

Sarah Doherty (Age 10)

Shiny

A spider's web lurks in the back yard.
Waves in the wind while it's on its guard.
Shiny and silver like nylon strings.
The spider spins it out of silks and things.
Shiny in the day and sparkly at night.
Ready to give an insect a fright.
Round and round the shiny web spins.
Sitting in the middle, the spider grins.
Caught in the web, a tiny fly
Fighting for his life as he is going to die.
The spider comes to gobble up the food
I think the way spiders eat is very rude.

James Desser (Age 10)

Living On The Street

I live on the street
Nowhere to go

Living in dustbins
Feeding off the scraps

My dog is
The only friend I have

Jonathan Dean (Age 10)

Twinkle Fairy

Dainty feet
Very neat
Teeny tiny
Sitting finally
Glossy glitter
They twitter
Kind of shiver
Small quiver

Maria Dempsey (Age 7)

The Tiger

His teeth are sharp icicles
His eyes shine like the clear sea
He darts like an arrow flying to his destination
He is a quiet mouse when he seeks his prey
He's like a trampoline when he jumps at his prey

Abigail Edwards (Age 10)

Why Me?

Why me?
Always me, always
It's not me, can't you see
Can't someone else be in trouble?
Why me?

Georgina Nicole Everton (Age 9)

The Magic Box Poem

I will put in my box

The swish of a soft silk dolphin on a summer's night,
Fire from the top of a spitting volcano,
The tip of a tooth touching a brush

I will put in my box

Three beautiful wishes spoken in French,
The last seagull flying away from the island,
The smile from a foal standing up for the first time.

I will put in my box

A fifth pony and a blue sun,
A leopard in the sky,
A monkey on a broom stick

My box is designed from glass, metal and steel,

With jewels on the lid and candy floss
And chocolate in the corners,
Its hinges are the jaw bones of a snake

I shall dive on a dolphin under the calm ocean,
Smooth waves of the Pacific Ocean

Then a crowd of tropical fish swim with us,
Then I will go to a beautiful island surrounded by surfboarders

Louise Eastcrabbe (Age 8)

When Tom Eats Noodles!!!

When Tom eats noodles,
He munches and gulps and slurps,
The noodles disappear with a gurgle,
He scratches the bread around the bowl,
Munching and polishing every mouthful,
He burps, gets up and leaves the table.

Martine Evans (Age 10)

Football

Football is my favourite sport,
There are lots of sports but football is my sort.
We all get dirty but I don't care,
If our team wins we go to the fun fair.
The goalie sometimes has to dive on the floor,
But after that they still want more.
Yesterday we won three - two,
Even though our best player had the flu.
Our team had so many cheers,
Whilst the other team had loads of tears.
We saw that the team was very sad,
So we shook their hands and made them glad.

Jessica Davy (Age 9)

All About Me

My favourite colour is blue
My favourite food is stew
Carrots, potatoes meat and gravy,
How about you!

I like my hair all spiky
I love to wear all Nike
Jackets trainers tops and trousers
How about you?

Football is what I like to do
Playing on the X Box and running too
Jogging sprinting long distance and racing
How about you?

School is really exciting
I like reading and writing
Playing outside and learning inside
How about you?

But my family has to be the best
I love them more than all the rest
My sister, my mum and my fluffy cat
And no-one can ever change that

Jordan Ewing (Age 7)

Walking Through The Farmyard

Walking through the farmyard,
What do you see?
I can hear a chicken clucking at me.
Skip through the farmyard
What do you see?
I see a horse galloping over a ramp.

Ellie Edwards (Age 6)

River Erme

River gurgling
Mossy rocks
Icky sticky mud
On the way to the sea
From a trickle
To a river
Sometimes a flood
Sometimes a river
Gets bigger
Gets smaller
River never stop
Bubbly water
River splits

Cherry Davies (Age 8)

The Fantastic Countryside

In the countryside
I can see a young, farmer's boy ploughing

In the countryside
I can hear the strong, brown, bumpy tree swaying

In the countryside
I can smell the fresh, clean air flowing

In the countryside
I can touch the silky, smooth hairs on my own friendly labrador

In the countryside
I can taste the sweet, red, juicy apples hanging

In the countryside
I feel energetic and I want run with all the cute little furry animals

Rebecca Elkins (Age 7)

Rapping!!

My names Kye,
And I am a guy,
I have a friend called Paul,
He is very cool,
I go to the swimming pool,
I have a great big ball,
I run a hall,
I'm very tall,
Loads of people lie,
That's why my names Kye.

Kye Edwards (Age 9)

The Eagle

The eagle is a wonder of the sky,
He has a very piercing cry.
He is so mysterious, you'll never know why
He always flies so very high.

To the other eagles he calls,
Over all the mountain walls,
As they fly past the mountain halls,
Watching all the winter wolves.

Edward Eggleton (Age 9)

Blue Concert

Last year I went to a Blue concert
I went with my best friend called Beth
Then, after the concert, I went a bit deaf!

When I got back home
I had a nice warm bath
Whilst downstairs
My sister was having a laugh
With her best friend Jane
Who was a real pain!

Then I got into bed to have a big sleep
But my bed
Was in a heap.

So I tidied it up
And had a dream
About strawberries and cream!

Heather Ewart (Age 9)

The Striped Rain Forest

In the night time rain forest,
When the moon rises,
The night time choir begins to sing.
In the night when the monkeys start to swing,
The tiger starts prowling,
The chimpanzee howling,
The tiger and the leopard taunting,
And the parrots squawking.
As the mighty tiger prowls through the rainforest,
The baboon screeching at its best.

When t he tiger sees his prey
The tiger starts growling
The chimpanzee night today continues Howling from
Once the tiger has caught his prey,
That is the end of his day.

Zachary Eley (Age 9)

Before I Count To Twenty

One I can't find my shoes
Two where's my lunch box
Three I've got knots in my shoes
Four five six I need a jumper
Seven I need a drink
Eight I need the toilet
Nine ten eleven got to get my chips
Twelve where's my teddy it is in your room
Thirteen I need to get my Game Boy to play in the car
Fourteen fifteen sixteen I need to let the cat out
Seventeen I need a book
Eighteen I need my coat
Nineteen I need to pack my lunch box
Twenty time to go

Kieran Ellis (Age 9)

Storm

It approached
The merciless rage of the storm.
The thunder bellowed with anger.
The tornado danced
With the sea that followed.
The sea swished nearer and nearer.
The frustration of the storm was all I could hear.
The lightning chased me round,
Backwards and forwards.
My heart was dying inside me.
The hungry waves devoured the shores.
The black clouds hungrily ate up the sun.
Will the world ever recover?

Jack Eden (Age 11)

Pink

It is the shyness you can feel in your cheeks,
The valentine feeling,
It is the giggle of a new born baby,
And the love of your family,
It is happiness,
It is the joy you feel on your 1st birthday
It is the soft wet nose of a cat

Sheryl Emery (Age 11)

Puppy

Care it
Love it
Stroke it
Feed it
Leave it
Wash it
Brush it

Georgina Edmunds (Age 7)

What's With The Burberry?

Why do chavs think they rule the school?
They shout out in lessons and spoil it for all.
They laugh at boffs and push the geeks,
But do you know what? We'd rather be freaks!

They hang around ASDA, what's the point in that?
They don't do anything but sit and chat.
They lurk in the parks where children play,
Graffitiing swings and causing dismay!

Swearing and drinking when they're underage.
Fake, cheap tracksuits are all the rage.
What chav is complete without their 'bling, bling?'
How tacky is that fake diamond ring?

They laugh at us now but we'll get them back,
When they serve us up a greasy Big Mac.
What's with the Burberry and the hooded tops?
Stolen goods are no good with the cops.

They think they're cool when they light up a fag,
Standing there with their JD bag.
This is a message to the chavs out there:
Call us what you want, we don't actually care!

Natasha Ennals (Age 14)

All About Me

My favourite colour is blue
My favourite food is stew
Carrots, potatoes meat and gravy,
How about you!

I like my hair all spiky
I love to wear all Nike
Jackets trainers tops and trousers
How about you?

Football is what I like to do
Playing on the X Box and running too
Jogging sprinting long distance and racing
How about you?

School is really exciting
I like reading and writing
Playing outside and learning inside
How about you?

But my family has to be the best
I love them more than all the rest
My sister, my mum and my fluffy cat
And no-one can ever change that

Jordan Ewing (Age 7)

Then They Came . . .

Life was so simple,
Once upon a time.
You could run free
Beneath a canopy of leaves,
While small sequins of sunlight
Would shine on your fur.

Then *they* came,
With their metal machines,
That dug up the ground
And destroyed the trees.
They cared not for you and the effect they had
They cared for the money - "Their hard earned cash".

And now look at you,
Once majestic and proud.
You're desperate and hungry,
Forlorn and dejected.
They've ruined your home.
But you must carry on
In your battle for life,
As they carry on, increasing your strife.

Elizabeth Egan (Age 13)

Pig

Mud slapper
Whizzy roller
Food snatcher
Fast trotter

Luke Edmunds (Age 8)

Puppy Power

Picked from my litter I happily sat
In a warm cosy car on my new fluffy mat
I gazed out the window and what did I see?
My brand new home and family!

I was given a fresh basket and toys anew
All waiting there for me to chew!
I've had plenty of biscuits and a lovely tea
Are all these things just for me?

I can't help my puddles 'coz I'm just a pup
But it takes only minutes to clean my mess up!
I needed injections - so off to the vet's
There it was crowded with different pets

I now go on walks even in the rain
Then I have to wear a coat (that's a pain!)
I'm sometimes naughty and sometimes funny
But that's just me . . . . . I'm Honey!!

Nicola Grace Ellwood (Age 9)

One Single Tear

From nowhere, it came,
Her single dark tear,
More would follow, exactly the same
Each one, holding the same tale.

I could see reflected her torment,
I could see the words of hate,
That poisoned her mind and soul,
The words that would lead her to a new fate.

In that tear I could see the cold blade,
It pours blood and rips skin apart,
The hate and loss of faith,
That destroyed and decayed her heart.

In that tear, I saw her despair and fear,
I could see her entire world,
In that one single tear,
Depression, hate and pain,
Now here's the worst part,
Before long, I will see my tear again.

Catie Fisk (Age 14)

Fairies Flying

Fairies flying round and round
They hardly ever touch the ground
Try and catch one if you can
But if you do I'm telling you
There's more in fairyland!

Molly Amelia France (Age 8)

Water

Look here comes the rain,
Drip, drop, drip, drop, drip, drop SPLASH!
Look it's still raining.

I'm very bored,
Drip, drop, drip, drop, drip, drop SPLASH!
Look there's the sun.

Here comes the rainbow,
Let's run outside,
Jump in the puddles.

SPLASH! Oh no, we are wet!
Let's drink some water
Inside the house.

Gulp, gulp, yum, very nice,
Looks like blackcurrant.
Tastes like . . .*water.*

Michael English (Age 10)

I Wonder . . .

I wonder the name of the soldier
that was shot like a bird on the ground.

I wonder the name of the soldier
that grimaced in pain at the Somme.

I wonder the name of the soldier
that was brave like a lion at Ypres.

I wonder the name of the soldier
that carried the dying to safety.

Was he my friend or foe?

Battle weary, filthy, wounded and sore
I wonder when it will my time to go?
I wonder . . . .

Katie Ellis (Age 10)

Lilly The Fish

Lilly the fish loves to swim
She always comes up when her food is put in
She always hides underneath the bridge
She lives on top of my fridge

I got Lilly when I was eight
She was small then
But now she's great
Lilly is scared that's what I hate
So that's Lilly my fish

Jade Evans (Age 9)

Mr Head And The Head

Mr Head said,
To go to the head,
The head said,
That Mr Head,
Had sent you to the head,
Because you were flicking heads.

The head said
To go to Mr Head,
Mr Head said,
That the head,
Had sent you to Mr Head,
Because you were flicking his head.

Right no more flicking heads,
Or I'll send you back to the head.

Cullen Evans (Age 10)

My Best Friend

This is a person
Who I think about all the time,
She is fun to play with
And if you go to her house
She will go crazy about you,
You will always have a friend
Because she will comfort you,
She is my best friend
Jessica

Sian Easterbrook (Age 8)

Sun Lord & Lady Moon

He rules with a spear, she rules for love
As they fight in their battle for Earth and above.
The Sun Lord he shines with power and strength,
His cape of pure light measures miles in length,
Yet when he must sleep Lady Moon shall then come,
And spread out the cold that makes fingers go numb,
With her cloaks and her veils through the night she does dance,
While the stars sigh in peace and whisper of romance,
Yet Sun Lord is impatient, before morning he rises,
But old Lady Moon is full of surprises,
With a wave of her hand she summons her troops,
Then the mist, rain and fog all gather in groups,
She readies her soldiers, the battle is near,
She places them well and waits without fear,
The sun Lord is angry, his temper ablaze,
The heat it is scorching, burning half crazed,
They battle for hours, for months, weeks and days,
Moon sent the tide and sun sent the haze,
They called in a truce to end all their plight,
Now sun rules the day and Moon rules the night.

Bethany Foxon (Age 12)

The Christmas Tree

One
Silky star
With silver sparkles
Two golden angels with glittery crowns,
Three Father Christmases with snowy beards,
Four running Rudolphs-the nosed reindeer,
Five stunning stars shining in the sky,
Six snowmen wearing silly hats,
Seven people wearing silky saris,
Eight stars peeking out saying Boo!
Nine sparkly lights glowing in the dark,
Ten twinkly costumes worn by snowy snowmen.
And there at the bottom
Of our Christmas Tree
Is
A
Great big present
Just for me

Alisha Everson (Age 7)

Shoes

Old shoes, new shoes, shiny shoes, dull shoes,
Red shoes, black shoes, pink shoes, blue shoes,
Green shoes, brown shoes, lots of different sized shoes.

One shoe, two shoes, four, five, six shoes
Any shoes you could imagine.
Spotty shoes, stripy shoes, velcro shoes,
Buckle shoes, children's shoes, wedding shoes,
Ones for special occasions.

Playing out scruffy shoes, dirty shoes, clean shoes,
Smelly shoes, nice shoes, ugly shoes, pretty shoes . . .
Just the kind of shoes I like.

Laura Esteves (Age 7)

If I Won A Hundred Quid

What I would do with a hundred quid
I would spend it on a super squid,
It would shoot lazers from its eyes
And bake really good lemon pies

What I would do with a hundred pounds
I would buy an army of ninja clowns
They would make me laugh and scare little kids
And they would team up with my super squid

What I would do with 10,000 pence
I would buy a really tall golden fence
It would go all the way up to 'heaven'
Super Squid, Ninja Clowns, Goldenfence, 11

Dan Edensor (Age 15)

Summer Cat In Custard

Summer cat oh summer cat
Playing around in custard
Summer cat oh summer cat
Goes split splodge splat!

Summer cat oh summer cat
Plays in my paddling pool
Summer cat oh summer cat
Do you think it's cool?

Summer cat oh summer cat
Can you do this double
Summer cat oh summer cat
You're getting into trouble.

Summer cat oh summer cat
Paddled out to sea
Summer cat oh summer cat
Is coming after me!!!

Rebecca Louise Evans (Age 7)

The Haunted House

When you enter the haunted house
You must step on a toe
If you don't
You will meet, a terrible foe!

The house is scary
When it creeps
You must be careful
Or the monster leaps

Never enter the house at night
Or you will get a terrible fright!

Jake Everett (Age 10)

Orange

A young deer
Cries for its mother
Bound to be
For each other

Galloping horses
Street lamps galore!
Red's younger cousin
And the devil's roar

Hypnotised by sunlight
Heads towards their king
Pretty little sunflowers
The beauty they shall bring

Catherine Francis (Age 11)

Remember

Every year in November,
It is common to remember,
On this special day,
When a poppy is worn,
Not replay,
But a for those who lost to mourn.

Thousands sacrificed their lives,
People died on both sides,
'Twas not at all an event to remember
Men were proud at first to stand and fight.

Ended in November
The poppys blow in the wind
On the day to remember
11 o'clock 11 is the day
The month 11th poppys sold and all do pay.

Natasha Ereira-Guyer (Age 11)

The Dark Fall

As we were standing by the lift
Our guardian pushed us down
We fell down scared and screaming
The only way to describe the fall was dark,
Darker than dark

It was a long drop
With no stop
Until we reached the bottom
We weren't going to survive
Unless there was a miracle

Then it happened there was a miracle
A net was in the way
We were saved but trapped in the middle

Matthew Faithorn (Age 10)

Winter Landscape

The world is motionless
Bushes huddle together to keep warm
White grass stands in a frozen parade
A delicate web of crystals hangs from twigs,
Twisted branches silvered.
Trees raise their frozen heads.
Colours fading.
Magical.

Levi Evans (Age 9)

Fireworks

Fireworks go bang and sizzle wallop
In the midnight sky
Exploded colours
Fill the air
As they get higher
They get faster
Like a formula one car

Edward Farrow (Age 9)

My Shadow

While I am at drama,
My shadow waits for me outside

While I am doing literacy,
My shadow rubs it out

While I am playing outside,
My shadow goes to sleep

While I am painting,
My shadow draws pictures

While I am eating vegetables,
My shadow is drinking lemonade

While I am reading poetry,
My shadow reads Mr Sneezy.

Megan Feist (Age 7)

Winter

When icicles hang by the wall,
And James the shepherd blows his nail,
William Poole logs into the hall,
And milk comes frozen home in pail;
When blood is nipped, and ways be foul
Then nightly sings the staring owl.
Tu-whit to-who! A merry note
While greasy Joan doth keel the pot.

When all aloud the wind doth blow,
And coughing drowns the parsons saw,
And birds start brooding in the snow,
And Chloe's nose look's red and raw
When roasted crabs hiss in a bowl,
Then nightly sings the staring owl
Tu whit to who, merry note
While greasy Joan doth keel the pot.

Molly Ford (Age 9)

Nightmare

A lifeless shadow creeping up behind me,
I turn, turn and turn, no one there
Walking through an endless maze.
The shadow still following quietly,
Tap, tap, tap.
But no matter how many times I look it disappears into thin air.
Suddenly,
Hundreds of shadows surround me.
I start running; they jump on me, BANG!
"Sarah, are you ok? I think you had a nightmare".

Sarah-Jane Eyles (Age 11)yu

Fear

Sprinting, sprinting for your life
Heart thumping like an elephant stampeding to war
Goosebumps as high as a rocky cliff
Sweating like the sun in space
Scared you are about to bungee jump off a helicopter 1000 feet above earth
The wolf is still chasing me
I stopped
The wolf stopped
The wolf opened his mouth!!

Samuel Evans (Age 9)

My Dog

My dog Monty is chocolaty brown
He's young and playfull and acts like a clown

Good old Monty so fluffy and round
To me he's worth a million pounds

He likes to run around on the grass
But sometimes prefers to scratch his a....e

Good old Monty so fluffy and round
To me he's worth a million pounds

Brown boy's favourite meal is roast beef
Then he chews on his bone to clean his teeth

Good old Monty so fluffy and round
To me he's worth a million pounds

When nightfall comes we both snuggle down
Now it's dreamland for my special clown

Good old Monty so fluffy and round
To me he's worth a million pounds

Alex Fraser (Age 14)

Monday Morning

Monday morning is here once more,
But for me it's unhappiness and tears galore,
I come into the classroom to jeering abuse,
My team has lost, that's their excuse.

"Oh Chelsea lost they're really bad,"
These silly jeers they make me sad,
And even though I shouldn't care,
A defeat for my team is really rare.

I just can't believe the fact that's there,
Chelsea have lost fair and square,
And the more I think about it
The more my stomach turns to a pit.

Next week and it's Monday morning again,
This time I walk in with a giant grin,
"Ha ha ha ha, three cheers, three cheers,
This time it's me giving the jeers.

Man. United have lost and I'm glad,
I really am no longer sad,
Everybody has a bad day,
That just has to be the way

Finbar Fitzgerald (Age 11)

The Country

The country is fresh and green,
And lots of animals I have seen,
Cows and sheep and pigs and hares,
There are lots of animals there.

Clean and fresh countryside air,
Grass, the best you've seen anywhere.
Crops everywhere, yellow and green,
The most natural I've ever seen.

Vegetables grow everywhere,
Here it's definitely not rare!
Sprouts and potatoes and peas,
Look around, you are bound to see.

Flowers, beautiful and nice,
You're bound to look at them twice.
The country is the place to be,
So why don't you go look and see!

Nicole Flatman (Age 12)

My Shadow

While I am screaming because England lost,
My shadow sits and plays quietly.

While I am playing with my friends
My shadow rests in bed.

While I am choosing my toy,
My shadow stays in the house.

While I am dressing up,
My shadow undresses for bed.

While I am wrestling with dad
My shadow is kicking a football.

While I am waiting for a friend,
My shadow moans.

Thomas Fern (Age 6)

The Moon

Sometimes when I go outside,
Way above the clouds do glide
On moonbeams, shooting to the stars
Which hide behind the planet Mars.
The moon looks down upon my town,
And shimmers with his golden crown

Hannah Furnival-Jones (Age 8)

Tanka

Mum, Dad, Leah and me
We are the Fox family
Comfort, joy and love
They give to me.
We are a Happy Family,
Always

Rachel Fox (Age 10)

Lighthouse

I am so strong, I stand so tall
My beam lets off bright light
It shimmers on the murky seas
And saves ships in the night

Powerful waves bash and crash
Thundering against my side
As ships pass - I light up their way
Saving many lives

I have such an important job
But I don't get any pay
My job is so fulfilled
Saving people every day

My job is great it's the best around
With wonderful views I see
The boats the people the weather the sounds
Fill my life with glee

Steph Foster (Age 13)

Watching York City

I go to watch York City with my dad
My mum and Nanna think we are mad!

They both like to go to Hull
But I think that is rather dull

York City play in red and white
On the pitch they look really bright

My favourite player is Andy Bish
When he scores I've got my wish

Yorkie the lion is very funny
He looks like a rat says my mummy

There are usually lots of people there
They are brilliant fans who really care

Once I saw York win five nil
The crowd all roared and it was brill

Dad shouts so much his throat gets sore
But the very next week goes back for more

I like to go because it's fun
Especially if we have won

I love to watch them whatever the score
I'll support them forever, win, lose or draw

Ruth Feasby (Age 8)

Mountains Of Fire

The lion is a powerful blasting machine.
It roars and echoes the land
The lion is in a colossal lava pool.
It is a huge amber creature
It is a violent monster

Bradley Foster (Age 10)

My Future

What will happen when I am gone?
What shall I eat and what shall I do?

When I am up there in the sky
Shall I speak to God or fly around all day long?

What will be left when I do stuff without my family
Will it be sad or will it be ok?

Will the earth still be there it's not up to me
It's up to the world?
So I wonder what it is like up in space?

Robyn Frampton (Age 9)

Jogging

Every day I go out,
In the early summer sun,
And it feels so comforting
Like I'm the only one.

The animals are waking up,
The birds starting to sing,
It sounds so lovely, sounds so sweet,
As the morning begins.

And as the sun is rising,
There's a glow over the hill,
Of red and gold and yellow,
In the sky that is so still.

And now I see the lights turn on,
In the houses on the street,
When commuters are off to work,
Hurrying on their feet.

So now the cars are on the road,
The quietness is dead,
So I return back to my house,
And I go back to bed.

Josie Griffiths (Age 13)

Skater

Skater
Skating slowly
Jumping, rolling, flipping
Nosegrind, kickflip, 5-0
Combo!

Harry Jay Furnival (Age 9)

Walking Through The Farmyard

Walking through the farmyard
What do I see?
I see a horse neighing at me.

Walking through the farmyard
What do I see?
I see a duck quacking at me.

Walking through the farmyard
What do I see?
I see a pig oinking at me.

Jasmine Filby (Age 6)

The Wind Up Clock

The hands are black,
The other is red,
The small one looks like it is dead.

It turns each hour,
And it's soo boring,
But it still ticks when you are snoring.

It seems to pass quicker,
If I don't snatch a look,
But doesn't work when it is shook.

People ask 'Why is it useful?'
I simply reply,
'How strange it is, that time flies by.'

The word is 'Clock',
When it goes 'tick tock',
So now you know what it is.

Without the turn,
There's no tick tock,
And then the clock will stop!

Alex Freeman (Age 11)

Fire!

Creeping slowly nearer,
The flames licking at my feet,
Eating all the plants,
Like a greedy little child

Smoke rising,
Like dust from a stampede,
I can smell it now,
Like in the smoking part of a bar

I hear it crackling,
As it eats away,
It's fine banquet
Of leaves and twigs

It's a vicious monster
Roaring like a lion behind me,
As if it's threatening me,
Telling me to run.

It's like a dangerous animal,
That doesn't want to die,
And keeps escaping,
It's now chasing to kill . . . me!

Holly Fleming (Age 11)

The Volcano Lion

The lion sleeping, not aware of what's in store for the land and people,
But then it wakes and it's angry and now you're its prey
With a terrible rumbling and roaring noise
It pushes off its blankets pounces into town
The people run but there's no escape
Now it's a ghost town but the lion is just sleeping

Rachelle Flanagan (Age 10)

Hide and Seek!

I hid motionless,
Breathing heavily.
It was silent!
Then I heard...I don't know what I heard,
But it wasn't human!
Maybe it's a little fairy, coming to tell me not to worry,
Or, maybe a....ghost haunting me for the rest of my life,
How long will I be here?
I hope I get found soon,
What if someone steals me and I never get to see mother again.
'Hide and Seek'
Those few words echoed in my head.
Hide and seek, hide and seek
I wish I had heard that, then I would be free from here.
The bed creaked, like a door with a rusty hinge.
It was like it was trying to whisper to me, telling me to get out,
I did.
What a mistake that was!
'Ahhhhhhh'.

Lucy Follows (Age 11)

The Seals That Swam

The seals that swam in the lake
Some people think that seals are fake

They swim around in the sea
I jump around and giggle with glee!

They swim and dive into the sea
My mum says "can you see".

When we're at home I said
"Have they broken a bone".

Rachel Froud (Age 8)

The Field

The field is green
The field is a scene
The field is a good place to be

The field has horses, sheep and cows
The field has animals having fun
The field has flowers, bushes and fences

The field is a good place to see
The field is a good place to be!

Katherine Feaviour (Age 8)

When I Go To School

When I go to school
I listen to the seagulls squawk past

When I go to school
I watch the cars go zooming along the road

When I go to school
I listen to people talking as I walk past

When I come home from school
I watch the sun set

Adam Flay (Age 9)

Friendship

At three the sun shone bright
It felt like someone had shone a light,
But when I was four a dark cloud covererd
It felt like the sun wasn't bothered,
Now I was at school
She wasn't that cool,
But now I am six
I have to fix
Our friendship forever,
But now we're together.
It felt like a rollerecoaster
Going up and down,
But now I'm up high it's bright
I can switch the light back on tonight.

Joanne Fuller (Age 10)

Acrostic Poem

D inosaurs sometimes eat meat.
I am a fierce dinosaur.
N o I shall not go out in the snow with you.
O h no I am afraid of dinosaurs.
S tegosaurus has spikes on his tail.
A nkylosaurus flies.
U p Pteranodon flies
R oar roar.
S tegosaurus has spikes.

Lauren Fuller (Age 5)

Colour Poem

Yellow is the colour of the sun
Green is the colour of the grass
Blue is the colour of the sky
Brown is the colour of the mud
Red is the colour of an apple
Pink is the colour of my bed
Orange is the colour of an orange
Purple is the colour of the grapes
White is the colour of clouds
Grey is the colour of wool

Jessica Freeman (Age 9)

Spring

In Spring children play outside with toys
Flowers grow out of the bulbs planted last Autumn in the dark
Baby animals are born on the farm soil
I like Spring

Jack Gowlett (Age 6)

A Vibrating Fluffball

A vibrating fluffball,
A whining call,

A litter box,
A small version of a fox,

A daily pouncer,
A big bouncer,

A creature not to be walked,
An animal that doesn't talk,

A fluffy mat
      To make me
         CAT.

Lucy Maria Fagan (Age 11)

Animals

Cats leap
Tigers roar
Parrots squawk
Dogs bark
Kangaroos jump
Robots crackle
But I am as normal as can be

Georgina Ford (Age 11)

Cake

Chocolate cake
Cherry cake
Icing on the top

Banana cake
Sultana cake
Eat until you drop

Birthday cake
Christmas cake
Homemade or from a shop

Carrot cake
Coffee cake
Keep munching, never stop

Easter cake
Wedding cake
Too beautiful to chop

Fairy cake
Angel cake
I think I'm going to POP!

Katy Foster (Age 10)

Snowflakes

Snowflakes drift back and forth
Like stars toppling over the night sky,
Staying forever never melting,
The deep dark soil covered with pure snowflakes.
It's growing heavier and heavier,
Until no land, no grass, no sight of Earth.
The world is gone.
Wrapped up in a cold, white nutshell,
The sapphire night sky starts to warm up beneath the fiery sun,
Earth is light,
Uniting with life
It's Spring,
All is living and alive.

Antonia Francis (Age 10)

Easter Comes

Easter comes with daffodils blooming
Easter comes with green shoots growing
Easter comes with baby animals squealing
Easter comes with the sun returning
Easter comes with children laughing
Easter comes with birds twittering
Easter comes with the Easter bunny hopping

Holly Fitzpatrick (Age 9)

The Mysterious Thing

The ancient house sat there all alone
As the moon glared at its walls.
Its shadow covered the lonely street
And the trees hands grasped it tightly.
All its curtains were closed without a gap
So no eye could witness the inside.

She heard the grand-father clock tick
There was only silence here.
While the rocking chair was motionless
And a cat was spying on her.
She could sense there was something here
When she heard a scream from upstairs.

She could smell the burning of wood
It was coming from the cellar.
She glared down through the floor-boards
Though she felt incredibly scared.
Then she curiously turned around
And that cat was staring back.

The grandmother's soul ran with her
Though the heavy, iron door was locked.

Innogen Gengatharan (Age 12)

The Rhyming Colour Poem

My favourite colour is light blue,
Just like our brand new loo.
The living room is yellow,
Like me when my dad bellows.
The sun is bright red,
Just like my vibrant bed.
I know someone who wears green,
The only problem is that she's mean.
My pen is pink,
But the strange thing is that the ink in't.
The wrapping of the bread is gold,
But inside all there is is mould!

Kerry Fowler (Age 11)

Rivers

Gushing flow
Winds blow
Big rocks
With docks
Green bits
Horrible hits
You're wet
Get set
Never dive
Stay alive

Luke Forward (Age 7)

Winter Song

Winter is coming it's Christmas
Time   snow fall
              snow fall
              snow fall
              snow fall

Nights are getting long days are getting
Short   snow fall
              snow fall
              snow fall

Snow is white and soft, mushy and
Slushy   snow fall
              snow fall
              snow fall

Nathan Forsdyke (Age 9)

Birthday

My birthday comes
    with balloons popping
My birthday comes
    with people laughing
My birthday comes
    with presents opening
My birthday comes
    with music playing
My birthday comes
    with pets dancing
My birthday comes
    with doorbell ringing
My birthday comes
    with family seeing
My birthday comes to make me old
    - so respect your elders!!!

Kirsty Gledhill (Age 8)

I'm A Lonely Child

I'm sitting on the stairs,
No-one else is there,
I'm feeling small and shy,
I may be about to cry,
A thick long tear runs down my cheek
It ends up at my feet, I'm sitting here in the street
I don't know who I will meet,
It's hard to tell your dreams
It's sadder than it seems,
I can hear a train, I'm in pain, it's started to rain,
Time for all our goodbyes,
Poor lonely child,
Gets upon a train,
It will not be the same.

Jupiter

After Mars
The king of all planets lay
With a red spot
Just like blood.
Orange and red stripes
Just like blazing fire
The giant on Jupiter
Makes his gas
Swirl around like a hurricane.
All the other planets are jealous
Why can't they have
Mightiness inside them?
Sorry
Jupiter RULES!

Emily Greenfield (Age 7)

My Shadow

While I am sitting on a comfy chair
My shadow is running around screaming

While I am saying my guineapig has chewed a hole in my coat,
My shadow keeps quiet

While I am thinking what to write
My shadow goes around not thinking

While I am looking at a horse,
My shadow doesn't look where it's going

While I am digging my garden
My shadow reads the newspaper

Emma Flanagan (Age 7)

The Golden Dragon

The vast golden dragon just waiting to erupt
Finally the time has come
He erupts like a rocket taking off
Exploding
The golden dragon still flying in the dusty air
The golden dragon making humungous flames trying to blow the thick dust.

Zach Gower (Age 10)

Cheese

Cheese cheese cheese
It makes me rather pleased
Cheese cheese cheese
I like to have it for teas
Cheese cheese cheese
I like to smell the smell of cheese
Cheese cheese cheese
So make me pleased by

CHEESE!

Alfi Gözacan (Age 6)

Animals

Monday's animal jumps and praises
Tuesday's animal says lots of phrases.
Wednesday's animal has a home to own,
Thursday's animal chats and chats,
On the phone.
Friday's animal cuddles,
Saturday's animal snuggles.
But the animal that is born on the Sabbath day,
Has a very happy day in May.

Leah Fox (Age 7)

Late Again

You are late and the bell has gone
Well my brother cut his hair off,
My dad got stuck up the chimney
My baby wet herself,
My gran lost her pet snake,
My mum got stuck in the car without the car key,
My grandad lost his gloves,
My cousin lay in and did not want to get up,
My dog couldn't stop attacking me.
Say sorry to the class for interrupting them.
Go and do your work.
Sorry Miss I have got nothing to write about.

Katy Forsdyke (Age 6)

Snow Storm

The icy cold white beast is all around me,
I call for help,
But my voice is drowned in its **deafening**
Screeeeech.
It surrounds me,
I call and call and *call,* but no one comes.
It is huddling around me.
I close my eyes in hope that when I open
My eyes I will be in my bed room, but,
No it's real...
I call and call, alas, no one comes,
I can't escape,
Well at least not now....

Natasha Griessner (Age 10)

Up On The Farm

Up on the farm my eyes can see
Beautiful, black cow mooing
Funny, yellow scarecrow scaring

Up on the farm my ears can hear
Lovely, black horse neighing
Fat, pink pig oinking

Up on the farm my fingers can feel
Soft, yellow chicks hatching
Smooth black cats meowing

Up on the farm my nose can smell
White, boiled eggs sizzling
Red, rosy apples falling

Up on the farm my mouth can taste
Sweet, gold corn waving
Lovely fresh air rustling

Up on the farm all of my senses
Alive and tinking

Erin Guyton (Age 6)

A Day In The Life Of A Crime Scene Investigator

Process the Crime Scene,
Dust for fingerprints;
Sift through the evidence,
Look for any hints.

Turn all the lights off,
Spray the Luminol;
Check for any blood spatter
In the room and hall.

Collect spent bullet casings
For later analysis,
Transport back to the Crime Lab
To scan into 'IBIS'.

Running DNA samples
Through the computer,
Checking for any 'priors'
To catch the perpetrator.

Yes!! We have a match
From the victim's fingernails;
Cops are off to arrest the suspect,
And now he's going to jail!!

Roxanne Gardiner (Age 14)

Watch Me Burn

Small smooth and thin
A dragon lying down
Breathing fire
Always growing
Trembling with fear

The death meets
The wicked
As red as lava
And thick black smoke

Oliver Fordred (Age 10)

Winter Is Not Like

Winter is the coldest season of them all
Winter will always be the coldest season of them all
Winter is not like summer at all
Winter will never be like summer still
Winter is not like spring at all
Winter will never be like spring at all
Winter is not like Autumn at all
Winter will never be like Autumn at all
Winter will not be like summer, spring or autumn
Winter will always be the coldest season of them all

Peter Griffin (Age 8)

Fairies

Goblins green and goblins small,
I cast this spell to make you tall,
As high as a palace you shall grow,
My icy magic makes it so.

Then steal Doodle's magic feathers,
Used by fairies to make all weathers
Climate chaos I have planned
On earth and here in fairyland

Paige Green (Age 10)

Outside

The trees dance as the wind whispers,
And as the clouds start to cry,
The thunder roars.

When the leaves fall,
They sway from side to side,
And the grass jigs about in the ground.

Inside another story,
Where electronics and civilazation takes over.

Kiri Gilmour (Age 11)

Dead Or Alive?

Up and down, bleep, bleep.
Up and down, bleep, bleep.

Life support eh, oh what a drag.
Lying all day, limp as a rag.

Nobody knows me, no one hears me.
My brain is still working, why can't they see?

I knew about my diabetes, I knew about the insulin.
Why didn't I take it? Why throw it in the bin?

I wanted to be noticed among all the fights.
Now I'm being noticed under the hospital lights.

I've been here one week two maybe three.
I'm trapped in a prison I just want to be free.

Oh God, please don't turn the machine off.
Mum, Dad, listen to me don't, don't turn it off.

Flick goes the switch, the whirring slows down.
Inside I scream - I'm not dead yet, I'm only 13, don't let me go yet!

Up and down, bleep, bleep.
Up and, and bleeeeeeep.

Gone

Emma Gavigan (Age 15)

Toucan And The Anaconda

I dreamed of a toucan,
A big colourful bill
Living in the tropical rainforest
Tossing the fruit with his bill.
I dreamed of a mighty anaconda
Powerful enough to tackle a bull
And make his empty stomach full
And crawls away to sleep.

Sadie Grief (Age 10)

The Railway

Here is a lady, there is a man,
There is a beaver making a dam;
Rabbits and cattle and birds go by,
Going so fast you want to fly;
Here comes the tunnel, there goes the light,
There goes a bear roaring with might;
Faster and faster things go by,
There is a fox that looks quite sly.

Iona Griliopoulos (Age 9)

Jump Or Jiggle

Elephants barge, bulls charge
Snakes creep, frogs leap
Kangaroos bounce, kittens pounce
Dogs wiggle, monkeys giggle
Parrots fly, cats cry
Cheetah cheats, tiger's eat
Deer runs, pigs grunt
Lizards crawl, lions roar
Corcodiles snap, sharks catch
Budgies flew, I went to the zoo.

Anojan Gnanakulasekaran (Age 9)

Rap Writer

My name is Kelly,
And I love eating jelly,
My best friend is Ellie,
Her best shoes are wellies,
She has a big belly,
She calls me smelly,
And we love watching tele,
With Keri,
I hope you like this rap,
Cos now I'm going for a nap.

Kelly Gent (Age 10)

Farmyard Animals

We are the farmyard animals, we like to play with you, some of us have green eyes, some of us have blue.
Some of us have white hair, some of us have grey, all the stable horses like to munch on hay.
I love the cosy kitchen, collage on the floor, I like everything about it, especially the new door.
Kitty's by the fire, dreaming of the sun, with you she will have quite a lot of fun.

Cows are in the field thinking what to do, they're longing for a meal, they want to moo at you!
They're black and white, they have long tails, when they're sad their moos are wails.
The sheep dog's in the yard barking like mad, don't pull his tail, don't make him sad.

Ponies in the paddock prancing around, waiting for their meal scattered on the ground.
Bridles and saddles hung up on the wall, worn out and old, ready for the market, ready to be sold.
Pigs are in the pigsty snuffling around, pushing for their meals dropped on the ground.

Sheep are in the meadow munching away, if they got the chance they would munch all day!
Geese and goslings waddling around, eating their meal flung on the ground.
Little goslings crying for their mum, waiting for her to come, come, come.
Small, gentle goats with long curly horns, have to watch out for those prickly thorns.

The sun has set, there's a breeze in the air, and a cream coloured foal is by her mare.
Everyone is settling down, away from the town.
There's not a peep or a sound and no-one awake can be found,
For it is dark, the animals are asleep..... even the very noisy sheep.

Holly Timmins & Honor Garbutt (Age 9)

Fog In A Dream

Fog into wisps, like hair unravelling.
A hole in the corner where light peeks through.
Gentle droplets of water trickle down my nose,
From the moist air around me.
Damp spots here and there floating like delicate fairies.
Muffled voices in the distance,
But where are they coming from?
Ghostly figures slowly appear,
As my stomach twists and turns.
As I step along the deserted road,
The world turns like a gigantic roller coaster.
Then I run with fear, through unknown passageways.
The fog clears and the sun shines,
And I find I'm at home, in bed,
Safe and sound.

Emily Gay (Age 11)

A Rat

A rat
Long scaly tail
Yellow sharp teeth
Mean red eyes

A rat
Smooth black fur
Small grey ears
Mean red eyes

A rat
Lives in the cellar
Or in the drain
With red eyes

Jack Garvin (Age 7)

The Wind

The wind is a racing lion
Going from strength to strength,
Pouncing on unexpected prey
Tearing up it's path.

The wind is a delicate butterfly
Fluttering its gentle wings,
Whispering to passers by
Kissing the flowers goodnight.

Chelsea Gaffney (Age 12)

Untitled

Seagulls squawk
Children talking
Dolphins swimming
Little girls gyming
Penguins sliding
People hiding
Kankaroos jumping
Monkeys bumping

Isabella Gore (Age 5)

Hope

If I were Lord of the Land of Hope
The sky would be as blue as the ocean,
The mystical moon shines.
Gazing at the picture, I see a smooth sunset slither over the land,
The bushes rustle as a bird flies over the moon tweeting as it sings.
With trees of green so smooth the cats eyes glitter in the gloom, while the breeze drifts around.

If I were Lord of the Land of Hope
The moon was an eye gazing upon me.
A hooting sound echoed around, bouncing off the walls.
The chapel door creaked open as if beckoning me in,
The silence felt spiritual as darkness descended.
Moonlight stretched across the land.
The stained glass window was as colourful as a rainbow
As the moon disappeared the colour turned austere.

Abbie Glover (Age 9)

Chocolate

Chocolate is nice chocolate is sweet
You could have a bar of chocolate for a nice little treat
When you go into a shop down an aisle
You will find a bar of chocolate on one of the shelves
There will be all different kinds some big and some small
Some Cadbury's chocolate some milk chocolate
You can get lots of things with the flavour of chocolate
You can get chocolate spread chocolate milk shake hot chocolate and so on.
I licke chocolate and I think you do too
So buy a bar of chocolate when ever you can.

Ross Goody (Age 7)

Up At The Farm

My eyes can see
Pink fat pig smelling
Big horse sleeping

My mouth can taste
Yellow pancakes cooking
Brown bread toasting

My nose can smell
Red rosy apples falling
Big smelly barn standing

My ears can hear
Blue tractor driving
Black and white dog barking

My fingers can feel
Soft cat meowing
Hard bricks falling

Ryan George (Age 7)

My Imaginary World

My imaginary world would be,
A place with no one else but me,
Animals and peace is all around,
Flowers and trees growing up from the ground.

I'd have a cottage in the country,
With a warm log fire and a chair so comfy,
Each morning the birds would be singing,
And throughout the day I'd be daydreaming.

On the grass the dew drops gleam,
I'd watch my reflection in the stream,
Never a cloud in the sky,
Touching the fish as they pass me by.

I'd love a world of my own,
Never a dead flower to be shown,
But I'm not in my own world,
I'm in this world!

Tiffany Gardner (Age 11)

Flower 'O' Wonderful Flower

Flower 'o' wonderful flower leaves swaying about in the air,
Your petals are dancing about across your stem.
Flower 'o' wonderful flower growing and leaving the buds behind,
Let's hope your fiery colours will begin to glow around the garden.
Flower 'o' wonderful flower go along and join the dance,
People will think you are amazing because of the way you prance.
Flower 'o' wonderful flower your beauty takes over the bulbs,
Your eyes glow towards my face.
Flower 'o' wonderful flower your beauty takes my breath away,
You sigh as you stare at the bees buzzing.
Flower 'o' wonderful flower you cry in the rain as you groan,
Your leaves grow stronger over your soft face.
Flower 'o' wonderful flower you brighten up the day,
Your petals are violet and orange too.
Flower 'o' wonderful flower you attract the butterflies,
Their wings touched your skinny stem before you died.

Romy Greenstein (Age 10)

Something

Something is here,
Something is near,
Closer and closer it creeps,
Closer and closer it sweeps.

Can everybody feel it?
I don't think so,
Humans can't feel it,
But the animals feel it.

What is this strange something you see?
Well it is not you or me,
So what is this strange thing?
It definitely can not sing!

It is pollution!

Victoria Gadsby (Age 11)

Snow Eternity

Icy crystals, spiralling from the dusty clouds,
Like distant stars falling, falling from above,
It is as silent as death himself,
But fear not, for you are with me now,
I, like a skeletal raindrop, who will pull you away,
Away forever.

You can't turn back,
You must break free,
Have to keep going,
Without really knowing,
The reason it is snowing.

I, for reasons unknown,
Should really make my exit,
Goodbye, as I pass beyond the realm of existence.

Pete Goodfellow (Age 11)

Hide And Seek

Icebergs big and high
Filling up the moonlit sky
Crack, creak, up comes a penguin's beak
Silver fish coming by,
Penguin snatches, says goodbye.

Through the air they dart they fly
With a thump and a glide
Penguin lands but must hide
With a bang and a shudder,
Baby runs to her mother.

Hastily they march away,
Safe to come back another day!

Sofie Gutteridge (Age 12)

War

People dead over there
Many of us just stand and stare.

What to do when lives are taken
What to do when families are broken.

People have different jobs.

People have different opinions.

But there is one that we all share
The fact that we all care about
The people dead over there.

Nathan Hitchings (Age 12)

Scared

As it goes round in circles,
Sprinting backwards and forwards,
Going faster every minute,
Flying up and down.
It was trying to swing me off.
I was screaming,
Telling it to stop.
But it wouldn't stop.
Why did I ever get on that ride?
It was like it would never stop
Sprinting from side to side
Then to another.

Dani Haines (Age 10)

Diary

Flicking through my pages rapidly
You finally find the page
Where you dropped your last secret
In that black ink, that tickled my white paper.
You tattoo me in butterflies and birds
Photos of friends, glitter and magic;
Making me look beautiful and divine.
I am as truthful as your best friend
And I can keep a secret for eternity
I wait for you when you are at school
And while I wait, I mediate
On wherever I get put
For you hide me in different places
When your brother reads your secrets
You shout and fight
And you lock me up ready to move house
But wherever I am still keep your secrets for
Eternity.

Laura Johnson (Age 11)

Singing To The Stars

Once there was a little girl singing to the stars,

In Africa,
All was quiet,
All was still.

Suddenly animals gathered all around
To listen to her beautiful song.

In Africa,
All was quiet,
All was still.

The star twinkled so light
Like a yellow sun in daylight.

In Africa,
All was quiet,
All was still.

Abigail Green (Age 10)

Competition

C ome and enter the competition
O n comes the spot light and sparkles.
Me and you can enter the competition,
P lease come and play
E nter please please please!
T urn in a competition
I n the house I sit.
T urning on the light
I have seen your poem
O h I wish I can win
N o-one can win.

Charley Gormley (Age 8)

Places

When the sea is cold,
All the fish go bald,
When the grass is wet,
The animals get upset,
When the frost stops freezing,
The penguins start sneezing,
When the mud is dry,
The worms wonder why,
When the leaves are falling,
Winter's calling,
When I'm tucked up tight,
In the middle of the night,
I think of life around me.

Lucy Green (Age 11)

The Witch's Kitchen!

The Potion pungent like the revolting smell of mouldy cheese,
A black, iron, cobwebbed cauldron bubbling over the orange haired flames,
There are no sounds....
Except the cackle of the witch's high pitched laugh that comes from her echoing potion,
The picture of her sister hangs on a golden nail,
Her black, ebony hat bends like a frog's leg,
The witch never fixes her broken broomsticks; she never makes a potion that's nice, happy or cheerful,
Indeed she intends on being nasty, moodier than monsters,
The air is hurling with the wind of a hurricane,
A black, iron, cobwebbed cauldron bubbling over the orange haired flames,
She finds eyeballs are good for potions and stew,
And shometimes she will stand over her cauldron stirring a potion for ages,
For this is where she makes them boiling, bubbling, spurting, nasty potions.

Charlotte Grainger (Age 11)

Rainforest Life

In the rainforest shade
The monkey swings
In the rainforest shade
The white bird sings

In the rainforest shade
The brave tiger will pounce
In the rainforest shade
The green frogs bounce

In the rainforest shade
The toucan gobbles fruit
In the rainforest shade
The great monkey will hoot

In the rainforest shade
The anaconda is dressed
In the rainforest shade
Everything's at rest.

Faye Gooch (Age 9)

Music

My shiny red guitar
With it's six metal strings.
I practice very hard.
Playing lots of tunes.

I like writing tunes
I like to play my friend's music.
I also like to perform.
I like playing my music.

I like playing with my friends
I like teaching my friends to play.
I like playing the guitar.
I like helping my friends play.

I like to learn to play the guitar.
I like my guitar teacher teaching.
I like teaching my brother,
I like to see my fingers stretching.

Thomas Herbert (Age 11)

Winter Comes And Goes

Hailstones come
Hailstones go
Freezing ice...   tobogganing in snow
                     tobogganing in snow
                     tobogganing in snow
Cold ice come
Cold ice go
Wet water...   fluffy snow
                     fluffy snow
                     fluffy snow
Ice come
Ice go
Snow white...   freezing snow
                     freezing snow
                     freezing snow

Andreas Georgiou (Age 9)

Killer Whale

The Killer Whale is a horrible beast,
It gathers up humans for his midnight feast.
It's black and white
And has a nasty bite.
Never go to the deep,
Because that's where he keeps,
His meal of humans!
Never go there or he'll gobble you up
I swear.
For he is waiting
Just waiting to get you.

So beware,
Don't go to his deep, dark lair,
As I said he's just waiting to get you.

Shannon Gallagher (Age 9)

The Creature

The creature that lives deep in a fiery home
Substantial
Powerful
Thunderous
Scoffs up all the mantle and breaths it upwards with a petrifying speed
Exploding though the crust of the earth
The creature rests
Waiting
Watching
For another chance........

Jamie Grey (Age 10)

Winter Song

Long winter nights
Short winter days,
Winter wet...winter dull
Winter dull
Winter dull
Winter dull

Winter comes
And winter goes
Winter cold...winter slow
Winter slow
Winter slow
Winter slow

Ice comes
And ice goes
Slippery snow...slippery ice
Slippery snow
Slippery snow
Slippery snow.

Matthew Gardner (Age 9)

Easter

E aster eggs, daffodils
A nd fluffy chicks
S pring is here
T o let them hatch
E aster time is fun, fun, fun!
R esurrection and death of Jesus Christ

Alex Giles (Age 12)

Easter

E ating all the Easter eggs
A re you coming Easter Bunny?
S o many smiles on Easter Day
T aking all the Easter eggs
E ggs, eggs, glorious eggs
R ip, rap, rip eating all the Easter eggs.

Jack Glover (Age 9)

Spring!

S pring is lovely
P retty butterflies in the air
R ose growing in gardens
I n Spring is woodland
N ew birds singing in the tree tops
G orgeous Spring.

David Gosling (Age 9)

Banana Split

Banana split
My favourite bit,
Is the ice cream in between.
Chocolate flakes, crumble and breaks,
Topped with squirty cream.

Cherry on top,
Sauce won't stop,
As it dribbles down the side
On a spoon,
I'm over the moon!
Altogether now open wide!

All gone now,
But my-oh wow,
That pud was really yummy!
The plate is clear,
The split's not here,
Its all gone in my tummy!

Cerri Gaskin (Age 10)

Star

Small twinkling, star high in the sky,
Shining like a medal, pointed like a spear,
The colours are gold and silver.
Stars blazing like a fire,
Dazzling like a diamond.
I think they are wonderful and lovely.

Rebecca Gulowsen Ekeberg (Age 8)

Snowbells

Snowbells
White twirling snow
Glittering sparkling
Twisting turning snowfalls to ground
Snowbells

Abbie Glover (Age 8)

Volcano

The black panther is waking!
The earth is shaking
The black panther sends out its mighty roar!
The hot steamy lava is scorching
Lots of smoke is coming
As the black panther builds up its anger!
The orange lava has turned to ash
The black panther is sleeping.

Abigail Gray (Age 10)

Through My Window

Last week outside my window,
I saw a washing line,
With clothes hanging off it,
Most of which were mine.

Last night outsisde my window,
Everything was dark,
I heard an owl hooting,
Which made a little dog bark.

Today outside my window,
All that I can see,
Is someone in the garden,
Waiting to play with me.

Tomorrow outside my window,
I hope to see some snow,
Then I will get dressed quickly,
And into the garden I'll go.

Each day outside my window,
A different scene I view,
I always am excited,
Because it's always new!

Hannah Gregory (Age 10)

Horse

Grass eater
Loves jumping
Fast galloper
Hay roller
Lazy sleeper
Cute creature
Great rider
Oat lover

Caitlin Gilding (Age 8)

The Wild Night

Running through fields of powder
My muffled footsteps growing louder
Northern wind blowing down my neck
Freezing parts of unclothed flesh

Silent landscape near and far
Above me shines some unknown star
A brilliant moon shines on this hour
Above me, in silence, tall trees tower

Near by, a wolf pack moaning
Across the landscape they are roaming
To find some prey, is their key
I have a horrid feeling that prey's me

Anna-Maria Green (Age 13)

Jim And The Boy

They laughed at him,
He turned away.
This happened to him every day.
They took his money, they pulled his tie.
But he tried to get by.

A new boy joined the class,
The new boy's name was Jim.
Jim came and sat next to him.
They became friends.
The boy told Jim about the bullies,
And he understood fully.

He advised the Boy,
Told him to tell someone,
Anyone about the con.
The Boy decided to tell,
He would tell his teacher,
The Bullies said "Oy! Preacher!"

As they cornered him, the teacher came round.
They left him safe and sound,
They never scared him again.

Carenza Harvey (Age 11)

Snow

Snow is falling all around,
Then it sets upon the ground,
It's really cold it makes me shiver,
Then it melts and becomes a river,
I like to play in the snow,
Then it says it's time to go,
Then it all melts away,
All this happened in just one day!

Ella Gower (Age 8)

Mr Muscle

My Dad is Mr. Muscle
Or so he likes to think
He's always causing trouble
When he's had a drink.

He trains with his mate Neil
Who thinks he's made of steel
But we all know that's a lie
He couldn't fight a single fly.

You ought to see them at the gym,
A baby could lift more
As for doing press ups
They can only do four.

Kayleigh Hickinbottom (Age 11)

Snow

Snow is falling from the sky,
When people are going by,
Off to home we are going,
Through the falling snow,
When will it stop falling?
I don't want it to its not appalling,
Mum says it's getting better,
I say I am getting wetter
When I am playing in the snow,
There are places to go,
Up the hill,
And have a thrill,
In the falling snow.

Kimberly Hunter (Age 8)

Friends

F riends are for ever
R eal friends
I nfant friends are for ever
E very friend is a good friend
N ever let a friendship die out
D ead friends are sad friends

Logan Gray (Age 10)

Amazon

A ngry alligator argued his way around
M ale monkeys mushed melons then
A pe appears around a tree
Z oe the Zebra zacked around
O ctopus Owen opened an oak tree
N aughty Nicole stole a Nintendo

Luke Garland (Age 8)

The Rainforest Nourishment

Hunting
Fishing
Growing fruits
Vegetables to survive
Cutting
Burning
Mining dams
Trees coming down
Farming
Growing Manoc Crop
Water to survive

David Griffiths (Age 9)

Adjective Poem

Cold is water
Colder is snow
Coldest is ice

Small is a dog
Smaller is a ladybird
Smallest is an ant

Big is a cat
Bigger is a Lion
Biggest is an elephant

Kelsey Guy-Brennan (Age 9)

My Dog

My dog looks after me
My dog eats
My dog exercises
My dog digs
My dog runs
My dog plays

Luke Gaskin (Age 7)

My Cat

My cat sleeps on my bed
My cat helps me on the Playstation
With the parts I get stuck on
He runs away from me
When I'm getting him
He hides from me

Tom Gaskin (Age 5)

Untitled

Gorillas swinging
Whales swimming
Piranhas drinking
People eating
Cows mooing
People booing
Birds flying
People dying
People eating
Pirates peeping

Ethan Gooderson (Age 6)

Animal Antics

Dogs digging in the enormous garden.
Cats catching all the birds
Hamsters sleeping through the day,
Budgies burying their sweet eggs,
Lions leaping over me with delight,
Zebras eating evening till night.
Giraffes grazing every month,
Crocodiles crawling on the mud.
Butterflies flying cloud to cloud.
Dolphins dreaming of the wide sea.

Tiegan Howe (Age 7)

Spring Flowers

Spring is here now with flowers.
Winters disappeared,
Everywhere I look
I see flowers called Snowdrops,
Daffodils, Crocuses that are yellow,
Green, purple and white.
They can go to sleep at night.

Samantha Hubbard (Age 7)

Orkney Haiku

Gold stones still and tall
Leafless trees of the Orkneys
The Ring of Brodgar

Zachary Goodwin-Baker (Age 8)

The Countryside

In the countryside
I can see big spiky trees waving

In the countryside
I can hear a golden rooster calling

In the countryside
I can smell bright orange carrots waving

In the countryside
I can touch a smelly dirty tractor

In the countryside
I can taste bright rosy red apples

In the countryside
I feel really happy

Harry Hitter (Age 7)

Tiger

On my way to school I saw a tiger,
It was a furry, tiger
It was a hungry, furry, tiger
It was an ugly, hungry, furry, tiger
It was a lost, ugly, hungry, furry, tiger
It was a big, lost, ugly, hungry, furry, tiger
It was a striped, big, lost, ugly, hungry, furry, tiger,
It was a fierce, striped, big, lost, ugly, hungry, furry, tiger,
And it stole my doll!

Aimee Hardy (Age 7)

The Animal's Day

Tiny Tim the Turtle swam to the terrifying trees.
Owen the Otter opened his oven.
Ricky the Rat ran to the right.
Tommy the Tortoise tidied his teatowel.
Isabel the Iguana went to his igloo.
Shona the Snake slithered silently through the shade.
Ellis the Elephant is very intelligent.

Peter Hutchings (Age 9)

Breezy

Windy, Breezy
Twirly, Swirly, Whirly
Daffodils are sprouting
HURRAY!

Murran Harvey (Age 9)

Animals, Animals

Animals, animals, lots to choose,
There are lots of them at different zoos.
I love the tiny ants,
With lots of tiny pants.
On TV programmes, there's lots to choose.

There are blood hounds, pugs and killing dogs,
There are even spotty, warty frogs.
Also, some fat cats,
And some vampire bats.
So there are some cats, bats, frogs and dogs.

Give the big elephants some big pies,
They are made from tiny butterflies,
They will eat all day,
Till the end of May.
And that is how much they love those pies.

Ashley Harris (Age 10)

My Magic Box

I will put in the box,

The first howl of a wolf at night and a lion's enormous roar,
The floating feather of a golden eagle, swooping over the moor,

I will put in the box,

The glowing of the moon at night,
The most beautiful red roses on the greenest rose bush
And the first colourful firework on bonfire night,

I will put in the box,

The brightest stars twinkling in the sky.

Jenny Harris (Age 8)

Brazil

B om dia!
R estaurants are very posh!
A mazing football players on the pitch!
Z ooming football players!
I t's really fun!
L ove the food!

Bradley Graham (Age 7)

Money

Money, money
Here and there
From far and near,
So spend and spend,
Until you've got
None near.

Connor Gordon-Smalley (Age 10)

Haiku

When I first saw snow
My mum and dads faces were
Filled with happiness

Lauren Hibbert (Age 11)

My Cat

My cat brings rabbits indoors.
My cat runs about.

Oliver Humphreys (Age 7)

My Lovely Mummy

My mummy is pretty
Wearing makeup is a pity
She is always chewing chewing gum
And by the way she's a jolly old chum.

My mummy is about 5 ft 3
She is not much taller than me
She can almost not quite climb a tree
And she says one day she will look up at me.

My mummy has long blond hair
And everyone said she was a cheeky mare
When she was my age she looked like me
And she will for eternity.

My mummy has sparkling blue eyes
She never tells lies
She will do anything for me
Like go to Pluto and back for me.

Abbi Hards (Age 10)

The Sea The Sea

Beautiful waves
Smashing and clashing roughly
Waves as powerful as a knight
Roaring and screeching
In the dark thunder night
The sea smashing at the sandy beach
Before stopping at my feet

The sea gushing and wet
Splashing uncontrollably
As the bright sun sets

Sweeping up the shells
Soaking them to death
Choking all the time
Running out of breath
Soaking all the walls
Along with all the men
Getting them all cold
Hitting everyone den

Jodie Hankin (Age 9)

Crashing On The Rocks

Crashing on the rocks
Waves upon the sky.

Making rocks into diamonds
On the seashore.

Dolphins leaping in the sea.
Mermaids swimming, curling in the crashing sea.

Watch the little girl making a sandcastle.
And doing a somersault in the sea.

A storm is coming.
It's getting worse!

Someone tell the lighthouse
To put the light on.

Emei Hong (Age 6)

Sum Poem

2 + 1 = Tiny Tom
6 + 3 = Look there's a bee
10 + 4 = there's a tiny door
5 + 7 = Let's go up to heaven
8 + 9 = Lemon and Lime

Jaren Groves (Age 6)

Square Eyes

I looked in the mirror and what did I see
My dad sitting in his chair watching TV
Dad you'll get square eyes by watching the TV
But all he did was nod his head and laugh at me

I went in the living room and what did I see
My mum sitting gracefully on the settee
Mum you'll get square eyes by watching the TV
But all she did was sigh and ignore me

I went in my bedroom and what did I see
My sister lily watching TV
Lilly you'll get square eyes by watching the TV
No I won't that's a load of rubbish dad told me

And as I said again and again
I know you're in a lot of pain
I know this isn't the time to go . . .

Ha-ha
I TOLD YOU SO!!!!!

Jody Hinchliffe (Age 10)

The Countryside

In the countryside
I can see golden corn moving

In the countryside
I can hear blackbirds singing

In the countryside
I can smell a smelly tractor

In the countryside
I can touch trees waving

In the countryside
I can taste orange carrots growing

In the countryside
I feel sad

William Hall (Age 7)

Foods

F ood glorious food
O ranges are oranger
O h I like food!
D eer I do not like
S o do you like food?

Thomas Gowlett (Age 8)

The Predator

Silent as the night,
Eyes blazing like rubies,
In the moonlight.
The predator...
Stealthily creeping by,
Under the vacant,
Starry sky.

The zebra grazing near,
Hasn't noticed
Predator creeping by.
Softly padding,
Towards its prey and...
Striking to the zebra's dismay.

All is quiet,
As silent as night,
Eyes blazing like rubies,
In the moonlight.
The predator...
Stealthily creeping by,
Under the vacant starry sky.

Emily Hill (Age 10)

From A Spring To The Sea

You start so high,
Coming from mountains in the sky,
You trickle your way,
To the rivers during the day.

I'm at the riverbank,
Waiting

Most people wait at the seabay,
But I'm right here watching you flow my way
I hear your thundering, mighty, roar,
You thunder your way night and day travelling to the distant shore.

I'm at the sea mouth,
Waiting

You travel at a rapid pace
Entering into an endless place,
Now you're colouring the shore so plain,
With galloping white horses swaying their mane.

I'm in the sea.

Luke Herdson (Age 10)

A Frosty Morning

It is as white as angel clothes.
As crunchy as half settled concrete.
It is really as cold as the North Pole?!
Sounds like a crisp packet.
The grass is as spiky as one hundred needles!
The frost changes as quick as a flash

George Hale (Age 8)

Carrie's War

Nick and Carrie on the train on their way to Wales,
They were all carrying berries in broken pails,
Carrie and Nick were sent to the Evan's house,
Where they saw a little mouse.

Mr Evan's was very strict,
While Auntie Lou was kind,
Mr Evan's hit you with his stick,
Mess, Auntie Lou didn't mind.

Mr Evan's,
Prayed all night,
And cared for the heavens,
With a bright light.

Nick went stealing food,
Especially ginger biscuits,
And went in a mood when he didn't have his food,
He was the greediest boy in the district.

Emily Hardy (Age 9)

Johnny My Donkey

His name is Johnny and he is my donkey,
He is a bit skinny and a little bit wonky,
His ears are big but he doesn't need a wig,
He likes to eat oats and he wears a big coat,
When he eats his hay it makes him bay all day,
He likes to eat dates and he's my best mate.

Ryan Harrison (Age 8)

In The Countryside

In the countryside
I can see a fluffy rabbit snoring.

In the countryside
I can hear a brown horse kicking,

In the countryside
I can smell a red rose waving.

In the countryside
I can touch a brown silky rabbit twitching.

In the countryside
I can taste cup of milk dropping.

In the countryside
I can feel happy.

Robbie Hives (Age 6)

In The Zoo The Animals Do. . .

In the zoo,
the cheetahs do,
running,
jumping,
and eating too.

In the zoo,
the penguins do,
swimming,
sunbathing,
and drinking too.

In the zoo,
the gorillas do,
roaring,
fighting,
and munching too.

In the zoo,
the snakes do,
slithering
sliding,
and hissing too.

In the zoo, the lions do??????

Jolly Hinks (Age 10)

Love

Love is like a dove
It can fly high
And reach the sky
But when it lands
Make sure you open your hands!!!

Alicia Hardy (Age 8)

The Hurricane . . .

The hurricane . . .
A horrid thought,
The strong and crashing wind
The tree swayer and brick breaker
The twirling trash and crying children
The killer that I hate,
The storm that might never come back.

The hurricane . . .
A horrid thought,
The vicious rain and silent snow
The fearing flood and flying food
The crash that stops the world from spinning
The killer that I hate,
The storm might never come back.

Stuart Henderson (Age 11)

OAPs

Old age pensioners,
Just like my gran,
Have ancient names,
Like Minnie and Stan.

Speak up! Speak up!
My granddad groans,
Rubbing his knees,
With aching bones.

"Everything's wrong" -
"The youth of today;"
"The price of things!"
You hear them say.

And as they get,
Yet still older,
Their eyes get worse,
Their wrinkles bolder.

But do not laugh,
This could be you,
A toothless wonder,
At eighty-two.

Matthew Holgate (Age 11)

The River

R iver gushing, water flushing
I cky stick mud joining the flow
V ery wet moss, at the side of the water
E very fish gliding through the clear water, and
R ocks in its way.

Isobel Howell (Age 7)

Phoenix

It swooped down like giant hail stone,
It ate its victims to the bone,
It flies so very high,
In the scorching, Eastern sky.

This legendary animal is as graceful as its name,
And from heaven it came,
When you see it do not say,
If you mention it to a local he will say, nay.

For if you do see the beautiful sight,
You will be blinded by the light.
People who say its name will come to death,
With bated breath
With a thirty foot wingspan,
And eyes the size of a frying pan.

Samuel Hughes (Age 11)

The Zoo

I really like to go to the zoo
A kid jumped out and said, "BOO!"
I like to walk around,
I don't make a sound,
When I meet the people in the zoo.

I saw a really big chimpanzee,
I don't think he liked me!
As he rattled the bars,
You could see all his scars.
Don't go too near the chimpanzee.

I was walking past a really big shark,
You could hardly see him in the deep dark.
He had sharp teeth,
They smelled of beef!
Look out for them when you see the shark.

But now it's time to go home,
Don't like to go on my own.
I walk really slow,
Don't want to go,
But now it's really time to go home.

Nathan Howells (Age 9)

Tanka

Sad and happy times
But always loving each other
Telling secrets of
Times spent and shared together
Standing by each side, forever.

Jordan Haworth (Age 11)

Up On The Farm

Up on the farm
My eyes can see
Pink, fat pig eating.

Up on the farm
My ears can hear
Red feathery cockerel crowing.

Up on the farm
My nose can smell
Little, dog, barking.

Up on the farm,
My mouth can taste brown bread.

Up on the farm,
My fingers can feel
Me stroking a lamb.

Josh Hives (Age 6)

Far Away Lands

Lands of perfumes carpets and sweetmeats
Saracen swords to mahogany boards
From mysterious souks and bazaars
To the palace of the Indian Raj
Silver and myrrh to cats that go purr
Incense and gold to silk in folds

The Jasmine laden fragrance of the night
Statues of Gods that give you a fright
Emperors and Sultans pursuits for Glory
In ancient legends sometimes gory

Ancient tombs and temples
Scholars with high credentials
The pyramids in all their splendour
Cairo's bars with grinning tenders

Camel trains and nomads mid the ever shifting sands
Cairo and Fez ever so grand
From Persia and Turkey
To the Dead Sea so murky
Travel and see all to the East
Where ideas and adventures spring up like yeast

Charlie Hancock (Age 12)

Spring Time

Spring time,
Flowers, sunshine,
Lambs running, playing games,
Cool breeze, blue sky, sun shining
SPRING!

Shona Hughes (Age 9)

Bakery

Freshly baked baguettes covered in jam,
Chocolate muffins rising in the oven,
Sausage rolls waiting to be eaten,
Cup cakes sprinkled with sugar.

£2 for a loaf
30p for a cake,
£1 for a sandwich,
All which the bakers carefully make.

Bread made with the finest flour,
Sandwiches prepared from scratch,
Lollies made for the children of the village
That taste rather sour.

Children run in and make a selection,
A muffin, a sausage roll, a jam tart,
Whatever you choose
Your taste buds are going to show some affection!

Molly Hyson (Age 11)

War

Struggling to find my feet I push myself up,
Exhausted, drained, dead on my feet,
We got no sleep in the sludge pit.
We leave the field to reach safety
Stumbling over dead men and horses.
Flares and shells whistle past me
I can't move with speed
I only have one boot my other foot is blistered and bruised.

"GAS MASKS ON!!!"

We struggle to fix the quire things to our faces
There is one man who fails to fix his mask
He coughs and chokes while his lungs fill with water
I watch helpless as he dies.

I struggle to see through the pea green gas
Bullets still whistling past.

Think how you, yourself would feel if you had witnessed this scene
As he's flung in to the wagon to try to reach safety.

Just imagine how I felt when I heard him choke and cough his life away!!

People say they died in glory for their country.
The people lie!!!

Bruce Hall (Age 13)

My Magic Box

I will put in my magic box,
The sound of the waves crashing
Beneath the rocks.

My box is styled from a horse's soft skin.
My lid is coated with the hot sun and
The silky skin of a snake.
The hinges are coloured with a cat's
Skin and duck's feathers.

Brittany Hewitt (Age 7)

My Magic Paint Brush

With my red I can paint roses.
With my blue I can paint sky.
With my yellow I can paint the sun.
With my purple I can paint flowers.
With my brown I can paint houses.
With my black I can paint the road.
With my red I can paint the school cardigan.
With my green I can paint the grass.

Aimee Hall (Age 7)

Fire

Burning, smoking, flames so bright,
Burn and burn all through the night.
Making houses burn to the ground,
Flames of fire go round and round.
Destroying families in the night,
Does this fire really feel right.
Killing trees,
Burning bees.
Filling the world with lots of smoke,
Like a big black killing cloak.

Ami Hardy (Age 10)

Cait's Poem

The man strolled down the street.
His Boom Box playing loudly in the heat.
The children followed on scooters and bikes.
Skateboards and roller blades anyway they liked.

They followed the man onto the tram.
They pushed their way on and caused a big jam.
Off went the tram to its destination.
They all fell out at East Croydon station.

Cait Heffernan (Age 9)

The Fierce Troll

Beware of the Troll it comes through the woods,
Its beady eyes are watching you everywhere you go,
Its sharp toenails are as sharp as knives running through the woods,
He smells like a dustbin,
His teeth are as black as the night,
So do not get any closer because he might bite?

Isabella Hathway (Age 8)

Lambs And Calves

Lambs are cute lambs are one of the favourites,
Lambs are born from sheep,
Lambs are really beautiful, and lambs drink milk from sheep.
Calves are baby Cows,
Calves are small when they are born,
Calves and sheep are a sign of Spring.

Lauren Hillery (Age 7)

The Magic Box

I will put in my box,
The roar of a greedy lion.

My box is styled from rubies and
Emeralds and Sapphires and stars.
The lid is decorated with slimy, slippery slime.
The hinges are constructed from red rolling lava.

Christopher Harman (Age 7)

Sight

Staring at the seaweed below the ocean's surface,
Pink and purple coral shining in the distance.
The look of the sand reflecting the sun's rays
Like the gold on an athlete's first gold medal,
The look of graceful life under water.

Glaring at the books piled up beside the counter
Bronze oak polished so you could see your reflection.
The look of children turning pages happily
Like a baby's first breath of air,
The look of graceful reading in the library.

Watching the floating icebergs go by,
Polar bears stamping their feet on the pure white snow,
Snowflakes so perfect that the white sparkled like glitter
Like a little girl's first smile
The look of graceful playing in the Arctic.

Katie Harris (Age 9)

Wake Up

S pring is finally here we can
P lay with all the blossom green, pink
R ed and blue these are some of the colours.
I n Spring the animals have
N ew born babies, see them
G row and blossom

Annie Hyman (Age 8)

Kitty, Kitty Cool Cat

Yo, I'm your darling
Yo, I'm your girl
Pet me, kiss me, and I'll do a twirl

Yo, I'm your darling
I am very proud
Pet me, kiss me, I like a crowd

Connie Higgins (Age 9)

Are You Real?

I see you in the daytime
I see you at night
You follow me everywhere
You're always in sight

I look in the mirror
You're looking back at me
You seem so happy
You're smiling with glee

But when you're next to me
You seem so real
Your fingers, your face
These things I can't feel

I have walked straight through you
You just stand and stare
Are you fake?
Or are you really there?

Rebecca Hawkins (Age 13)

Get Your Jumper On...

You won't go to the park if you don't put your jumper on, I'll count to 12.

One. *I can't find it,*
Two. It's under your bed,
Three. *I've got it,*
Four. *I'm coming,*
Five. Put it on,
Six. *It's too tight,*
Seven. *Can you help me,*
Eight. No!
Nine. *Please.*
Ten. Alright then,
Eleven. *I can't get my head through,*
Twelve. *There told you I could do it.*

Joshua Hendry (Age 8)

A Parrot

I have a parrot,
That ate a carrot
It waddles
It toddles,
He likes to squawk,
I make him talk,
So I called him...
Torky.

Matthew Henighan (Age 8)

Rain

Sprinting down to the ground
Making puddles
As they tip-toe across the ground.
Making roads like a river
Getting deeper and deeper
By the second.
Raindrops are dancing like they're
Loving it.

Beth Haines (Age 10)

Operation Table

Death is inevitable,
It's quite clear.
But for some,
Like me,
It's closer than near.

The monitor bleeps,
Constantly.
But now and
Again,
It changes it's key.

Angels are visible,
To me anyway.
But to others,
It seems,
They're much further away.

I'm on my way out,
Not staying around.
As my brain
Goes dead
There's a long, dull, sound.

Joshua Hale (Age 12)

The Eagle's Song

Neither walk nor run can I,
But I swoop with my wings,
And I have,
Speed, speed, speed.

Neither lips nor toes have I,
But I scrabble with my claws,
And I have,
Speed, speed, speed.

Neither fins nor gills have I,
But I have a sharp beak,
And I have,
Speed, speed, speed.

Neither farm nor forest need I,
The open moors are where I dwell,
And I have,
Speed, speed, speed.

I master every glide,
I catch and devour my prey,
And I swoop with,
Speed, speed, speed.

Fiona Anne-Marie Hollin (Age 11)

Death

The sky was dull dark and grey
In the park children playing
Children on the sea-saw
Children on the swing
Then it came
It took them
All except one
He ran as fast as he could
But he was taken too
Every second someone's taken
Only every forty-five seconds someone's born
Life carries on
But soon there will be,
Nothing left

Katrina Hughes (Age 11)

Manny Mats Eating Bats

This is the tale of Manny Mats,
Who was always found eating horrid bats,
One day she ate and ate,
Then it was too late,
Poor Manny Mats was a bat.
She tried to fly, fell and landed flat,
And that was the end of Manny Mat.

Albana Hasani (Age 9)

My Pets

I have three pets a rabbit, guinea pig and a cat,
With them I like to have a chat.
My pets are special to me,
I like to have a laugh with them and go "he he".
My cat sleeps on my bed,
His stripes are orange and red.
My guinea pig is shy
And I don't know why?
I have a great big bunny.
He bites my finger and thinks it's funny!
I love my pets they're great
And they'll always be my best mate!

Isabel Hewitt (Age 9)

What Is Orange

Orange is the colour of the beautiful sun set.
Orange is the colour of the traffic lights shining in the night.
Orange is the colour of my head of my goldfish swimming in the water.
Orange is the colour of the hot fire.
Orange is the colour of a pumpkin outside a door.
Orange is the colour of the oranges falling off a tree.
Orange is the colour of some leaves falling off the trees in the breeze.

Dylan Hurdus (Age 8)

Rhyme Poem - The Jester

There once was a young prince from Leicester
Who ordered a funny court jester

He had great fun that day
Till the jester ran away

The king he searched everywhere
Down low and up in the air

He found him later that week
In a place that was cold and meek

The prince he was pleased
But the jester was not!!!

Jamie Heavens (Age 11)

Waterfalls

It smells fresh and clean
It looks as blue as ink
It sounds like cars on the motorway
It feels cold as it smashes against your hand
It makes me feel relaxed all the time.
It bubbles like oil in a saucepan.
Waterfalls are the best!!

Jamie Harrison (Age 10)

Crazy Tudors

Terrible Tudors were really torturistic,
Reading about them makes you go ballistic
Henry the VIII was a real slob,
All in all he did a terrible job.
Elizabeth was a pain in the neck,
I guess her Kingdom thought what the heck.
If you were unlucky to be Henry's wife,
Be warned you would almost certainly lose your life.
Henry desperately required a son,
He got one eventually after two daughters had come,
Not all his wives were divorced, beheaded or died,
One in particular named Catherine Parr survived.
I'm glad I live now and not then,
Because I don't think I'd reach ten.

Kayleigh Hardwick (Age 9)

Chased!

My knees knocking
Like door knockers that never stop

Eyes water
Like a flood of rain

I shiver
Like a person in t-shirt and shorts in the Arctic

My mouth goes
As a land with no water

My heart beats
Like a gigantic giant invading the city

My teeth are chattering
Like chains rattling

My feet
Have big weights on them

I open the window and then . . . .

Bethany Howse (Age 9)

Chased

My heart was thumping
Like a giant and an elephant stomping on my chest

My mouth was as dry as a rock
Coming out of a firey volcano ready to explode

My eyes watered
Like a waterfall falling down a rocky mountain

My skin is shivering
Like I'm in shorts in the Arctic ocean

Daniel Hodgson (Age 9)

Under The Sea

Deep down in the clear, azure sea
The water sparkles like diamond rings
Scuba divers glide like seagulls up above
They glide over the bright, coloured coral
Tropical fish dart, sword fish fight
Sharks dart in and out
Of the swaying seaweed
Clams open and close like a child's mouth
Octopuses move their tentacles like they are trying to fly
Getting short of oxygen it's time to rise
I take one last look down below.

Charlotte Hollinshead (Age 11)

Pony Poem

Ponies can be grey
And jump round the hay

We can plait ponies up
Then run away

Ponies trot and
Have large knots

Ponies snuggle up
In lovely warm bays

Ponies eat
Every day

Ponies charge
Throughout the day

Through the woods
And in the hay

Ponies love
The hot Summer days

Jessica Holmes (Age 9)

Luke Flood

The tale of fat, chubby Luke Flood,
Who's always drinking blood.
Always on the streets at night,
Looking for people to horribly bite.
Goes out roaming with blood red eyes,
And yet another person dies.
Grey skin, fat feet and hands,
Scrumptious blood, OH NO! **BANG!!!!**
As one man said,
Too much blood then you're dead.

Benjamin Hann (Age 9)

What Is The Sun?

The sun is a golden gem
Flickering in outer space
It is a golden face
Smiling down at you

The sun is an orange ball of fire
Soaring round and round the night sky
It is a golden bullet
Dashing between the trees

The sun is a golden eye
Looking down at you
It is a golden flower
Dancing up and down

Bethany Hubbard (Age 9)

Silence

The sky was dark, the moon was bright,
But no ghoulies or ghosties were hunting that night.
No boogeymen waited to give me a fright,
Just silence.

The trees in the forest, leaves making no sound,
No strange hybrid spiders scurried on the ground.
No screechy wailing for which banshees were renowned,
But silence.

A reflection of the moon shone in the lake,
But there were no vampires - no need for a stake.
There were no footprints like a Bigfoot might make,
Only silence.

So as I stood there, no ghost frightened me,
Yet I was still scared of the true enemy.
And it was not a werewolf or demon or yeti
'Twas silence.

Charlie Hudson (Age 11)

A Rat In A Hat

I saw a rat
On a mat.
I almost forgot I have a cat
Who likes to eat the rat.
My cat's name is Freya.
He is a good basketball player.
I don't know why you chase the rat.
He always hides under the mat.

My name is Jordan I am a bat,
But I am not very fat.
I have a fat cat
Who always sleeps on the mat.
He only gets up to chase the rat,
And the rat hides in my old man hat.
I hope this is a good joke,
Because the man who did this smoke
But he is a very good bloke.
He is now picking up a can of coke.
I hope you liked this rhyme.
I am now escaping a crime.

Jordan Hay (Age 13)

Evening Comes

Evening comes have a bath,
Go down stairs have a laugh
Mum makes tea while I play with my puppy,
After that go in to my room,
Turn on TV watch till twelve,
Go back down stairs sneak a lolly,
Get in to bed and read a horror book,
Phone my friend have a chat,
Then when I hear mum come I'm off to bed

Dominique Haywood (Age 9)

Springtime

The Springtime sun is shining
Not too hot, but warm
Flowers looking beautiful
Spread round the garden lawn

Lots of colours, lovely smells
Washing on the line
Sitting on the patio
Oh yes, I love Springtime

Kelly Harvey (Age 9)

Being Chased

Running, running for my life
Knees knocking like a rattle snake shaking its tail
I feel cold like I live in the Arctic
Eyes watering like a gigantic rain storm in rage
Mouth dry like a hot, dry, sandy desert
My hair stands up on end like lots of mountain peaks
I kept running
Trying to get away from the griffin
He was catching up with me
I ran into a cupboard
But the griffin smashed the door down
Aaaaaaaahhhhhhhhh

Brogan Hollomon (Age 9)

Performing . . .

I like to play the piano
It's such a lot of fun
I play it at the weekend
When my homework's done

I also like my dancing
I do modern, tap and shows
I also appeared at Christmas
In the Peter Pan panto

On Thursdays we do choir
The singing is really great
Soon we're doing a concert
I really just can't wait

Thomas Holmes (Age 8)

Skiing

The sound of people overtaking,
The sound of others crashing,
The sound of the wind rustling the trees,
This is what you hear when you're skiing!

The taste of creamy hot chocolate,
The taste of hot tomato soup,
The taste of a chocolate snack,
This is what you taste when you're skiing!

The touch of ice cold snow,
The touch of a freezing lift pole,
The touch of a prickly fir tree,
This is what you touch when you're skiing!

The smell of distant coffee and tea,
The smell of scorching soup,
The smell of steaming hot chocolate,
This is what you smell when you're skiing!

The awful sight of people falling,
The sight of people coming past,
The sight of little children playing,
This is what you see when you're skiing!

Pippa Harrison (Age 10)

One Hundred Years From Now

One hundred years from now
It will not matter,
What kind of car I drove,
What kind of house I lived in,
How much money was in my bank account,
Nor what my hair looked like.
But the world may be a better place
Because I was important
In the life of a child!

Faith Haywood (Age 13)

My Rabbits

My rabbit Honey is his name,
He's brown with black stripes.
Cute and cuddly but loves to play,
With everyone throughout the day.

My sister's rabbit Spud is his name,
With white fur and patches of brown.
He's jumpy, lively and fun too,
Looking after him is something to do

Jumping and flipping in the garden,
Together having fun.
They snuggle up warm and tight,
When I put them away at night.

Sam Harvey (Age 13)

My Mum

My mum is very kind,
If I hurt my brothers she doesn't mind.

If they hurt me,
She will always see.

She never lets them in my room,
If they do she shouts with a boom.

If we're apart she'll write a letter,
Just to make me feel better.

If she ever wants a drink of coffee, in a mug,
Instead I will give her a big hug.

If I sleep out I start to miss my mum,
But to make me better I start to hum.

If she starts to worry because she's run out of money,
I'll give her some bread and honey.

My mum is the best,
The best of the rest.

My mum is the best in the world!!

Ellen Haley (Age 11)

Once I Saw A Rainbow

Once I saw a rainbow up in the sky,
Once I saw a rainbow up very high

Once I saw a rainbow above a tree,
Once I saw a rainbow that surprised me

Once I saw a rainbow as bright as the sun
Once I saw a rainbow and that's me done

Bronagh Hanley (Age 9)

Death

Everyone mindless,
Knowing of what will come,
Yet still abusing their lives
Like lambs to the slaughter,
They run around aimlessly,
Living life aloud,
Some even claiming their own,
Some claiming others,
Life is a joke,
Death is the punch line,
It is unstopable, inevitable even.
All are claimed by its mindless wrath,
It needs no excuse,
Death merely exists to execute

Callum Hough (Age 13)

Colours

Here he comes
Blonde haired god
Blue jeans tight
White teeth sparkling
Doesn't notice me

Here she comes
Red hair perfect
Pink skirt tiny
Tanned legs flawless
Hanging on his arm

Here I stand
Black shoes awful
Pale hands sweating
Green eyed monster
See me staring

Here she runs
Purple nails grabbing
Brown mud flying
Red faced loser
There they go

Mikala Hough (Age 15)

Rain

Rain falling from the sky,
falling down, into my eye,
from the mountains way up high,
yes it's falling from the sky.

The rain makes puddles very deep,
it gets my feet very numb and weak,
as I look around I see,
rivers that are filling up so deep.

Lili-Mae Hewitt (Age 10)

Space

It is an amazing place,
Freezing cold and boiling hot,
The very place, every other is not,
The center of communication,
Lots of satelites, space stations,
The first astronaughts went up,
Their fingers crossed, wishing for luck,
Suddenly the thing we require to live, gone,
The air it is not there.
In space a cavity,
There is, no gravity,
It is so different from Earth,
Extremly unlike Perth,
Space is so unique,
It makes me feel so weak.

Matthew Hunter (Age 12)

Seeking Light

Hiding in a dark shadow from my home,
I wait; wait in the darkness of London,
I wish I was royalty, sitting on my throne,
Then I would be happy and safe.

My dear mama is dead,
She got shot by the police,
She was so fragile, like a piece of thread,
Don't leave me, your turning Femi into an angry beast.

My uncle is missing,
My papa's not here
So now I'm not talking, just listening,
Stopping my icy cold tear.

I hear my brother crying,
It hurts me so much,
But my papa could be dying,
I just want to feel his touch.

Hiding in the dark shadow from my home,
I wait; wait in the darkness of London.

Bianca Jeacock (Age 12)

Sight

I look at the sun from the hillside,
My eyelids slightly closed as the light beats down.
I see the laid back sheep gently grazing,
The cows ambling,
The horses trotting,
The fields below me stretching out towards the valley,
The colours of the sun blending into a dim orange glow,
As it slowly slips beyond the horizon,
And the moon rises into it's nightly reign.

Samuel Hewitt (Age 11)

A Day Out

Being on the seaside is such a treat
As I listen to the waves breaking in front of my feet
I can hear the soft music of the funfair ride
And the excited yells of people inside.

I sink my feet ankle deep in the sea
I stare at the caves surrounding me
I watch the waves as they roll back and forth
And I see the gulls flying north.

The noise on the beach is getting loud
And I am surrounded by a buzzing crowd
I turn around and start to roam
For I am heading home.

Millie Hubbard (Age 11)

Stage Girl

Awaiting in my tutu, I stand at the edge of the stage.
I feel my toes wriggle, as though they're in a cage.

I can see every smiling face, looking up in awe,
Up at the ballerina, who I simply adore.

My butterflies start stirring, my neck burns up as well,
I place my hand upon my stomach, as my heart begins to swell.

As the ballerina exits, I can hear a sudden buzz,
I get ushered up on stage, as my face begins to flush.

But as the lights shine on my face, I can see the audience no more,
I perform my dance spectacularly, this is what I have been preparing for.

As the lights on stage dim, I can hear an utter din,
I am given a bunch of flowers, I have practised this for hours.

Sophie Holt (Age 13)

Border Collie

Running after sheep with speeding power.
Black and white colours flowing in the wind.
A helpful friend with lots of companionship.
Panting tongue after a hard days work.
A great sheep dog and always will be.

Emma Hooker (Age 8)

Football Cinquain

Football
Is the best game
But all the games I've played
Someone always goes OTT
Always.

Joshua Horne (Age 9)

Tornado

T ornados are nasty spinning things
O ur homes being ripped apart
R aging winds getting faster and faster
N ow everything's getting destroyed.
A ll around things getting sucked up in to the icy eye.
D own in the shelters people hide all cold and scared
O ur homes are destroyed there's nowhere to go.

James Harris (Age 9)

I Have A Dog

I have a dog called Bart,
For a dog he's incredibly smart,
If someone's at the door,
He will bark.

He hate's cats,
But he loves to sleep on his mat.

Aaron Haynes (Age 10)

The Wardrobe

It waits to be opened,
Standing still but I can see the doors opening,
Like a mouth talking,
Hating the way I look at it,
Jealous how I get to move around without anyone noticing.
I hear the creaking of the doors like coughing.
The handles are like eyes watching over me,
The clothes inside it moving like a heart pumping,
He seems scared as if I am going to pull a body part.
It seems wrapped up in its own little world,
Keeping my clothes inside all warm,
But wanting to get out.

Laura Hamburger (Age 11)

A Wild Thing

The eagle-headed wild thing,
Is a feathery frenzy,
With terrible claws.
It is mad and wierd,
Mysterious and loud,
Lively and wild.
It is terribly mean,
Energetic and funny,
Silly and strange,
This eagle headed wild thing.

Amy Hughes (Age 7)

Holy Relics

Like the pure grass of life he carried on,
To seek where he would find his destiny.
Through happiness and sorrow he went on.
He carried on although he could not see.
Eternal power is found inside his heart
He has no ears yet still he could hear sound.
A will so strong that he would never part
With his time walking on this holy ground.
But people feared this tot'lly inn'cent man.
They thought he was from a band of witchcraft
They attacked him and struck him to the ground,
But those people were superstitious and daft.
That is the life of the chosen ones,
Reduced to sacred spirits and bones.

James Ireland (Age 11)

Gran Can You Rap?

She rapped past the market she rapped past the school
She said to a little boy yo I'm cool
I could hear a voice saying listen man
But I knew straight away that it was gran
I'm the best rapping gran this world's ever seen
I'm a slip-slap trip-trap rap-rap queen

Craig Hunter (Age 10)

Viking Poem

Vicious vikings sailed to sea,
I saw them from England but not just me,
Killing monks that got in their way,
I saw it all happening on the 17th May,
Nasty people killing everyone,
Giants of the seas but now they're gone.

Matthew Hyslop (Age 9)

Horses

The horse is the most graceful thing that I've ever seen,
It moves so gently,
The soft of its muzzle is like velvet,
It's as swift as the wind,
When it's free it's as calming as lavender.
It can be as dark as the midnight sky,
Or as light as linen.
It's coat shines in the summer's sun like glass,
The horse is a precious thing, which should not be broken in
Spirit like porcelain,
But treasured like gold.

Bethany Harvey-Cook (Age 12)

Halcyon Nights

As I withdraw to face the stunning night sky
I study it, showing off its admirable stars.
I hastily cool down and breathe in the
Comforting scent.
The darkness darkens.
To the humming owl I heed.
Suddenly I feel so safe, so secure,
So festive and gleeful.
I hum too, after the fright escapes.
The long grass gently hugs me.
I trudge to the beckoning house,
Sighing joyfully.

Hiba Ismail (Age 11)

Finley

F inley is...
I nteresting
N ever stops walking.
L icking lolly pop's.
E ggs are my favourite food.
Y um yum.

Finley Hickey (Age 6)

Love

Love is a dove
Fluttering from my heart

Soaring through the open sky
Seeking an open heart,
With love that's waiting there

Scott Haynes (Age 12)

Animal Poem

Scritch scratch the cat ate the rat
The mice ate the cheese
The dog ate the bone
He was very hungry
The pigs were having a mad bath
The chickens layed one hundred eggs
And they were discoing in the hen house
The horse kicked the bird
Oh no the bird in the sky he flew into the fly

Alexandra Hamilton (Age 6)

Fear

"Listen, look, what's going on?"
Footsteps, footsteps getting louder,
"Run, hurry don't look back."
Heart beat getting faster like a horse galloping around inside you,
"Stop, no noise except your heavy breathing like a big panting dog."
Tension building up like a python squeezing its prey.
"Wait, what's that over there?"
"It looks like a ball of matted hair with teeth like dark knives!"
Run, trip, 'SMASH'!
Yuck, the smell of rotten mean and a growl like thunder . . .

Rosanna Haigh (Age 9)

My Cat Lucy

My cat Lucy doesn't like foxes.
But she likes to sleep in cardboard boxes.
She is a little pest.
She likes to bring birds in from a nest.
She also likes to bring in other presents which she thinks is nice.
But we don't like the mice.
She is far from dull.
She likes to sleep in my brother's room.
She pretends to be a doll.

Stephanie Hunt (Age 10)

Once I Saw A Rainbow

Once I saw a rainbow, with a lovely ruby red
Once I saw a rainbow, with an orange as bright as the sun
Once I saw a rainbow, with a yellow as sparkly as gold
Once I saw a rainbow, with a green as green as an emerald

Once I saw a rainbow, so long I couldn't see the end
Once I saw a rainbow, swaying in the sky
Once I saw a rainbow, as graceful as a swan
A little bit of rain, a little bit of sun,
Put them together and your rainbow has just begun

Emily Hunter (Age 9)

Animal Antics

Dog digging in the dirty soil,
Cats catching mice in the kitchen.
Fish swimming in the deep blue ocean,
Lion lazing in the hot sun,
Horse galloping across the Meadow,
Tigers lunging on each other,
Elephant eating by the cool water.
Rhino running across the plain.
Guinea-pig gnawing in it's cage.
Rabbit nibbling on a carrot.

Craig Johnson (Age 8)

Tornados

T ornados spinning round
O ur homes nearly destroyed
R aging round to scoop us up.
N asty things happen to us
A ll around breaking things
D oing things to stop them
O pening shops to stay alive
S topping when it wants!

Patrick Huxley (Age 9)

Mysteries Of The Rainforest

Fog on the floor
Mist in the tree
Trees swaying in the wind
Frogs croaking
People hunting hunt leopards

Leopards hiding from danger
Monkeys chattering to other monkeys
As people hurry up
Sloths climbing up the tree
As leopards go by in a hurry

Chris Inwood (Age 9)

An Acrostic Poem

D espite everything around, to all noise and movement you are heedless.
R olled up in your sleepy thoughts, lost in another world: It seems ceaseless
E nrobed in warm covers, you drift from mortal tire.
A rmed with the days happenings, you dream of your desires.
M agic clouds caress you, and warmly sing you to relax.
I llusions of good and bad events cause your mind to inchance
N othing can wake you from this beautiful dream land
G entle reflections embrace you as you sleep in angel's hands

Jacqueline-Noemi Hughes (Age 11)

The King Who Could Not Sing

There once was a King,
Who could not sing,
Although he tried so hard.
The Queen, his wife,
Said "how you screech
It really is not fair."

"It's lessons, dear that
Would be good
So go and learn to sing
You'll come back
With a lovely voice
Just in time for spring"

By Spring it was harmonious.
The Queen was overjoyed
No longer did she have to hide
When the King began to sing.

Javier Iglesias (Age 11)

Frozen Beauty

I owe it all to you, my one true love
For your frosty gaze and your frozen stare
You are delicate like a new-born dove
And for your safety I take utmost care
But why should such beauty come at a cost
But for you, I'd pay all and anything
Without your uplifting beauty, I'm lost
And in my eyes you are but everything
I cry tears of sorrow when you are finished
And beg for you to come back to my world
And when you do, my hope is replenished
I never sit in the corner, all curled
And lying still, while I bitterly scream
For my much needed, beloved, Ice-Cream

Ben Illsley (Age 12)

Vicious Volcano

The lion lives deep deep in the mountains
Roaring
Berserk
Malicious
Like screaming waterfalls
Leaping, killing all the plants and trees
Soon the lion cools with smoke

Luka Hunter (Age 9)

Madness! Confusion!

Bombs falling out of the sky like rain
Water trenches full of death
Machine guns firing and explosions everywhere
Fear! Pain!
My anger keeps me fighting
My wet, muddy boots gave me blisters.

Adam Hughes (Age 9)

Black

It's the silence of death,
It's an evil scream
It's the reapers scythe
It's the death call of raven
It's the last thing you see . . .

Sami Hakim (Age 11)

Mountain Of Fire

The hulking volcano is rough edged
Lava lakes tumbling down
Lava waterfall
Lava is boiling if you touch it it will scar you for life.
Orange slime bubbles over melted rock.
The volcano is ready for another explosion.

Josh Hill (Age 9)

Anger

Anger is like a dark hole,
It tastes like frozen jelly,
It smells of sewers,
It looks like a dead stream,
It sounds like echoes in the corridor,
It feels like you're burning

Nathan Hubbard (Age 11)

Fear

Running, running for your life
Sweat like a charging river down your face
My mouth as dry as a sizzling sausage
Someone's watching like an eagle
Chattering teeth like a rumbling earthquake
And then I hid in the cupboard and then . . .

Thomas Hewett (Age 9)

Winters Poem

S pring is soon Winters just begun
N ails go pink and fingers go numb
O ver the hills the snowflakes fall
W hat a beautiful sight after all
F rosty snowman standing in the cold
L akes iced over twinkling like gold
A nd whistling wind howls through the trees
K nocking on doors "let me in please"
E nd of Winter now is Spring

Chantelle Isaacs & Sophie Lang (Age 10)

Dinosaur Acrostic Poem

D iplodocus has a long neck.
I do not like T-Rex
N ow, I definitely do not like T-Rex.
O ver Pteranodon goes.
S ometimes they do have spikes.
A nkylosaurus has a lump on his tail.
U p flies Pteranodon.
R ex is big.
S tegosaurus has four spikes on his tail.

Joel Johnstone (Age 5)

Fear

Sprinting, sprinting, for your life,
Heart thumping like an elephant stomping through your chest
A tornado was catching up with me,
Lips dry like a deserted Sahara desert,
Spinning, spinning like a whirlpool sucking in fish,
Stuck to the ground like cement sucking me into the ground,
It was closer than ever now,
Can't swallow like a vault closing . . . .

Liam Huxtable (Age 9)

The Wind

The wind is a ghost, swooping through the sky.
Gliding through the clouds gathering speed.
Destroying everything in sight.
Howling its painful cries.
Sweeping people off their feet.
It tosses boats into hungry waves.
And then it stops, fading into darkness.

Sophie Heuze (Age 14)

Elephants

Elephants are enormous, massive,
With gigantic tusks and whopper, huge, big bodies.

They are grey, dangerous, noisily trumpeting, charging,
Incredibly protective, fierce, muddy, water spurting,
Thumping feet, swishing tail, grass eating, group keeping,
Lots of eating, sizeable, big, huge, gigantic, massive,
Enormous ELEPHANTS!

Nicola Ingles (Age 8)

The Sea

Beautiful bright sun glistening on the sea
Protecting it like a blanket
Calm and crystal blue
Softly dancing in the breeze
At dusk the sun is low in the sky
The sea starts to thump the rocks
Until it rages out of CONTROL!!!!!!!!
FInally it turns to dawn everything is peaceful

Tiffany Jones (Age 10)

Wings

If I had wings
I would touch the soft feather of a bird.

If I had wings
I would smell the fresh juicy fruit.

If I had wings
I would hear the owls at night
And sometimes I would fly and look down at the view.

Syed Nazmul Islam (Age 8)

Pet Planet

I love pets all sorts of pets
Cats that scratch
Rabbits that twitch
Dogs that bark in the park
Parrots that peck on my neck
Hamsters that scurry in a hurry
So I love pets all sorts of pets.

Beth Johnson (Age 9)

Winter Song

Winter comes
Winter goes
Icy snow
Winter Slow
Winter slow
Foggy snow
Rivers icy
Animals hiding
Slippery ice
Quiet hiding
Winter snow
Silent all
Around all you can hear the
White snow . . .
Winter snow . . .
Winter snow
All you can hear
Is the foggy white snow

James Irvine-Cullen (Age 8)

Lambs

Lambs are fluffy
Lambs are cuddly.
I like lambs such a lot.

Lambs drink milk
Lambs get shaved
Lambs are good fun.

When it's winter
The fluff comes back.

At last spring,
Is here hip hip hip hooray.

Billie Judson (Age 8)

The Dinner Ladies

The people who clean the dishes
The people who make our food
The ladies who grant our wishes
To make the afternoons good.

The people who watch us play
The people who keep us safe
They take care of us every day
In every single way.

They over see our games
Children get along
They know most of our names
And we sing a football song.

The dinner ladies

Nathan Jones (Age 7)

The Roamer

He walks town to town, with a bag on his back,
Not knowing where to go,
Settling down is out of the question,
Seeming to, like a tidal flow.

Nobody questions his profound disposition,
Curiousity is one of his main traits,
He doesn't care for his awkward position,
Nomadic lifestyle is one his fates.

City to City, Town to Town.
Wondering in which place to stop,
Seething with stillness, yet he smiles,
Searching his settlement from bottom to top.

We don't question the roamer,
He's like one of the family,
'How does he do it, where will he go?'
Yet he seems to roam quite happily.

Rini Jones (Age 12)

Fireworks

Catherine wheels like roundabouts
Spinning and screeching
Rockets like a once in a lifetime
Experience
Firecrackers like a twirling multicoloured
Flare blazing in the dark night
Banger like a fountain shooting in the sky
Roman candles like a magical shower
Flying in a spiral

Their deafening, colourful and spectacular view!

William Jones (Age 9)

Would You Be Mine?

Could i ask you if you would be mine?
You have the radiant, eternal beauty divine.
My heart would break if you would say no,
For if this happened, where would I go?
Even if the flames of hell barred my way,
Nothing will keep my love for you at bay.
If the winds howl and rattle your window pane,
That will be me saying I am in pain.
My love for you is so strong,
That I could control the Earth and nothing could go wrong.
Like the star, moon and sun worshippers of old,
I can bring you the pleasures of gold.
But this much I can say,
You are my stars, my moon, and my sun combined.

Abbas Jivraj (Age 12)

Jack Frost

One morning I lied awake in bed,
When I heard a knock at the door.
I got up and trudged down the stairs,
The sound of creaking on the floor.

They knocked again,
I asked who was there.
No-one answered,
So out the window I stared.

The door swung open,
The frost attacked me.
Jack Frost had arrived
And there stood he.

Jody Jones (Age 13)

The Easter Rhyme!

In Spring it is sunny,
And the sun brings the Easter bunny
The Spring brings the rain and sun,
But most of all we have lots of fun!

The leaves laugh in the wind,
The sun makes the girls get their hair trimmed.
Spring brings love and joy,
To every little girl and boy.

At Easter time I wear my bonnet,
It's freshly decorated with daffodils on it.
All birds love to sing,
As church bells ring!

Chantelle Jackson (Age 10)

Easter

E ggs, eggs, glorious eggs
A nice day out
S uper delicious chocolate eggs.
T reats for everyone.
E aster bunny is coming tonight
R ip up the crinkly paper.

Elliott Jagger (Age 8)

Soap

Slippery soap slides across the floor,
On the floor it spins around and around like a spinning top,
Around it goes like a merry go round,
Perfumed soap smells good enough to eat.

Rachel Johnson (Age 8)

The Magic Box

I will put in the box; My rabbit 'Bubbles' playing with me,
     The bracelet of my Great Aunts, who was so kind and caring
     The eyelash of a child.

I will put in the box; The twinkle of the last star in the sky at night,
     The picture I drew of my mum with my brother,
     The first time my cousin clung on to me.

I will put in the box; The first word my brother spoke,
     The tuneful laugh of my Aunt,
     And a dogs first bark.

I will put in the box; A snowy day in Winter,
     The full moon growing in the night sky,
     And a birds first tweet.

This is what I would put in the box.

Rebecca Johnstone (Age 11)

Sports

Sports can be fun,
Sports can be dumb,
Sports can be weird,
People like horse riding,
People like skydiving,
People even like to run,
Some sports are for girls,
Some sports are for boys,
Some sports are even for both,
There's sport for young,
There's sport for old,
There's sports for middle aged folks,
Some may hate sports,
Some may love sports,
Some just even aren't sure,
But this is what I think about sports they're great that's for sure!!!!

Charlotte Jones (Age 10)

Taste

T omatoes on top of a pizza,
A pples and honey, my mouth is watering.
S oup is trickling down my throat,
T angerines all juicy and sweet,
E ggs with sausages and bacon.

Rowan Jones (Age 11)

Once Upon A Time...

Once upon a time there was a frog green and slimy,
He sat on a log that was brown and grimy,
He said 'I need to confess
That I love the pretty princess'
So he gazed at her castle that's shiny.

Once upon a time there was a princess that liked McFly,
She was really sad she looked to the sky,
Because her dad said,
On his death bed,
That he was going to die.

Once upon a time the queen told the princess to
Stay in bed because she had the flu.
Before she had a kip,
She kissed the frog on the lips,
And he turned into her prince that was new!

Once upon a time the princess missed her dad,
But she wasn't really that sad,
She a fling with the frog,
On that grimy log,
And she's glad she hasn't met any other lad(or frog!)

Ellis Jephtha (Age 12)

The Animal Man

When the animal man comes to town,
You will never see a frown,
He brings animals from fish to monkey,
Possibly even a donkey!

As he brings his owl,
You will hear a howl,
I stroke the owl with my hand,
It flies up, over African Sand.

Using magic from a wizard,
He conjures up a lizard,
I feel the lizard's scaly skin,
He starts making a massive din.

When the snake comes around,
It tries to climb to the ground,
It is really thin,
With it's very rubbery skin.

Sam Jackson (Age 11)

My Poem

I love my sister
Because
We sing songs together

Sammy Jo Jones (Age 14)

It's My First Day Of School

It's my first day of school,
And everything's cool.
I go out the house,
As quiet as a mouse.

I walk down the path,
WIth my mates having a laugh.
I turn the corner,
And found my new school's much taller.

Everyone smiles,
Everyone shivers.
Everyone stares,
Everyone fears.

I enter the building,
Expecting teachers to be there.
But when I look around.
There's nothing, just air.

I've now been fed,
And I'm lying in bed,
Looking back at my day,
Really it seemed OK.

Hannah Jones (Age 12)

Man In Blue

Down, down, down,
In a freefall,
No-one can stop him,
Dropping in a shower of rain.

He has hit the surface hard,
He has landed in a reservoir,
Is pulled under and spat out,
On the other side of a monstrous dam.

Down he rushes in an
Ever widening stream,
Through a city he flows and is
United with old friends.

Outside the city he starts to slow up,
Poisoned by sewage,
Factories are killing him as he twists,
Turns and meanders.

He comes to the delta at a slow pace,
Splits but merges into the sea.

Now he roams in the shape of white horses,
Forever surfs the free oceans.

Philip James-Pemberton (Age 10)

Animals

Scritch, scratch the cat ate the rat
The pigs in the bath
Oh no the hens have two mile eggs
The house is a tip
The dog and the cat have trashed the farm
Oh no the farmer and his wife are back what a mess

Nicole Kelly (Age 7)

The Iron Man

Where did I come from?
Those stars up there.
At least I'm free.
I can hear the sea around me.

Why did I just jump off that cliff?
Will anybody find me here in this soft peach stuff?
I'm lying here in little bits.
Where the rest of my body is I do not know.

It is morning and I'm still lying hopelessly here.
Did I make it through the night?
But I am not afraid I am the mighty iron man.
Though I hope nobody is on the hunt for me.

Chloe Johnston (Age 9)

Look At Me

Look at me, I'm a star!
I'm on the football pitch
It's what I do, for my career,
You know I'm filthy rich!

Look at me I'm a star!
I'm centre stage again
It's what I'll do when I'm older,
I'll always entertain.

Look at me, I'm a star!
I'm a brilliant cook
But now I'm getting bored again,
I want to write a book!

Look at me, I'm a star!
I'm a wicked writer
But who needs that
When what we really need
Is a superhero fighter!

Look at me, I'm just a kid
I don't do anything
There's lots of time
Left to choose but for now. . .
I'll just cruise!

Devin Kahraman (Age 8)

Easter Poem

E aster time
A baby frog could be born
S ome baby birds could be falcons
T reats from the
E aster bunny
R un and find your eggs

Declan Johnson (Age 7)

The Mermaids

Swimming through the water
Jumping over waves
Collecting pearls from giant clams
And hiding them in caves

Swimming with the dolphins
Playing with the fish
Sitting where they like to sit
And make a magical wish

Watching children on the beach
Having great fun
Sitting down to a picnic
With sandwiches and buns

Jessica King (Age 8)

Snow

The snow
Destructive as it falls
As it touches your skin
You shiver
It settles on a mountain
And then...
The untamed snow thrashes and crashes down the mountain
And then silence...

Then snow kills the plants
Makes them shiver
But the cows and sheep trudge through it
The children play and have fun
Throwing snowballs
Making snowmen and sledging
Their parents watch
Gracefully
Thanking the precious snow.

Matthew Johnson (Age 11)

The Flight Of The Butterflies

Don't you love it when butterflies fly,
Right across the deep, blue, sky?

In the air, amongst the trees,
Flying in harmony with the summer breeze.

When emerging from the cocoon in spring,
It shows the beautiful life within.

Its flight, soundless, no concept of time,
And while we watch, *our* time goes by.

Flying high, fluttering low,
And once they land, their contentment glows.

When near the end of their short life,
They march on, the flight of the butterflies.

James Kirby (Age 13)

The Countryside

In the countryside
I can see tall golden corn.
In the countryside
I can hear big green leaves rustling.
In the countryside
I can smell red strawberries growing.
In the countryside
I can touch fresh green grass growing.
In the countryside
I can taste juicy blackberries squirting.
In the countryside
I feel excited and I was jumping.

Rachel Jackson (Age 7)

An Autumn Walk

Wind blowing
Cheeks glowing
Leaves crunching
Shoulders hunching
Conkers falling
Owners calling
Dogs chasing
Squirrels racing
Home coming
Microwave humming
Soup steaming
Faces beaming

Emily King (Age 10)

Snakes

Snakes slither
Snakes climb
Snakes bite
Snakes crunch
Snakes spit
Snakes kill
Snakes are long
Snakes are big
Snakes can swim
Snakes are strong
Snakes are scaly
Snakes are my friend.

Nathan Judson-Richardson (Age 10)

Football

The ball jumped
Then somersaulted
Air walked into the net
With a mighty bang

The shirt whistled
The grass cheered
For the team
Then bounced with delight
As England won the cup

The seats clapped
As the ball pounced into the crowd
The net collapsed
As the stadium went wild
With a boom

The grass was muddy,
As the players licked it clean
The stadium disappeared
With a flash of magic.

Lauren Jordan (Age 11)

A Walk On The Beach

On a cold winter's day the rain poured down,
with the wind howling all around.

We drove to Exmouth beach to have some fun,
we wanted the dogs to go for a run.

We walked along and picked up pretty shells,
the dogs wold walk off and track other smells.

The greeny blue waves crashed violently on the sand,
the water splashed on my freezing cold hand.

The yellow sand dunes were very bumpy,
I nearly fell over, it was so lumpy.

In the distance you could see people's sailing ships,
and there was lots of sticky green seaweed lying in strips.

On the beach, there's lots of little streams
and there were no people selling ice-creams.

It was time to go, I felt quite sad
because it was a great walk that I had had.

Rosie King (Age 8)

Horse

Good sniffer
Great runner
Grass eater
Tail swisher
Great jumper
Fly catcher

Samuel Jones (Age 8)

Silver Stars

Silver stars stare in the night.
Gassy gold topaz colour,
Shows up the dazzling night.
Stars shine all night long.
They're huge but sparkly and enormous and stare in the night.
But I think stars are as great as anything in the night.
And they shouldn't scare.

Annabel Knight (Age 7)

Friends Are Like Stars

Friends are like stars,
They are what shine out in your life,
They are what brighten up your day.

Friends are like diamonds,
Always sparkling,
Always precious.

Friends are like log fires,
Always able to cheer you up,
Would you really want them to be cold?

Friends are like mind readers,
They can look at the smile on your face,
And know that you're heartbroken.

Isobel Kitching (Age 13)

Sonnet On Death

Why oh why must we be taken by him
He removes us from our loved ones
For what, a lesser amount of the seniors
And an increase of the young and healthy.
He leaves us depressed and alone on earth
Why oh why does he do this
Just to leave us on this planet alone and scared
Why must he do this although it is his work
Why do I ask for these things
With lack of point the final question I must ask
Is why does death have to exist
Other than to keep us depressed
And so we know of our demise
Why does he take us to our graves
And to our after life in the underworld

Matthew Robert Knock (Age 12)

Hung On A Cross

Torturous death hung on a cross, that's how he is going to die.
Don't they know it's the Son of God, who they've chosen to crucify?

Can't they see he's innocent; Done no wrong, committed no crime?
Sent here by his Father above, to fulfill His mission divine.

His face so white with streaks of blood, on his head a cruel crown of thorns.
How could they do it to this man? It's Jesus Christ they mock and scorn!

King of the Jews; It's just a name, he doesn't want to steal the throne.
His kingdom isn't here on Earth, it's in his Father's heavenly home.

His cross a burden on his back, lesser than the weight on his heart.
He knows the world depends on this, in God's plan he must play his part.

His breathing slow and laboured now, three hours he's been hung on high,
The air is still, the crowd silent, His final moments drawing nigh.

A last effort to speak his word, "Oh, Father forgive them!" he prays.
His dying words upon his lips: "They know not what they do," he says.

His mother, Mary, stands and cries her tears of love and grief and pain.
Above the sky is dark and grey, tears from Heaven falling as rain.

Marika Kinsey (Age 15)

Friendship

When I was born I had one friend,
I knew I'd have her until the end.
When I grew up, she was there
Looking after me with loving care.
When she wept and when she cried,
It made me wince and wished I'd died.
When she was happy, she gleamed with joy,
It was like playing a brand new toy,
When she got older, she got new friends,
She'd never forget me, we were friends 'til the end.

Jadene Joy (Age 10)

Best Football Player

R ock shock goals
O ver the keeper
N ever better than him
A lways curls it
L ow and high shots
D efence brilliant
I f only he would play for England
N ever misses a skill
H e is a hell of a player
O ver in the box

Anthony Kelly (Age 10)

The Sounds Of The Outside

The sounds of the outside, a peaceful place to be,
It is like a secret hideout only meant for me,

The blowing of the trees whispering in my ear,
The tiny little footsteps of the baby deer,

All the trees are dancing, moving as it's Spring,
Maybe they are dancing to the birds that sing,

The sun is shining, the blue skies are out,
This is what the outdoor sounds are all about.

Gemma Knight (Age 12)

The Flea The Bee And The Tree

One day there was a tree
That had a beehive
One day a flea flew by
And the bee said goodbye
So the bee opened his mouth
And shut it again but
There wasn't anything in there
So the bee said goodbye
To the hive and flew
Through the sky so high
Then he caught the fly
So high up in the sky
And then the bee ate it up
And he didn't miss it!

Olivia Kingscott (Age 8)

Love

I'm standing here on my own
All alone
In the middle of darkness
I can't see a thing
Now I'm here
I need love in my heart to survive

I need somebody to hold me tight
Make me happy
For the rest of my life
Cause love is stronger than loneliness
You can conquer all your fears

I'm nobody without love
No one knows me
I'm in the dark like a shadow left to die
Sadness takes over me
And now I can't see
And the smile upon my face fade's away
So I'm standing here on my own
Waiting
Waiting
Waiting for love to come to me

Ambreen Kauser (Age 14)

Battle

Remember years long past
With fire and cloven steel
With fire coursing through the skies
And war biting at your heel

We laid all things to rest
With our soldiers in the ground
Forgot the ways of war
And how the battles sound

We fought across the land
Across each bloody field
Too many people died there
But each refused to yield

And fallen blood did stain the guns
That cut all through our foe
But as the day drew on and on
Our tired guns did slow

Tell me how we lost it,
Why did the world fall apart?
With years without guidance
When did the chaos start?

Nick Keirle (Age 15)

Iced Bun

One iced bun in the baker's shop
See you on Monday for Vernon.
One iced bun in the baker's shop
Put it in Vernon's pot.
One iced bun in the baker's shop
Down Vernon's tummy.
One iced bun on the tree top
Put it in Vernon's pot.
One iced bun in the baker's shop
Along came Vernon with a penny one day.

Vernon Kingsley (Age 10)

Winter Days

Trees void
Frosty air
Icy streets
Wind tear

Sun frozen
People shiver
Flowers drop
Postmen deliver

Christmas is coming!

Fraser Kent (Age 8)

Frosty Morning

Flowers droopy and sad
Breath like steam
Tingly fingers and toes
Under the frost the grass was gold
Bird feeders empty
Sky grey
Red berries covered in frost
When I pushed down on the frost it made a pattern
Wrap up warm!

Lewis Kempson (Age 8)

Holidays

I love holidays.
Holidays are the best.
I like holidays.
I love holidays so much
I wish I could go on holiday.
Places like a pub,
With cheese, a happy meal with a drink.
Milk shake!

James Knight (Age 7)

Colours

Red's for blood,
Black's for the dark hole,
Brown's for sweet, sweet chocolate,
Yellow's for custard,
Brown and red are for sausages,
Orange is for orange squash,
Green is for vegetables, yucky vegetables,
Red's for Arsenal,
Blue's for Ipswich,
Red's for sun burnt people,
Black's for coal,
Black's for burnt food,
Green, yellow, orange, red, purple, blue are all in the rainbow,
Black and yellow are for a bumble bee,
Red's for a tomato and apple,
Brown's for brown sauce.

Luke Kearney (Age 8)

Ocean Travel

If I could travel
the oceans blue,
these are the things
that I would do.

Fly with puffins
under the ocean.
Dive with seagulls
and find a blue potion.

Cling to the tail
of a rolling shark.
Leap with dolphins
in the cold and dark.

Jordan Latimer (Age 8)

Pigs

I like pigs
They snort around their sty
With might
They never fight
They don't like flys
They roll around in the deep boggy mud
They eat their fill until their heart is content
That is why I like pigs

George Kitchen (Age 9)

Amber And Me

On the beach
I play with Amber.
Share a ball.
Under the sea are
Starfish and crabs.
Octopus swim,
In the sea.

Kieran Kemsley (Age 10)

Twilight Star

Twilight star
Twilight star
Twinkling light
Shining bright
Wishes known
Heart ships unknown
Shining stars
And clocks strike thirteen
Magic waterfalls
Leading to lands with unknown names.
Unicorn horns and dragons wings.
Roses sparkling red with shimmering green stalks.
Blue ribbons and wedding bells.
Sparkling blue lakes and tropical trees.
Magical lands and flowers
With rainbow coloured petals
Pegasus wings spreading out wide
A magical land for me and my friend.

Danielle Kennedy (Age 9)

My Cat

My cat,
Plays with a bat.
My cat's paws
Tap at the door.
My cat's teeth
Bite through beef.
My cat's tail
Moves like a whale,
My cat's ear
Can disappear!
When I look at his eye
He winks, saying goodbye.
His smelly feet
Reek like meat.
He sprints and walks,
He seems to talk.
He smiles,
When licking tiles.
He soundly sleeps,
Curled up by my feet.

Sam Key (Age 9)

Shadow

Where the monsters lurk
In the middle of the night
Where the ghosts and skeletons
Make you scream in fright

Where the cobwebs swing
In the eerie black
Where the spiders crawl
Under the door crack

The shadow the frightening
Most evil thing
The supernatural hiding place
Where the bats do wing

Lying in your bed
Where you can't be harmed
Is the place to be
When the vampires call around.

Toby Jones (Age 11)

Frosty Morning

Flowers droopy and sad
breath like steam
Tingly fingers and toes
Under the frost the grass was gold
Bird feeders empty
Sky grey
Red berries covered in frost
When I pushed down on the frost it made a pattern
Wrap up warm!

Lewis Kempson (Age 8)

Fear

Running, running for your life,
Sweat rushing down you like a river
Frozen, frozen like a statue with bricks on your feet
Breathing, breathing heavy and fast
Just like you have gone into the past . . .

Andrew Kett (Age 9)

Spring Poem

R ain rain is in spring coming down like tears
A pples are green and so are pears and grapes
I n spring daffodils glow like a big fat sun
N ight time is dark owls come out
Y oung animals are born in spring

Olivia Louis (Age 8)

The Sea

The calm and silent sea
Contains unique life
Suddenly destructive
Tsunami fifty metres tall
Crashes all the life from the beaches
Leaves nothing as if was never there . . .

The calm and silent sea
Contains unique life suddenly . . .
Huge forces of flashing lightning
Unbearable winds
And the powerful great blue
Destroys cities and towns
Snatching life with a flash.

The calm and silent sea contains unique life.
Don't be fooled it's deadly!
Or is it? . . .

James Kapondoro (Age 11)

Dinosaur

D inosaurs are scary
I hate dinosaurs
N o way I want to play with dinosaurs
O h no a dinosaur is coming!
S cary dinosaurs
A dinosaur was sleeping
U p I go
R oar!
S top

Megan Lynch (Age 5)

Friends Forever

Friends to cheer you up
When you're feeling down
They are always there to help
Makes you feel like part of their family
Warm and friendly inside.

Blane Lumley (Age 10)

Spring

Spring time
Beautiful plants
Trees growing their leaves back
Curling twisting turning plants
Great Spring!!!

Ty Lee (Age 9)

My Autumn Poem

What does Autumn mean to me?
I look around what can I see?
The leaves change colour and fall off the tree,
Amazing colours golden brown, yellow and orange
As they fall down.

Crunch, crunch, crunch,
A great Autumn sound,
I love to run through the leaves
When they lie on the ground.

Autumn is my favourite season
Why people don't like it I know no reason
Maybe it's because summer has gone,
I don't mind what people say,
Give me squelching autumn any day

Jordan Kay (Age 9)

My Pony Called Steel

There was a pony called Steel
Who, I thought was unreal,
He was so good
When he rolled in the mud
He got so dirty, a great deal.

He was such a good little boy
That I bought him a stable toy
When I gave him his hay
He tossed it away
Oh what a good little boy.

I cuddled and brushed him each day
And of course I fed him his hay
We rode in the school
He splashed in a pool
Oh what a wonderful day!!

Geneva Grace Low (Age 8)

If I'm Black If I'm White

If I'm black or if I'm white,
And I don't worship the same God as you might,
What's the point of making fun?
After all God has made us one,
Treat me like I am your mate,
Or if I'm taking you on a date,
If this is what the world is like,
Nobody would be hurt or get into a fight,
If I'm black or if I'm white,
What is it to you?
No colour, no size,
Treat me like you would treat yourself.

Keshav Kapoor (Age 12)

Gadgets

Gadgets, gadgets here and there,
Gadgets, gadgets everywhere.

Made by a crazy little man,
Sitting in a lab in Japan.

Computers, laptops and pda's,
Make me go hip hip hooray.

Fiddling around with them as much as I can
Everyone knows me as the gadget man!

Imran Khan (Age 13)

My Autumn Poem

Big and little leaves whirling around
Going everywhere not making a sound

There's so many colours like red, orange and brown
And when they fall off the trees they twist and turn and go all the way down.

The days get shorter and the nights get long,
And when you hear the wind whistling, it's like a song.

In Autumn it gets much colder,
The trees shed their leaves and the wind becomes bolder
Autumn is love and I am another year older.

Molly Kay (Age 9)

Anger's Rage

The pain of securing anger hopelessly hurts,
Holding it in soon announces failure.
Time and pain becomes an enemy,
With every second pain grows stronger.
My insides toughen,
Discovering rock trying to take the pain.
The pain soon breaks.
Making my feelings happy but the victim troubled in fear,
The anger gushes out of my fists and mouth.
Surrounding the victim mercilessly,
After a while the anger runs out.
The victim still drowning in fear.
I'm hoping, just hoping anger doesn't call on me again.

Samar Khan (Age 10)

Change Of Weather

One winter morning I was in bed lying
Not to awake until the birds were crying,
After a night of wind and showers
Freezing to death the little flowers.
The winter weather had been so cold,
It was making my skin go wrinkled and old,
The freezing winter just seems so long
And everything went very, very wrong.
At last the sun's turn had come
To take over the weather and make us not glum.

Kaiwen Liu (Age 10)

The Fierce Dragon

A dragon awoke from the lair
He had slept in for hundreds of years
The steam blowing from his nostrils
Could blow away the sky
His eyes were like glass balls
If they dropped they would smash
His tail could take down a forest
His teeth were like swords
Nobody could fight him
His fire would burn down a crowd
His claws were so sharp
They could take a thousand people

Chloë Lacey (Age 7)

Silver Baubles

Silver baubles falling from the sky,
Covering us in white,
Like a blizzard swirling around,
But then "BANG!"
The icy coldness of the snow suddenly
Overcomes you,
You feel bitter, not right,
You lose control,
Then you stop -
It's gone.

Catherine Lewis (Age 11)

Waiting In The War

1914

Dear Diary...
This place is a market of pain and suffering,
The sudden silence plays with your mind
Waiting, just waiting...
When death comes it hangs in the air like a cloud in a thunder storm,
Shells boom, it's a deafening sound.
My time will come where I will be buried for ever...

The thunder storm came, this time worse
And the toxic cloud took my brother.
The silence is greater
Without him I'm almost insane.
Waiting, for a shell to come and take me
I'm waiting, just waiting...

Me and my brother would sit in the trenches
And sing as the bullets ripped to the sounds of the beat.

Diary...
I may never write again
For this war is my death, and I'm waiting...
Just waiting...

Joe Lambert (Age 10)

Senses

Sound   When you're on the beach you can hear,
The sea with your ear.
You can also hear the whooing wind,
And the wind blowing the bin bags being binned.

Smell   You smell the flowers in the spring.
You smell the soup on the stove, Ping!
It's ready, we also smell the sweetness of sugar
And the sourness of salt.

Sight   We see some children laughing merrily
And bullies punching angrily.
Either way we see, nice and nasty things.

Touch   You use a hand to feel the soft cat's fur
And the firm straight whiskers.
You also feel the ice in winter.
Ouch, you got a splinter!

Taste   You can taste sweet, sour, bitter and salty things
Like sweet treacle and a sour lemon,
Plus a bitter, pecan nut and a salty packet of crisps.

Hannah Lester (Age 9)

A Walrus

A blubberous thing, as fat as a Sumo wrestler,
His beady eyes look for something to eat.
His teeth are as sharp as a machete.
His tail tapping like a human tapping his finger.
As grey as a street, he grabs a fish and eats
Like a starving man.
His layers of fat are like cliffs,
His teeth are like Greek Pillars shining in the Arctic sunlight.

Joel Loynds (Age 11)

I Love Dogs

Dogs, dogs, I love dogs,
Even German Shepherds,
I know one that is called Tom,
He looks like a Leopard.

Dogs, dogs, I love dogs,
I wish that I could have one.
I would take him around the world,
Even to tiny Taiwan.

Daniel Loe (Age 10)

My Kitten - Heather

I have a little kitten called Heather,
She's grey, fluffy and as light as a feather.

She is tiny but tough,
And when she plays, she's very rough.

She likes attention and is always number one,
She pushes her brother out of the spotlight and has lots of fun!

When she's sleepy, she's nice and cuddly,
She even falls asleep on my dear Duddly.

That's my gorgeous Kitten Heather,
We will always be together.

Lucy Lovelock (Age 12)

Winter

Winter comes
With a touch of frost
Winter comes
With adults getting cross,
Winter comes
With some jasmine white snow,
Winter comes
With hats and gloves,
Winter comes
With family love,
Winter comes
With a lot of ice,
Winter comes
With an expensive price.

Courtney Leader (Age 9)

Sid & Zig

Once there was an elephant
His name was Sid
On a long walk he began to pant
So from the sun he hid

When Sid was hid
Something stirred
Sid became very timid
Only to discover it was a tiny bird

Sid asked the bird his name
The bird replied my name is Zig
Would you like to play a game
Yes, let's play tig

Sid and Zig began to play tig
Sid found it hard
Because he was so big
This isn't natural because I am a baird

Sid and Zig decided to chat
It was too hot to play
Zig lent sid a big sun hat
Sid said thanks it will help me on my way

Sophie Larard (Age 8)

Walk Around The Moon

As I look up to the sky.
The moon is the one who shines into my eye.
A bird flew over my head.
Made me think does the moon hold the dead,

Above my house flew a ghost.
I wonder if the moon has a coast.
And I found a little thing.
Does the moon have a king.

As I came to the roof.
The moon itself has past its youth.
I get to a ship that takes me.
To the moon that I want to see.

I fly and fly up in the sky.
We fly very high.
As I see the cheese rock.
I gaze at the new clock.

As I sit upon a crater.
Where I saw all the dater.
Now I walk around the moon.
Before I leave, I hope the earth has not come to doom.

Freddie Lampen (Age 11)

Monday's Child

Monday's child is a super walker
Tuesday's child is a rubbish talker
Wednesday's child can't stand cold
Thursday's child is really bold
Friday's child is oh so mad
Saturday's child is extremely sad
But the child that is born on the Sabbath day
Is really fond of eating a takeaway

Matthew Lees (Age 8)

Touch

Touch may be good or bad, nice or nasty,
Cactus plants have spikes that prick you,
A shark's tooth could stab you painfully,
My fluffy cushion is really soft,
Sleek furry cat is good to stroke,
Glaciers are cold enough to hurt you,
Lava, hotter than hot, will burn you badly.
So many things to touch in the world.

Tom Lees (Age 10)

Kitten

Very sweet
And neat
Eating meat
With feet
Slurping milk
On silk
Waving tail
At males
Very purry
But blurry

Alisha Lamble (Age 7)

Animals

I like dogs because they are fun
They make me laugh when they start to run

I like lions when they roar
I like their lovely big paws

I like rabbits when they eat the grass
They are all fluffy when they come out of the bath

I like lots of animals
And they are all my friends

Megan Lane (Age 7)

My Mini Cooper

My dear little red Mini Cooper,
It's quick and it is super duper.
It speeds down the road,
With only me as its load,
My dear little red Mini Cooper!

This cute little car that I own,
Is so beautiful and it's well known.
Only a berk,
Would buy a big Merc,
All you need is a Mini to own!

Everything's chrome on this Mini I own,
Everything's glistening and bright.
It's all very great,
With the waterproof paint,
Sat on my Mini, please don't spill that Sprite!

James Linsey (Age 11)

Flamingoes

Flamingoes are pink,
Flamingoes drink,
Flamingoes love the sink,
Flamingoes think, and drink at the sink
Flamingoes wink
Flamingoes link to another wink
The Flamingo lays an egg in May
Flamingoes fly,
But they go by.
Flamingoes are a bit white and they are bright
And they live in a sink
Flamingoes drink a pink drink.

Annie Kelly (Age 8)

Parklands

These four walls, they're closing in around me
As I curl up in a ball embracing my knee
A hand on my shoulder it feels so firm
But when I look up he pulls his arm away
Wiping it obsessively like he would a germ.

He pulls me up and throws a tissue in the bin
But not before wiping the dribble from my chin
I look at his hair and then feel my own
It's prickly and greasy, I can't
Remember the last time I used a comb.

I glance round the room knowing everyone's fate
But I don't like to be seen in this awful state
All these years on my own are taking it's toll
Whilst taking to an imaginary soul
I just want to get out of this mental home.

Marissa Laing (Age 12)

Storms At Sea

Storms at sea are blue and wet,
Storms at sea makes whales go splat,
Storms at sea just like that,
Storms at sea can make the sky go black.

Storms at sea are like a lion,
Storms at sea get louder and louder,
Storms at sea make the sea bubble
Like a frying pan on the double.

So next time you're going out to sea
Make sure there's no storm heading for thee.

Edward Lampen (Age 9)

My Time

Gripping the outer sheet firmly
I shook the pillow harshly;
I reached out...

Turned my head.
I saw my room flooded with a mystical pale orange glow.
I heard the gentle buzz of a moth attempting to escapethe clutches of the bathroom light,
I smelt the comforting waft of fajitas creeping slowly up the stairs,
I tasted the wash of Morrison's new improved whitening fresh mint toothpaste,
I felt sound, secure, safe, like all worries had been wiped from the world...

I turned the knob,
Flicked the switch
And let the familiar drone wash over me,
Overwhelm me,
Drown me,
As it had done so many times before...

Bethan Llewellyn (Age 9)

Tsunami

It's coming closer...
And closer...
Like a blanket covering a bed
People are seeking a high building, any building?...
Panic takes hold throughout the city
The flood is coming

It's coming closer...
And closer...
Like a blanket covering a bed
The raging sea is growing
People still scurrying for safety
Crash! It's here!
People screaming here, there, everywhere
While the raging sea crashes through the windows of buildings

It came...and it has gone
The city is covered in sea
Dead bodies are...
Floating in the water
It's like a city among the dead
Starvation...Death....Hell!

Chris Leventis (Age 11)

On A Summer's Day

On a summer's sunny day,
The children go out to play,
On the beach the children stay,
Greeting people "Good ay mate!"

Sophia Lang (Age 10)

Spring Means

Spring means watching little lambs being born
Spring means sunshine
Spring means Easter rabbits bouncing in the meadow
Spring means seeing little chicks being born on farms
I love Spring.

Charlie Lee (Age 9)

Spring

In the spring it gets warm
And the flowers come out
In spring I can play in my garden
The leaves on the trees are green
And baby animals are born
Spring makes me feel happy

Hayden Layton-Bullock (Age 6)

Ye Olde Nite Hags

Ye olde nite hags,
Do watche with spite,
Ears of raven,
Eyes of sprite.

Ye demons leer,
As if to bite,
Their frames bente,
Their faces wite.

No holy spirit,
Do dwell in site,
Whilst in the claspe,
Of hellish nite.

They turn and grype,
Their long steeds tite,
For when at last,
They seeke their flike
AWAY! AWAY!
Ye dawnin' lite.

Karen Legg (Age 14)

Easter

Fun Exciting
Eating, drinking singing
Chocolate eggs all over the place
Church!

Declan Lewis (Age 8)

My Cat

I've got a cat called Ted
And he loves my colourful bear
If you ever want to find Ted
I'm sure he will be on my bed

Helen Low (Age 8)

Dog

Loud barker
sheep rounder
good sniffer
Brilliant hunter
good digger
Bone licker

Chloe Lovett (Age 8)

School Poem

S chool, school what can I say? Please read on and have a nice day!
C lassrooms, classrooms you can get lost, mustn't be last at any cost,
    whether you're new or whether you're old, get a map or so I'm told.
H aha it's not finished yet, there's still the lessons don't forget;
    love them or hate them it's just the same, they're all part of the whole school game.
O h, those teachers can nag, nag, nag, "don't drag your feet, don't swing that bag."
    but they're only doing what's good for you so just relax and you'll pull through.
O f course there's the homework you have to do, even though it's boring it's good for you.
L ast of all, I have to say, school, school is everyday!

Emma Lewis (Age 13)

Sunny Summer

Summer
Lovely bright summer
Fanning yourself, too hot!
Laying stretched and sunbathing
Boiling!

Georgia Lewis (Age 9)

The Blue Sea

On the cold grey
Stones O sea!
The blue sea waved
Around splashing on rocks
The blue sea roars.

Kailen Lewis (Age 9)

Rugby

Rugby can be good, rugby is the best
Rugby can keep you fit and healthy
Rugby got invented in 1886
Rugby is rough and rugby is tough
It is very very hard
Rugby has a sin bin for ten minutes
And you can get sent off
For the whole game

Nathan Lamb (Age 8)

Walking Through The Farmyard

Walking through the farmyard
What do you see
I can see a cow mooing at me

Walking through the farmyard
What do you see
I can see a horse gallop at me

Nathan Lovett (Age 5)

Ocean Travel

If I could travel
the oceans blue
these are the things
that I would do.

Go on the beach
and get a bat.
Sit on a log and
whack a mat.

Go on the ocean
in a boat.
Paddle the oars.
Float on a moat.

Looking at the eagle
flying over the sea.
Oh I think I see a snake
I think it's drinking tea.

Austen Lane (Age 8)

Huntress

A distant clock strikes twelve
This is the midnight, witching hour
Although the moon shines, large and full
An eerie darkness looms

As her shape flits through the shadows
The moonlight seeks her out
She hunts, senses alert, intense
Feline grace and agility, she stalks her prey

Suddenly, a stray moonbeam finds her face
Reflected in burning, emerald cat's eyes
It dazzles, glows, gleams
Betraying her position, giving her away

It's then that the huntress strikes
An elegant, fluid movement
Teeth and claws glint in the moonlight
This power can't be tamed, it is wild

Sarah Manning (Age 15)

Number Poem

Number One
Chocolate Bun
Number Two
Chicken Stew
Number Three
China Tea
Number Four
Sugar Galore
Number Five
Honey from a Hive
Number Six
Chocolate Sticks
Number Seven
Cream from Devon
Number Eight
Eat at the Gate
Number Nine
Hey that's Mine
Number Ten
Same Again

Olivia Lowther (Age 9)

Days Of The Week

Four o'clock Friday I'm home at last
Time to forget the week the week that has passed

On Monday I got wrong, because I swore
I cried and banged into a door.

On Tuesday I scribbled all over my work,
Sammy laughed and called me a jerk.

On Wednesday I tripped on a chair,
I frowned and said "it was not fair".

On thursday Laura Crouchy yelled
She jammed my thumb it hurt and swelled

On Friday lunch I had some pie
I smashed my plate and told a lie

Four o'clock Friday I'm home at last
Time to forget the week that's passed

Sophie Mason (Age 9)

Sum Poem

1 + 2   = a fat kangaroo
2 ÷ 2   = bird flu
3 - 1   = a beautiful swan
4 + 4   = a big door
5 + 5   = a beehive
6 + 6   = a pile of bricks
7 + 7   = go to heaven
8 + 8   = a piece of steak
9 + 9   = I am really fine
10 + 10= I am in a den

Kaid Mavrou (Age 7)

One, Two, Three...

One otter, old and hairy,
Two tiny T-rex's tickling tigers toes,
Three tickling turkeys,
Four fat frogs frying on a pan,
Five flying fish flying in the air,
Six scorpions sliding down a hill,
Seven sloths sitting on New York,
Eight eels electrocuting elephants,
Nine newts needing chocolate,
Ten turtles tearing T-rexs.

Jordan Law (Age 9)

What Is The Sun?

The sun is an amber yoyo
Whizzing through the sky
It is beautiful in colour
But it is also slow as a fly

The sun is a golden ball
Bouncing in space
The sun has survived
A long time into the human race

The sun is a yellow gem
It shines like a rose
It flickers in the sky
And really shows

Reuben Lane (Age 8)

The Darkness Is...

A trapped deadly enemy waiting to snatch your life away from you.
The devils pathway.
The unlit deep depths of the Abyss,
A welcoming to a daunting, shadowy black blanket,
An opening to hell's hand,
The frightening pit underneath your bed,
The stars twinkling,
The grim reapers murky coat,
A world where unpleasant animals are,
Where the light can't get in,
Where the bad spirits curse you,
An empty feeling in the root of your stomach
Where silence is all around,
A witches nasty cauldron.

Emma Lawrence (Age 11)

Snow Mountain

If I were Lord of Snow Mountain
Where the air is as cold as ice
The people are full of contentment.
Gazing at the picture, scarlet scarves strangle snowmen,
Crunch,
Crackle.
I'm dumbfounded as the snowman's eyes glitter at me mercifully.

The snowman's frown turns upside town
As appears on his shoulder
A small snowman child
His son stared at him joyfully,
The only person in his family
They've never been apart and they never will be.

Helen Lister (Age 10)

Sum

1 + 3   =   look at me.
9 + 10 =   amen.
6 + 7   =   go to heaven.
5 + 8   =   get the gate.
2 + 4   =   knock at the door.
1 + 10 =   a smelly hen.
2 + 5   =   a bee hive.
3 + 8   =   a metal gate.
4 + 7   =   go to heaven.
5 + 6   =   get your bricks.
1 + 2   =   kick my shoe.
3 + 4   =   knock at the door.
5 + 6   =   pick up your brick.

Dylan Miller (Age 6)

Hamish

The Autumn day was dry and crisp,
Cliff path winding and deserted,
Seagulls screeching, soaring high in the sky,
Waves crashing against the rocks
Pebbly ground beneath my feet,
Boats bobbing in the distant sea,
I could hear a whimpering....
A white fluffy creature cowering behind the rocks
Lost and alone, cold and shivering,
It was a dog, Hamish was his name.
I scooped him up, walking briskly
Back, up and, up the twisty path....
A woman rushed towards me,
Thankfully it was the owner,
Hamish...., safely back where he belonged!

Abbie Loka (Age 10)

I Hear Them Coming

I hear them coming
I hear him crying
I see how he's struggling
I see how he's trying

He thinks he'll get away with it
But he is very wrong
He thought I wouldn't take it
He thought I wasn't strong

He won't bother me now
He is far away
I think it is finally safe
For me to go out and play

Molly Magee (Age 12)

The World Cup

4, 2 is the score,
The crowd is quiet in their seats,
Hoping the whistle will blow soon,
Sweating, biting nails, trembling,
Hope rising,
Come one, come on, only a minute to go,
The gold cup glistening in the sun,
Will it be ours, only 40 years have we waited,
Ten seconds more, 9, 8, 7, 6, 5, 4, 3, 2 ,1,
The whistle blows,
Silence then shouting, cheering, clapping,
Happiness beyond words,
Ours again in 2006.

David Lipscombe (Age 10)

A Chinese Shar-Pei

A saggy bundle
A loud tumble
A cuddly toy
A naughty boy
A guarding machine
That may seem mean
An expert at 'puppy eyes'
But that's no surprise
A real Chinese
A home to flea's
A catalogue to make me
A DOG!

Fenella Rose Maguire (Age 11)

The Sea

Water skipping
Over jagged rocks
Seagulls calling
Ships floating
Fish frightened...
By the sea
So unpredictable
And overpowering
Waves crashing
Sea running after you
The tide getting closer
The tide getting closer
Run...
Run...
Run...
The waves are coming
In the sunlight...
Shimmering.

Jack Lucas (Age 11)

My Shadow

While I am screaming at my mum
My shadow is talking to my dad

While I am playing netball with my mum
My shadow is sitting on the chair nicely chilling

While I am shouting Manchester who won
My shadow is whispering for Chelsea

While I am eating fries and hamburgers
My shadow eats fruit and vegetables

While I am choosing some sweets from pick and mix
My shadow is going to the dentist

While I am laughing like a hyena
My shadow is weeping like a lamb

Lauren Mistretta (Age 6)

The Fire Mountain

It sounds like a rumbly tummy,
Gurgling because it's hungry,
Red dribble starts coming out of it's mouth,
It's rather fat,
It's going to explode,
All of a sudden, bang it goes.

Hannah Lewis (Age 10)

The Rainforest Rhyme

Tree frog jumps from branch to branch,
Sloth having an afternoon doze,
Coati venturing in the tree tops,
Squirrel monkey leaping from tree to tree,
Keel-billed toucan seeking fruits high in the canopy,
Funny Oropendula frantically takes off,
Piranha snaps his jaws!

Kizzie Mountain (Age 8)

Every Good Thing After School

I am going to the swimming pool,
That's a good thing after school.
Then I will play with my toy Gaul,
That's a good thing after school.
Then I'll pretend to be cool
That's a good thing after school.
Anything can be good after school!

Freya Lance (Age 7)

Untitled

Racing through the air, 100 mph,
Open the door, very slowly,
Connection to earth,
Kelly we've done it, the flag's on the moon.
Everybody threw us a party when we got home,
Tonight we're going to celebrate, till the morning comes.

Olivia McKay (Age 13)

Is It A Dream

I can hear nothing but silence lifting me up into a world of white
I can feel a shudder of coldness as a flake catches my hand, wrapping its bitterness around me
I taste a freshening snowflake on my tongue sitting for a second then sharply melting deep inside me
I see a vicious blizzard of white falling from the heavens above
This new scene stands in front of me am I dreaming?
I stopped,
I stared,
It was real I was there!

Aimee McNair (Age 10)

Sweets

I like chocolate,
I like sweets.
I like toffees,
They're so neat.
Lemon sherberts,
Turkish delight.
I like to munch and grunch,
ALL NIGHT!

Haribo gummies
Make me feel funny
Mars Bars and Milky Ways
Make me smile all day

I just love all kinds of sweets!
Even though my mum says they are bad for my teeth
I just don't care
And I never want to share
My sweets are all mine
And you would have a hard time.

Just trying to get hold of my yummy scrummy sweets!

Alex Mehew (Age 6)

Months

January is bitter cold
February is wet through
March is windy everywhere
And April doesn't have a clue

In May you hear the blackbirds sing
In June you feel the sun
July I feel is the hottest month
And August you can have fun

September again it starts to get cold
October, the wind blows
November black nights are looming
December it starts to snow

Ryan Meredith (Age 12)

My Family

I love my mummy because she waits and
I love her because she stands at the gates
I love her cooking when it's good
But when it's bad it tastes like mud.

Daddy buys me toys but when I say
I don't want them he makes a lot of noise.
My brother Jacob likes football
And he is very tall.

Alisha Mather (Age 6)

Ocean Travel

If I could travel
The oceans blue
These are the things
That I would do.

Fly like an eagle
Over the sea,
Dive like a dolphin
Just like me.
Go on the ocean
In a boat,
Go to the beach
And find a goat.

Sail on a boat
And shout "AHOY."
Go on the beach
And find a toy.

Jump like a fish.
Swim like a shark.
Hunt with an eagle.
Run home before dark.

Thoren Musselwhite (Age 8)

My Toffee The Hamster

My Toffee is a softie,
And likes to sip on my coffee.
He likes to nibble on his honey nuts,
But I say NO BUTS!

My Toffee likes to sleep all day,
But then at night he comes to play.
He always likes to climb around,
But sooner or later he'll hit the ground.

My Toffee likes to play away,
But needs exercise everyday.
OH, how I love my Toffee,
In each and every way!

Hannah Mehew (Age 8)

Spring Is Here

Spring is here
Winter is gone
Every Spring
I see daffodils
The sun is like
A golden ball
So hot
It melts the ice
Spring is my favourite season

Connor Lazenbury (Age 7)

How Can This Be Me?

How can this be me?
Sitting here in this pit,
How can I make you see,
I hide my sadness with wit?

Most of the time I wonder
When will this massacre end
All around me, guns like thunder
But I stay here and defend.

Always I am thinking,
Will I leave here alive or dead?
Sat in this muddy trench sinking,
Oh how I long just to be warm and fed.

Waiting here in hell,
With my friend alongside me,
Then flash, he's gone, he's fell,
And suddenly I feel as lonely as can be.

The next words that I hear,
Are "Up and over the top",
The words I most fear,
And I pray, "Please God make it stop"

Laura Murray (Age 14)

Walking Through The Farmyard

Walking through the farmyard,
What do I see?
I see a duck quacking at me.

Walking through the farmyard
What do I see?
I see a pig oinking at me.

Walking through the farmyard
What do I see?
I see a sheep baaing at me.

George Morris-Jones (Age 5)

My Naughty Behaviour

I slapped the teacher,
So it was a dare
What could I do run away in scare?
She moved me down to fifteen minutes
All I had to do was be good,
But it didn't work out,
All I did was mess about
Can you tell me how to be good
'Cos now I really think I should

Amy Morris (Age 9)

The Road Ahead

My life is black for I cannot see the road ahead,
I am not here when the sun is shining,
Though I am here when the moon is dead.

I will not be here when you look for I,
Yet here when you think not,
Though I see no cloud in the sky.

When the sun begins to die and wane,
I will be hurt and battered,
Though feel no pain.

My life begins and ends at dark
The length of my life the size of a pin,
Not hear will I the loudest dog bark.

My life is ended,
My life is gone.
It had no purpose,
No meaning.
But to reach its end,
However glorious or joyful
Though now it's finished,
So for another I shall wait happy or hurtful.

Matthew McConnell (Age 12)

The Hot Countryside

In the countryside
I can see a shiny rabbit hopping
In the countryside
I can hear the soft cold wind blowing
In the countryside
I can smell the yellow flowers opening
In the countryside
I can touch a black dog running
In the countryside
I can taste a crusty sandwich munching
In the countryside
I feel excited

Adam Musrati (Age 6)

Late Boy

You're late
What have you got to say for yourself?
Well Miss it goes like this Miss
My nan had chicken pox,
My hamster died
I had the flu and not only that I had a bat on my hat
I got stuck on my mum's lap
OK now get on with your work please
Miss I've got nothing to write about

Rebekah Murray (Age 7)

I Am White And Here Are My Thoughts

Anxious because of the laws I have to keep,
Peculiar feelings of separation,
Apart and weeping in the nation,
Reading the newspapers I began to despair with myself,
This Apartheid we have does not make sense,
Hero Nelson Mandela we call,
Encouraged we stand together to fight injustice,
I begin to know the joy for the very first time when this,
Demanding country is for the blacks and not just for the whites.

Sohail Kashif Mahmood (Age 9)

Rap Writer

My names Rosie and I'm here to say
That I like to rap every night and day
My dogs called Chester and he's really cute
He likes to run away with the loot
The loot is the dog biscuits and he thinks they're yum
But my favourite food is chewing gum
He thinks he's a kid but he's really not
He always smashes the flowerpots
I am nine and he is seven
We don't take him holidays even to Devon
He's just a little puppy inside and out
He sometimes gets into a pout
It's time for me to say goodbye
Everything I've told you is a lie

Rosie Metzner (Age 9)

Flowers

Pink ones, violet ones, all different kind of ones
Purple ones, blue ones, and all kind of different ones
Round ones, oval ones, and all kind of shaped ones
Star ones, square ones, and very, very tall ones
Smelly ones, and old ones, and all different kind of ones.

Zoe Moore (Age 7)

In The Sunny Countryside

In the countryside
I can hear a black furry skunk searching.

In the countryside
I can hear a camouflage bird flying.

In the countryside
I can smell the honey bees making.

In the countryside
I feel the green grass waving.

Jordan Mather (Age 7)

The River Thames

The River Thames is wide
And it also has a very strong tide
The barrier goes up and down
To stop the flood in London town.

Boats made from different wood
Brings factories all their goods
Pollution sent the salmon away
Only the blood worm could stay.

Connor Murray (Age 9)

Animals

The slithering, sliding and striking snake
And the rib snapping crocodile,
Are both reptiles.
The rigid, ruthless rhino,
And the quick, pouncing tiger,
Are both mammals.
The fast fighting falcon,
And the aerodynamic eagle,
Are both birds.
The black and white great white shark,
And the Amazons piranha,
Are both fish
What do they all have in common . . .
All vertebrates.

Charlie McCarthy (Age 11)

Moon . . .

The moon is shining bright,
As it twinkles in the darkness.
It is ghostly white
As it twinkles in the darkness
The moon is enormous

Natasha Martin (Age 8)

Ing Words

Seagulls squawking
People walking
Zebras crashing
Mummys mashing
Dolphins swimming
Tigers springing
Cats scratching
People catching
Dogs fetching
People stretching
Frogs leaping
Cows sleeping

Megan McGuire (Age 6)

All My Games

I like playing all sorts of games
Some with counters and others with names
Spiderman, Fantastic Four
Lara Croft crawling through a door

Chicken Little, bouncing on his head
Charlie and his grandparents,
Sharing the same bed

All my favourite Playstation games
Are in the rack, sorted by names
Some are old, some are new
I've even got one with Winnie the Pooh

Skating, surfing, running and driving
When I play them
I'm really excited

I look forward to Christmas, when the games roll in
But the best times of all
Is when I win!!

William Mehew (Age 6)

What Is The Sun?

The sun is a golden gem
Glittering in the sky
It is spinning through the clouds
High up in the sky

The sun is a golden bullet
Floating round
It is flickering into outer space
High above the trees

The sun is a golden crisp
Burning in the sky
It is flying over trees
Hiding behind the trees

The sun is a yellow pineapple
Sparkling red and amber
It is a dancing flame
Bright and colourful

Megan Manly (Age 8)

Snow

I twirled and turned down to the ground
Waiting for someone to pick me up
I fall in the air into your hair
I am very cold when you hold me
I come down on your head
And I came down when you were in bed
I look like bubbles in a bath
And when I come down you might laugh
When I come down I do not look like a clown

Rebecca McCulloch (Age 7)

Autumn Days

Leaves falling
Branches swaying
Squelchy footsteps
People playing

Plants dropping
Wind blowing
Ice-cream keeping
People going

Jerome Marcel (Age 8)

Smoky The Dragon

I had a pet Dragon called Smoky
His fire had all burnt out
He has got green eyes without a doubt
He has bright shiny scales
His tail is like a spear
He's got sharp pointing claws
And teeth as white as snow
He lives in his mountain lair
With all his gold as well
One day he ran away to live above the clouds
I wish that he would come back to me one day
It's a shame he never did.

Kelly Morgan (Age 7)

The Seaside

Waves are crashing on the rocks
Shells are shining in the sand

People walk up and down as
Waves come swooping in

People swimming, splashing in the sea
As happy as they've ever been

People making magnificent sandcastles
Digging holes and jumping from the pier

It's fun being at the seaside

Olivia Mellet (Age 6)

The Spell Poem

This is a spell to change the time.
The main ingredients is lemon and lime.

Put a bit of humming birds tongue,
Then add a bit of human's lung.

All these things go in the pot,
Then I'll have to drink the lot.

Trouble, trouble make it rubble,
Make it as twice as double.

Flies wings and frogs legs,
Newt's eyes and chicken's eggs.

Gerbils claws and dragon's scales,
Snail's antenna and a rat's tail.

Trouble, trouble make it rubble,
Make it as twice as double.

Eagles beak and sunny weather,
Cat's whiskers and peacocks feather.

Dead butterfly and rabbit's tummy,
Horses hooves and baby's dummy.

Trouble, trouble make it rubble,
Make it as twice as double.

Tina Malinic (Age 10)

Horse

Fast trotter
Hay eater
Noisy neigher
Carrot eater
Tail wagger
Heavy stamper

Jessica Matthewson (Age 8)

Gone Forever!

When someone dies,
They're gone forever,
Their presence has left you,
No more kisses, never ever.

No more goodnight kisses,
Or lullabies,
"It's OK, don't be scared!"
Mother used to say as I cried!

Although she isn't really here,
She is in my heart always,
Whenever I need her, she's there,
Standing by my bed or in doorways!

Her spirit will guide me,
and never leave,
In times of trouble,
Her warm hugs I'll keep.

I won't ever stop missing you,
You'll always be near me,
this I know is true,
I love you very much Mummy,

Goodbye, I'll see you soon xxxx

Cara McPherson (Age 13)

Motorbike

Motorbike, motorbike,
You're the best,
Even when you're in a mess,
Jumping, speeding over jumps,
No slowness in the bumps,
Even if you're really small,
Motorbike, motorbike you're really cool.

Jack Mighall (Age 10)

Nigeria

Nigeria, Nigeria you can't explain how beautiful is Nigeria,
With the beautiful colours and plants Nigeria,

But then there's London how grey and dull that is London,
The people are mean but some can be kind
With the beeps of horns and the shouts of people, who have lost their mind,

Living in London is like living in a sewer apart from there are people and shops,
Which sell lollipops but even with all that you're really all alone in London,

So that is Nigeria and that is London, Nigeria with beauty and London with the sea of grey.

Peter McNally (Age 13)

Swimming

Swim in the sea at half past three
Swim in the sea at quarter to three
Swim in the garden at half past two
Swim in the tree at quarter to two
Swim in the flowers while getting stung by a bee
Swim in the grass getting tickled by a bee
Swim in the river and get out with a shiver
Swim in the bath and have a laugh quick as a flash but try not to splash
Swim in the car but don't go far
Swim in the ocean watch the waves in motion
Swim in the clouds and shout out loud
Swim in the pond with the fishes and swans
Swim in the pool it is really cool
Swim in the lock on your front or back butterfly and crawl you can swim them all
Splish and splosh and have a wash
Swim all day long and all through the night don't worry you will be alright
Swim all the time it will make you feel fine

Emily Mangan (Age 7)

Ariel

Open sky
Can dive
Have friends
Naughty girl
Proud father
Love Prince
Evil sea witch
Have tail
Human again

Emily Mellis (Age 8)

Who Has Seen The Wind?

Who has seen the wind?
Neither I nor you:
But when it is hailing and the gates are squeaking
The wind is dashing through.

Who has seen the wind?
Neither you nor I:
But when it is dashing the trees are falling
The wind is howling by.

Bonnie Macey (Age 8)

Seasons

Spring is in the air
New life is everywhere
Birds returning from migration
Bears come out of hibernation

Summer means lots of fun,
Fantastic holidays in the sun
Eating ice cream around the pool
But best of all - no school!

Autumn leaves fall from trees
Kites are flying on the breeze
The pitter patter of the rain
Sliding down the window pane

Winter woollies knitted by mum
Keep me warm when having fun
Sunlight glistens on the snow
Bury the jumper - she'll never know

Lucy Mitchell (Age 9)

The Best Time Of Spring

Spring is where the glittering flowers grow,
Easter is right here.
Easter is better than playing with dough,
And chocolate will appear.

Sometimes in Easter parents bake,
Children wonder what it might be.
Really delicious brown and cream cake,
And easter is what you see.

Spring and Easter have bright and red flowers,
Sometimes there is yellow ones too.
The Easter bunny has lots of good powers,
As wide and as tall as a shoe.

Easter is a really happy time,
I also love decorated eggs.
Easter will get the church bells to chime,
But not as quiet as a wooden peg.

Talia Muncaster (Age 11)

The Day I Got My Hamster

The day I got my hamster,
I played with it all day.
It ran around the house,
I was glad it was here to stay.

I named my hamster Cheddar,
Because of his love for cheese,
He really is so special,
And runs around his wheel with ease.
I take him out to play with me every single day,
And close my bedroom door so he doesn't run away.
He likes to scamper around the floor,
He loves to gnaw the door.

I really like my hamster,
We are the best of friends.
My mum however is not so keen,
And here;s where my poem ends.

Matthew Morrow (Age 10)

The Sea Song

The sea played music
Whilst the whales danced
In the moonlight
While the sharks had their
Midnight feast
And the fish
Did the congo
The shrimps
Did the macarana
The party had started.

The Titanic sunk in fear
The anchor chinkled like coins
The shells somersaulted out of the way
The angel fish did the salsa
The boat watched with joy
The seaweed swayed to the music
The icicles stamped on empty cans
And that's how the sea played its song.

Ellie Montgomery (Age 11)

Christmas

Christmas outside is
Sledging down snow covered hills
Christmas outside is
Trees with sparkling lights
Christmas inside is
Hot fires and presents under the tree

Alasdair Monney (Age 8)

What's Spring Like?

Daffodils are growing.
The juicy grass is growing
From the muddy ground.
Little baby lambs have been born.
The lovely spring has appeared.
Planted seeds popping up from the ground.
Spring is here!

Lucy Manly (Age 6)

The Polar Bear

The polar bear strides through the frozen, crunchy snow,
In Alaska the temperature is extremely low,
He jumps into glacier waters for something to eat,
A colossal salmon would be a treat!

The polar bear rapidly slides on a glaze,
For the animals in the Arctic it is the latest craze,
The polar bear's fur is soft as a pillow,
Like a soft breeze that moves through the willow,
His shiny black eyes stand out in the snow,
His massive paws leave traces below.

The polar bear looks awfully sweet,
But if you annoy him, you might be his meat,
With the penguins the polar bear might seem to play,
But really he is sneaking around for his prey,
With the little cubs it is fun to play,
After an exhausting time they slide into their cave at the end of the day.

Melina Mukherjee (Age 10)

Summer

The sight of the
Gently flowing stream
And the vast forest
Surrounding,

The sound of a
Baby bird's chirp
And the breeze rushing past
The quietly rustling trees.

The soft smell of the
Multicoloured flowers
And the sweet smell of
The refreshing Summer scent.

The taste of the
Delicious red berries
With their pure
Running juice.

And the wonderful feel
Of a tug on my line
And the pull of
A big strong fish.

Joe Moran (Age 11)

Summer Days

Grass shines
Sun rise
Flowers blush
Every size

James Moore-Morton (Age 7)

Me And My Friend Sam

My friend Sam,
Does not like ham.
We both like football,
Sam is very tall.
When we have fun
It's normally in the sun.
When we're on the swings
We do lots of things.
We both eat pasta
But Sam eats much faster.
When we go to the shop
We get some pop.
Wen we're not in school
We play in the pool.
We both eat chips
And spit out orange pips.

Me and my friend Sam.

Ryan McSweeney (Age 9)

Rainforest Poem

The rainforest area, covered with trees,
All of them are topped with leaves.
Birds that nest in the canopy,
Laugh and sing with the Asian monkey.

Down comes the rain that hits the floor,
All of the animals run.
Taking shelter for their care
To get out of the rain and sun.

Hippity, hoppity, jumping frogs
And the climbing sloth.
Jumping, swinging, flying,
I do love them both.

Singing birds in the morning,
Golden petaled flowers.
Swaying trees in the breeze,
Here comes the rainy showers.

The fog that floats on the floor,
Holds no winter.

Luke Mortlock (Age 10)

Bob

There was a man named Bob,
Who could not get a job.
He won the bingo one day,
And now can pay,
But sadly became a slob!

Callum Moore (Age 11)

The War

We used to have such great times,
But now we do jobs and let out wines.
All we hear is yelp, yelp, yelp,
I suppose we need a little help.

When we were young we had good fun,
Run little children, run, run, run.
We played with out gas masks all day long,
And sang our little battle song.

When the war's over dad will come home,
I can't even speak to him over the phone.
I want him back in my arms,
To keep him out of all the harms.

So happiness throughout the years,
Will fill me with loving tears.

Harry McGowan (Age 11)

Phantom Wolf

Look to the skies, there's a full moon tonight
If you're out in the woods then you're in for a fright,
The Phantom Wolf has taken flight

If you hear a bone-chilling howl
Stop, stand still and listen for a growl
And don't be disturbed by the hoot of an owl

Running through the forest, away from his past
Your own heart beating really fast
In a world of your own, you wish it would last

A loud noise brings you back to your senses
You look at the wolf as his whole body tenses
As if he is manning all his defences

He throws back his head and howls at the moon
It really is a mournful tune
Sadly, it'll end so soon

The Phantom Wolf shall rest in peace
Although his power will not decrease
Even though he is deceased

Look to the skies, there's a full moon tonight
The Phantom Wolf has taken flight.

Rebecca Morgan (Age 12)

Joy

Joy is pure white,
It smells like slowly melting chocolate,
And tastes like warm drinks on a cold winter night,
It sounds like a choir singing a wonderful song,
Joy lives in a cosy, welcoming home.

Alice Murphy (Age 10)

The Coming Of The Night

The blue angel's work is finishing,
It is time to move on,
His army of clouds that fill the skies,
Are slowly turning orange.

Apollo is leading the sun,
Down to find another place,
The night is threading through it's lace,
To slowly settle down.

The night Princess is starting to stride,
Filling the night with her pride,
The blue sky has gone away,
Now the darkness rules.

Torran McEwan (Age 10)

Space

Space . . . . !
Our leading face,
Creator of planets,
Watcher of creatures,
Watcher of features.

Comets . . . . !
Its rage of rocket,
Ice and dust thundering past,
Masters of target,
Masters of hard-hit.

Planets . . . . !
Some as tough as granite,
Others as miniscule as ants,
Circles of life,
Circles of ice.

Stars . . . . !
All from afar,
All servers of light,
Sights of names,
Sights of flames.

Elliott Mason (Age 11)

Snow Land

Snow is white like a fluffy cloud,
It flies across the dark night cloud.
It goes past the moon and the sky
It just keeps shooting by.

Christopher Millar (Age 9)

The Angry Farmer

The angry farmer sits in his chair
Doesn't look but does stare
He sees a bird eating his crops
He starts to think then starts to rock
He thinks of poison he thinks of a gun
He thinks of anything to make the bird run
He could not think after having a drink
But then an idea popped into his head
He must have been bumping his head on the bed
He decided to jog far, far away
And then he wouldn't be a farmer again.

Tillie-May Merritt (Age 10)

Dolphins

What gorgeous creatures,
Splashing in the sea.
They've got millions of admirers,
And one of them is me.

Just beneath the waves,
Where the dolphins talk and play.
They say hello,
And agree with plans with an OK.

They have forever lasting smiles,
They are never sad
They've got a shiny back,
And are never bad.

They jump out of the water,
Then back into the blue.
The babies stay with their family,
As they should do.

Jamie Leigh Mackintosh (Age 10)

My Rabbit

My rabbit runs about a lot
Hides a lot
He sits on my lap everyday
He sleeps in the hutch
Eats in the hutch

Jazmin Marshall (Age 6)

Music

Music is . . .
Instruments playing
Shining cymbals smashing together
A guitar . . .
Throwing powerful notes at you
Beautiful blue drums
The beats getting faster
Music is . . .
The beats
Beats that are fast and getting faster
Beats that are slow and getting slower
Beats getting faster and faster
And faster
Then all of a sudden it STOPS!!!!
And then starts again
Getting slower
This time
Then nothing
Pure silence
Music is . . .

Paige Ashley Moore (Age 11)

Bullies

As I stand here all alone,
I begin to cry and groan.
Because as you stand there joking,
I sit here choking.
As I struggle for breath,
You hear me and act deaf.
Soon my time will all be gone
As another has just begun
You'll wonder where I have gone,
But you killed me with your tongue.
No more taunting could I take
So my life I did take.
It's your fault I died.
Every night I cried.
But in your mind you know
It's your fault I did go,
It's your fault I am dead.
It's your fault I took a shot to the head.
But now your old toy,
Is now a dead boy.

Rory Maginess-Roberts (Age 15)

Summer

Seaside glowing
Swimming, walking, playing
Hot sunshine warm summer
Breeze time
LUNCH TIME

Olivia Middlebrook (Age 8)

The Night Princesses

T'was the night
I held my lantern high
When I saw three figures
Dart past very fast

Each with a golden crown
On thy black hair
Each with black
Chain mail dress

They pulled darkness
Along thy path
Foot prints so dainty
They didn't show in the grass

They lifted off into the air
Golden magic full
But I didn't need the clue
I knew they were the Night Princesses

Iona McEwan (Age 10)

Sugar City

If I were Lord of Sugar City,
The sugar would be as sweet as honey,
The silver-whiteness dazzling me,
Hunger haunting me,
Slurp, I can taste the marvellous sugar,
Crunch, it's so delicious,
I can see sugar ants walking into sugar shops,
Marching up sugar mountains,
It's a beautiful City.

If I were Lord of Sugar City,
The sugar ants would troop,
Blowing trumpets when they got to the top,
They'd call "Attack!" to the other ants,
The sugar cubes would tremble as the ants attack,
Tumbling down, down, down, into blackness,
The ants, disappear with the sugar,
I wonder, sprinkling sugar in my tea.

Clare Mawson (Age 9)

You Are Late

Well my brother fell in the chimney
My dad fell asleep in the tree
My dog ran away
My nan cut her knee
My grandad fell down the loo
My sister locked herself in the loft
My mum fell asleep on the cat

Get on with your work

Please Miss I have nothing to write about

Caleb Marriner (Age 6)

Miss Ferguson's Poem

M iss Ferguson is my FAVORITE teacher!
I s she good at LAUGHING or NETBALL!
S houting is her best!
S ue Turner she likes the most!

F un is what she likes less than shouting!
E xciting objects she has today!
R elazing and resting she likes the most!
G lug...Glug....Glug....what did you say!
U nderstand math's now Miss Read!
S un's shining let's go out for some fresh air!
O h! No! A naughty boy!
N o! No! No! IT IS GOLDEN TIME!
 THE END!

Zoe Mallett (Age 7)

The Frosty Planet

If I were Queen of the Frosty Planet
Where it's as cold as a freezer
It would be so relaxing.
Gazing at the picture, I see frost fur,
Rustle, crisp, pad as they start to stroll.
Fresh white snow is a mass of footprints,
Now they are dancing
Jumping to the moon.

I start to munch,
My hand is deep down,
Rattle, crunch
Snow slips through my icy fingers,
I run towards them
The polar bears skip about and celebrate,
Because I am the only queen of Frosty Planet.

But only until tomorrow,
When the golden sun will open it's huge red mouth,
And shine through my window.

Layla Myers (Age 9)

Happiness

Happiness is there when I need him
Rolling around and walking calmly
He looks like a small fuzzy tennis ball
So no worry can scare me.
His nose is a button his eyes are bright and
There is his cheeky grin that will not fright me.
He moves so jolly with not a scare in this world.
He makes me so strong so no worry will beat me
I am so lucky because happiness lives with me.

Cathy Morris (Age 11)

Easter Has Come!

Easter has come,
With daffodils dancing in the sun.
Children have fun decorating their eggs,
While baby lambs are trying to stand on their legs.

Easter eggs are very yummy,
All the chocolate in my tummy.
Spring is here time for joy,
Time for fun for every girl and boy.
Every year spring is here,
Ready for bunnies to appear.

All the donkeys plodding along,
While the children sing a song.
White fluffy bunnies hopping around,
Coloured easter eggs rolling on the ground.

Beth McGoldrick (Age 11)

Ocean Travel

If I could travel
the ocean blue.
These are the things
that I would do.

Dive in the sea
and search for magic.
Beware of the shark,
it could be tragic.

Sail on a boat
and shout ahoy.
Go on the beach
and find some toys.

Swim in the sea
and find some potion.
Lay on the beach
and wear sun lotion.

Swim in the sea
and find a band.
Eat a pea
and play in the sand.

Gemma Morgan (Age 7)

Star Sounds

Telling the sound of
Rocks the house
An instrument to love
True rock and roll
Oh a great big sound
Chords for you to play on it
A great instrument
Start playing on one now
Tell everyone it rocks
Everlasting sound
Rock out the house

Nathan Mitchell (Age 8)

The Fox

I hear horns,
Hunters getting ready

I smell fear
And danger
Coming for me.

I see hunters
With their dogs!!
Oh. . . Oh. . .

Cheyenne Mackenzie (Age 10)

Books!

Happy books, sad books
Good books, **BAD** books

Short books, looooooong books
Quiet books, song books

Round books, **square** books
Cat books, bear books

Thin books, thick books
S-l-o-w books, *quick* books

Scary books, **funny** books
Rainy books, sunny books

Big books, small books
Short books, tall books

Pull books, **flap** books
Pop-up books, trap books

Trick books, clue? books
Old books, new books

I love books, you must agree
So, let's chop down another tree!

Ryan McGrath-Johnston (Age 10)

Ben Flatches Death

This is the tale of Ben Flatches,
He always plays with matches.
Then one day he burned his toes
And even burned his baggy clothes
Then he burned his nose.
His mum said "How are your toes?"
Then he bought new clothes,
His mum said "Don't burn those."
The fourth day he was burned to his skull.
Then his mum said OH, NO . . .

Luke Marshall (Age 9)

Friends

My name is Kelli
I'm very friendly too,
What's your name?
Elizabeth? Hey!
Would you like to be my friend?
You could stay to tea,
We could play with my dolls or watch TV,
Friends are fun,
Friends are kind,
Friends will help you anytime.

Kelli McArthur (Age 10)

The Colours Of Life Unfolded

Orange is the sunset gleaming at you,
Green is jealousy from the depths of hell,
Blue is elegant, soft sky filled with clouds numbered 1 to 9
Red is anger from the devil's blood
Yellow is happiness blooming with buttercups
Black is the shadow hanging over you and causes depression
These are some of the colours of life unfolded

Shari McLaren-Sterling (Age 12)

Giraffe

G lorious, tallest beautiful giraffe became
I rate when his great mate, Adam the ape,
R an off and
A te all his grapes.
F lirty flamingo was a wise old bird fearing the worst suggested!
F riends are forever and may be they should share!
E ventually after a time Giraffe and Ape were the best of mates.

Amy Mohr (Age 10)

Sunset

S pread your toes across the sand and watch the sunshine fade.
U nderneath the sand the crabs are buried deep.
N o sound but the rolling waves and the wind in the palm trees.
S ealife's asleep the ocean is silent.
E verything is still, nothing moves but you.
T he moon and the stars are beginning to appear.

Samantha Maitland (Age 10)

The Feelings Of An Old Piano

The little ones claw and bang
And mash and bash my fingers,
But the tall ones are kind and light
Then there is loneliness all through the night.

A boy, a boy is that his name?
I'll name him Jim.
He plays me with angelic grace
Unlike the other little ones with fingers like mace.

Jim feels my fingers and presses them down
And I just sing, sing and sing.
This note, that chord, this areppegio, that scale,
But wait Jim's looking quite pale.

They say that he is sick
Will he live to play me again
Now no-one ever comes.

Christopher Marriott (Age 11)

Friends Poem

F antastic friends to play with,
R unning, racing, having fun.
I deas to share.
E ncouraging you to do your best.
N ever letting you down.
D oing things that we all like.
S pecial friends for evermore.

Jamie Malone (Age 9)

Brazil

B om dia!
R aining rainforest!
A mazing footballers!
Z ooming people!
I t's great!
L ung's of our earth!

Grace Martin (Age 8)

Colours

A red rose
An orange ball
An indigo plum
A blue jumper
A beautiful rainbow
To shine on us

Rosario Marciante (Age 11)

Ocean Travel

If I could travel
The oceans blue
These are the things
That I would do.

In the cold windy sea
Swim with a shark.
It's a stormy day
In the dark.

I get a net
And catch a fish
On a noisy day
In my dish.

Jump like a frog.
Dive like a fish.
Run in the dark
And find a wish.

Georgia Norbury (Age 7)

Nature

A turquoise forget-me-not drifted on the stream,
Its petals were as small as an ant.
Its fragrance smelt so sweet,
Bees came from all around to see it.

A golden leaf floated down,
It danced around like a baby ghost.
It landed so softly as though it were a feather.
A little insect crawled on and nibbled it.

A robin chirped in his wonderful nest,
His chest as red as paint.
He flew around his oak tree,
As the robin chick sang merrily

A ladybird scurried up a stem,
Her spots as black as coal.
She reached the flower at the top
And sniffed its fragrant smell.

Naomi Mercer (Age 10)

The Protective Ring

As the warm wax trickles down the smooth white candle
It flickers in the shadowy dark room
The wax suddenly wander's down like a lava ball
And blasts on the tin foil

Around the flame is a protective ring
Like the ring around saturn
Smouldering smoke the colour of the flames shadows
Flickering like a rocket lifting
And burns like the beautiful sun

Jemma Munro (Age 11)

Somerset

A nice summer day when the sun is setting
To see the colours fade together
And turn into the midnight sky.

Maddie Newman (Age 9)

Under The Sea

Under the sea, it's a great place to be
Under the sky, like a great huge pie
I like to swim in the sea, with a great big fish and me
The seaweeds green and the sharks are mean
I wish I can see, the great big bottom of the sea.

Aaron Neale (Age 8)

My Limericks

There was a young man named Dave,
Who decided to live in a cave,
He lost one sock,
And was sick of rock,
So he ended up just listening to rave.

There once was a dog that was fat,
Who sat all day on his mat,
When there was a huge race,
He finally got up from his place,
And was beaten by a young small gnat.

There once was a cobblestone path,
That people walked to the local cafe,
But little did they know,
There was a monster below,
Waiting to let out its wrath.

Jacob Marshall (Age 12)

My Dad

Nose picker
Ice-cream licker
Late snoozer
Pub boozer

T.V mad
Always sad
Football crazy
Always lazy

Hannah Mundell (Age 10)

Fantasy Haiku

Bowser in the Dark World.
Bowser in the Fire Sea.
Bowser in the Sky.

Rhys Manning (Age 11)

Earl

There once was an old bloke named Earl
Who woke up thinking he was a girl.
He then got in his car, and drove to a Spa
And then got his name changed to Pearl.

Cameron Morrish (Age 12)

Nature

As the sun shines brightly on the sparkling lake,
A red squirrel jumps out from his hiding place.
Fluffy white rabbits, a family of robins,
And a colourful woodpecker starts tapping a large tree.

Many animals sit around the water,
Feasting on worms, nuts and dandelion leaves.
A beautiful bird starts chirping sweetly,
Trees start swaying to the music.

Candy floss clouds, a cute grey cygnet,
Silvery fish, green slimy frogs,
A pink flamingo and the shining sun,
Are all humming along to this lovely song.

Tulips and daffodils, roses and daisies,
Swaying in the sunlight,
Wanting to dance all around the lake
All day till the moon is out.

Rosie Mercer (Age 10)

Life

In the galaxy,
There is earth, fire, and water.
People died from the ice age. They then came back from
Animals who survived, fish, apes and others.
Apes learnt how to build, their faces changed,
But they never knew about the galaxy until now.
Life is not what it seems.
LIFE is like time.
Life is the most delightful, astonishing experience
EVER!

Samuel Moody (Age 9)

What Am I?

A white tower with a silky body.
A crown on top that changes colour.
When the flame is lit a light shimmers across the room.
The mix of colours make it so beautiful

The flame moves with the wind
It has a shield of light that protects it
Like a king with a wonderful crown
A flickering movement in the wind.

The flame burns, the wax melts like lava.
The soft wind livens the flame each time.
The smoke travels like an animal needing a home.
The wicks end glows gradually fading
The light of the world it seems to me.

Rebekah Mumford (Age 11)

Animals

Big or small
Or tougher than a brick wall
We love them all

Slim or fat
Or even wearing a hat
We love them all

Fast or slow
Or even ones we don't know
We love them all

Snakes or bats
Or spiders or rats
We love them all

And God made these animals
For the health of the world
And that's why we love them all.

Rebecca Moore (Age 10)

Volcano

A mouse in front of a lion,
The scream of death is heard a mile away.
The hill has one companion.
Death.

The cloud has covered an area.
A deserted ally way lays empty.
But still the cities cry one word,
"Goodbye."

Conor Murphy (Age 9)

Monkey

Once I saw a monkey,
Climbing in the trees,
Eating some bananas,
And throwing some at me!

First it was quite lonely,
Just him and me,
Then came some other monkeys,
1, 2, 3!

The monkeys were all grooming,
Eating bugs yummy,
I climbed up to meet them,
They tickled my tummy!

Chloe McClure (Age 11)

The Three Bears And The Sleepy One

On a summers day,
In a cottage made of hay,
Lived three, fluffy, brown bears,
Mamma bear woke up late everyday,
And forgot to cook the breakfast,
The breakfast,
She forgot to cook the breakfast.

So everyday,
They had KFC,
It was chickstrips,
And a basket full of chips,
And finally they had their breakfast,
Their breakfast,
They finally had their breakfast.

Lydia McQuiston (Age 11)

The 5 Senses

I touch sand and sharp rubble.
I taste cold oily fast food.
I see graffitied boarded up buildings.
I hear traffic jams and disgruntled drivers.
I smell traffic fumes.

I touch silky garments.
I taste fresh fruits.
I see green pastures.
I hear streams and birds.
I smell flowers and spicy herbs.

Oliver Martin (Age 12)

My Teacher

My teacher Miss Wold
Sits in her chair
And fiddles with her long hair.

My teacher Miss Wold
Helps me when I'm stuck
And she never gets rough.

My teacher Miss Wold
Is so kind
She makes me feel like I want to swing on a vine.

My teacher Miss Wold
Is the best in the world.

Joanne Murdock (Age 8)

Summer Comes

Summer comes
            With the leaves growing
Summer comes
            With the rivers flowing
Summer comes
            With the children playing
Summer comes
            With the high priest praying
Summer comes
            When the teachers don't have any fuel!
Summer comes
            When the kids rule!!!

Connor Menon (Age 9)

Fireworks

Banging and bashing, the people go aahh.
Popping and fizzing, the people are watching.
Crying and crackling, the dogs are barking.
Sizzling and flashing, the colours are in the dark sky.
Screeching and whistling, the audience are amazed in the crowd.

Roxy Newberry (Age 12)

Stars So Bright

The moonlight night with stars so bright
Prickly and sparkly corners of stars.
Which you want to touch but you just can't.
You shelter your eyes from the glaring stars.
When you look at stars they're dancing around.
Twirling and swirling as they turn around.
Who want to make you dizzy
But you're too clever.
They can sparkly, dance, twirl and you might not even know if they fall on you
Now the night sky is turning into light.
And the clouds are covering the stars.

Komal Maqsood (Age 11)

Poetry Day

P eople reading poems through and through.
O ne poem being the winning one.
E ndless lines of imaginative ideas.
T reacle tart being passed by, as participants laugh and cry.
R eading , reading the competition goes on
Y es!! I've won!

D aft poems being scored low, good poems being scored high,
A silence while the judging goes on.
Y es!! Another person laughs and another person will sigh.

Sam Medford (Age 11)

Billy Bob

There once was a boy called Billy Bob,
Yes there once was a boy called Billy Bob
He had a great fall on a wall and he didn't know
What to do, so he called his mum and she gave
Him a lift, and then he was quite okay.

Now this boy called Billy Bob he knows all the books
You can say, he knows all the sums you can fire at him
And he will never let you down; you can't catch him out,
He's always watching you so be on the look out.
You shouldn't try to tease him because he's got lots of combats,
And he will always beat you and you shall never win.

Alex McKeown (Age 10)

Sound

When I go to the theme park everyone is squealing their heads off,
You could hear from a mile away,
When I go to the beach I hear the sea gulls splashing into the water.

When I go to a football match everyone is either whooing or booing
When I go to a cricket match there is no cheering.
No whooing or booing.

When I go the local library no one squeaks or makes a sound,
Everyone is completely silent.
When I go through the woods at night,
I hear the howl of the wolf and the toot of an owl.

Alex McNie (Age 10)

Monster Under The Bed

Monster under the bed, heavy breathing, wet drool on your carpet.
Then it jumps up and lands on your bed,
When you see the true identity of this monster from underneath your bed, it horrifies you,
It opens its mouth and shouts something terrible, which will knock your socks off. BOO!!
As the monster draws back the curtains there's your mum saying,
"Hurry up you're late for school, otherwise the monster under the bed will come and get you".

Bethany Nicholson (Age 9)

Tiger

Tearing food
In mood
Eating liver
Before shiver
Too bad
You're had
I'm fat
That's that

Regan Mullen (Age 7)

Cats Jump

Cats jump
Cats leap
Cats sleep
Cats eat
Some cats are bad
Some cats are good
Some cats are lazy
Some cats are old
Some cats are young
Cats are middle aged
My cat is perfect just right

Gemma Newton (Age 7)

Summer Days

Boiling streets
Bees flying
Screaming children
People lying

Crowded streets
Blue sky
Branches still
Birds fly

Jorja Newman (Age 8)

Rain In Baghdad
(After "Snow in Madrid" by Joy Davidman

Faces turned upwards, gazing fixatedly at the sky,
They did not know what to think, nor do, nor say,
And the reasons they were there slipped to the back of their minds,
And guns clattered to the tarmac from hands on both side.

They felt it splash on their faces,
And on their skin, dark and white.
Then slowly a smile curled the upheld faces,
And helmets and balaclavas were thrown to the floor.

A vacuous silence fell, so much emptier than usual.
Gone were the gunshots, explosions and shouts.
And their expressions were ones of gleeful surprise,
For once something gentle was falling from the skies.

Dominic Merchant (Age 12)

Mountain Of Fire

The earth is shaking
The devil is waking,
The devil is angry.
The devil is throwing parts of the mantle,
The streets are on fire.
The devil has settled back down,
The silent streets.

Daniel Morris (Age 9)

The Crocodile

His skin is like armour
His teeth are long, shining curving scimitars,
His eyes are like a sly hawks,
And his tail is a lethal broom sweeping
Those who come near.

His legs are thick tree stumps,
He talks to death before he kills.

Jack Margolis (Age 10)

Haiku

Dogs and cats stolen
Terrified of being killed
Owner crying, dog missing.

Rose Newton (Age 11)

Rainbow

I know a pen
All the colours of the rainbow
It helps me write
It gives me ideas
That make me glow

Holly Miles (Age 9)

Noses

I looked in the mirror,
And saw my nose.
It's the funniest thing,
The way it grows,
Stuck right out where it shows,
With two little holes where the breathing goes.

If you ever want to giggle and shout,
And you can't think of what to do it about,
Just look in the mirror and then,
No doubt,
You'll see how funny <u>YOUR</u> nose sticks out!

Katie Mehew (Age 10)

Sade's Poem

I miss Nigeria, that was my home,
Where I felt safe.
I'm now in London, it's not very safe.
The people were friendly, back in Nigeria
Here they're not, they're ignorant and mean .
It's far too big and far too noisy
I don't know my way around this enormous place.
I want to go home, home to my mama,
But she's not here, and won't be coming back.
Uncle Tunde has been missing, for quite a while now,
I hope he does appear, I really hope he does.
Papa may be in danger, I want to see him once again.
I wish he would return, safely home to me. . .

Charlotte McMahon (Age 13)

Six Ways Of Looking At The Leaves

When they dance in the air and drift around
It is like they are spying on you

And the shape is like eyes gleaming at you
And you just want to step on them

They are red and brown and lovely to look at
And you want them up

And when they fall off trees and made you slip on the ground
And you just want to get rid of them

And when you touch them they are all rough and bumpy
And slimy when they are wet

Hannah Marshall (Age 9)

Yu-gi-oh

Y ou need Yu-gi-oh
U nless you are dead
G ood players win
I deas will help you
O butter is really good
H ave you played your cards right

Jacob Milburn (Age 10)

Hedgehog

Hedgehog,
Rusty copper,
A ball of spines,
Hidden under autumn leaves,
Shuffling, unhurried,
A dry, brown holly leaf.

Catherine Maddox (Age 11)

My Fox

I'm a fox,
I am so scared and terrified
I don't want to be dead
Not now, not ever

I feel pain everywhere
I can hear the dogs
Chasing me so fast.
I can smell blood and death,
Coming for me.

I love my family
I just do,
But will I soon be dead?

Indiana Mackenzie (Age 10)

My Boring Teacher

My teacher is so boring I always end up snoring,
With a yawn and a sigh,
I think I'm going to die,
Her voice goes on and on like a never ending song,
DONG, DANG, DING
I wish the bell would ring!!!!!

Amy Noble (Age 10)

The Farmyard

Walking through the farmyard
What do I see?
I see a tractor looking at me

Walking through the farmyard
What do you see?
I see a sheep baaing at me.

Wesley Nkala (Age 6)

The Big Beach

Sunset,
Toy jet,
Volleyball,
Yum food stall,
Sun cream,
Like a dream,
Swim in the sea,
Happy as can be,
Make a castle,
With no hassle
Bucket, spade,
Fun parade,
All on the sunny beach for people to enjoy!

Charlotte Marino (Age 9)

Fredrik's Family

Aliens come in different sizes.
This one's doing exercises.
He munches in the morning, he jumps in the night
His name is little Fredrik and he is ready for a fight.

His mum is called Louisa, his dad is called Mike.
His mum and dad are dangerous like little mediamites.

His brother's called Thomas, his sister's called Kate.
They're punking dudes with shining shoes like Aliens irate.

But little Fredriks left alone and gets a lot of smacks.
He's a naughty boy just like Roy his best best mate.

Hope Millar (Age 9)

The Wolf

There are noises from the town
The wolf awake, he is very angry now
He stands on four paws
He rips open the earth
And gathers red hot lava
He puts it on the volcano
And lets it trickle down the slope
The lava crashes into the town
There are shrieks and screams
The wolf smirked
And when all was quiet
The wolf quickly settled back to sleep

Rhiannon Noke (Age 10)

My Favourite Fireworks

A Catherine Wheel spins round and round.
Like a roundabout on a playground.
It gets faster and faster and makes a whizzing sound.

A rocket flies high into the sky.
Faster than an aeroplane and goes kaboom when it explodes.
It showers and sparkles red, white, green and blue.

A golden shower zooms up into the air like a shooting star.
It stops a moment. And then bangs in the inky midnight sky.
Like a golden umbrella, which showers twinkling golden rain.

Rory Miller (Age 7)

Sport

The netball court dreams of not getting stamped on,
The rugby ball wishes of always going through the posts.
The cricket bat wonders when it's next going to hit a six,
The football screams when it hits the post.
The Lords cricket grounds reminds everyone where the Ashes were played.

The hockey stick sweeps up victory,
The swimming pool hopes to be free like the ocean.
Wembly stadium cheers for England,
The rounders bat whacks a full rounder.
The baseball bat misses a strike.

The tennis racket smashes the ball across the court,
The volley ball was slammed into the net.
The badminton bat swipes out the shuttlecock,
The football socks cheered as Rooney won the cup.
The rugby pitch cries as it is torn up by the players.

Johanna North (Age 10)

154

Sadness

It feels like the street is all sad and lonely
And there is nowhere to go

It tastes like my food has got a big sad face
And is all iced up.

It smells like an old street in New York city.

It looks like loads of people going down the road all sad.

It sounds like a loud noise is going through the house
And you don't know what to do.

I'm Sorry

Connor Martin (Age 11)

You Are Late

You're late said the teacher,
Why are you late?
Well it's like this Miss,
My Mum won't stop watching TV,
My Grandad locked himself in the garden,
My mouse fell in the milk bottle,
My Nan got stuck in the toilet,
My baby knocked the fish tank over,
My sister wet herself,
And my brother fell off the ladder.
Now get on with your work.
Please Miss I have nothing to write about.

George Nicola (Age 6)

4 O'Clock Friday

Four O'clock Friday home at last
Time to forget the week that's past

On Monday morning we had maths
At break time we had some laughs

On Tuesday Afternoon when we were at break
It was my birthday so I had a cake

On Wednesday Morning we did R.E.
After that we had P. E.

On Thursday lunchtime I had a chat
At break time someone stole my hat

On Friday morning we went to the computer suite
For my dinner I had a real treat

Four O'clock Friday I can't wait
For I am going to my mates.

Hannah Nixon (Age 9)

Sum Poem

1 + 2 = look like you.
3 ÷ 4 = knock on the door.
10 + 9 = hang your washing on the line.
5 - 6 = look at the sticks.
7 + 8 = look straight.
6 + 9 = all of the time.
10 + 10 = smell a hen.
6 + 3 = look at me.
2 + 4 = knock at the door.
7 + 6 = pick up sticks.
5 + 8 = look straight.

James Ormrod (Age 6)

Untitled

Wagon driver
Football striker
Real stinker
Little tinker
Big fat heart
Sure to win at darts
Loves you always
Who am I?

Sarah Nelson (Age 11)

The School Monster

Please miss, help he hides under my desk,
He makes a big mess,
But if you chuck him out
He would let out a big shout.
It wouldn't matter if he chews your shoe,
But it would if he eats you.

He has red eyes and green skin,
He picks his nose and sucks his toes
Sometimes you can find him in the bin.
Having a little dose.

Please miss, help
He is hiding under my desk,
He's made such a mess.
Should we ring 999?
Then everything will be fine.
But I don't think the police will believe us,
I don't think they will come,
So I can say one more thing,
RUN!!!!!!!!!

Lewis Nyman (Age 7)

Colours

What is yellow?
Yellow is blonde hair
Yellow is fresh lemon
Yellow is bright sunny flower
Yellow is shiny butter

What is red?
Red is a sweatshirt
Red is spinning fireworks
Red is a big balloon
Red is a rosie red apple

What is green?
Green is fluffy grass
Green is tiny runner beans
Green is a huge stork
Green is a big frog

Louis Nicoll (Age 7)

In The Spring

Spring, Spring
Green leaves shooting
Everything is pretty
Children play at the park
Cafes open for lunch

Edward Nourse (Age 5)

Hamster

H uddling in his bed
A fter nibbling his food, runs around,
M unching with his sharp teeth
S illy and climbing new things,
T asting and smelling
E very day new treats
R umbling and rattling in his cage

Isabella Nicoll (Age 9)

Fear

He heard creaking on the floor
And the slamming of a door
His heart pumped with fear
Could it be a ghost quite near
Broken tiles fly through the air
Trees screech on the window
The air twizzles through the air
Ghostly faces in the curtain.

Liam Newell (Age 9)

Will You Accept My Love Unto Your Heart?

Will you accept my love unto your heart?
As so cold as a frosty winter's morn,
If you just let your hard mantle of stone
Be broken, split into thousands of shards,
One small shard could penetrate the ice
Surrounding a heart of gold to be loved,
Thus letting my heart flow to you, my dove;
Or to separate our love at a price,
But that will not happen, my future wife.
Though Death, Hell and Disease should bar the way,
For I will meet them in combat and say,
You will let us go forth to experience Life
To go forth into Heav'n, to meet our Lord,
Jesus Christ, our hope, our shield and our sword.

Tom Nichols (Age 12)

The Dragon Of Fire

The dragon shoots out like a rocket,
Gigantic,
Thunderous,
As big as Mount Everest,
Lava explodes from the dragons jaw,
Fiery,
Throwing rocks with it's bare claws.

Oliver O'Grady (Age 9)

Snake Attack

The snake who lives deep under ground
Sleeps silently and calmfully
When suddenly it strikes and spits out its venom 20 metres high.
It coveres the land people run and hide
The venom destroys the town below
It hisses and spits for a few minutes more.
Then settles back down to sleep.

Charlotte Needham (Age 9)

A Beautiful Waterfall

A waterfall
Is very tall
It is shimmery with a glisten
It sounds like a swooshing sound listen
The water is gently flowing
Dropping like it's snowing
It's gleaming like the sun
A waterfall is very fun.

Chloe Oliver (Age 10)

Mrs. Lock

Mrs. Lock stands out in the crowd
Rosy red cheeks and very loud
Mrs. Lock looks young and healthy
Has a sense of style and is very wealthy

She keeps herself young
And up to the minute
With walks in the park
Chatting to everyone in it

Her handbag is huge with zebra print
Full to the brim with tissues and mints
She wears silver shoes that are ever so pretty
It is said that she wears them for dancing in the city

The children love her stories
About what happened in her past
When she was young and stunning
She wished time wouldn't fly by so fast.

Katie Nicholls (Age 14)

Countryside

Underneath the sweet countryside
With rabbits and hares, the countryside, is unhappy.
Pigs snort, sheep charge and horses clomp their feet,
The wind whistles the cobra's song,
While the grass and field dances.
The blizards and storms, bails silently
Rolling across the bare fields,
The cars run up the bumpy lane -
All because it's having a bad day.

Hdia Nour (Age 11)

What Is The Sun?

The sun is like a yellow pineapple.
Oval and prickly with spikes.
Fruity and juicy that melts in your mouth.
Warm refreshing and something I like.
The sun is a firing ball with tentacles.

Jake Parker (Age 7)

Ocean Travel

If I could travel
The ocean blue,
These are the things
That I would do.

Cling with a starfish
Glide with a sea-horse,
Hover with dolphins
And rush to the rivers source.

Do the locomotion
At the bottom of the ocean,
Going mad with a
Bit of motion.

Frolic with a whale
Soar with a hammerhead,
And before you know it
Your back in your bed.

James Orledge (Age 8)

Let's Play Today

Let's play today in the playground
All day and play football,
Run and jump,
Up in the playground
It's fun in the playground,
Play with the hoops
When the bell rings we scatter inside.

Fern Norris (Age 6)

Come On Spring

Come on flowers
Grow, grow
Let's see your lovely faces.
Come on trees
Lets see your lovely leaves

James Nourse (Age 5)

The Pacific Ocean

On Monday the pacific ocean laughed happily as the fish tickled its salty waters,
On Tuesday it got upset as the children splashed its waves,
On Wednesday it got angry and started yelling and shrieking and it's waves grew high,
On Thursday the pacific ocean invited its friends and family over and they flooded the land,
On Friday it grew quiet as it drifted off slowly to sleep,
On Saturday it fell ill with a cold and it had to stay in bed all day,
On Sunday it got better again as it laughed happily as the fish tickled its salty waters.

Emily Neal (Age 10)

The Empire State Building

One thousand feet tall,
One hundred stories high,
This grand wonder can touch the sky.

It lives in New York,
In the U.S of A
This grand wonder you can see fom miles away.

It's just so famous,
Anyone from anywhere would stare,
This grand wonder that stands high in the air.

The tallest building when it was built,
Looking down on Manhattan and all it's fun,
This grand wonder touches the sun.

It's new friends the Twin Towers,
In whose shadows it lay,
Another grand wonder now sadly gone -
Been blown away.

Andrew Norman (Age 11)

School Days

When my school day is over
And all my work is done
I rush off home with my mum
To play and have some fun

When my school day is over
"Wow" my spelling test was just fine
I rush to my mum who waits for me
And shout "Certificate number 9"

But now my school day is over
As we have an Easter break
Two weeks off Easter holidays
Eating jelly and ice-cream and cake

But now my school days are over
And I talk to all my friends
About my school days good and bad
From beginning to the end.

Johnny Piccou (Age 7)

The Sun

When I was riding on my camel through the desert,
I could feel the boiling sun.
I had to put my sunglasses on,
And say "that's me done."

In France in the swimming pool,
I couldn't stop licking my ice cream.
I then put my cool sun cap on,
I got so wet in the swimming pool.

On the beach I had so much fun,
Because there was so much sun,
That was my family, and that was what was done!

Jack O'Neill (Age 8)

My Brother

My brother John is only three,
He may be wee, but he can climb our tree,
Sometimes he's like a cat,
The way he sprawls around our mat,
He takes my toys and pulls them apart,
The way he arranges them I don't think is art,
If I dare to play with his toys
He says "Get off, they're only for boys,"
My brother John is my bestest friend,
But why does he drive me round the bend?

Laura Orr (Age 8)

Snow

It glistens, it falls like rain, but it's softer and slower.
It shines like the sun but it's much colder.
It falls out of the clouds but it's not hail,
Do you know what it is?
It's snow!

It shoooootssss past peoples heads
It's monsterous.
It's snow!

Alistair Neal (Age 8)

Spring

Spring is coming
See the blossom trees
Flowers bursting open
Hurray spring is coming
Everyone's shouting we love spring
Lots of sunshine falling onto the ground
Some little clouds like cotton wool
Float across the sky.

David Nevitt (Age 8)

My Garden

The grass is green so are the leaves.
The roses are red the snowdrips are white.
The soil is the colour of oil. The twigs are brown so
Is the ground. The roses are red the violets are blue. The
Trees are tall the grass is small. The herbs have a strong smell
The grass doesn't have a smell. The herbs are wide the trees are slim
But not that thin. The gravel is hard the grass is soft. The grass is swaying
But the trees aren't playing. The grass is growing the seeds are sowing the rain
Is flowing and we aren't knowing. The snowdrops are opening the winter roses are
Closing.

Adam Norton (Age 8)

Chocolate

Yummy! Yummy!
Chocolate in my tummy
I don't care if it is
In the baby's hair or
Up the baby's nose
I don't care

I really don't care.
If it is in toffee sweets
Or on my feet
I think chocolate
Is very Neat.

I think chocolate
Is great.

Georgina Peachey (Age 7)

Treeland

If I were the lord of trees,
The snow as white as milk
Happiness is everywhere, happiness is good.
Gazing at the picture, the mini mountains migrate,
Slam! A brick falls, Crash! another one.
The snow slept on the ground.
I looked up but could see nothing,
For the snow is getting thicker

The church bells chimed fiercely
It was so loud, the snow on the houses quivered.
The birds squawked.
The birds flew away, with their graceful black wings.
They land on a snowy roof
Far away, the world begins to thaw.

Karina Olsen (Age 9)

Animal Antics

Dogs digging in the enormous garden
Cats purring on people's laps
Hamsters sleeping in their playful cage
Fishes flowing through the water
Horses galloping over the fields
Tigers terrorising animals that trespass
Gorrillas growling in the jungle
Budgies burying some seeds
Crocodiles crunching in the water
Lions roaring in the darkness

Paige Oliver (Age 8)

Anger

Anger is an evil spirit running through your body,
Taking over you,
Making you feel furious.
It's a bad tempered spirit.
Anger demands others talk with indignance,
It produces words to make other people enraged,
You feel left out and alone.
As the anger converses with you in a slow voice,
It echoes in the darkness.
Making you feel lifeless.

Daniela Oliveira (Age 10)

I'm The Coolest

I was walking down the street
With a really groovy beat
I think I'm the best
And the coolest in the west.

William Oram (Age 9)

Spring Flowers

Spring flowers are daffodils and snowdrops.
Snowdrops white as white.
Daffodils swaying in the wind.
Daffodils yellow as the sun,
The spring has begun!

Otis Pick (Age 7)

Snow

It glistens, it falls like rain, but it's softer and slower.
It shines like the sun but it's much colder.
It falls out of the clouds but it's not hail,
Do you know what it is?
It's snow!

It shoooootssss past peoples heads
It's monsterous.
It's snow!

Alistair Neal (Age 8)

My Dad

My Dad has large brown eyes,
My Dad wears multi-coloured ties,
He loves chocolates especially mint,
At Easter and Christmas he gives a hint.
He goes to work every day,
He teaches science in a fun way.
My Dad's jokes drive me round the bend,
But best of all he's my friend.

Isabel Odysseos-Beaumont (Age 9)

Letricorn

Through the woods the Letricorn came
With spurts of flame and a golden mane
With a smile I rode its back
Tumbling down the hill we were attacked
The Letricorn reared up in the air
And it may be fair to say,
That we got away.
I woke up in bed hoping I would see it another day.

Frances Oakes (Age 11)

Dinosaur Acrostic Poem

D inosaurs are dangerous
I like dinosaurs
O h no dinosaurs are coming
S tegosaurus has spikes on his back
A nkylosaurus has armour on his body
U p in the sky they fly
R oar!
S tegosaurus runs away from T-rex

Leanna Orchard (Age 5)

The Country Side

When I walk through the country side I see.......
The due on the grass sparkling like diamonds,
The birds flying like fire works,
Men ploughing the fields,
My shadow alone on the ground.

When I sit in the country side I.......
Watch the animals run like the wind,
Smile at the faces in the clouds,
Listen to the breeze,
Stare in amazement at the beauty of nature.

When I listen to the sounds of the country side I hear.......
Birds chirping like little alarm clocks,
Rustling leaves,
Tracctor engines blaring off in the distance,
The silent sound of my breath.

When I am in the country side I.......
Walk, sit and listen,
To the wildlife that surrounds me,
The country side is beautiful,
I think it's a magical place to be.

Courtney-Alice Pochin (Age 11)

Seasons

Snow is falling,
People are slipping,
Cats are shivering,
Dogs are barking,
WINTERS HERE!

Rain is showering,
People are gardening,
Flowers are sprouting,
Trees are budding,
SPRINGS HERE!

Sunbeams are shining,
People are sunbathing,
Bees are buzzing,
Butterflies are fluttering,
SUMMERS HERE!

Wind is blowing,
People are raking,
Leaves are falling,
Hedgehogs are hiding,
AUTUMNS HERE!

Fionnuala-Aine O'Connor (Age 9)

All Year Round

Spring has it's glories blooming out of buds
Arriving in all rainbow colours like they should.
And with a touch of sunshine and April showers
They all become really great looking flowers.

Summer is better: rays of sun and clear blue skies
Breezes upon Castle Hill to help the kites fly.
Riding bikes here, riding bikes there,
Riding scooters, everywhere.

Autumn is OK too: leaves flying in the air
A touch of orange here and a bit of brown there.

Winter is best though: lots and lots of ice and snow
Church bells ringing, Christmas bells jingling
And wondering what Santa will be bringing

Mary-Kate O'Brien (Age 9)

The Sea And The Sand

The sea, the sand, all in the same place.
Swim to the other island, if it's not too far.
Do not worry, fish don't bite.
Only the sharks bite.
Crabs lie on the sand.
They bite too.
But not as hard as the sharks!

Harrison Phillips (Age 7)

My Cat Nemo!

My darling Nemo
I like you so,
More than anyone would ever know.

You irate me,
Annoy me
And get in my way,
But that's the way I want you to stay.

Nemo, Nemo you can be charming,
Now that.......is quite alarming.

There is not a lot of words I can use to describe you.
But promise me one thing, you will do.......

Is be you, my darling Nemo.

Titi Otaru (Age 11)

My Friends

F unky friends
R iding horses
I won I won
E nd of the show
N ever ride a horse again
D ad agreed with a funny grin
S top right now!

Alyssa Oates (Age 8)

Sade And Femi Poem

Scared and alone with nowhere to go
No one to turn to what can we do?

Lost in London, try to keep strong, for the sake of Femi, where did we go wrong?
I hope Papa's OK and Mama Buki, I wish we could just go home.

Scared and alone with nowhere to go
No one to turn to what can we do?

What happens next, and why won't Femi talk? All I know to do is walk and walk and walk,
Where is our Uncle? Maybe he's dead, I can't help but think that we might be next.

Scared and alone with nowhere to go
No one to turn to what can we do?

At least now we're safe. And going to school, Mrs Graham is nice but Kevin is cruel.
Moving again, how much can we stand? Femi's still silent, still haven't heard from Dad.

Scared and alone with nowhere to go
No one to turn to what can we do?

We live with the Kings, it's our new home, a bully at school won't leave me alone.
At least I've made one friend, she's great to me, back in Nigeria, I hope Papa's free.

Josh O'Brien (Age 13)

Sports Number Poem

Number one
Football fun

Number two
Hockey too

Number three
Penalty

Number four
Football galore

Number five
Watch it live

Number six
Hockey sticks

Number seven
Sports heaven

Number eight
Sports are great

Number nine
Half way line

Number ten
Play again.

Kristopher O'Hare (Age 10)

Big Cat

Fastest cat
Easy catch
Big scratch
No Kittycat
Not fat
Killing cat
Break laws
Sharp claws

Connor Newman (Age 8)

Untitled

River Erm
Very loud
Evaporated cloud
Fish fall
Feed ducks
Clear blue
Real silver
Wet rocks
Big plants

Daniel Opie (Age 8)

A Year As A Small Prickly Animal

Stretching
Hunger, hunger
Looking only for food
All to taste a delicious worm
It's Spring!

Yawning
Feeling the heat
As he lies in the shade
Knowing that he is still too hot
Summer.

Watching
Seeing leaves fly
Their beautiful colours
Swirling into him, with the wind
Autumn.

Sleeping
A ball of warmth
Although the cold sneaks in
He waits for the flowers to peep
Winter.

What am I?

Hedgehog

Jonathan Phillips (Age 10)

Dinosaur Acrostic Poem

D inosaurs are big.
I n the forest there is a T-rex.
N o dinosaur had hands.
O n a tree there is a Pteranodon.
S ome dinosaurs had armour.
A nkylosaurus has little spikes on his back.
U p goes Pteranodon.
R un Stegosaurus T-rex is here.
S tegosaurus is good.

Owen O'Leary (Age 5)

Frustration

My head almost like a volcano erupting
I keep thinking, "what will happen, will I
Get a letter sent home to my parents?"
"Will they send me to boot camp?"
I felt like sprinting away into the air.
I heard the door slam, echoing through the corridor.
Then clip clop, the devastating noise of teachers' shoes.
I knew what to expect.
I could tell it was crunch time for me.
I wish I was invisible!

Rachel Perry (Age 11)

The Vicious Dragon

The dragon bursts out
Viscious
Fierce
Menacing
Thuds on the ground
Lava spurts out of his nose
The dragon slows down
Settles and sleeps.

Bethany Newell (Age 10)

Parts Of Life

Cows mooing
People booing
Birds flying
People dying
Fish jumping
Kangaroos stumping

Jake Pritchard (Age 6)

Untitled

You can see the crown of thorns
I can taste the blood.
I can smell dead bodies
I can hear cries from the crowd
I can touch the cave with Jesus' body inside.

Christopher Price (Age 9)

Happiness

It's come to live in my room, Happiness,
It's changed my dark grey walls to pink.
Sunlight knocks on the door,
And is peering through the windows.

Her eyes are hearts,
Her nose is round.
Her smile is fixed,
Her small feet tip and tap waking up glee,
And scaring my worry.

She is as cute as a bunny,
As soft as silk,
As pink as candyfloss.

I hope she stays forever,
Or my worry won't go away,
I've never had so much fun in my life,
Thank you Holly for today!

Rosie Pringle (Age 11)

Days Of The Week

Monday is a funday because we have maths.
Tuesday is a snoozeday because we have a nap.
Wednesday is a wetday because it's very damp.
Thursday is a darkday and you need a lamp.
Friday is a pieday when you have pie fun.
Saturday is active day when you have to run.
Sunday is whatever you want because its a sunny day.

Molly Palmer (Age 9)

Chased

Heart, thumping like trees falling heavily.
Light, I am a feather falling from the sky.
Empty, like my organs have been sucked out.
Dry, mouth dry like it has not rained for a million years.
Hair, your hair is 10 needles sticking through fabric.
Ready, ready to run faster than before.

William Potter (Age 9)

Best Friend

This person who I'm talking about is my best friend,
She always makes me laugh,
She cheers you up when you're down
She's the best friend anyone could ever have
She's Sian

Jessica Pratt (Age 8)

My Mum

My Mum is very funny,
She makes my day bright and sunny.
She teaches me to cook and sew,
And ties my hair up in a bow.
In the day we run and play,
Then we dance the night away.
On holiday we have great fun,
Building sandcastles in the sun.
In the garden we play in our wellies,
And have a picnic eating jellies.
My mum makes me look pretty,
She buys me nice clothes when we go to the city.
We play the piano and sing lots of songs,
And often she helps me when I think I've gone wrong.
My mum never leaves me out,
But if I am naughty she sometimes can shout.
At the end of the day when we watch T.V,
She gives a hug especially for me.
I will always love my mum whatever we do,
And I know my mum will always love me too.

Hannah Payne (Age 8)

Mrs. Chadwick

Mrs. Chadwick is the best,
Better than all the rest.
So clever and hip, she does an Elvis impression with her lip!

Mrs. Chadwick, Mrs. Chadwick, how can I say,
Happy and jolly everyday.
Good and kind, she knows all right,
Mrs. Chadwick enters there is light!

Fit and bouncy she knows she is,
Full of vim and fizz.
Encouraging and FUN!
Quick as a flash the work is done!

Garton's gain is our loss,
She'd make the world's greatest boss!
Music, music, music that's what she likes,
Sings like an angel in that mike!

How do you cope? It's so good,
People would do it if they could!
But now Mrs. Chadwick it's time for you to go
The best teacher in the world so...

COME BACK AND SEE US!

Sarah Pearson (Age 11)

What Is The Sun?

The sun is a glowing ball of gas
Floating miles away.
It is a one pound coin
Tossed high into space.

The sun is a hot air balloon
Glowing it's fire high in the sky
It's a piece of toffee
Bobbing around in the wind.

The sun is a gold medal
Winking at you from above.
It is a shining beach ball
Thrown too high in the sky.

The sun is a golden pyramid
Floating up to heaven.
It is golden frisbee
Cast high in the clouds.

The sun is a golden bullet.
Shot high in the air.
It is shining boat
Sailing on the horizon.

Jemma Reddaway (Age 9)

Dog Crazy

Dogs are helpful in many ways,
Some guide people along in their days.
So listen carefully and you will see,
Cats are about as useful as a tree.
But dogs are still brilliant at giving love,
So it will be sad when they go to the heavens above.
So make the most of the time you've got,
Care for them if they're cold or hot.
So now it's clear to see,
I'm DOG CRAZY crazy me!

Kira Pattenden (Age 8)

The Dark

I don't like the dark
Because of the noises.
I can hear dogs barking,
The TV on.
People talking,
It's so scary.
I can hear mum and dad
And the wind blowing.

Matthew O'Connor (Age 7)

Alliteration

One wet waiter washing windows.
Two tanks tackling two tables.
Three thumbs thinking thickly.
Four fish fighting fifty freezers.
Five fruits falling fast from France.
Six sizzling sausages sulking in the sand.
Seven scientific socks sitting in the sun.
Eight elephants eating everything.
Nine naughty knuckles knitting nothing.
Ten turtles tickling twelve tins

Tyler Pryer (Age 8)

Little Birds

Birds like to fly,
In the sky.

They like to cheep,
And weep.

They peek at their food,
And flutter like butterflies.

They like to live in trees.

Reesha Patel (Age 6)

Under The Sea

Under the sea
Where nobody goes
Fish swim about, up and down
The sea crashing side to side
The sun reflecting from the deadly sea
Who knows? Nobody knows . . .

Under the sea,
Where nobody goes
Eels and turtles
Dolphins and sharks
Octopuses and death
Who knows? Nobody knows . . .

Under the sea
Where nobody goes
On the surface,
We hear the boats and see the oil
The further down we go,
The quieter and darker it gets
But where are we going
Who knows? Nobody knows . . .

Sophie Parles (Age 11)

The Butterfly Dances

The butterfly dances upon a bobbing breeze,
A single raindrop within a monstrous ocean,
Its eyes see nothing but rolling fields and sunny skies,
It hears naught but the bird on the sun-blessed morn.

While in the weakened hearts of men,
Rest nightmares of blood and pain and fire,
A soul and mind consuming monster,
Word-made wounds but foul wounds inspire.

The butterfly with wings of ocean blue,
Flutters through its bubble-wrapped realm, -
Rose-tinted eyes reveal a rose-tinted world, -
While purity conceals the darkness and smoke.

Upon his bone-made throne sits Death,
Spinning pain with human tongues,
He looks to swords and bombs and guns,
But never does he peer upon the butterfly.

Never will the butterfly know,
Of all the misery on this blackened planet,
No tainted blood will smear its pure blue wings.
And still the butterfly dances.

Jack Powell (Age 13)

Lambs

When lambs are born they have to drink a lot of milk to get stronger
But when they get older they have babies
Which run about to get energy and do exercise so they can get strong
So they can fight their enemy to get food for themselves.

Hannah Pedley (Age 8)

Countries Together

Country to country, people to people, Chinese say to Spanish, what is your country like?
Spanish say, hot and humid, Chinese say, rich and bold.
Together they join a circle, all the way round the world.

Country to country, people to people, Africans say to French, what is your country like?
French say, fashionable and garlicy, Africans say, dry and poor.
Together they join a circle, all the way round the world.

Country to country, people to people, Scottish say to Germans, what is your country like?
Germans say, tough and wet, Scottish say, joyful and cold.
Together they join a circle all the way round the world.

Country to country, people to people, English say to Japenese, what is your country like?
Japenese say, friendly and quite wealthy, English say, grateful and sometimes chilly.
Together they join a circle all the way round the world.

Other countries from near and far, talk about where they live,
And together they join the circle, forever,
All the way round the world.

Connie Power (Age 11)

Animals

Number one,
Rhinos weigh a ton,
Number two,
Cows moo,
Number three,
Flamingo knees,
Number four,
Tigers galore,
Number five,
Bees in a hive,
Number six,
Lots of ticks,
Number seven,
Hedgehog heaven,
Number eight,
Elephant's weight,
Number nine,
That cat's mine,
Number ten,
Say it again!!!!

Victoria Patton (Age 9)

What Is The Sun?

The sun is a glittery frisbee
Flickering into space
It is a golden cup
Flying high in the sky
It is a hot air balloon
With fire coming out in the breeze
It is a golden pancakes
Spinning through the air

Jodie Pike (Age 7)

Alien Wars

Zap, spaceships flying
Bap, aliens dying
Alien wars
No laws!

Wham, saucers exploding
Bam, guns loading
Alien wars
No laws!

Laser guns out
Aim? No doubt
Alien wars
No laws!

Terrorizing army
Blind me
Alien wars
No laws!

Rhiddhit Paul (Age 8)

The Colour Collector

The blueness of the ocean
The red you get in roses
The green of the football pitch
The pink you find on noses

The orange of a Cheshire cat
The browness of a collie
The black on a fluffy mat
The lemon of the lolly

The cream of the rubber
The yellow of a banana
The purple of a clubbers hat
The white of a pony gymkhana

The clearness of a snow flake
The violet you see on a fairy
The peach of a sponge
The indigo of a canary

Kirbi Pryer (Age 9)

Excitement

It tastes like your favourite meal
Every day of the year,
It smells like victory and success,
It looks like a glorious sun
Shining upon a wonderland,
It sounds like 1000 rejoicing angels,
It feels like you're dressed in
Royal silk that dances around you,
Excitement is like a
Celebration brewing in your heart.

Jamie Poulton (Age 11)

Green

Green are the leaves swaying in the breeze,
Green is the grass, hiding the busy bees.
Green in the grasshopper, hanging on to trees,
Green is the frog croaking behind the leaves.

Green in the nightmare that comes out when you sneeze,
Green are the foods like Spinach, Broccoli and Peas.
Green is the paper shining in the sun,
Green in the icing on my favourite bun.

Green is the colour of a grass snakes skin
Twisting and turning with a horrible grin
Green is the knee bruised and knobbly,
Green is the medicine horrid and wobbly.

Green can be a nightmare and make you run,
Green can be beautiful and full of fun.

Dhriti Paul (Age 7)

Summer Time

Summertime is beautiful
It starts when the blossom fall

First the lambs are born and bred
Then it's time to paint the shed

Flowers turn up through the ground
Most of them are large and round

Bunny rabbits everywhere
Jumping, hopping over there

Ducklings paddle in the stream
Looking like it's just a dream

The sun shines strong and very bright
Although it is a lovely sight

The summer is the very best
When it's warm and in the west

Sophie Perry (Age 14)

Horse

Hay eater
Apple muncher
Carrot cruncher
Tail swisher
High leaper
Polo sucker

Taylor Robinson (Age 8)

My Brother

I have a big brother,
His name is Benjamin Marc,
His hair is blonde,
His eyes are blue,
And they have a little spark!

He lives away at uni,
He has a small room,
It's full of all his gadgets,
And his music goes BOOM!

He has to cook and clean himself,
He cleans his room with a cloth,
His room is very dusty,
And that makes him cough!

I don't care what he does,
But I know I love him,
He is the best brother in the world,
And I want to show him!

Madison Parton (Age 9)

The Christmas Tree

One
Sparkling star
Silver sharp ends,
Two funny Santas laughing,
Three skaters skating round the tree,
Four flittering fairies flying,
Five crackling crackers cracking,
Six red wrappers with sweets inside,
Seven tiny Christmas trees with a star,
Eight baubles silver and shiny,
Nine snowy snowmen shooting snowballs,
Ten chocolate coins covered in silver and gold.
And there at the bottom
Of our Christmas tree
Is
A
Great big present
Just for me

Alex Pointer (Age 7)

Spring

S pringtime seeds grow into flowers
P eople grow flowers in their gardens.
R oses bloom and turn red.
I n springtime it's brilliant when it gets warmer.
N uts hang in the trees and the birds peck them.
G rass grows green and looks beautiful.

Jack Roe (Age 6)

School

When I first saw school it gave me a fright,
Why did I have to see this terrible sight?
I saw it in the pouring rain,
I hoped I would never see it again.

When I got inside it wasn't so bad,
But seeing the teachers was quite sad,
And when it was home time I felt good once more,
But from all the writing my hand was quite sore.

On the second day it was better still,
But this was only because I was ill,
I got to stay at home and watch TV all day,
But I'm not allowed to run and play.

But sometimes in our class it is quite cool,
And sometimes I think school can rule,
On most days it can be quite fun,
Especially when I get all my work done.

Adam Place (Age 9)

167

An Amazing Sight

When I opened my door what did I see?
Something that totally amazed me.
A teacher with a smiley face
What a sight for the human race.
Why was he smiling? What could it be?
This was something that puzzled me.
I looked straight at him to see what he had.
I saw he had nothing I was surely going mad.
He usually would curse me, frighten me, or scare
But this I was not scared of
Strange he was usually like a bear.
He handed me a paper I wondered what it'd be.
A little tiny school report on which he graded me
An F I had been given this made me really sad.
Now I realised that I really was not going mad.
The reason he was smiling now obvious to me
Was in fact the rubbish grade which he had given me.

Edward Purse (Age 12)

Jupiter

I am really big
I can see the solar system
I see Earth especially
Because of it's lovely colours
My colour is duller than Earth's
I like Earth's best.
I am made from hydrogen gas
Not from lovely seas.
So if I am the king of Planets
I command you to make me beautiful!

Samuel Potter (Age 8)

The Great Race

Dancing Dingo, Hippy Hamster and Slow Salamanda
Are off on a race,
Off they go,
Hippy Hamster is in the lead,
Here comes Dancing Dingo who overtakes him,
Slow Salamanda has barely crossed the start line.
Hippy Hamster gets on his moped and zooms away,
But what's this,
Slow Salamanda suddenly speeds into the lead.
Dancing Dingo however has disappeared
Oh there he is
Coming out of the ground
In a monster truck
He squashes Slow Salamanda he fights back and gets on a pogo stick.
He leaps into the lead and wins
In 2nd place Dancing Dingo and last
Hippy Hamster.

Bran Pick (Age 9)

Up On The Farm

Up on the farm
My eyes can see
Green lettuce growing.

Up on the farm
My ears can hear
Brown horses neighing.

Up on the farm
My nose can smell
Pink pig rolling.

Up on the farm
My mouth can taste
Red juicy apple crunching.

Up on the farm
My fingers can touch
The green swaying grass.

Elizabeth Penwill (Age 7)

Animal Poem

Horses trotting in the stable
Rabbits racing round the garden
Dogs barking up a tree
Cats hissing around me
Fish swimming in the tank
Koalas clinbing around Australia
Kangaroos killing around their pen
Pandas nibbling on bamboo
Peacocks pinching in the morning
Dolphins diving in the blue sea.

Rachael Poole (Age 7)

In The Countryside

In the countryside
I can see a black rabbit eating

In the countryside
I can hear a tractor rattling

In the countryside
I can smell a juicy apple hanging

In the countryside
I can touch a soft fluffy rabbit hopping

In the countryside
I can taste a banana growing

In the countryside
I feel really happy

Finlay Payne (Age 6)

Conversation Poem

"Hello"
Said Mr. Fellow.
"How are you?"
Replied Mr. Boo.
"What are you doing today?"
Called Mrs. Whoday.
"I am going to the shops."
Replied Miss Potts.
"Can I come?"
Desperately said Mr. Plum.
"I need to buy a lot food."
Said Mrs. Mood.
"OK,"
Excitedly said Mrs. Kay.
"What time?"
Asked Mrs Lime.
"It is up to you."
Said Mr. Lew.
"Let's go now."
Replied Miss Bow.

Loretta Pyle (Age 10)

Sniffing Through The Mud

I can see the mud,
I can see the blood,
I don't like sniffing at gory bodies,
With their bloodshot stomachs.

Woof, woof, woof, woof,
That's what I did when I found a
Soldier dressed in different shades of green
It smelt like it had been there for centuries.

I can smell the gas,
I can smell the odour of the dead, rotted soldiers,
I hate seeing the soldiers,
Coughing and screaming for help,
While green smoke surrounds them.

I'm sniffing through the mud because I've been
Taught to follow instructions from my owner,
I also do it because it's my job to sniff
For the soldiers that fought for our country.

Vijay Patel (Age 13)

Tears Of Sadness

A homeless heart trapped in blankets of tears.
Gushes of thunder and rain pouring down on my empty mind.

Tamara Parsons (Age 10)

Memories

In my head, a little chest
Sitting in a corner
It lies open, clear to see
What's inside, time will tell

Bottles, toys and baby blankets
All neatly folded away
No longer needed anymore
Keepsakes for my adulthood

Odd gloves and picture books
All safely put away
Schooldays, now beginning to read
Kept for memories

Time tables, ties and make up
Books and pens galore
Bus pass and mobile ready
For next days middle school

What will enter the chest next?
I don't know, do you?
We'll just wait and see
Only time will tell

Jasmine Perkins (Age 12)

Raindrop

We are born every second, then split into pairs.
For a young baby raindrops, nobody cares.
The soft white candyfloss, my heavenly bed.
The only shelter to rest my head

Why should you care? It's not like
I will do anything with my life. It's a hike
From baby to splash just a short little walk
But my views aren't heard. I can't talk

Now I am falling, straight through the sky,
And the world that you love, is just rushing by.
The laughter, the smiles, the cries of pain;
The joy and the sadness, it's just not the same.

I'm nearing the ground, I just can't think
The bruise of the building, the smoke and the clink
Of a key turning. Those little things you
Couldn't live without, but to me, it's a view.

Then SPLASH! I hit the cold dark land,
My one life is over, but it's not all bland
For a few little drips of me will escape
And back to the pure little clouds we'll traipse.

Rio Richardson (Age 12)

Sense

The best things in life don't make sense!
None of the following are to our expense.
Love, beauty is another,
It's in the eye of the beholder.
They give us the ammunition as people, to be bolder.
Even humour doesn't make sense,
If you think about it -
Who can explain what people find funny?
I can't understand some people's sense of humour,
For love or money!
I laugh at everything people don't find remotely amusing:
Most people find it confusing!
When you first meet somebody,
You haven't got to worry about making them happy;
Everything you do makes them smile,
They love your wacky style.
You're fun without even knowing it.
None of this makes sense, you have to admit!
To me, it's the insistence of making sense
That doesn't make sense.

Lucy Powell (Age 15)

Koala

On my way to school I saw a koala,
It was a baby koala,
It was a cuddly, baby koala,
It was a sleepy, cuddly, baby koala,
It was a lost, sleepy, cuddly, baby koala,
And it was hanging upside-down on the monkey bars.

Alice Rennison (Age 6)

Policeman

I see him there, standing tall, a towering figure above.
Although his face is hard and stern; his heart is full of love.
A smart and super uniform, shines out from all around.
He stands out in the crowd, his polished boots firm on the ground.

In his eyes, a certain glow of bravery stands out.
His voice sounds like the thunder, as he begins to shout.
He warns the dangerous drivers and keeps the neighbourhood well
Prosecutes the evil people, watching what they sell.

When you hear a smashing; perhaps of someones window.
Here in a flash of 999 the great policeman will show.
His face seems determined, to capture those nasty men,
His kind, gentle smile calms all the little children.

The bravest job in all the world, not enough pay,
He doesn't do it for the money but for the way
He can have that satisfaction having helped the country.
When he sleeps at night, he's known to all the county.

Lizzy Parry (Age 13)

Rabbit!

It's cute
And it's
Small it
Doesn't
Grow tall
It's hard
To catch
And it's
Name is
Patch it's
Hopping
Mad it's
Never sad
When it's
In the
Mood it
Eats good
Food.

Annie Richardson (Age 8)

My Pony Prince

Fast racer
Good chaser
Slow runner
Loud shouter
Sleepy feast
Fairly bad
Glary dad
Greedy biter
Seedy sitter

Katie Peard (Age 8)

Football Players

F abregas
O leguer
O wen
T hierry Henry
B eckham
A liadiere
L edly King
L ampard

P aul Ince
L uke Young
A shley Cole
Y akubu
E to'o
R onaldhinho
S teven Gerrard

Jake Preece (Age 13)

My Cold, Sad Life

Part 1

Again; commuters come and go, in rain
Or shine. No one helps me, I am as
Lonely as a bullied child at school.
No, no one ever stays, they always go
On their way.

I, I used to wink at children as they went by,
But now I cry. I wish to die.
A victim of vandalising vandals; always die.

Everyone used to come,
Until one day I saw someone
Axed away. I was a murder suspect.

Part 2

The mountainous machines will come,
I will be done, my end is near,
Death's my fear.

Sam Puntan (Age 13)

Storm

As it approaches,
The merciless storm crawls nearer and nearer.
As bleak as the starless night sky,
It thunders down all it could achieve.
The noise was deafening.
The sky flashes.
Then the roar of thunder
Crashes down.
Slowly it starts to fade away
And leave its devastation behind it.

Alex Pryor (Age 11)

Wild Thing

If I was a wild thing,
I would be hairy.
If I was a wild thing,
I would also be scary.
I would eat people!
And never clean my teeth.
I would kill anyone,
Who came near me.
I would guard my territory.
I would be lazy.
I would climb up trees.
Sometimes I would eat leaves.
Whenever I needed to hide,
Into a bush I would slide.

Louis Pantziarka (Age 7)

Easter Is Here!

Easter is here, time for joy,
For each and every girl and boy.
All kinds of flowers start to grow,
Whilst the racing rabbits hop to and fro.

I love the sweet summer smell,
The easter eggs taste really well.
In the Spring, people having fun,
In the park, eating their hot cross bun.

Chocolate, chocolate in my tummy,
Chocolate, chocolate is so yummy.
Sending and receiving Easter cards,
Running and running for miles and yards.

Chicks are hatching in the dancing sun,
They are singing joyfully and it sounds really FUN!
Happy Easter to everyone,
I hope you enjoy the hot Spring sun.

Samantha Robinson-Duff (Age 10)

Carrie's War

Bombs rained down on London town
Children were sent away
Carrie and Nick with their suitcases brown
Went to the Evans' to stay.

Nick loved to sneak a little biscuit
Every now and again
He was the greediest boy in the district
Mr. Evans thought he was a pain.

Alex Pridmore (Age 9)

Sound And Smell

Sound

Save me, please, save me!
Oh the sound, help it's awful!
Uneven tones flat out of tune.
No, no, there's more!
Dad please stop, be quiet!

Smell

Smoke of a cigarette in the curtains,
My nan puffing away,
Even though she knows how bad it is for her.
Loving my nan so much I don't know what to do.
Life is so precious, don't waste it!

Alice Penfold (Age 11)

Winter

The park rang with a still silence, so cold
White, crisp snowflakes blanketed the ground
No one dared to leave their houses, to be so bold
As to skate on the pond the ice had crowned.

The pond twinkled and glistened in the rare winter sun
It shone on the frozen pond as if to say,
"Ice, what mischief have you done?
For what you have you will repay!"

And as the sun began to fade
And the snowflakes ceased to fall
The ice most definitely repaid
And melted and was no more.

Harriet Phillips (Age 14)

Why?

Why can't I have seventy pounds?
When can I have it?
Who will get me it?
Why can't I have seventy pounds?

Gina Savery (Age 8)

English Poem

Football is the Sport of Kings
When you hit it, the ball goes 'ping'
Shots and tackles
Offside and goals
Whatever you want the sport, it holds
Whether a player flying down the wing,
Or a player crossing the ball,
This sport has everything
It has it all.

Nic Pocock (Age 13)

People

People, they come and go like rain and shine
I don't, day after day,
Year after year.
I am rooted to the ground like a tree.
I see the world rush by as if time
Is carving its way into my soul.

I talk but they don't listen - they never do
They pass through me and hardly notice I am there;
I always hear them, chatting, shouting,
Laughing, like life goes on.
It doesn't.

People, I shelter them,
But who shelters me?

Jess Puntan (Age 13)

Untitled

Long is shark
Longer is fishing rod
Longest is tree

Small is a boy
Smaller is a cat
Smallest is a banana

Big is a man
Bigger is tall
Biggest is an elephant

Cold is water
Colder is snow
Coldest is ice

Joseph Reynolds (Age 9)

Haiku - Landscape

First I was empty
A barren land in darkness
Skyscrapers planted.

Dominic Roberts (Age 12)

A Scary Poem

I am frozen in a car
And I am going to a bar
But it is in the middle of the night

I see a bear
Standing over there
It comes closer
And it looks like a scary poster.

Luke Page (Age 10)

Seasons' Haikus

Morning dew
Pretty coloured cob
Prances round

Deep turquoise pool
Summer Rainbow
Reflect on Miracles

New school year
Leaves changing face
Harvest Festival

Child of God
Desert Town
Place of hate

Felicity Robinson (Age 14)

What Am I?

An orange glow shimmers in the darkness
Hot melted wax drips like blood.
Dances around a bonfire swaying to and fro
But so gently
A blue sapphire an autumn leaf jumping about.
White wax like a blanket of snow in a cylinder shape.
As you blow the flame out a scent of smoke drifts into the darkness.
The room is cold and still.

Danni Potter (Age 10)

Ghost!

Ghosts are howling,
Screeching, growling,
People back for threats.
Death is so cruel,
Everybody hail to the pumpkin ghoul.
If you scream, at the sight,
You'll be dragged right into the night.
So remember, in front of death,
Try not to lose your head.

Joel Proudfoot (Age 10)

When I Dance

When we dance as a three
There's Jade, Laura and me
Disco and pairs in our 70's flares
My favourite is tap
And there's a move called '*The Flap*'
I stand on my toes
In a ballet pose,
I pirouette, a spin on one foot
Pointing my toes.

Charlotte Phillips (Age 11)

Easter Days

When Easter comes it comes and,
When Easter goes it goes but the,
Best bit of Easter is when it melts the snow,
So when the snow melts we all shout hurray!
Until the grass comes out,
For a brand new day,
As we look outside we see the
Easter eggs we collect them in our arms,
We put them on the table
Until the next day comes.

Hannah Powlesland (Age 9)

The Kranky Kroc

The Kranky Kroc is a beast with a big fat belly
Exactly like a jug of jelly
If you tell him anything he will kick you out
If you enter his mansion he will roar and shout
He will offer you coke which is very, very light
And sing you some songs which may give you a fright
Until well after midnight
When he'll say with some hot choc
There's nothing in this world
Like the songs of a Kranky Kroc

Amy Philburn (Age 9)

Out At Sea

I sat under the old oak tree
From there I could see the glistening sun
There were hundreds of old navy ships
Riding on the seas crest and dips
One in particular caught my eye
It was so old and beautiful, it made me sigh
What I would give to be able to ride on that ship
What I would give to feel the salty breeze on my lip
To live a life at sea
To have no troubles but just to be
Instead I am here, all alone
With nothing to do but moan,
Moan about how I wished my life would be
If only...if only I was out at sea

Rajesh Patel (Age 12)

Fruit

Juicy apples are my favourite treat,
For a snack they're hard to beat,
They're red and green,
They're pristine clean.

Sweet sticky pineapple is nice to eat,
It's much much nicer than chewy meat,
They're golden yellow,
They're spiky and mellow.

Cool green kiwi is a lush tangy bite,
You peel the hard skin with all your might,
Makes your tongue fizzy
You may feel dizzy.

Beth Pollard (Age 11)

Fields And The Countryside

Tractors, there they are patrolling the fields like robots,
Ploughing the fields,
Turning them from green to brown.

The crop grows, the colour of corn yellow as
The sun on a summers day,
Being carted off as bales, like bricks on a pallet.

Combines, massive great things,
Only taking thirty minutes to harvest a whole field,
I can smell the frashness in the air.

I can hear birds singing in the hedges,
I pick a blackberry off the hedge, I eat it, it is so sweet,
The thorns, smooth but as sharp as a knife.

Matthew Poll (Age 12)

The Lion Acts In Charge

He acts in charge and is mean and hairy,
But proud and fierce and sometimes lary,
As quick as lightning and relaxed,
Lives in wild and hunts in packs.

He's a predator not prey so
Nothing nor no one gets in his way,
You and I are its food,
So don't make him grumpy or in a bad mood.

Emi Pell (Age 9)

52 Bars Rest

Cheap plastic seat,
Sweltering heat,
52 bars rest,
Even though you think you're the best.

Compulsory concerts,
Ridiculous mess,
Pointless experience
And 52 bars rest.

Mind you, there's no burden of playing
On my chest,
No chance of screwing up
With 52 bars rest.

The Germans are laughing and hooting,
Mocking us dead.
It feels like they're pointing a gun at my head
Loaded with 52 bars of mind-numbing rest
This poem's about orchestra,
In case you hadn't guessed...

Ben Robinson (Age 13)

World Peace

World Peace would be a great thing,
Then the magpie wouldn't lose a wing.
There would be no more wars,
So the cats wouldn't lose their paws.
World Peace would be a great thing,
Then the pigeon wouldn't lose a wing.
There would be no more fires,
So the people wouldn't become diers.
World peace would be a great thing,
Then the crow wouldn't lose a wing.
There would be no more fights
Then people would have safer flights
World Peace would be a great thing,
Then the chicken wouldn't lose a wing.
World peace would be a great thing.

Conor Ruane (Age 9)

Teenager

TV watcher,
Soap lover.
Old lady scarer,
Annoys their mother.
Greasy food lover,
Healthy food hater.
Pop music singer,
Get out of bed later,
TEENAGER.

Sam Pester (Age 12)

Stormy

The ship set sail
As fast as a whale
While dolphins jumped
The crew got drunk
While the storm was brewing.

The cargo rolled
While the ship's cat strolled
The cook's pot fell
As the crew gave a yell
Before a tidal wave.

The ship was moored
The crew went over board
The water was cold
But the Captain was bold
He jumped into a rowing boat.

He rowed to land
Where there was lots of sand
Although he survived
He never tried
To find his way home!

Hannah Robertson-Steel (Age 11)

Lions

Lions have...
Eyes that shimmer
In the sun.

Lions have...
Tails that sway
When sensing guns.

Lions creep...
Slowly on their prey
Chasing, killing through the day.

Lions can be...
In a zoo
With other animals too.
Where they may be
Fast or slow
Watch out!
You never know.

Gemma Pearson (Age 10)

The Months

January is the king of cold, frost and rain
February is like a huge swimming pool
March is terribly windy, enough to make you insane
April is however moderate, whether warm or cool.

May sees trees and flowers bloom
And June has sand, beaches, sun
Boiling July, but they're all too soon,
August arrives to pick the corn it has won

Lovely fruit has September got
But decay begins in October
Cold, frost, November's got the lot
All is lost, in desolate December

The months are now done
And Christmas is here
Lets have lots of fun
And Happy New Year!

Sacha Rond-Alliston (Age 11)

I Know A Pen

I know a pen
It's full of blood red
It draws my pictures
Of the living dead.

Tom Pearce (Age 8)

Spring Means

Spring means Easter
Spring means little bouncing lambs
Spring means rabbits hopping around the place
Spring means playing outside late at night
I love Spring.

Abbie Rawlings (Age 9)

The Rain Did Fall

The rain did fall
Upon the ground,
And hit my head
So I fell down.

I toppled over
And bumped my head,
And ended up in a hospital bed.

Lying still
Doing nothing,
My purple lump was thumping, thumping.

When I got up out of bed,
It was then that I realised I was dead!
I walked towards the pearly gates,
And St. Peter said "Hiya mate!"
I screamed to myself,
It was all over
And then I woke up,
As light as a clover!

Nicolle Rudd (Age 12)

The Tsunami

The sea waits,
Waits patiently.
The temptation begins,
The water bolts in,
The universe rumbles,
The trees are knocked over by the sea,
The wind unites with the roaring waves
Like millions of soldiers, invisible ones, coming to
Attack the country.
The Air Force of the wind and soldiers of the
Waves attack together.
The water secretly moves out in triumph!
Wood scattered everywhere,
Boats turned over,
Weak houses defended helplessly.
Devastation!
Lost lives!
The attack was named

'THE TSUNAMI'

Lavangan Raveendranathan (Age 10)

If I Could

If I could hold you in my arms,
For just another minute of the day,
I'd tell you how much I care and how my love will never go away.

If I could touch your lips so soft,
Knowing that you would smile,
I'd wait around for you to come and make it all worthwhile.

If I could change the day we met,
I'd give you my heart again,
But then you turn with tears and tell me,
I think we're better as friends.

If I could make you laugh once more,
I wouldn't let you leave,
Because every night, I sit here and think,
As I cry myself to sleep.

Yet these are just my fears,
Of what I have to come my way,
And I'll happily wait a million years,
Before I see this day.

Matthew Roseblade (Age 15)

The Agitated Weakness

We're agitated and proud,
We've got rid of Christ,
We're standing in the crowd
The big hostile crowd.

We're upset and still loved,
They've got rid of Christ,
We're standing in the wind,
The sharp but gentle wind.

Long gone has Jesus,
Delighted! Yes we are,
Our plan has worked,
Yes! our evil, cruel plan has worked.

Long gone has Jesus,
Strong-willed! yes we are,
The King is dead,
Yes! the King of Jews is dead.

Laura-Mae Read (Age 10)

Mornings

We wake up in the morning to "get out of bed it's time to get up you sleep head."
We feel groggy and tired and ever so weak
All we want to do is go back to sleep.
We drag ourselves up and start to get dressed
It's school in a bit we have to look our best
We pick up our bags and are off on our way
Its off to school for the rest of the day

Oliver Revill (Age 8)

Femi And Sade Grieve

Femi and Sade, seeking asylum,
Their mother has died by the shot of a gun.
Heartless, meaningless, pathetic murderers,
That pulled the trigger don't deserve the right to breathe.
Within a blink of an eye or the clap of a hand,
Their worlds and lives have changed.
Poor Sade and Femi no longer have a mother,
To care for them, to love them, no mother to depend on.
The events that followed could never shock them,
For what has been done is shock enough.
A wound, a scar is left in their minds as a memory.

They now are in London with little hope their father is still alive,
He will no longer have strength to walk or speak.
He'll be tired, exhausted, dying with a few breaths remaining,
The truth had been released but the police couldn't handle it.
They take a life, and they will take more to come,
They don't care, they'll never care,
All they leave in their path is devastation.

Edward Reardon (Age 13)

Snow Season

Snow is finally here!
Apart from thunder you can find
No one with fear.

It drops so lightly all day long,
You can definitely tell if your not wrong.

As bright as the clouds high above,
More brighter than a perfect dove.

As soft as soft could be,
Wait until next time and you will see!

It always has to be right,
That radiant gleaming shine of white.

If you want to know how to have fun,
Aim at your friend and through a ton!

Joseph Ryan-Hicks (Age 10)

A Summers Day

On a beautiful summers day,
The flowers blooming bright.
The sun is beaming down,
With a fashion of light.
The luscious green grass,
Reaching for the air.
Birds are singing sweetly,
And glide with such care.

On a beautiful summers day,
A warm breeze fills the sky.
Bee's buzzing so lazily,
Will make honey by and by.
Children play, laugh, and sing.
Loving the summer sun.
Sliding down the hillside,
Rolling one by one.

Megan Richardson (Age 10)

My Dad

My dad is the best
Because he is better than all the rest

My dad is very funny
Always asking for money

My dad is very cool
And very good in the swimming pool

When he's got jobs to do
He pretends he's got the flu

When I play on the PS2
He says have you nothing else to do

When my mum makes some food
If he doesn't like it he goes in a mood

Luke Rice (Age 10)

I'm Late

You are late, why?
Well my dad was stuck on the roof.
My brother broke his leg.
My baby wet his self.
My sister was hiding.
My mum was washing up.
My nan fell down the stairs.
My snake bit me.
My dog was fighting.
My cat fell off the tree.
My friend hurt his self.
Oh well just get on with your work
And next time, just say you're sorry
Miss, I've got nothing to write about.

Tyler Rogers (Age 7)

A Snowflake's Journey

Faster, faster and faster again
Hurling forward, a never ending journey.
Hitting the ground at full speed, STOP.
I never know where I am going, never getting
A chance to think why.
In the world a snowflake is tiny thing, icy
Cold and wet.
Drifting through wide open spaces and falling
To make children happy.
That is my job and I like it.
Now I must be patient and wait for eternity,
Till the world is a block of ice and it is time
For me to carry on my journey onwards
Through the vortex of space.

Kate Rist (Age 11)

Lions

It's the lazy lions rest hour and all is peaceful,
The soft yellow sand blows over their huge brown paws,
The wind rustles their huge manes and the orange sun shines on their backs,
When the big chief lion roars everybody knows it's time to get up and start the hunt.

The lions split into three groups,
The big chief lion spots a gazelle, he pins his forget-me-not eyes on it and gets ready to pounce,
He gets ready to run and whoosh he's off, in the chase round the tree and then....he gets it.
He drags it back to the pride,
Three small baby lion cubs bounce out from behind the tree.

They all dig in and fill their stomachs,
They flop onto their sides,
They make loud groaning sounds because they've eaten too much,
They drop their heads and shut their saucer eyes and go to sleep.

Chloe Robertson-Steel (Age 9)

The Life Of The River

It's born from rain, snow and mist, springing into gullies and pools.
A fickle trickle of widening streams, fast and shallow, jagged and rocky,
Like a puppy chasing, bouncing, jumping around.

Leaping into a waterfall, narrow, steep gorges
Playful as a child falling, cascading, splashing and sploshing,
Plummeting and pouring, plunging into a pool.

it's youthful energy wearing away the rock,
Foaming and spraying, the current pulling, sucking, rushing about.
Then slowing, meandering, wider and deeper, maturing like a turtle taking life
At it's own easy pace.

Joined by tangled tributaries like spaghetti knitting together.
Through towns and villages and open fields,
Through big curved bends and verdant greens. Leaving behind old friends.

In oxbow lakes, in ponds and pools.
Meanders on across the plains and starts to split up
Like a family that's falling out.

Flowing into the delta near the end of it's life
Like fingers reaching for the sea.

Finally the estuary, a new taste in it's mouth, of surf and shells, of sand and salt.
Goodbye to the land, hello to the sea.

Patrick Rutter (Age 11)

Winter Times

Snow going round in the air like a tornado
Icicles glitter in the caves
Thistles freeze in the snow
Snowflakes melting in the breeze
Cuddling your hot water bottle as the snow falls
In the bitter cold wind we build snowmen
Ducks walking on the cold thick ice
Lampposts frozen on every street.

Mark Reece (Age 11)

My Magic Body

With my hips I can wiggle a hoop.
With my mouth I can speak the truth.
With my teeth I can chew my food.
With my hands I can pick up a book.
With my eyes I can see my friends.
With my heart it can pump my blood around.
With my nose I can breath in.
With my ears I can hear everything.

Ellie Reynolds (Age 7)

Sight

Look I see a Giraffe and a Lion.
I see a book and oh, a pen.
I see a playstation and a poster.
Look at all these wonderful things.
They are all in sight, all for our eyes to spot.
So be thankful to be able to see.
Don't waste it all on TV and video games.
Have you seen Barcelona? It's built for sight.
Look at that candy, I bet it makes your mouth water.
Don't waste sight for the time you have.
So don't waste it!

William Roberts (Age 10)

One, Two, Three...

One orange octopus opened it's eyes immediately.
Two tigers tidying the toilet.
Three T-Rex's trampling on the trees.
Four frightening frogs sitting on a log.
Five fat freaky fish swimming in the sea.
Six swans swimming in the stream.
Seven snakes snarling at me.
Eight elephants stomping on a tree.
Nine nice newts but being naughty.
Ten tiny tigers tearing away leaves.

Daniel Rawlings (Age 9)

School, School, School

School, school, school we have it everyday,
Monday to Friday, literally the whole of the week,
We have school this long, September to May,
No school on Saturday, none on Sunday,
The next thing we know is school on Monday.

School, school, school what could I say,
Two hours of homework after 6 hours a day,
Maths, English, Science, Latin and French,
One hour of lunch just sitting on a bench,
That's the hard life of school.

School, school, school I'm tired of saying that,
I'm so bored I feel like a cat on a mat,
So bored in English more in Maths,
I try to rhyme and it sounds like that.

Only if I was talented
It would be easy at school
I should try not to copy and try not to look cool,
Oh well it's only 243 days left at school!

Prajith Rakunathan (Age 12)

Big Tiger

Tiger, tiger I love you
I saw you in the zoo
I saw you coming close to us
And my cousin was getting scared
Even I was
When I saw your big sharp TEETH

James Richardson (Age 7)

Spring!

Lady Spring is in the country side,
I heard her coming,
Spring makes the flower buds open up,
Spring is doing this by her silver shining light.

Queen Spring is in my garden,
I saw her making the new green grass grow,
Spring was painting the bright colours on the trees,
There she was melting the snow and ice.

Lady Spring is in the park,
I see her coming,
Spring makes the new baby animals to come out,
Spring is doing this so the new world can come.

Queen Spring is in the neighbourhood,
I smell her coming,
Spring makes the new trees grow,
Spring is making the world full of colours.

Georgia Ring (Age 9)

Number Poem

Number one
Football fun
Number two
Skating shoe
Number three
Go for a ski
Number four
Sports galore
Number five
Do a dive
Number six
Gymnastics
Number seven
Flip to heaven
Number eight
Go over a gate
Number nine
Cross the line
Number ten
Do it again!

Lindsay Ruddock (Age 10)

The Wind And The TreesS

As I look outside I see the breeze,
Rip the leaves from the trees,
To carry them all around,
To scatter upon the ground -
To send my thoughts to those I love,
To send them with the birds above.

Edward Reynolds (Age 9)

Ocean Travel

If I could travel,
The oceans blue,
These are the things
That I would do.

Drive to the beach.
Get on a boat,
Dive in the sea,
And see a goat.

Go in a boat.
Jump in the ocean.
Swim some more,
And smell some potion.

Run and run.
Find a dog.
Play with it,
And hold a frog.

Deeksha Raju (Age 7)

Five A Day

Five a day
That's what they say
They're grown on trees and under ground
They're sold by the kilo and the pound
They can be cooked or eaten raw
We find them in our grocery store
They can be large, they can be small
If we eat enough they'll make us tall
They're orange, green and red
Fruit and veg is what we should be fed
There's strawberries, apples, tomatoes too
These fruits are very good for you
There's carrots, greens and kidney beans
These veg will keep us healthy in our teens
So eat up your collie, apples and pears
And when we get old we'll be able
To run up the stairs.

Lewis Revill (Age 11)

The Graveyard

In the light came a fright
When I walked home with a light
In the darkness I saw a stalker.

It was a scary night
The moon shone bright
Among the birds that took flight.

At eight o'clock
The moon light stopped
And out of the ground came a terrifying sound.

Zombies and ghosts came out the ground
With gargoyles which seemed to be round
Around a table they were quivering
People that saw them were shivering.

Joshua Reaney (Age 11)

Excuses

I was abducted by aliens,
They tugged and pulled and got me into their ship,
They had lots more people,
They tied me up with invisible electric ropes,
I screamed and shouted but I soon calmed down,
And then I had a brain storm,
I started talking about myself and said,
I don't brush my teeth,
All I eat is chocolate,
I have not had a bath in two years,
But it was all a lie and they all got so annoyed.
They stuck a handkerchief in my mouth,
But I kept on talking so they let me go,
And that's why I'm late for school.

Jack Rolfe (Age 9)

The Beach

Waves whispering to their friends
Kites showing off their moves
Wind driving people off the beach
The sun not sure to come out.
People see the sun is rising
The wind roars as it's now a
Sunny day
Kites gliding to the ground
Waves now chatting to the swimmers
The sand decided to burn
Whoever walks on it.
Everyone loves the
Beach.

Rebecca Russell (Age 11)

The Three Little Pigs

Once there were three little Piggy Wiggys
Who all build housey house each.
The first made it out of muddy-wuddy,
5 seconds later wolfy wolf came he made
A very loud shouty shout.
Wolfy wolf said "I will, will, will blowy blow down your house."
So the muddy-wuddy house fell down.

The second piggy-wiggy build a house of sticky-wickys
Then the wolfy wolf came by and blowed down the sticky wickeys house.
Then he didn't blow down the third house it was made out of bricks.
The wolfy wolf ate the first pig and the second piggy-wiggy.

Alexander Robinson (Age 10)

Mythological Creatures

Mermaids jumping through the air
The red blooded,green-eyed Minotaur giving people heart attacks in Greece
Magical fairies soaring through the air and flying in the sky
Blood thirsty dragons mouth watering over meat
Loch Ness scaring you out of your wits

Cameron Stewart (Age 9)

Happiness

Happiness is a puppy.
Playful and jumpy,
Smelly and muddy
But ever so cuddly.
With glass eyes and muddy paws,
It likes to eat apple cores.
He's adorably small,
A cute wet nose,
It likes to get squirted with a hose.
Its ears stick up when it hears
Another puppy so cute and cuddly.

Katie Reeves (Age 11)

The Alien

"We come in peace,
Foolish little earthling.
Take me to your leader.
Hurry up. I'm waiting.
Screaming isn't going to help.
No, I'm not a hallucination.
Or a trick of the light.
Forget it. These earthlings are too primitive."

WE WILL RETURN.
Is next year okay?"

Ollie Roberts (Age 11)

The Sky's Gems

The stars are...
A drop of silver paint
The lights of the world
Gems in the sky
Glowing neon lights
A sprinkle of hundreds and thousands.

The sun is...
A golden football in the sky
A colourful disco ball
A finger print of paint
A ball of fire.

Hannah Read (Age 12)

Kennings Poem

A super sprinter
A door dinter
A bin raker
A person waker
A hare chaser
A track racer
A high flyer
An alleyway crier
A mans best friend
They sometimes go round the bend
A catalogue to make make me
DOG!

Moses Ralph (Age 10)

Darkness

Sit in the darkness
Silent, still
A tiny light flickers
In the corner of a room
Don't stray nearby
Keep away, far away

The light, so tempting now
Take a chance
Step over, closer
In the corner of a room
Bend down, reach out
Start to fall forwards, can't scream now...

Tanya Reap (Age 13)

My Life In England

I life in England, because I move here.
Before I lived in Poland. Poland is not good state,
Because we do not have work,
People have to stay at home.
Living in England is easy, because my mum has work.
UK is very good state by in comparison with Poland.
My first three months living in England been terrible,
Because I miss my polish friends, my school and my family.
I'm crying, because I left my childhood, I said:
"I won't go home." my mum was very sad,
She tried to help me.
Now is alright, I have very good friends,
I'm happy.

Monika Rink (Age 14)

Snowflakes

S nowflakes are so cold
N ot even a drop of warmness
O n the road all alone
W hole of England is covered in snowflakes
F alling so delicately
L aughter and fun
A ll melting
K nowing it's snowing makes you smile
E very snowflake is so crispy
S inging beautifully.

Shannon Randhawa (Age 8)

Benjy Is...

Benjy is playful
Benjy is soft and cuddly
Benjy is brown and white
Benjy is good at catching balls
Benjy is fast!
Benjy is kind to children
Benjy is good at hiding bones
Benjy is great at digging them up again
Benjy's wet nose touches my hand
Benjy is my dog!

Annabel Reed (Age 7)

Walking Through The Farmyard

Walking through the farmyard
What do you see?
I see a pig oinking at me.

Walking through the farmyard,
What do you see?
I see a chicken clucking at me.

Alex Rhodes (Age 6)

My Dog

My dog is fat
She always chases a cat
But she ripped up my hat
Everyday she lays on the mat
When she got hurt I cried and cried
But she still looked beautiful
I love my cute dog I pat her every night.

Kelsey Royal (Age 8)

Dolphins

Diving dolphin in the sea
Come on dolphin you'll never catch me.
So let's have a race in the sea.
I will win, you will lose!
You are a mad dolphin and you are cute
I will beat you all the time
Big or small I'll beat them all.
Any time!
Anywhere! I'll beat the dolphins!

Jodie-May Rowles (Age 7)

Spring Time

Spring is coming
I know it's on it's way,
My mum and dad have told me
I can now go out to play.
Flowers in the garden,
Birds are on the trees
That's a lovely way.
To make everyone be pleased.

Charlotte Roberts (Age 8)

Storm

Flashing lights
Outside my window.
The crashing sound of the lightning in the sky.
The wind rustling
Through the leaves on the tree.
The rumble of the thunder
Like an angry giant up high.
The sound of the rain
Pit pattering down the window.
Then silence.
As the sun appears in the sky.

Georgia Robinson (Age 11)

Walking Through The Farmyard

Walking through the farmyard
What do you see?
I see a pig oinking at me.

Walking through the farmyard
What do you see?
I see a sheep baaing at me.

Walking through the farmyard
What do you see?
I see a dog barking at me.

Kallumn Reynolds (Age 5)

One, Two, Three...

One orange opened our only oven
Two tangerines tried to tie these shoe laces.
Three tango tried to teach their teachers
Four frightened fish fainted
Five flattened frogs fished
Six slimy smelling silly slugs
Seven sunk ships infested by sharks
Eight enormous energetic elephants.
Nine naughty newts nipped my leg
Ten tarantulas tried to sneak out of the jungle.

Ben Roberts (Age 9)

Food

|Spaghetti and meatballs the Italians eat
Sushi and Tempura a Japanese treat
When in France frog's legs and snails you might try
Go to the States for burgers and fries

In England roast beef and Yorkshire is great
Germany could well give you sauerkraut on a plate
A shrimp on the Barbie is Australia's thing
Wherever you go, food fit for a king.

Georgina Rutty (Age 10)

Walking Through The Farmyard

Walking through the farmyard
What do I see?
I see a dog barking at me.

Walking through the farmyard
What do I see?
I can see a duck quacking at me

Walking through the farmyard
What do you see?
I see a sheep baaing at me

Caitlin Rushmer (Age 6)

The Sea

I shout and I roar so loudly that people get scared.
I even crash up against the rocks when I am angry.
When I am calm I come up to you and whisper in your ear
And when I come up to you I crawl like a crab.
When I am kind I let you play with me.
When I am grumpy I am dangerous and kill.
When I am moody I don't talk to you.
When I am happy I give you a home.

Amy Ross (Age 10)

The Seaside

I like to make holes
In the sand.
I buy ice-cream,
Fresh air outside
On the beach.
I jump in the sea
With my armbands on.
I look for crabs, make
Sandcastles, play catch.

Ronnie Riley (Age 7)

The Moon Is...

A lump of cheese nibbled by mice
A vortex taking you back in time
A friendly face flying high in the sky
Waving to children walking by
Bouncing ball, glowing gem
Sending your sparkling spies
Rounded present
So, so pleasant

Megan Rippon (Age 11)

Monkeys

I think monkeys are really cool
They prance around
While acting the fool
Monkeys eat fruit
They climb up trees
Swing on vines
Like a flying trapeze
They live in jungles
Scratch their fleas
Get up to cheeky tricks
And do as they please.

Richard Roberts-Popham (Age 8)

Rhyme Poem

There once was a fat old pig,
And he liked to go and have a dig.
One day when he went out,
He heard a very big shout.
There was a person up a tree,
Who was being stung by a bee.
So the pig went for help,
But decided to muck about.
And the poor man was stuck up the tree!

Rosanna Ryder (Age 12)

No Man Is An Island

Upon a bleak and distant shore
Curling tongues of midnight lap,
Whilst a bleeding figure sits, tight
His footsteps swept to stormy seas.

'I love you' was shattered on stagnant minds.
The sunlight fled from his island,
Yellow skies rain silent tears
As he falls endlessly to darkness.

Annie Ritson (Age 14)

What Every Girl Wants

To be rich and famous, wear flares and frills
Enough money to fill all the shop tills
To have diamonds, pearls and expensive rings
All the girls want these things

An oversized mansion and a reliable man
To go to Barbados and get a good tan
A room full of chocolate and a golden dish
This is every girls wish!

Hannah Roberts (Age 11)

School

School, school,
Wish we could play pool,
We fight like mules,
But work like little angels,
Our teachers teach you,
Then they eat you,
Learning mentors,
More like Dementors!

Jillian Georgina Raw (Age 11)

Maths Is So Great

My maths teacher is so great
A times table test can be hard
The sums I like most of all
Hard work ends at last
Some people got it wrong
But at least they tried their best
Maths is so great
I want to do it again and again.

Stephanie Rose (Age 8)

The Moon

The moon has a face like a crystal -
Clear,
It shines on the shops by the seafront and the pier,
On streets and fields and harbour quays,
And rugby men with dirty knees,
The loud animals and noisy people,
And the church and the steeple,
The glowing light that we call the moon,
If you can't see it now you can see it, soon.

Hannah Ralph (Age 9)

One, Two, Three...

One orange, oyster, old and odd.
Two tiny, turtles, tickles a tiger.
Three turquoise, tigers, tumbling there and here.
Four fierce fighting fish.
Five flies yawn all day long.
Six sick snakes, sick as can be.
Seven stupid snails sleeping with me.
Nine newts and nuthatches.
Ten talking turkeys, talk away in the night.

Samantha Ring (Age 9)

My Journey

One great reefshark swimming into the depths,
The deadly rattle snake swallowing his prey,
Off to Antarctica now
A pack of reindeer delivering presents,
Off to England now
In the forest a harmless robin keeping watch,
Further into the forest I saw....
A scurrying rat coming to get me,
I ran and ran and finally I'm out of the forest,
What a journey I have had today!

Amy Reddaway (Age 11)

One, Two, Three

One orange opened our oven
Two teeth tickled the television
Three turtles took two twins and a tigger
Four fighting funny fat frogs
Five firefighters fighting to put the fire out
Six satsumas sitting on a seat and eating
Seven silly sausages sat on sofa
Eight eggs eating easily through an Easter Egg
Nine naughty noisy nutty gnats
Ten tarantulas hiding in the tree

Owen Shaw (Age 9)

Dumb Dog

He's the dumb, dumb dog
Of our cool, cool house
That's why he's
Chasing a mouse

Daddyo, daddyo
Chase that dog
Daddyo, daddyo
There's a frog

I'm hap-hap happy
I'm fa-fa fast
Like a che-che cheetah
Never last

Scott Sadler (Age 9)

Ben The Monster!

Ben the monster
Is totally barmy
So big he is broad and bold
And slightly stubbery
And can be highly boisterous
And boring

Ben lives in a skanky, smelly, sickly
And slimy tree stump
It is mucky, mouldy and horribly manky!

Ben likes to riot
So he rumbles and roars
People call him
The raging rebel!

Jo Sanders (Age 12)

Ploughing

The engines groaning
Like a bumblebee dying
Towing the plough along

The plough starts dragging
The hard m ud into rows
The seagulls come down

The worms are picked up
The farmer gets bored
But at last he has finished

Benji Spinks (Age 12)

Don't Open The Window

Don't open the window!
You could blow yourself away!
There's a 50% chance you will land in a pile of hay,
Don't open the window!
There is a draft,
And if you open it that would just be daft,
If the window was open
(it would be a very bad thing)
And guess what . . .
Your arm will be in a sling

Megan Spark (Age 10)

Crocodile

Crocodile
Splashing as it catches his prey.
Crunching
Wild beast bones
Smashing heads
With other crocs.
Among the rocks
Gliding through
Calm waves.
Sliding
Onto the bank
Then...
SNAP!
Wanting to be
Dominant male
With a chance
Especially when you are
A twelve foot long
Crocodile...

Chris Routley (Age 11)

Being Yourself

Have you ever wanted to be different?
Ever hated being you?
Choked with envy, turning green?
Or just wanted a different scene?
Wanted to be more grown up?
To be a baby again?
Wanted to go back in time?
Or just whiz into the future?
Do you daydream about a different life?
Wonder what being someone else would be like?
How would you feel?

Now just picture yourself now, and all the things you have.
Forget about the things you want, leave them all behind.
The past is the past, the present now, the future far away.
No-one can plan your life for you, so don't just waste it away.

Be you.
Be happy.

Jess Smith (Age 14)

185

Chelsea

C helsea are the best, better than all the rest
H ernan Crespo scores a goal the fans all start to cheer
E veryone goes wild when John Terry scores a fantastic goal
L ampard is the best, better than Henry
S ounds of the crowd, when they score a goal
E veryone cheers for us Chelsea
A fter all we are unstoppable

Jack Sherrin (Age 10)

Gran Can You Rap

She rapped to the dog and she rapped to the cat
She rapped to the maid who's as blind as a bat
She rapped to the butler and she rapped to the maid
She rapped to the baby while it happily played
I'm the best rapping gran this world's ever seen
I'm a hip-hop tip-top rap-rap queen

Abbie Ramplin (Age 10)

While The Battle Was Going On

One night I heard a fright,
While the battle was a rattle,
I was supposed to go out shopping,
But my head was still popping,
I had to leave the kids behind,
But Martin said, "He would be kind",
There was a lot of trouble
While I felt like a bubble

Sophie Shiner (Age 11)

The Home In The Dark

I know a house that's spooky and dark
It has never shown light not a bit not a spark

I have been inside just once or twice
But I only find rats and mice

And a few cobwebs on the ceiling
So when I think I'd better get going

I hear a faint noise that gets louder and louder
Until I shout "There's a ghost in this house
I need to get out!"

I run around saying "Oh it's so bad"
And then I wonder what made me so mad?
I open the door, step out and I run back home

At last! Safe back home!

Sukhinder Singh (Age 7)

Six Ways Of Looking At Rabbits

Rabbits paws are very bumpy
Rabbits eyes are shiny
Rabbits claws are sharp and long
Rabbits fur is soft as silk
Rabbits ears are floppy
Rabbit toes are tiny

Daniel Sargeson (Age 9)

Gran Can You Rap?

She rapped in the pool
We thought it was cool
Then she said I've got to go
I'll be back tomorrow
She rapped on the playground
Then looked around
Everybody listened they didn't make a sound
"I'm the best rapping Gran this world's ever seen
I'm a tip, top, yip, yap rap, rap queen. "

Amy Wheatley and Leigh Stanger (Age 10)

This Lovely Country

In the countryside
I can see a grey smooth horse smiling

In the countryside
I can hear a horrible red hunter stomping.

In the countryside
I can smell the green shiny tree burning.

In the countryside
I can touch the fluffy bright animals running

In the countryside
I can taste the lovely tasty food cooking.

In the countryside
I feel very happy.

Grace Sturman (Age 6)

Teacher

I hear the shuffling, as the children sit down,
The teacher stands there, like a king with a crown.
He signals for us to open our books,
Giving us one of his dirty looks.
"Prepare for a test!" my teacher shouts,
Passing this test is one of my doubts.
I scribble the answers as quick as I can,
My sweat blows off, from that ever-buzzing fan.
Silence remained as we called out our results,
How I hated these mean and foul adults.
I feel nervous after my turn, he calls:
"Honestly child, when will you learn?!"
Prepare for a retest young man, tomorrow!"
My heart sinks and is filled with sorrow.

Faris Shoubber (Age 12)

Empty Room

You bang on the walls to let yourself free,
You can't find a door to release your soul,
The darkness scars you, it makes you cry,
The tears flow down, unstoppable cold,
There's a freezing breeze it cuts your face,
There are voices, screaming, crying, calling out,
The pain is unbearable, it makes you scream,
Screaming out loud for someone to help,
No-one comes, you stare into the dark.

Natasha Spiller (Age 14)

A Snapshot Of London

We woke up excited in anticipation
And rushed to get ready before heading to the station
The train looked imposing and sped along smoothly
Fields and hills and towns shooting past me
We pulled into Euston and ran past the hoards
To make our way to Madame Tussaud's

Kylie Minogue, Davina McCall
Actresses, royalty, we saw them all
Hollywood, Bollywood, Ashwari Arai
Then off to Westminster to the London eye
High in the sky, the Palace's Mall
The Telecom Tower, Big Ben and St Paul's

Our final stop, the Natural History Museum
Dinosaur skeletons, so amazing to see them
No time to see everything and read all the words
Insects, elephants and creepy, staring birds
Tired and hungry, with aching, heavy legs
We're not excited now, we just want our beds!

Nazish Saeed (Age 9)

Football Match

My favourite game is football
I think it's really great
I play it after school
With Nathan he's my mate.

Manchester United are the best team
My cousin has seen them play
That would be my top dream
It might happen one day.

The Ref blows his whistle.
When there is a foul.
It sounds like a pistol
And then the players howl!

William Spencer (Age 7)

Dinosaurs

D inosaurs eat other dinosaurs.
I am a dinosaur.
N ever have I seen a dinosaur.
O h no a dinosaur.
S ome dinosaurs eat plants.
A dinosaur is scary.
U p goes Pteradon.
R oar said T-Rex.
S tegosaurus has long spikes.

Phoebe Stelling (Age 5)

Seasons

Summer brings happy feelings,
Outdoor swimming pools,
Picnics on the moors,
Playing on the beach,
This is Summer.

Autumn brings wind and rain,
Beautiful trees starting to moult,
Woods paths covered in leaves,
Holidays are cheaper,
This is Autumn.

Spring brings baby creatures
Full of new born happiness,
Jesus on the cross,
Three days later rising again,
This is Spring.

Winter brings fabulous snow,
Rivers and lakes begin to freeze,
St. Nicholas begins his long journey,
This is Winter.

Benjamin Stephenson (Age 9)

A Poem

I stand in the tunnel listening to the crowd
When I walk out they are very loud
We kick off to make the game start
Off down the wing is where I dart

I get a good pass so I can turn
I put in a bad cross that's a part I need to learn
The ball is easily turned away
I just need to carry on and play

It falls in front of a team mates boot
The call from the crowd is for him to shoot
He hits it with his left
The header in the box was deft

The ball nestles in the back of the net
Now I need not fret
We held on to win
Inside we open the gin

We are the Champions again!!

Matthew Spargo (Age 13)

Is That Too Much To Ask?

Don't walk by,
I am calling out S.O.S.
I'm not just sitting here,
I really need your help.

I don't speak your language,
But my message must be clear,
I haven't got food or water,
And I'm freezing cold out here.

The only home I have,
Is this wet cardboard box,
With the rain pouring down,
And the wind gushing in

So all I ask is one thing,
Please take me home,
Don't do what my owner did,
Love and care for me,
Is that too much to ask?

Bethany Slingsby (Age 10)

Thunder And Lightning

I can make the sky cloudy and dull
Knock down trees and block your path
I can flash and spark and make you scared
When I am angry I can boom and bang
Sometimes I can set fire to your shed
Your cats and dogs will go and hide
I can keep you awake with my chaos
And you can't stop ME!!

Nathan Simpson (Age 10)

Friend's Poem

Hard worker
Happy player
Kind person
Best buddies
What are we?

FRIENDS

Joanne Small (Age 11)

My Friend

Every since I came to school I've always had a friend,
Who'll always stick with me until the very, very end.
She'll be my friend forever and she'll always stay with me.
Lots of people dream of having friends like that you see.

She's bright as a button, always happy, never sad.
To have a friend, a friend like my friend, always makes me glad.
I can make a fool of myself in front of her.
She may think I look stupid but she'll never say a word.

If I snore or if I dribble when I'm in bed at night
Or if I'm scared of the dark and only like the light.
She'll never make fun of me, never laugh or jeer.
To have a friend like her always makes me want to cheer.

She rings me up when I am ill and when my nose is snotty.
This brilliant friend I'm talking about, yes, that's it. It's Lotte.

Alice Spencer (Age 11)

Animals

Cheetah is as warm as a heater,
Lion is as strong as a piece of iron,
Bear is so greedy, he does not share,
Mouse is so fat he can't fit into his house,
But not me can't you see.

Rabbit loves eating carrots, it's a habit,
Fox is so poor he lives in a box,
Dog is so weird he rides on a log,
Snake likes drinking strawberry shake,
But not me can't you see.

Cat is so stupid he sat in his hat,
Pig is so hairy that's why he is so big,
Horse is so fit because he went on a course,
Sheep is busy he has so many papers in a heap,
But not me can't you see.

I'm not as stupid as Cat who sat in his hat,
I hate strawberry shake unlike Snake,
I'm not as fat as Mouse who can't fit in his house,
I'm not as poor as Fox who lives in a box,
But this is me can't you see.

Karan Shah (Age 10)

The Earth

On earth what will be left to eat and drink?
What will it be like when I grow up?
At night the flow of water still runs
But what will be left when I grow up?

Shane Simpson (Age 9)

Sox And Rox Hates The Fox

I've got two rabbits
Obviously I teach them good habits
They're twins
They fit easily in bins
Their favourite place is in a box
They sleep all day
And then they play
They're always lying down asleep
All we need to do is take a peep
After a few weeks . . .
I took a peek
Where's Sox and Rox!!!
They've got eaten by a fox
It was my fault I thought
For a rabbit I shouldn't have bought
The next day the fox came out
Ready to scare me with a shout
I should fight this fox
Until it gets chicken pox

Maathusha Srikhantha (Age 10)

Thoughts About The ICEHOTEL

While people bake,
All eating cake,
Others freeze,
With each breeze.

Snow, ice,
All nice,
The Torne River,
People a'dither.

Snowmobiles,
Lots of seals,
Sculptures and art,
Will all break a heart.

Meet James Bond,
Who is very fond,
Of a girl,
With many a'curl.

Each year,
It disappears,
Rebuilt again,
And again!

Charles Smith (Age 10)

Biscuits

"Cooking biscuits, Scooby Doo biscuits"
Denis the Menace biscuits, cookies too.
I love cooking biscuits do you?
Dinosaur biscuits, marshmallows too!

Jack Straw (Age13)

Ocean Travel

If I could travel
The ocean blue,
These are the things
That I would do.

Fly with seagulls
Under the sea,
Swim with dolphins,
Fish for tea.

Dive with an ape,
With a can.
Frolic with seals,
Meet a man called Sam.

Soar with starfish.
Hunt with a shark.
Leap on a whale.
Fly home before dark.

Thomas Smith (Age 8)

Sports

Number one
Play ping pong

Number two
Footie shoe

Number three
Casualty

Number four
Play some more

Number five
Do a dive

Number six
Gymnastics

Number seven
Swim to Devon

Number eight
Pass to a mate

Number nine
You're doing fine

Number ten
Practice again

Rachel Stevens (Age 10)

My Family

I love my brother
Because he is good at football
He makes me feel happy and safe.

Ben Panton (Age 13)

Mirror Mirror

Mirror, Mirror, on the wall
I am going to a ball
Can't decide what to wear
Shall I wear ribbons in my hair?

Mirror, Mirror, on the wall
Who shall I meet at the ball
Will it be a handsome prince?
If I'm lucky I'll catch a glimpse.

I will curtsy, he will bow,
We will dance all around.
Spinning till we fall to the ground.

Mirror, Mirror, on the wall
I'm so happy, last night I had a ball.

Mollie Sturges (Age 10)

The Amazon Rainforest

The natives used to see the wildlife
In the Amazon
Where have they gone?

We used to see pictures,
In books of monkeys and birds
Now all we see is destruction.

On TV there used to be,
Scenes of tropical trees,
Now there's sawdust and mud.

Zoos are filling up with species,
Of monkeys that could be
In the jungle wild and free.

There used to be nuts and fruits
For the natives to feed on
Can they survive on wood?

The natives didn't mind
The monkeys humorous calls
And the snake bites they gained.

But I guess the machines do.

Jack Stevenson (Age 9)

Fishing

Children are swimming in the sea.
Boats are out looking for fish.
The sun is shining hot.
People looking for fish.
The fish are nice.

Cain Seviour (Age 5)

The Haunted House

A haunted house still and alone
With a creaky door and broken windows
A squeaky floor with no-one there
Creepy pictures watching you
Spiral staircase going around
Hairy spiders hanging down
Giant cobwebs brushing your face
Make you shiver down to your toes
In the hall fast and small
I run from a ghost that I cannot see
In the big dining room
I hear a moaning and groaning
A clanking sound comes from the attic
A scream from the kitchen
I run and run
Never dare to go there!

Hannah Smith (Age 8)

Up On The Farm

Up on the farm my eyes can see
Lovely, long corn swishing
Green, pink dragonfly, swooping

Up on the farm my ears can hear
Noise, pigs oinking
Loud, blue tractors rolling

Up on the farm my nose can smell
Bubbly mud spreading
Yellow honey running.

Up on the farm my mouth can taste
Lolly red apple dropping
Frothy brown cows milking.

Up on the farm my fingers can feel
Very small baby rabbits hopping
Furry, brown puppy yapping.

Up on the farm,
All my senses are alive and exciting.

Bronwyn Sellick (Age 6)

Frost

Frost on the boat
Flowers praying for more sun

Frost on the berries
Leaves like old wrinkled faces

Frost like grass cut short and sharp
Steam like a boiling kettle

A field of frost
Shadowy background of pale trees

Nose like an ice-cube
Cheeks like snowballs

Fingers all numb
Hungry birds

Sky still, sad and dull
Ball of frost waiting to be thrown.

Sarah Stock (Age 8)

At School

On Monday at break they played football with me and then we played dirtball
On Tuesday they helped me do my homework, I as pleased it was hard
On Wednesday they gave me a snack and gave me a lunch pack
Yesterday in games they helped me score a goal, then they helped me out of a hole

Today when I threw up, they helped me clean it up
The weekend is here, I am free, but I can't wait till next week

Joshua Symes (Age 9)

Aeroplanes

The machines go up and down
They even go left and right
Some fly thousands of miles,
Maybe across the isle
You may have been on one,
Or maybe even five,
And most likely to survive
You board these locomotives
Where hundreds also do
Some you say, might die
I included too
But you are safe, my friends,
I assure you here and now
Piloted by trained superiors
These magnificent beasts are called
AEROPLANES

Joseph Sherratt (Age 12)

Memoirs Of An Orc

I run around completely wild
To no person I have ever smiled
I smell like rotten fish
From last year my favourite dish
Above all I hate all stinking gnomes
I eat them with butter on my scones
I think I'll go to Searing Gorge
On my way to Iron Forge
There there was an epic drop
to the auction house start the lots!
I'm going across to Gnomearan
To get some gnomes to eat with my clan
Just then I was savagely attacked
And my skull was completely cracked
Now I'm cursed to be a ghost for 20 years
When I get back I'll buy some beers.

Zander Spiller (Age 11)

The Box Of Magic

In my box I'll have
The first sunbeam in the morning,
The last star in the sky
The cuckoos first flight

The angels heavenly song
The owls call in the night
The baby's first cry

The smell of schools best cooking
The scent from the finest flower ever made
The smell of the salty sea on a sunny Sunday beach

The chocolaty taste of a flake in a pink strawberry ice-cream,
The softest marshmellow from a creamy milkshake

Grace Shorten (Age 9)

My Brother Ed

My brother Ed has a <u>very</u> big head
My brother Ed's head <u>won't</u> get out of bed!
My brother Ed <u>loves</u> his teds.
<u>Sometimes</u> I would like my brother Ed <u>dead!</u>
My brother Ed loves cricket balls that are red.
My brother Ed's Pencils <u>are</u> made of lead.
My brother Ed doesn't like to be called Ned.
My brother Ed <u>needs</u> to be fed
However he <u>will</u> eat in bed!
My brother Ed's <u>best</u> friend is called Jed.
My brother Ed has a <u>bun</u> in his head
Because of all this we call him
Ed Ted with a bun in his head!

George Shelley (Age 11)

The Hat

The sense of Cashmere against my face,
As it touches my skin I feel the need to embrace.

The softness of the magenta wool,
Over my head I try to pull.

As the ice white snow flutters upon my hat,
I attempt to push it off with a gentle pat.

As I rush home a few minutes later,
I place my hat on the radiator.

Where he can dry and start to warm up,
For the next day to come, when he'll have more luck!

Simran Sandhu (Age 12)

What Is The Sun?

The sun is a golden bullet
Shooting through the clouds
It is a yellow penny
Flicked into space.

The sun is a shining sequin
Floating across the earth
It's a golden gem
Knocked into the sky.

The sun is a toffee apple
Shot into space
It is a red balloon
Floating into space

Jake Symes (Age 8)

Spring, Easter

S pring is like a burst of new life
P osies and possums
R ainbows and flowers
1 n the middle of your garden are sun rays
Nice hot sun
G reat

E gg-stravaganza
A mazing
S tunning light
T he last supper
E xciting
R evolution

Natasha Sunter (Age 9)

School

School is great, school is great,
Especially the sports and break
Football and lunch
Basketball and break,
School is great, school is great!

School is great, school is great,
Especially maths and I.C.T.
Maths and lunch
I.C.T. and break,
School is great, school is great!

School is amazing,
No time for lazing!

Eloise Shuard (Age 12)

Briny Rice With Spice

My brother is very precise.
All he will eat is briny rice,
And he won't take one bit of advice,
He just says,
Rice, it is nice it might need a bit of spice then it's truly nice.

Now mum would be very concise,
When giving him her advice,
And would call, one day you'll pay the price
Unless you do the extensive exercise.

On the contrary dad would say come on guys,
And heave us out the door as we say our goodbyes,
Usually he would take us to the library or some where not very nice,
But this came to us as a pleasant surprise,
He took us to Frankey Bennies,
For curry and rice.

On our return home dad said we had gone for exercise,
But mum could sense the guilt on our eyes,
And bellowed, son look at your size,
Not very nice, even with spice,
Now go and take some exercise!

Shankar Saanthakumar (Age 12)

Poetry

George and Matthew, they're two dogs
Drive their horrid mother up the wall
Faith and Jodie make more howling
Than a grey smooth hippo in the hall.

Michaela Saunders (Age 9)

The Seasons

Spring is when flowers start to blossom
And the sun begins to shine,
The days get much lighter now
As we all adjust the time.

Summer brings the bright hot sun
Children can now play outside,
Go on holiday and swim in the sea,
Run around with each other and hide.

Autumn is when the leaves change colour
And gradually they fall,
Lying crisp and crunchy on the ground
Seen and heard there by us all

Winter, we hope for snow to use our sledge
It's exciting as Christmas is near
Holly with red berries cover the hedge,
As Christmas trees, presents and people bring cheer.

Owen Smith (Age 8)

Monsters

Green and smelly
Warts on the face
Flying through the sky,
To a cave, their base.

This is not true,
What people say,
But witches are real,
Just like demons grey.

They live in your mind,
They won't go away.
They make you fear,
Every night and day.

There is another monster,
Even greater than this.
They tear through the world,
Leave not even a wish.

Monsters are in this world,
But you can't always see,
The real monsters,
Are humans, you and me.

Philip Smith (Age 13)

My Dog

My dog Megan
Can sing to heaven,

Hollie Smith (Age 7)

Warm Fire

Snowflakes come
And snowflakes go
But warm....warm fires
Warm fires
Warm fires
Warm fires
Snowflakes falling
Snowmen are gathering
But warm....warm fires
Warm fires
Warm fires
Warm fires
Snow blizzard come
And snow blizzard go
But warm....warm fires
Warm fires
Warm fires
Warm fires

George Sherrin (Age 8)

On The Farm

Up on the farm my eyes can see
Yellow small corn swaying,
White baby ducks quacking.

Up on the farm my ears can hear
Big black dog barking,
Blue metal tractor chugging.

Up on the farm my nose can smell
Brown sticky pigs rolling,
Smelly old farmer groaning.

Up on the farm my mouth can taste
Rosy red apple hanging
Butter brown bread toasting

Up on the farm my fingers can feel
Soft yellow straw laying
Fluffy ginger Tom cat purring.

Up on the farm
All of my senses are alive and singing.

William Savage (Age 6)

Ocean Travel

If 1 could travel
The oceans blue
These are the things
That I would do.

Swim like an ape
With a black old cape.
Fly with a bird
And eat lemon curd.

On the beach
I had a nap.
When I woke up
I met a nice chap.

Play with seals
Under the sea.
Find black eels,
"Ouch" it stung me.

Gallop like a sea horse.
Hunt like a shark.
When I've done all of that
I run home before dark.

Michael Sullivan (Age 7)

All About The Sea

The sea is smashing and roaring on the rocks
The sun is shining on the sea
And the sea lions swim on the seabed
The seagulls sit on the sea top
As people swim in the lovely sea

Ashley James Smith (Age 9)

Tanka

Never ending love
Throughout the rough, tough, bad times
The Smith's house is care,
Me, Mum, Dad, Rebekah share,
Very special memories

Charlotte Smith (Age 10)

Politically Correct

What is wrong with the world today,
When freedom of speech is kept at bay,
Why are we not allowed to say what we think,
Due to worries of offending people,
Eskimo's now known as Inuits,
Fat people called horizontally challenged,
Short people - vertically challenged,
And nativity plays banned,
What has the world come to?
When we aren't even allowed to celebrate Christmas in public,
In case we contradict other peoples religious customs,
Even though they still celebrate their festivals,
The government has gone insane,
And all these stupid things are just a pain!

Dan Smith (Age 14)

Anger

It was unstoppable
The anger kept on chasing me
I couldn't breathe any longer
Then I collapsed
It ran through my body
I jumped up
I couldn't escape from frustration
I felt as if I was on fire
I was burning up
My fists clenched
Anger let go and left
I still felt fear
It was terrible
Would the anger leave me alone or come again?
I hope the world is safe and the anger never calls on me again.

Migena Sadikaj (Age 11)

Steam Trains

Whistle blowing
Toot, toot, toot.
Sounds like a recorder playing.

Large shape
Huge, huge, huge
Looks like a giant sausage.

Snow is falling
Flutter, flutter, flutter.
Looks like cotton wool.

The sky is darkening
Dark, dark, dark,
Looks like a black hole.

Holly Samuels (Age 8)

Cocktails And Politics

Grab your glad rags, sugar, there's a world you've got to save,
Gush some sequined ideology and let the flashbulbs rage,
Splash it on the headlines like martini hits your glass,
Toast limousines and liberalism, not forgetting foie de gras.
This is cocktails and politics, honey.

There's a craze amongst the socialites for benefit, welfare,
Pink champagne socialism, the world's without a care,
Tango with a journalist as you twist about the floor,
Smile as you explain blue's not in fashion anymore.
This is cocktails and politics, honey.

Step out in stilettos, darling, speak to entertain,
Frame policy with lipstick as red as your campaign,
Hide behind your botox, keep voters' eyes naive,
Caviar society wants something to believe.
This is cocktails and politics, honey.

Patricia Scurfield (Age 16)

The Winter Song

Cold nights in winter
Fluffy snow clouds
But snow . . . snow falls
Snow falls
Snow falls
Snow falls
Hail stones falling
Winter's calling
But snow . . . snowmen
Snowmen
Snowmen
Snowmen
I cry puddles on the ground
Wrap up with warm clothes
But snow . . . snowflakes
Snowflakes
Snowflakes
Snowflakes

Carter Scott (Age 9)

Monster Cat

My cat is no ordinary cat
O of course she is
N aughty and mischievous but . . .
S arah can be nice in the day but . . .
T he night is kind of weird . . .
E r she kind of turns into a . . .
R ight monster to be precise she turns into a

C at that has BIG BIG fangs with a black coat
A nd she isn't a pretty sight but . . .
T his cat Sarah no matter what she turns into she's the best, to me anyway!!!

Scarlett Stock (Age 9)

The Black Jaguar

As black as the night he is,
With his black, satin fur he glistens,
Feline-like, he glides gracefully, holding his head dignified.
His eyes are moonless, yet susceptible to an unforeseen motion.
He has mighty paws, with razor sharp claws.
He listens intently for a slight murmur from a humble creature to pounce upon
His eyes scan the landscape for his threatened target
While stalking his prey, he stands motionless, like a statue, eyes fixed upon his current victim.
Faster than the speed of light, quicker than the human eye,
He dashes across the African plains pursuing his chosen quarry.
He looms in the shadows to doze, out of sight from poachers.
As black as the night he is, the starless, elite Jaguar.

Lois Swinnerton (Age 13)

On My Table

On my table I will put
A golden ray of sunshine upon a rainy day,
Also on my table I will put
A diamond carved glass full of ruby red fire and emerald green grass,
I will also put
A glass cover filled with sapphires and gold.
I will put
A never pop bubbled bowl filled with raspberry red and every drop of sugared snow
I will put
One thousand drops of coloured rays with scents of snowdrops and rose
No ordinary table will hold these wonderful things
But a table made of cloud and golden dust
My table is amazing!

Emily Senior (Age 10)

Sports

Number one
Football fun
Number two
Hockey too
Number three
Penalty
Number four
Footy galore
Number five
Watch it live
Number six
Hockey sticks
Number seven
Sports in heaven
Number eight
Sports are great
Number nine
Half way line
Number ten
Do it all again

Matthew Smith (Age 10)

My Friends

My friends are so cool,
Me and my friends rule,
We love to party,
We are all arty!

Meet my friend Lily,
She is so silly,
She loves to play pranks,
She loves to sing and dance!

Meet my good friend Loretta,
She loves receiving letters,
She has long curly hair,
And she likes the fun fair!

My friends are coming round today,
They're coming round today to play,
To have some fun,
Under the warm sun!

Jessica Tellyn (Age 10)

Penalty!!!!

Our best player, sprinting through
Ripping the defence apart then
THUD!! He hits the deck... *PENALTY!!!*
The Ref blows his whistle and points to the spot
Eventually, after a big argument, he steps up and shoots...
GOAL!!!
It's all over, the opposition are near enough crying
What a game!!

Ryan Slater-Davis (Age 13)

My Colour Poem

Roses are red violets are blue
You know that I love you

Buttercups are yellow
Blackberries are purple,
You know my brother he goes burple,

Rainbows are colourful
With brushes of fun,
You know it's like a colourful gun.

Jordan Smith (Age 9)

Snow

I can hear the trees rustling
And the gusty snow landing
Landing like the fastest
Rocket in the world so existed
Am I with the taste in my mouth
And the rich air I can feel upon me
And the little twinkle I get when the
Snow gets to me

Jamie Smith (Age 10)

The End Of The World

The sun has shattered
The moon has skipped away
Hell and earth have clattered
There is no night and day

The people of earth are dying
And there is nothing we can do
The newsmen are lying
There is no hope for you

But the sun will not shatter
And the moon won't skip away
So don't get scared and chatter
You can live a final day

Charlie Saunders (Age 10)

Frog

Good hopper
Hard stopper
Good jumper
Hard dumper
Easy grow
Not slow
Easy grip
Fantastic flip

Daniel Sansom (Age 8)

Which Pet Fish

Fish so bright which shall I buy,
Silver and blue and green scales.
How will I choose.
From so many fish.
Many like one big scales.
Some with patterns with stripes
And many different shapes and patterns.
But that one there is the queen!!!!
How much, I'm having it.
Am I aloud?
Of course.

Francesca Savio (Age 8)

Easter

E ggs, eggs, glorious eggs
A re you enjoying easter.
S o many eggs, glorious eggs
T reats for you and me.
E aster bunny hops out of an egg.
R ip rap treat for easter.

Samantha Scott (Age 8)

Read Away

Long stories short stories
Small print large print
Colourful pictures illustrated diagrams
Reading is fun

Thick books thin books
Fiction non-fiction
True facts tell us a story
Imagination running wild
Reading is fun

Long poems short poems
Small print large print
Informative text rhyming text
Reading is fun

Hannah Slowen (Age 10)

When I Was Young

When I was young
I played all day long
For three whole years,
Lots of fun no tears
Life was an adventure
And the rest of my life spent working

Why is the world full of . . .
Cars, houses, McDonalds
Why is it not full of
Green fields and children playing in the streets
Fresh air to breath and where you can . . .
Climb all over things (like tanks in museums) not . . .
DO NOT TOUCH!

Alexander Stead (Age 9)

Landscape

Landscape rolls for miles,
Breeze through hair whistled.
Along winding roads
I see rabbits in fields
Singing sweetly nested birds
Clouded skies block the sun,
The world is turned dark and cold
The clouds disappeared and the sun comes out
Light and warmth engulf me
I smell all the plants
I see all the colourful flowers
Beetles and grasshoppers chirping
The grass is soft and moist

Josh Sharman (Age 11)

The Graveyard

The darkness crept up on me,
As quiet as could be

I want to get out of here,
But where I fear

My feet got heavier, as heavy as lead
With every footstep I tried to tread

The moon shines like a florouscent light
On the gravestones in the dead of night

The rotten dead people cry to be alive,
But it's not their fault they couldn't survive.

Sadie Sharman (Age 11)

Winter Sun

Rays of golden sunshine
Brightly gleam my way,
Knowing that it was something
I should wish for every day.

Pouring flames that burn the ice
Awake me with commands,
To stroll along the front
And kick the yellow sand.

Soon a red setting sun
Has fallen down below,
Gone off for a holiday
Whilst we enjoy the snow!

Emma Smith (Age 11)

The Shoes

If you don't put your shoes on we won't go to the park.
But.
No buts I'm going to count up to ten 1 -
But I don't know where they are.
They're under the bed.
But they have knots in them.
2 - *Oh Mum stop, can't you help me?*
3 - That would be cheating.
Oh Mum! But all right then yes! I can't untie the knots.
I told you to untie your knots before you take your shoes off. 4, 5, 6, 7 -
Oh Mum stop, where are my socks?
They're in the shoes where you left them.
I need some time and anyway you know I'm not good at bows.
8 - *I've done one shoe.* 9 - *Now I've done the other.*
10 - And we're off to the park.

Rataba Saud (Age 9)

It Stands Tall

It stands tall, as white as a cloud
It sits still, like a stone statue
A sudden blaze of light,
The flame is lit.
Bright like the sun,
But bigger
It carries on flickering,
On and on
Until the wick dies
Smoke swirls up like a whirlpool
And the flame ends

Jake Seviour (Age 11)

Sight

The baby blue sky
Beaming down upon the earth's excited subjects,
See the black and white gulls circling,
Their heads bowed against the sun's blinding rays
In all its glory I give you the earth!

A deep black vacuum
Revealing burning balls of gas,
Like a master piece in a crummy art gallery,
You can't miss them, in all its glory I give you space!

Kirsten Sutherland (Age 10)

Can You Rap?

My dog is really silly
And he doesn't like me
I tapped him on the back
To see if he could rap

Can you rap Muzzy
Can you rap? Can you Muzzy?

He opened one eye
Me, I'm the best rapping dog
I'm the best

Toby Stupple (Age 9)

Hurricane

When I am angry
I terminate all your happiness
Unfortunately I do not mean to terrorise all your family
But I can not help it

I'm all you have got
But you cannot stop me
My strength stops you instead

My voice is very low with rage
As I roam over you land
I rip the floor up with my powerful voice

Macaulay Spensley (Age 11)

Spain

S unny Spain,
P eople playing football,
A tomato fight,
I t's time to try the food.
N ow it's time to say Goodbye.

Laura Savio (Age 8)

Scissors

Scissors, scissors, scissors we had ten pairs at noon
And now we only have two
We'll stay here all day
We'll stay here all week,
We'll stay here all afternoon
If we have to!

Miles Stock (Age 8)

Hyacinth

Last October like a baby in a cot,
I was planted in a blanket of damp bulb fibre,
I was put in the cupboard all cold and dark,
I could hear the shivers of fear from the other hyacinths around me.
I was taken out again later in the year,
Yellow shoots had appeared on my head,
As if I was ready to grow up with the other plants around me.
I was put on a windowsill in the sun,
I was on a holiday!
I was awake with a purple dress of flowers on me,
I had a perfume that you could smell for miles.

Amy Stock (Age 9)

Floating Feathers

Whizzing round and round like gleaming white darts
Falling to the floor, they twist and turn
And assemble in a heap on the fresh blurry grass.

The frost biting me as I carefully walk
So I don't disturb the birds tweeting
As they look for a place to hide from the cold,
The frosty nature floating all around me . . .
Suddenly the feeling STOPS
As a car goes speeding past

Roberta Sarson (Age 11)

There's A Monster In The Swimming Pool

When I came home from school,
And I looked in my swimming pool,
I saw a Stompasaurus rex,
He was as scary as a witch,
He was as green as the Grinch,
And as heavy as a fast food freak.

He was as big as a house,
And talked as much as a mouse,
So I went to see if he was very nice,
He was as nice as nice can be,
So I said to my mummy.
Can I keep him as a pet please.

Ellie Skinner (Age 11)

Fireworks

F ireworks banging and exploding in the sky
I n the night are colourful fireworks
R ound and high and low they go
E xploding in the sky glittery and sparkly
W ow, all the people say as they glitter down
O ver heads they fly and go bang
R ound people's heads as they watch with amazement
K eep watching don't miss it
S ilvery and sparkly bright in the sky

Daisy May Bodicea Smith (Age 9)

Easter

E aster is full of joy
A nd everyone is excited
S pring is when Jesus rose from the dead
T idy for Jesus to arrive
E ver lasting Lord
R ising from the tomb

Ethan Strickland (Age 9)

Dinosaur Acrostic Poem

D inosaurs are gentle.
I am scared of dinosaurs.
N o he is coming to eat me.
O h no he is scary.
S tegosaurus has got spikes.
A Pterandon is big.
U p Pterandon went.
R un run run fast.
S tegosaurus is a plant eater.

Nathaniel Stratton (Age 6)

What Am I?

Fire-breather
Flesh-eater
Arms-sharper
Tail-ripper
Human-murderer
Brain-thinker
Claw-scratcher
Wing-hitter
Blood-drinker
Hell-maker
Creature-snatcher
Mammal-glider

Jack Sandiford (Age 10)

Spring Means

Spring means love
Spring means sunshine
Spring means animals
Spring means flowers
Spring means Easter rabbits
Spring means singing
Spring means happy faces

Daniel Strain (Age 9)

A Gog A Gog

A Gog a Gog
It lives down your bog
It creeps out at night looking
For some light, it really stinks
And it always blinks
A Gog is green and smelly
And it wobbles like jelly

Callum Smith (Age 10)

Journey Through The Forest

Monday in the forest I saw . . .
A moaning monkey munching a monstrous melon
Tuesday in the depths of the forest I saw . . .
A tiny tiger playing tig with a tortoise
Wednesday I widened my eyes and saw . . .
A weird Winnie the Pooh wailing at me
Thursday I thought I was going to die because . . .
I tried to do a runner but a tiger tickled me
Friday I fried a ferret but it . . .
Franticly fired its business at the fire and me
Saturday I sighed and saw a . . .
Snake smiling at me (it was scary!!!)
Sunday I spotted a . . .
A scrumptious sausage getting eaten by a sausage dog

Katy Strange (Age 11)

Silly Lily

My name is Lily
And I'm very, very silly
I have twinkle toes
And a little piggy nose
My feet are small
And I'm not very tall
I have a father and mother
Sister and brother
In my nice small bed
There's my nice small Ted
And in my comfy pyjamas there's ME!

Rachel Smith (Age 8)

Flowers In The Spring

Sunrise in the morning
Flowers are growing.
Colours of the rainbow.
Pink, purple, blue, red and yellow.

Flowers make me happy.
Flowers make things beautiful.
Especially in my garden,
Pretty flowers everywhere.
Down the road and to the pond.

Harriet Seabrook (Age 7)

Creepy Crawlies

Creepy crawlies are small
They're not like a ball
But they're not cool
They're as small as an ant

Some are as black as a bat
They're not fat
They can not bat a ball
They would fall

Shadae Staines (Age 9)

Maia's Easter Poem

E very day I am looking forward to Easter
A lovely little chick in my garden.
S pring is lovely
T he birds are singing
E ggs hatching
R un for spring

Maia Sherbersky (Age 7)

Chocolate Cake

I know a pudding that is yummy.
I know a pudding that is scrummy.
Chocolate cake, chocolate cake.
Yummy, scrummy chocolate cake.
Sticky, icky, chocolate cake.
Chocolate cake is creamy
Eating it is dreamy.

Chloe Smith (Age 7)

Chased!

I was sprinting, sprinting for my life
My heart was thumping, thumping like a gigantic giant stomping on my chest
It was a goblin it was chasing me
I started to shiver, shiver like I had jumped into snow in shorts and a t-shirt
I started to sweat, sweat like I was under the sun when it was 206°
I was stuck to the ground like a statue
My hair stuck up like needles sticking up through fabric
I opened a door and then . . .

Robert Smith (Age 9)

Lion Poem

I am the colour of scorching desert sand,
I am scary, fierce and ferocious,
I have a long fluffy, furry orange tail,
And a big mouth, with sharp yellow teeth inside,
I am king of the beasts,
Though when people see me they all get really scared,
ROOOOAAARRRH!

Holly Simmons (Age 8)

Random Flying Pig

F lying around
L oves eating cheese
Y ou will know it when you see it.
I t's an amazing invention
N ever dying,
G limmering just like it has been polished.

P ink with wings and a snout,
I s always on the move,
G ood food to eat!!!

Tom Smith (Age 12)

Rivers

Rivers gush, rivers slush
They make ripples which gives me giggles,
They pick up peat which I think is sweet.
They make waterfalls like big walls,
Ducks awake all day and night,
And sometimes giving me a great big fright,
They sparkle from the yelllow sun
And now my poem is over and done!

Timothy Stephenson (Age 7)

Four Ways Of Looking At The Sun

The sun is like deserts,
Beating down on you.

The sun makes holidays for you,
And you can play on the beach too.

When you look at the sun
It is bursting with brightness.

The sun is yellow
It is like a giraffe.

Jack Short (Age 8)

The Teacher

The teacher says stop being so tough
The teacher says stop being so rough
The teacher says now it's R.E.
The teacher says then it's P.E.
The teacher says if we get all our work done
Then we will all have fun

Oliver Sharp (Age 7)

Stay Safe

Walk down the road look left and right
Look and listen and keep in sight.

When it is dark don't get lost
Or you will get a fright.

When you are playing
With friends around
Tell your parents
So you can be found.

Oliver Slaney (Age 7)

Summer Days

Lovely flowers
Buzzing bees
Grass growing
Silver weeds
Burnt skin
Bright sun
Town busy
Chocolate bun
Nearly summer!

Megan Studdert-Kennedy (Age 7)

Dinosaurs

D inosaurs are scary.
I don't want to touch a T-Rex.
N o I am not going to touch it.
O h no the Dinosaur is coming.
S ome dinosaurs fly in the sky.
A dinosaur is called T-Rex.
U p in the sky they fly.
R un run the dinosaur is coming.
S ome dinosaurs eat meat.

Talia Shefik (Age 6)

The Ferocious Dragon

He roams the land with fiery breath and teeth the size of long swords.
His wings are furled upon his back and when he is in flight
He is the size of a small aeroplane.
His scales are shiny red.
He has spikes on his back the size of knives
And claws the size of swords.
His tail's like an enormous arrow with a hooked end.
His eyes are yellow like a cats.
His fire is orange, blue and red
And he lives in a lair on a mountain range.

Benjamin Sanders (Age 7)

Animal Poem

Have you ever had a wiggly worm in your pants?
Because if you do, watch out or it will squirm.

Have you ever had a bear wearing your socks?
You might be surprised.

Have you had a panda wearing your dress?
Because I know you will scream.

Have you ever had a duck wearing your underpants before?
Because if you have, it will peck you.

Daniel Sierwald (Age 7)

Chased

Running, running for my life,
As fast as lightning striking.
Eyes watering like a waterfall inside my head.
It's getting closer now.

Frozen, frozen like a statue with extra cement
Dry mouth like the Sahara desert in summer
Goose bumps as tall as Mount Everest
Breathing, breathing like a train at full speed ready to burst
Heart thumping like an elephant stomping through my heart.
This five foot monster getting near then . . .

Laura Short (Age 8)

Easter

E aster bring lovely eggs!
A ll eat a lot of chocolate!
S o much chocolate and more chocolate later!
T oo many bunnies arriving!
E aster is full of fun and joy!
R ip, rip, rip it's all mine!

Rebecca Sellers (Age 8)

Bullied

Stomach churning,
Eyes burning.
Head pulsing,
Heart racing.
Teeth chattering,
Fingers fiddling.
Mind worried,
Eyes wondering.
Toes tingly,
Knees shaky.
Mouth dry.
Asking why?

Dale Tarr (Age 11)

In The Countryside

In the countryside I can see
A grey sparkling blackbird
In the countryside I can hear
Wet sloppy water dripping
In the countryside I can smell
Sweet mangoes swaying side to side
In the countryside I can touch
A silky black rabbit hopping
In the countryside I can taste
Massive green watermelons on the trees
In the countryside I feel happy

Jasmine Thompson (Age 6)

Fat Cat

There once was a cat who was very fat.
Her best friend was a rat
Who wore a green hat.
One day the fat cat
Sat on a mat.
She squashed her friend rat,
And that was that!

Charlotte Saunders (Age 8)

James Wales

This is the tale of James Wales,
Who always ate snails.
He got slower then as well,
He got a solid shell.
If he walked he left sticky slime
He said "I can't be dead, I'm only 9".
One morning he got snail eyes,
He tried to be very wise.
He shrunk so small,
He bashed into a wall.
He got stepped on and died.
His mother cried and cried.

Zoya Tajammal (Age 9)

Best Friends!

Best friends always there
Even when you're not there with them
Sure enough you'll stay together in life
Trusting you can always count on best friends.

Friends always stick together
Real friends never lie
Interesting facts come from best friends
Everything you can always share with best friends
Never ever argue with best friends
Dancing is a way to get together
Sure it works I've tried it.

Emily Thomasz (Age 8)

My Magic Poem

With my red I can paint a poppy.
With my blue I can paint the sky.
With my green I can paint a stem.
With my pink I can paint a flower.
With my black I can paint the night sky.
With my brown I can paint a winter tree.

Eleanor Stott (Age 7)

Jaguar

Jaguars have powerful pounces,
Jaguars have spotty faces,
You think that Jaguars have chicken pox
But they have normal spots
Jaguars run very fast,
Jaguars hide in the grass.

Nathan Stevens (Age 7)

Spring

S pring is wonderful
P oppies in the garden
R abbits bouncing in the field
I n the garden it is a wonderful place
N othing is better than Spring
G reat Spring

Sophie Smith (Age 8)

The Cat In The Tree

The cat in the tree said
The dog was fun playful and nervous.
It was bumpy and crazy.
"No" said the dog.
"I am not like that at all."

Anna Stephenson (Age 7)

Rainforest

With a bird's squawk
and a harpy hawk,
in the trees
there's lots of bees.
It's a sort of place
(a sort of race)
with the trees on top
beneath it's hot.
Here is a test:
We must keep forest
where it lives best.

Samuel Tyler (Age 8)

Sound

I love the sound of the birds and the bees
I don't understand why they don't love me.
The birds sweet chirpy song
And the mellow hum that last for too long.

At night they go away and the owl hoots to me.
Later that night the wolves start to howl,
Then the crickets play their smooth violin.

The doorbell rings, my mum starts to chat.
Then I remember the sound of the birds and the bees
And how they made me so happy.

Remy Thompson (Age 12)

What Love Defines

I thought love was just a tingling of the skin,
But who's to know what love defines?
I thought I was lucky for you to be mine,
But when you cheated,
I couldn't believe I was so blind . . .

I thought we would be together forever,
You made me feel special,
I thought there would never be a never,
But I guess I was wrong . . .

After everything we've been through,
After every special moment we had together,
It meant nothing to you.
The moment you went off with her,
Everything special we had just faded away . . .

And I wish I could be your tear,
To be born in your eye,
Live down your cheek,
And to die on your lips . . .
To show all the tears that left my eyes.

Linda Tran (Age 14)

Brazil

B om dia!
R aining in the Amazon!
A wesome dancing in the streets!
Z ooming fireworks popping in the carnival!
I love the sights in Brazil!
L ots of animals in the Amazon!

Alex Thurston (Age 8)

Anger

Anger smells like a baby's vomit.
Anger feels like a scorching volcano erupting inside you.
Anger tastes like an extra hot curry running down your throat.
Anger sounds like an everlasting, ear aching scream.
Anger is the colour of blazing orange in a fire.

Dyna Tlemsani (Age 9)

Summer

Summer
Flowers sprouting
Boys play football every day
The sun is shining in the sky
Football!!

Jack Trinder (Age 8)

Best Ever!

My family is one of the best
That there could ever be,
And it isn't just because of the fact
That it includes me!

First you have my parents,
Helping all the time.
Like cooking, washing, cleaning,
And helping me with this rhyme!

Then you have my older brother,
Bossing me about.
We always seem to start a fight,
And kick and scream and shout!

Finally there's my younger sister,
The weirdest of the lot.
She's loud, mad, funny and crazy,
I think she's lost the plot!

My family is one of the best
That there could ever be,
And it isn't just because of the fact
That it includes me!

Gabby Tyler (Age 13)

Spring Time

Spring time
Warm sun shining
People's flowers growing
Flowers growing over the fence
Play time!

Nicole Sliney (Age 8)

Sensory Garden

I like
Running
Trees
Flowers
Sleeping

Max Snell (Age 14)

Adam

A dam is . . .
D aft
A lways eating ice-cream . . .
M ore than anyone else

Adam Thomsett (Age 6)

Chased

Running, running for your life like a cheetah chasing its prey
Throat, throat as dry as an elephants graveyard
Breathing, breathing like a tornado wrecking everything in its path
Panicking, panicking like a dog watching fireworks!!!

Why is this dragon
Chasing me!!!

Kyle Turner (Age 9)

My Sunshine

My sunshine is a great big yellow ball
As bright as the brightest star,
My sunshine is a pink cat's eyes
Glowing like yellow sapphires
My sunshine is a waterfall
Falling like the air in mid air
My sunshine is . . .
LIFE!

Charlotte Theobald (Age 11)

Fire

Fire is like a bad rumour
Spreads faster than a heart beat
Nobody likes them but many start them
Not knowing how deadly they are
Once started they are uncontrollable
The damage is already done
Before they can be stopped

Rachael Topping (Age 14)

Chased

Running, running like a wolf chasing its prey,
Breathing, breathing like a train at its fastest
Panicking, panicking like a rabbit being chased by a fox
Panting, panting like a dog that has just ran a mile
Eyes, eyes watering like a river rushing down the hills
Throat, throat so dry it's hard to swallow

Lauren Tottman (Age 9)

Friends

Friends are glue
They stick to you
They never let you go
They are like family
Friends are always there for you

Ryan Thomas (Age 9)

My Dragon

My pet dragon is a humorous fellow,
Whose nostril heat is really quite mellow,
For it warms up my marshmallows, to runny proportions,
And makes the pink liquid turn into Jell-O!

He sits on an armchair,
His head proud in the air,
With his tail wag wagging
To help dry my hair!

His skin is red like a hot air balloon,
His teeth are yellow like the dying moon,
His manners are honestly second to none,
But he has problems with using those plastic spoons!

I love my dragon, and he loves me too,
I would never have put him into a zoo,
Because he is my best friend, from beginning to end,
And he's there for all to view!

William Trow (Age 14)

I Have A Zoo

A dingo was playing bingo
When a kangaroo went boo
A zebra went to Scarborough
Because he needed the loo.
A tiger drank cider
And then went to China

I brought a pithen in
Who's name is St Ivon.
A gorilla named Godzila
Who acts like a chinchilla
A giraffe named Paul
Who is very tall

It is noon now
Do you want to see the baboon
Before I close my zoo.

Sam Turner (Age 7)

The Frog And The Dog

The frog on the log with the hog and the dog
I have a job which is really odd,
I sat on a log and saw a frog having a jog
I carried on walking to my job
I came by a boy I saw the log by the frog
The next day I saw a hog having a rest by the dog
The log was there
So was the frog and the dog

Charlotte Thompson (Age 8)

The Welsh Dragon

There was a dragon that lived in a lair.
His claws are as shiny as Snow White's hair
Red horrible scales and long red wings
Sharp spiky teeth,
Bright red flames
A huge long tail
Large pointy horns
Green bulging eyes and a long red tongue

Courtney Tinton-Curr (Age 7)

Dog

Cat catcher
Bath scrubber
Big dribbler
Night sleeper
Long walker
Loud barker
Farmers best friend.

Emily Spanton (Age 8)

Super Summer!

Summer
Hot sun glowing
You run and play all day
The sun glows all day
When you play
Sun bathing

Leah Toop (Age 9)

Laura My Sister Watches Too Much TV!

Laura, my sister, watches far too much TV
I'm surprised she can even see unlike me - I don't watch TV

I settle down with a good book
Or maybe help my dad cook then I look

And Laura my sister is watching TV
I'm surprised she can even see unlike me - I don't watch TV

She doesn't even go to school
She thinks she's too cool I tell her she's being a fool

Laura, my sister, watches far too much TV
I'm surprised she can even see unlike me - I don't watch TV

I came home from my after school club
My Mum and Dad were at the pub and Laura was watching a film called Sub

Laura, my sister, watches far too much TV
I'm surprised she can even see unlike me - I don't watch TV

I walked in the room and guess what I saw,
Laura lying on the floor not watching TV, but doing a jigsaw

Laura, my sister, watches far too much TV
I'm surprised she can even see unlike me - I don't watch TV

Then she saw me all of a sudden she stood up and screamed
                    I HATE TV!!

Sarah Taskas (Age 10)

The Five Senses

Sound

The sounds of people cheering after a goal of a football match.
A lovely concert, violins in the orchestra, drums, flutes, clarinets in the band.

Sight

A wonderful sight of colourful rainbow, where's the pot of gold?
Seeing the amazing language for the deaf people.

Smell

My mum frying the evening steak, that glorious smell.
The rich smell of perfumes, they are all different in their own way.

Taste

A fabulous plate of food is placed in front of you.
Your mouth starts to water, that salty seafood, that hot spicy tender chicken in a curry.

Touch

You walk into an antique shop, all the smooth or rough items.
Carvings or engravings on wood. There is rough plastic, sharp glass, soft wool.

Mia Tozer (Age 10)

Fire

The flames jump in the air like jumping grasshoppers
Burning everything in its way.
The fire is running around like dancing fairies
Spreading its wavy arms all around the room.
Stinging all creatures in its way.
The fire erupts into a city of burning flames.
Like a massive volcano.
Death awaits you if you touch the hideous beast which are flames.
It gets bigger and spreads like falling rain.
The fire is like a river floating around the room.

James Taylor (Age 10)

Fear

The night sky wraps fear around me.
Dark night in the woods.
I hesitate in the darkness.
By myself.
Fear takes me further into the woods.
The darkness haunts me
As I go through the
Spooky woods of doom!
The trees shiver
And stir the night sky.
Fear takes me around the bends.
As I run I don't know
Where I am going.
Help!

Nathan Tidman (Age 10)

What Is The Sun?

The sun is a ball of fire,
Soaring through the skies
It is a golden penny
Being flicked into outer space.

The sun is a toffee apple,
Glowing in the clouds.
It is an amber eye,
Looking at the earth.

The sun is a red hot gem,
Burning in outer space.
It is a golden bullet
Flaming and zooming through space.

Harley Taggart (Age 9)

Life On The Line

The tunnel stands quiet wide and proud,
Then comes a train tall and loud,
I stand on the track my head is bowed,

It's coming . . .

Speeding past houses roofs made of thatch,
Leaping through the tunnel like a flame from a match,
I close my eyes and wait for the catch,

It's coming . . .

Hurtling out of the tunnel going round a bend,
The speedy Mallard's Journey is coming to an end,
I stand on the track my life I will lend,

It's gone . . .

(and so have I)

Victoria Turner (Age 12)

Bed Time

Get in the bath now
Wash your body
Are you nice and clean?
Now you're nearly ready

Dry yourself here's a towel
Now it's getting late
You still need to brush your teeth
And be in bed by eight

Put your pyjamas on
Read a story
The one about
The fish called Dory

Get into bed now
You know God cares
There's one more thing to do
And that's to say your prayers

Billy Teather (Age 6)

Our Headmaster

M is for music, played and sung.
R is for reading stories out loud.

G is for guitar in assemblies played.
L is for Literacy and Numeracy too.
E is for entertainment making us laugh.
N is for nature watching and learning.
N is for nice, kindness and care.
Y is for yes, what he usually says!

Jodi Tarr (Age 9)

Sammy The Boy Barbie

This is the life of Sammy Teds,
Always seen eating Barbie heads.
Suddenly he grew long gold locks
And started to wear beautiful frocks,
His lips got red as roses
And he started to do girly poses.
Wears blue eye shadow like the sky
And changed his name to Nye

Morgan Jake Thomas (Age 9)

My Big Sis

I refer to her as she or even an it,
As I enter her room she has a raging fit!
Shouting and screaming in a high pitched screech,
Pulling a face like a tag on leach.

Her boyfriend's coming round, I think he's from outer space.
There's a funny perfume smell in her room and she's putting powder on her face.
Now there's the lipstick, I laugh with a frown,
She's going to crack the mirror one day, she looks like a clown.

She or it is bigger and older than me, it really isn't fair,
Why can't she have bunches and silly ribbons in her hair?
Why is it that I have to eat all my meals with all the yukky slop,
She comes in, grabs a bite, out again! Meal times a flop!

Now sometimes she or it is nice and my feelings are in a muddle,
When I sit and cry a lot she gives me a big cuddle.
I know I get her into trouble with mum and the arguments I don't miss,
But I love she or it a lot because she is my BIG SIS!!!

Alexandra Thorne (Age 10)

My Teacher!

My teacher's like no other I've seen
She wears her old costumes from last Halloween.
When reading a book about a magical broom,
She decides to run around the room.

She asks us questions that are always in rhyme,
And she expects the answer in double-quick time.
If we're naughty she locks us in her den,
While wrestling a rubber and a silly old pen.

For homework she says that we cannot play
Or watch TV for the rest of the day.
My teacher's either totally insane,
Or she's a genius with a little brain.

But whether it's madness or her teacher powers,
I don't think it matters because I know that she's ours!

Nicole Tizzard (Age 10)

The Three Little Pigs

The three little pigs
Set off with their wigs,
To build a new home,
They saw a gnome.

And one asked if he could have his wood,
And the other asked for mud,
And the other used bricks of course.

The wolf licked his lips
And had several kips,
Just then he blew the wood house down
And pinched a crown.

Then he kicked the mud house
And won a mouse,
He couldn't try blow the brick house away
So he'll try another day!

Lucy Tillotson (Age 10)

Dominic's Pets

In his bedroom, Dominic kept,
Ten sick rats with chopped off toes
Nine black widows who were his foes
Eight serpents with rotted teeth
Seven wythor dragons with masters
Six fire birds with angry eyes
Five arctic dragons which was a surprise
Four griffins with tired wings
Three Texas dragons with golden shillings
Two Arabian dragons with skinny legs
And ONE . . . GUESS WHAT?

Dominic Thewlis (Age 8)

I Have A Dog

I have a dog called Milly
She is very silly
She jumps up in the window
Then she saw a dog called Bingo
Bingo is tall but Milly is small
When we take Milly for a walk
She runs away while we talk
But when she goes to sleep
And silent we keep

Alicia Thompson (Age 10)

Raiders In The Night

Creeping through the night,
Keeping out of the light.
Ere the break of day,
To earn their pay.
They plunder and rape,
Yet no-one's seen beneath their cape.
Picking locks and sitting upon a rock,
Their bows do they knock.
Their targets remain unaware,
As the sound of death hums through the air.
The money is soon gone,
Also taken is a scone.
They're creeping through the night,
Keeping out of the light.

Samuel Thorp (Age 13)

Rap Writer
(On the . . . . wait 2 seconds)

My name is Harriet,
And I work in Marriot,
But I like . . . riding chariots.

I have a bunny,
And he likes it when it's sunny,
But he misses . . . his mummy.

I go to Cranbourne school,
And it doesn't have a pool,
But it still is . . . sorta cool.

That's the end of my rap,
But it don't have any gaps,
Now I gotta go . . . for a nap.

Harriet Thorne (Age 9)

The Music Of The Spheres

Calm, still, silent
Is this a dream?
Why are there no wars?
This is lovely

All the guns gone
Quiet as the wind
They all listened
Carefully
To the music of the spheres

All you can hear is music
Peaceful music
Calm music
Gentle music

Richard Taylor (Age 9)

A Picture Of You

I know a felt tip
Full of blue
It helps me draw
A picture of you

Robert Tunstall (Age 7)

The Hunter

The agile black shadow of a hunter,
Dances down rippling, green plains,
And the swift silhouette of a hunter,
Darts between narrow winding lanes.

The penetrating eyes of a hunter,
Glow eerie in the light of the stars,
And the merciless face of a hunter,
Bears the burden of death and its scars.

The impeccable nose of a hunter,
Aids it in pursuit of its prey,
And the relentless speed of a hunter,
Dares anyone to get in it's way.

Now the tossed back head of a hunter,
Calls out and appeals to the moon,
And the ear-splitting song of a hunter,
Warns its victims that blood will shed soon.

The whistle sounds with a bleat from the hunted,
Who is pounced from beneath the unknown,
And the sinister carcass seen at daybreak,
Serves as its own tombstone.

Charley Turton (Age 11)

I Watch . . .

I watch it demolishing, destroying,
It thrashes and thunders . . .
The ground trembling
From the hurricane,
Tearing houses from the earth
The towering dark clouds
Threatening us,
Rain streaking from the sky,
Ripping trees from their homes,
Invading our neighbourhoods,
The roaring wind
Deafening your ears!
The torn sky shaking!
And through all this, I watch . . .

Lauren Tiller (Age 11)

Chimpanzees

Chimpanzees live in the trees,
Chimpanzees never eat fleas,
Chimpanzees always see bees,
Chimpanzees are lively and funny
Chimpanzees love lots of honey

William Thornley (Age 7)

The Mysterious Creature Goes

Trudging through the snow,
The mysterious creature goes.
Timid like a sheep,
The mysterious creature goes.

Dangerous claws it thrashes,
The mysterious creature goes.
Running through the winter snow,
The mysterious creature goes.

It spies a lonely rabbit,
Charging on its prey.
Only to find the prey not there,
Home it's gone to stay.

Its stomach makes a thundering noise,
In its tender hole,
Oh how it wished it had some food,
To eat it whole and whole.

Trudging through the snow,
The mysterious creature goes,
Trekking for its edible food
For it must eat some so.

Helena Tipper (Age 11)

Motocross

That wonderful smell of petrol,
Check your oil it should be full.
That wet dripping mud, falling of the engine,
Racing along, you're sure to win.

Those great chunky tyres, gripping in the dirt.
Let's hope you don't get hurt.
Dropping off the clutch,
Revving a bit too much.

Wheelie off the start line,
That silvery shiny cup, is sure to be mine

You're going very fast, the wind rushing past.
You slid off your bike,
Not a very pretty sight,
Someone obviously wants a fight.

Hear the sirens screaming,
Because you heard something ping.
You're looking pretty ming,
That must really sting.

Tom Twyman (Age 12)

Teachers!

Children from Bury,
Teachers from Mars
Having a drink,
Up at the bars.

Headteacher sitting,
Up at his desk;
Papers are everywhere,
Phew what a mess!

Headteacher washing,
Up at the sink.
Look at the toilet,
Pooh what a stink.

Teachers all smoking,
Having a chat.
Well that just explains it,
Now how about that.

Children all running,
Out in the cold,
Headteacher said,
"Teachers were sold".

Ryan Tooke (Age 9)

Fireworks!

Crackling and sizzling colours shoot swiftly up into the night sky like deadly bullets,
Banging and bashing explosions fly through the air,
Screaming and screeching the young children hide behind their parents like petite lambs
And wrap their hands around their ears,
Hissing and fizzing the catherine wheels spin speedily around and around
Popping and flashing the small sprinkles of light fall frequently down to the grassy ground.

Alice Vanstone (Age 12)

The Christmas Tree

One
Silver star
With shimmering snow
Two funny Santa's going Ho! Ho! Ho!
Three chocolate bars in purple packets,
Four crackers going off Boom!
Five frosty fairies with funny wings,
Six silver stars lighting up the room,
Seven silly snowmen with silly things,
Eight glowing moons shining in the dark,
Nine singing Santa's holding candles,
Ten twinkling fairies wearing a crown.
And there at the bottom
Of our Christmas tree
Is
A
Great Big present
Just for me

George S.K. Turner (Age 7)

Ocean Travel

If I could travel
the oceans blue,
these are the things
that I would do.

Go to the ocean
in a boat.
Go to the beach and
find a goat.

Go on a boat and
shout "ahoy".
Go to the beach and
find a toy.

Dive with a whale
and eat a grape.
Cling to the tail of
a big fat ape.

Chloe Trigwell (Age 8)

Story Of A River

I start from a droplet in the sky,
I fall down from very high

I land in a beautiful, peaceful stream
It's like having a magical dream

It's the beginning of my journey
Towards the Silver Sea

Rushing and gushing
Bubbling and splashing

Breaking rocks as I go
Eroding pebbles as I flow

I go past forests, fields and towns
I see seasons, hills and downs

My blue waters now get dark
All pollution from an Industrial Park

One last waterfall, one sharp bend
My adventure is now coming to an end

Finally, I'm now ready
I'm now steady
To join the shimmering Sea

Lion Thibault (Age 11)

Fear

Running, running for your life
Pale as a vanilla ice-cream
Breathing, breathing heavy and fast
I was a running rocket sweating in the heat
Teeth chattering like a dice in a cup
Running, running for your life
Knees knocking like a rattle snake shaking its tail
The creature looked like a frog
I couldn't look back

Max Tipping (Age 9)

The Man At The Top Of The Pyramid

One fine day in July
I saw a man at the top of the pyramid
I don't know what he was doing or why he was there
Perhaps he fell and broke his hip
He broke his hip and down he fell
One fine day in July
I saw a man at the bottom of the pyramid
I don't know what he was doing or why he was there
Perhaps now he's broken his leg.

Sam Tithecott (Age 9)

The Cat Next Door

The cat next door,
Explores everywhere.
The cat next door,
Flies in the air.

The cat next door,
Roars like a lion.
The cat next door,
Is made out of iron.

The cat next door,
Is as black as coal.
The cat next door,
Is hard to control.

The cat next door,
Is tremendously small.
The cat next door,
Can kick a ball.

Now you know the cat next door,
You might not be able to live anymore.

Biriantan Umasuthan (Age 10)

Spring

Spring is here!
Come and see spring!
Daffodils are everywhere
They smell really nice
They look pretty and yellow
They are in hedges and gardens
They pop up in spring.
Come and see spring!

Alisha Van Raat (Age 7)

The Moon Is . . .

A big ball in the sky
A huge hunk of cheese
A dot with no light
A midnight torch
A dim lamp light
A thing with no heat
A giant grey ball
A light stealer
A white star
A glowing guide

Jaz Tuckett (Age 12)

Friends

Friends are for sharing,
Not for keeping,
Be nice,
Be kind,
Share toys,
Make clubs,
And remember,
Friends are for sharing,
Not for keeping.

Friends are for kindness,
Friends are for happiness.

Friends are for laughter,
Not for tears,
Play games,
Make plays,
And remember,
Friends are for laughter,
Not for tears

Ruth Trevelyan (Age 8)

War

On the ground thousands die,
While in the air fighter planes fly,
Over everybody cold hands crawled,
Every soul unfairly mauled,
Out of nowhere cannons flare,
Death over everyone bare.
Miles away families cry,
Death they hope a terrible lie.

Jack Tranter (Age 10)

Storm

Thoughtless and heartless
A dangerous beast hunting for prey
Lightning, flashing everywhere
It strikes . . .
Until quiet . . .

It crashes and bashes
Like a death machine
Killing anything . . . anyone
It strikes . . .
Until quiet . . .

It's windy and blows
It attacks and kills
It comes and goes
Then . . .
It strikes . . .
Until quiet . . .

Lucy Tearle (Age 11)

My Rose

My rose that once was fair and bright,
As any blossoms were,
With petals blushed , thy shade was loving,
Thy beauty true and sure.

But now, thou has a wrinkled mane
With petals faded dry,
Thy wilted stem that once stood proud
Is now gone, with a sigh.

Yet, thy beauty remains, although dry and dead
Still your flower appears as the one that grew,
A reminder of forgotten past
And hope of the returning dew.

I will always remember your gentle sway,
The thorns that prick when our flesh did meet.
In memory your life lives on,
Visioned fragrant, soft, and sweet.

Georgina Willis (Age 12)

The Whistle

Standing between the posts
I watch the kick-off
As the ball comes towards me
My heart beats . . . faster and faster
The cool wind chilled me to the bone
Suddenly . . . thud! I saved it!
The ref blew the whistle . . .
We won!
The crowd went wild.

Michael Taylor (Age 10)

The Sunny Countryside

In the countryside
I can see small boys jumping

In the countryside
I can hear sweet, grey rabbits hopping

In the countryside
I can smell the sweet, juicy apples hanging

In the countryside
I can touch the golden long corn waving

In the countryside
I can taste the green fat cabbages growing

In the countryside
I can feel a sweet rabbit hopping

Ryan Watling (Age 6)

Cats

Soppy, sweet
Very neat
Soft furry
Very purry
Drinking milk
On silk
Lovely soft
Likes lofts
Glowing eyes
In disguise
Waving tail
In mail
Crossing string
Can sing
My cats
Chasing rats

Chloe Ellen Thompson (Age 8)

Green

Green is grass that grows
Green is envy and jealousy
Green is a fish's scale
Green is a dragon tail
Green is a book's colour
Green is a marshy land
Green is a tree's leaf
Green is a plant's stem
Green is a pelican sign to go
Green is fir trees
Green is a chameleon
Green is a seaweed swishing
Green is the colour of murky water
Green is when you're sick

Green is my best colour in the world

Sivanandarajah Vishnuthan (Age 10)

Tsunami

Suddenly there was a thundering noise,
Like a volcano erupting.
The noise was deafening,
And the ground was cracking . . .
The gigantic wave came from the sea,
It was a Tsunami.
It crashed to the ground,
Hundreds of screaming people,
Walls breaking and falling,
People climbing on anything.
To get them away from the black water.
Thousands of lost homes,
Then silence . . .

Joe Verbena (Age 11)

Hennock Is

Hennock is:

A shining fort on the top of an emerald hill,
A tiny egg in a high nest deep in a forest,
A snake outlined with houses,
A glistening star on the top of the Christmas tree,
A beacon shining in the distance on a pitch-black night,
An amulet safely enclosed within the moors,
A star blazing on the night sky,
A fading match lit in a dark cave,
A child in the big world.

Zak Tamlyn (Age 9)

Winter Song

Snowfalls quickly and snow is wet
Jack Frost . . . snow cold
Snow cold
Snow cold
Snow cold
Snow flakes fall at night
Ice is frozen . . . snow slow
Snow slow
Snow slow
Snow slow
Hail stones crashing and one hard and
icy
Windy night . . . snow flakes
Snow flakes
Snow flakes
Snow flakes

Haydn Tossoun (Age 9)

Race Horses

Horses begin the race,
They canter really fast.
They start to get a quicker pace,
Then they gallop faster than fast.

You can't even hear their feet,
With the crowd roaring really loud.
Someone tries to cheat,
But don't succeed with the others racing past.

The crowd gasp, it's true,
One horse so much in the lead.
Over the finishing post he flew,
Everyone's really amazed.
The horse called lightening wins.

Jenni Visuri (Age 10)

Walking Through The Farmyard What Do You See?

Walking through the farmyard what do you see?
I can see a sheep looking at me.

Hopping through the farmyard what do you see?
I can see a cow looking at me

Jumping through the farmyard what do you see?
I see a pony looking at me.

Swinging through the farmyard what do you see?
I can see a pig looking at me.

Matthew Venn (Age 5)

When Rosie Eats Pasta

When Rosie eats pasta,
She munches, crunches and blows bubbles,
The pasta goes plop into her groaning mouth,
The little bit of water goes zooming down her throat,
Down goes the pasta, skiing down the mountain with a swoosh,
Wee, bang, the pasta is in her deep, dark stomach,
Where it sends back up a burp!

Stacey Vincent (Age 11)

Fear!!

Fear is a big black cloud,
It tastes like a dry block of mud,
It smells like dust flying around near your nose,
It sounds like guns shooting, getting closer and closer,
It feels like hands are tightly wrapping around my throat
It looks like a dark alleyway

Paige Vincent (Age 10)

A Man I've Never Seen

I collided with a man I've never seen,
He had the biggest mouth and he looked very mean.
He had a great big nose but had only one eye,
He was a giant and wasn't the kindest guy.

After the huge collision, I fell on the floor,
He picked me up as gentle as a doe.
He asked me in a kind tone if I was alright,
I looked at his face and saw a wonderful sight.

The manners he had was the kindest ever,
I learnt that I would never judge a book from its cover, NEVER.

Tharshan Umasuthan (Age 12)

Walking Through The Farmyard

Walking through the farmyard
What do you see?
I see a horse neighing at me

Walking through the farmyard
What do you see?
I see a pig oinking at me

Walking through the farmyard
What do you see?
I see a sheep baaing at me

Lauren Vicary (Age 6)

Walking Through The Farmyard

Walking through the farmyard
What do you see?
I see a horse neighing at me.

Walking through the farmyard
What do you see?
I see a hen clucking at me.

Hannah Wicks (Age 5)

Bunnies

Bunnies are shy
Bunnies are cute
Bunnies have lots of fur
Bunnies are funny
Bunnies have lots of grass to eat

Kyle Thomas (Age 8)

My Cat
(In memory of Tiddles)

I have a cat
She's not round and she's not fat
She sleeps on the sofa
Because she doesn't like her mat
What do you think about that?
We named her Tiddles
We nearly named her Sox
She likes to play in a cardboard box
She is a bit of a hunter
As sly as a fox
That's my cat
I love her lots and lots

Matthew Waters (Age 7)

Love Is . . .

Love is like a desert
Going to let the people free

Love is going
Like a river

It is going to fly
In to the sky

Going to see the love
To fly and to fly

So we make a
Girl to fall in love

Lucy Upham (Age 7)

A Girl's Mind

Make-up, clothes, jewels, hair
Make the boys stop and stare

Pretty girls, dresses, hats
No more school girly plaits

That boy's fine, so he is!
Was that boy waving at me?

Curls, straight, wavy
I look gorgeous in navy

Zara, Ravel and don't forget Schuh
I need an outfit shiny and new!

Eleanor Warder (Age 13)

The Sun

I don't care what you say
I like the sun
I like the way it shimmers
All through the day

I don't care what you say
I like the sun
Because when the sun is out
There's animals about

I don't care what you say my friend
I like the sun I like it best
When it's out all day because
I have more time to spend

Carli-Ann Wilcott (Age 8)

Easter

Easter, Easter is coming soon,
Chocolate eggs and toads on stalls.
Big ones, small ones, fat ones, thin ones,
Short chocolate, tall chocolate and all chocolate.

Easter, Easter is coming soon,
The Easter bunny dressed in pink.
Green outfit, yellow, red outfit, blue,
Bringing chocolate eggs to you!

Easter, Easter is coming soon,
A holiday from school,
Yay, hip, hip, hooray.
The Easter bunny coming to see you,
Easter, Easter is coming soon!

Robyn Withers (Age 12)

The Silhouette House

The silhouette house stood on its own,
Empty, disowned and left all alone.
The soft flutter of birds,
Small shadows of bats,
The loud squeaks of mice,
Meows of cats,
The ripples of water flooding the floor,
The smell of animals down the hall,
Webs of spiders netting the door,
The buzz of flies caught in them all,
The walls covered in ivy all the way.
All this was meant to be silent.
Maybe it used to be, but now,
The silhouette house stands tall and true,
Full of life, just waiting for you!

Gemma Vaal (Age 13)

Land, Sea And Jungle

The world beneath my feet,
Spread out like a huge multicoloured sheet,
Blue, red and green,
Such a wonderful, artistic scene!

The waves beneath my feet,
Spread out like a huge bluish, greeny sheet,
Crabs, fish and whales,
Jump in a boat and let's set the sails!

The jungle before my eyes,
Full of tropical birds from the skies,
Vines and creepers high,
Growing on taller till morning is nigh!

Catherine Whatley (Age 9)

In The Countryside

In the countryside
I can see
A black and brown horse trotting

In the countryside
I can hear
A fluffy cockerel clucking and crowing

In the countryside
I can smell
The fresh golden corn swishing and swaying

In the countryside
I can touch
A mad dog barking

In the countryside
I can taste
The sweet juicy blackberries squashing

In the countryside
I feel happy just like walking

Megan Ward (Age 7)

Blossom

B lossom starts to bloom in a beautiful way
L ovely light pink
O h so pink and pretty
S pring flowers
S hines in the summer sun
O pens in a gorgeous way
M agic blossom everywhere

Zoe Titmuss (Age 8)

The Hurricane

The Hurricane is a rampaging rhino
A natural conqueror of the seas
Splitting families and friends
Like a paper trimmer.

This hater of man wants revenge
It only wants to cause mass destruction
In the north east south and west
And will not stop until the entire world
Is in panic.

From the mountains of New Zealand
To the metropolis of the Big Apple
A time for destruction
Is at hand!

Rory Wall (Age 11)

Bingbong Land

It was a dark night,
In Bingbong Land
All the fiddles were willing to give a hand
All the faples gave up a fight.

Then one day . . .

Someone lit the light
And someone nicked the maples
And this wasn't good news for the faples
Someone had stolen the fighter

Selif was afraid . . .

Everyone went and bought him a frap
Then did him a curtsy
Then again, bought him a murtsy
And sent a map

They cast them together,
And made a sauce and
Got everything back.

Rachael Williams (Age 10)

The River

It sounds like a roaring tiger
It feels like a slithering snake
It looks like dark blue ink
It makes the rocks like a charging rhino
It flows as gently as a butterfly
It is as cold as ice
I like rivers

Scott Venables (Age 10)

Happiness

It's come to live in my room
It skips around and goes boom
It's small and furry
It's eyelashes are nice and curly

Her cheeks are red and rosy
Her fur is all cosy
Her nose is tiny but pokey
Her hair is shiny and straight
With her furry little paws
She only walks around with indoors

She bounces, she booms
She travels around my rooms
She's all nice and bliss
It's happiness

Skylar Wiggins (Age 12)

The Pink Dolphins

The beautiful pink dolphins,
Gracefully slid through the velvety water.
Their gentle bodies reflected the blazing sun.
As their fellow friends glided towards them.

They rolled their pretty, but pale bodies,
And slipped through the slick sea,
Then splashed back down into the water.
They looked as special as a beautiful sunset.

Their bodies were small with a pale pink shade.
They were as smooth as silk made into a dress.
As all dolphins were, the pink dolphins were extremely kind and calm.
They grew to be the loveliest animals in the whole of the sea.

A scent so sweet drifted from them.
They smelt like newly picked roses on a bright summer day.
Animals were drawn towards their special scent.
Then swam away relaxed and content.

The dolphins were the only pink ones in the entire living world

Katie Walker (Age 10)

The Joy Of Easter

In Spring the daffodils dance,
While the lambs on the hills begin to prance.

Easter is a time when lambs are born,
Flowers blossom on Easter morn.
Easter is a time for a lot of joy,
For every little girl and boy.

The children eat their chocolate delight,
Whilst new born chicks take their first bite.
At this time of year Jesus rose,
While everyone decorates eggs with bows.

When it turns dark, you can eat a hot cross bun,
Especially made by your mum.

Ryan Watkins (Age 11)

Blackbird

He shivers slightly,
He's alone,
He's scared.
There's no one with him,
No one to comfort him,
An orange glow catches his eyes.
Dawn,
The world springs to life.
A new found energy grows inside him.
He spreads his wings and soars into the air.
He chirps joyfully,
He lands in a bird bath, splashes about,
He's happy.
Safe.

Conor Willis (Age 10)

Dolphins

In the sea dolphins swim eating fish
Along comes a shark and scares him away
Dolphins come another day

In the sea dolphins swim eating crabs
Along comes a whale and scares him away
Dolphins come another day

In the sea dolphins swim eating shrimp
Along comes an eel and scares him away
Dolphins come another day

Chris Whatley (Age 9)

Oh My Dear Cat

I gave my cat away
Last week on Wednesday
I wimped and I cried
And also I sighed
Throughout the long whole day

Oh how I miss my cat
Who used to sit on my mat
It's so sad he's not here
Oh I do fear
How he's getting on at his new flat

Laura Beth Winstone (Age 9)

Senses By The Sea Shore

Touch! Feel the ripples against your feet, the sand so warm
Touch the pine trees, feel how prickly they are
Feel the wind on your face and the sun burning your neck
Your hair is being pushed in your face

Taste! Taste the sweet, sour, bitter and salty,
Tastes of the sea food
Tasty pineapple smoothies lift up your hearts
And the tender apples all juicy and red

Sight! See the sea creatures all around you
Spot the jellyfish as it comes near
The white singing horse rushing towards
See the beautiful sights

Sound! Hear the pounding hooves of horses splashing in the water to cool down
Listen to the wind through the trees nearby
Hear the flying fish splash around,
Hear the crabs scuttle on the ground

Smell! Smell the salty smell of the sea
Smell the delicious sea food
Smell the ice-cream and the smoothies
Smell the smoke from a bonfire nearby

Rosie Webber (Age 10)

Polar Bears

A polar bear is like

A big white ball of fluffy cotton wool
A white teddy bear
A living cloud drifting across the ice cap
A playful child

A polar bear is also like

A white tiger that is angry
A hungry, sleepless lion
A dangerous weapon
A great white hunter

Anna Western (Age 12)

Losing Someone!

You were here but then you went,
An angel from heaven had to be sent.
Your face was pale it made me feel
My head was spinning like a wheel.
When you died my soul died too,
My heart started to crave for you.
I walked home in bitter sorrow,
My face looked sad my spirits low.
Your spirit is with me even today,
It's with me at work; it's with me at play.
I remoulded my mind out of clay,
To keep me going day by day!

Lauren Wright (Age 11)

Christmas

Christmas outside is snowy and white
It is fun going down the snowy white hill
And having a mini snowball fight
Getting your dad covered in snow

Christmas inside is warm and cosy
It is exciting waiting for Christmas
So come and open all your Christmas presents

Evie Wright (Age 8)

The Sea

The sea is furious Lion,
Fierce and terrifying.
Roaring when it hits the rocks,
With his sharp claws and frightening teeth

Time upon time pouncing on the land
CRASH, CRASH, CRASH
Lonely lion,
Washing its gold shining mane

Ellis Waugh (Age 11)

The Monster

The monster is coming creeping down the stairs
When it comes and attacks you you will never stop
Nor stare at the monster coming down the stair

For the monster is coming
Coming down the stairs

For the monster has got great big eyes
For the monster has got great big boots
And when you come for drink
The monster will come and creep up on you

The monster is coming creeping down the stairs
When it comes and attacks you, you will never stop
Nor stare at the monster coming down the stair

The monster will get you
When you come for a drink

The monster is coming creeping down the stairs
When it comes and attacks you you will never stop
Nor stare at the monster coming down the stair

He is going, going to bed
And now he is watching you rest your big head

Abbie Wardman (Age 9)

The Magic Box

I will put in my box,
The smell of cheesy pie and the scent of roses

My box is styled from
The moon and the stars and the planets

The lid is decorated with rockets and aliens

The hinges are fashioned from the toes of aliens

Rachael Worley (Age 7)

I Can

I can feel the fur of the woolly black bear,
I can smell the dirt from its golden hair,

I can hear the sound of little birds crying,
I can see the sight of small creatures dying,

I can taste the fruit from the juicy mango tree,
I can hear the sound of the small buzzy bee,

I can see the sun setting far away,
I can feel the warmth as it drifts away.

Georgina Winfield (Age 12)

Up On The Farm

Up on the farm my eyes can see
Pink, fat pigs splashing
Yellow chicks wings

Up on the farm my ears can hear
Black sheep dog barking
Yellow bees buzzing

Up on the farm my nose can smell
Beautiful horse hopping
Black and white cow smelling

Up on the farm my mouth can taste
Lovely red apples ripening
Farmer's wife cooking

Up on the farm my fingers can feel
Fluffy chicks hatching
Baby lambs sleeping

Up on the farm
My full body senses
Alive and singing

Katie Ward (Age 6)

Colourful Horse

A colourful horse
Gracefully trotting,
Powerfully trotting
Shy, but elegant
Proud and gentle,
Sleek and shiny
Lovely horse
Trotting, trotting, trotting

Lydia Worton (Age 8)

Pig

Messy eater
Fat stomper
Dirty roller
Loud muncher
Belly bumper
Water slurper
Hay cruncher
Apple squirter
Root digger
Ear flopper
You are pink but I like you!

Joseph Welton (Age 8)

Fair Trade

It all starts at the crack of dawn
The boiling sun as thousands rise

The hardest workers in the land bossed and booted down the path
Into the field of grief and pain
The hardest workers kicked and pushed
By the lazy boss
The lazy boss hammered and forced to kick and push
By the supermarket chain
The supermarket chain made to hammer and force
By the people

So what it comes down to is you
But what can you do one person in millions?
I'll tell you it's easy simple as can be
One word I'll tell you take it from me
Fair Trade

Rosie Wilson (Age 13)

Spring

S pring is lovely
P urple bluebells on tall trees
R abbits hopping and bouncing in the fields
I n spring everything is new
N othing is better than spring
G reen leaves on the beautiful trees

Ben Walton (Age 8)

A Young Girl

A young girl was walking on a hot beach one day,
When a sudden gust of wind just swept her away.
Like a big angry dragon or a dangerous bear,
The breeze held her close as she spun through the air.

At a breathtaking speed she hurtled and flew,
Confusion, tension, no time to argue.
Until the wind slowed and she was able to breathe,
As she swept through the air with the world at her feet.

She zoomed over Florida, Vermont, NYC
People looked up as she called out in glee
And then came Europe, a looming blue menace,
She hurtled past Berlin, past Paris, past Venice.

Africa looked like an endless dry desert
Pyramids majestic without any effort.
Asia came next in this quick worldwide tour
First Malaysia, then Thailand, and last Singapore.

Then with a loud thud and a smack to her feet,
There she was standing right back on the beach.
The sun was still shining, the waves still flowed past
Nothing had changed, but the memories would last.

Bethany White (Age 14)

Valentine's Day

Valentine's Day, Valentine's Day
Everyone's kissing,
Everyone's in love
Everyone's getting married,
I love you, I love you,
It's Valentine's Day!!!!!

Rebecca Websdale (Age 7)

You're Going Now

Pack your things,
Get in the car.
Go on the plane,
You're going far.

London boring,
Lagos now.
So, so beautiful,
But you're going now.

Don't forget us,
We won't forget you.
Pray for your Mama,
And stay in you two.

Stay away from police,
And stay on your feet.
Leave soon,
Where you're going
It might not be very neat.

My beautiful children,
You're going now.

Emilie Westcott (Age 12)

Up On The Farm

Up on the farm
My eyes can see
Some yellow corn sweeping

Up on the farm
My ears can hear
Some puppies barking

Up on the farm
My nose can smell
Some yellow poo stinking

Up on the farm
My mouth can taste
Some dead pheasants cooking

Up on the farm
My fingers can feel
Some musty mud squelching

Up on the farm
All of my senses
ALIVE and EXCITING

Joshua Wymer (Age 7)

Pony

Polo muncher
Carrot cruncher
Clippety clopper
Trip trotter

Rebecca Watson (Age 8)

Cats

I have a little cat
Very good to me
Black, white and grey
My cat is a she

It comes out shopping
My parties and more
When I come home from school
She is waiting at the door

My cat came from Florida
My dad brought her back
It was very hot there
She was in his backpack

My cat is my favourite
My pride and joy
My cat is the best cuddly toy.

George Wheeler (Age 6)

In The Forest

Things that move in the middle of the night,
They hide in the shadows and give you a fright.
With their long spiky legs that shuttle and crawl,
I wouldn't like to come across one at all.

But the things that slithered across the floor,
Aren't as beautiful as the things that soar.

Buzzards, vultures and the mighty eagle,
Don't compare to the sea-salt seagull.

They shriek and squawk,
They hate to walk.
They make their nests in a church steeple,
Their favourite food is chips from the people.

Now we're getting off the track
From the forest animals so let's go back.

Deep in the jungle where the lion roars,
Cat like eyes and great big paws.
All the other animals cower in shame.,
When the mighty lion shakes his mane.

Harvey Wain-Williams (Age 11)

Water

The water is flowing like an arrow through the sky
Crocodiles blowing bubbles to make trouble in the jungle
Birds singing people fishing in the jungle
Waterfalls falling onto rocks making big big splash!

Jonathan Webb (Age 10)

Mr Tough

Two black eyes and a broken toe
That's what happens when you play with Joe
He's big and scary and boy he's tough
The only game he plays is let's play rough
He's shaved his head so he's almost bald
He looks quite puny but that's you fooled
Wears Doc Martens and yes he can kick
Think he's bright? No he's thick, thick, thick
He'll start up a fight, teacher comes running
Joe will skip away "he's so cunning"
Teachers think he's sweet, a sugared plum
How thick are they, it's Joe that's dumb
He gets away with anything, even teacher respect
If he's in a fight, there's no effect
But if I were to run up to you
Spit in your face and stamp on your shoe
None of the teachers will let it pass
Make me miss break time and sit in my class
I now know why Joe's number one,
HE'S THE HEAD TEACHER'S SWEET SUGARED SON!!!!

Sarah Walker (Age 11)

223

In The Countryside

In the countryside
I can see a dirty horse sleeping

In the countryside
I can hear a little cockerel crowing

In the countryside
I can smell black mud squirting

In the countryside
I can touch a smooth dog walking

In the countryside
I can taste crunchy carrots growing

In the countryside
I feel warm running

Joshua Woodward (Age 7)

Sun Poem

The sun is,
shining,
setting,
smiling,
sizzling,
scorching,
setting,
summery,
shining

Joseph Witchell (Age 7)

The Countryside

In the countryside
I can see
A fluffy white rabbit hopping
In the countryside
I can hear
Golden shiny corn waving
In the countryside
I can smell
Sweet juicy blackberries growing
In the countryside
I can touch
Some soft red roses brightening
In the countryside
I can taste
Rosy red strawberries squirting
In the countryside
I can feel
The cold air blowing

Daisy Wilson (Age 6)

Shadows

His shadow haunts him
He looks at a suit of armour, creaking at every turn
His stepping echoes around the corridor
He stops as a door creaks, a chair rocks
He runs out into the cool, crisp wind
Tall oak trees stand sparse on this cold winter night
He hears a rustle, but no, it's just the wind
Or is it?
He enters a clearing, rustling leaves all around him
His name is called three times
"Michael, Michael, Michael"
The sweet voice, like honey, beckons to him
BANG! He falls down, down, further
He is suddenly back in his own world, sitting on the carpet,
Staring into all of space and time.

Holly Walker (Age 12)

Walking Through The Farmyard

Walking through the farmyard
What do you see?
I can see a pink pig
Oinking at me

Jumping through the farmyard
What do you see?
I see a wild dog
Looking at me

Tom Walker (Age 5)

The Firework Poem

Whoosh, bang, sparks shoot up into the sky,
A rocket zooms up high high high.
Catherine wheels dazzle as they whizz around,
All birds and animals are nowhere to be found.

Pink shooting stars exploding in the dark night,
The Roman candle, gives off a radiant light.
Bang, screech, thud and scream,
Is this part of some terrible dream?

I twirl the dazzling sparkler which gives off a bright glow,
Crackle goes the fire, as the smoke starts to blow,
Dancing flames start to rise,
As the bright orange colour hurts my eyes.

Suddenly it all starts to quieten down,
Children are going to sleep all over town.
The flickering fire decreases as the night goes on,
Ashes and embers left and all the people are gone.

Lauren Winder (Age 10)

Sleight Of Hand

'Roll up! Roll Up!' Cried the showman, the strangest sight to see,
He span around and waved his hand, beckoning to me.
'Roll up! Roll up! the quickness of the hand deceives the eye!'
But I managed to spy a movement that he planned.
He knew I saw this tricky move, and retorted with this speech;
'The quickness of the hand deceives the eye, '
And what a sight to see; this odd man speaking jovially
'Find the pretty lady!' He cried, looking shady,
'Just a pound a bet, you can win a fiver *that* you won't regret!'
He winked at me and carried on,
But he did not know I was a Magician
I palmed his illegal profit and placed it in its owner's pocket.
Hereby ends the tale,
If you see a conman, looking pale,
Just say; 'Find the pretty lady, just a pound a bet,
This is one gamble that you won't regret!'
Just say this, and looking flushed,
The card shark will say 'If I must,
Find the pretty lady, just a pound a bet
This is one gamble that you won't regret!'

Tom Wallace (Age 12)

Hunting

H unting is ok in a way
U gh! another gun's going off, I can sense it
N o no to hunting
T oo bad hunters
I say that hunting is polluted
N o no no no no no man please don't shoot!
G reat it would be (that man had to shoot)

Mark Wreford (Age 8)

Best Friends

Friends are there for you always
They are in your life forever
They stick up for you, never hurt you
Make you feel warm and happy like the sun
They feel part of your family
Everybody needs a friend I know I do

Vicky Wills (Age 11)

Black Rose

I started.
I grew open from a tiny seed,
Not knowing what I would become.
I stretched up, just like I was waking.
Then the bud came, I still didn't know.
I opened like the others
Not knowing that I was different.
They; they bore beautiful red crowns
Beautiful as they were they were cruel
They laughed. I wondered. I felt it.
Rain splashed down, cold, and smooth
Forming a puddle in front of my leaves.
I saw this beautiful transformation of the mossy ground.
Then I saw me.
I couldn't hear a thing
I couldn't taste or smell.
All I could see was the reflection,
The terrible sight of me.
Black, were my silky petals.
I stopped.

Jessica White (Age 11)

Jungle Jingle Jangle

Lions chase prey
Trees in wind sway
Birds sing and fly
Monkeys in trees high
Gorillas grooming
Bumble bees zooming
Caterpillars crawling
Ants are hauling
Dark Dingy Jungle

Snakes a slithering
Sloths a' dithering
Their homes protecting
Silently selecting
Leaves very wet
Traps being set
Hunters shooting
Animals hooting
Dark Dingy Jungle

Xav Warburton (Age 10)

Winter Time Song

Long days come
Long days go
Winter snow . . . winter slow
winter slow
winter slow
winter slow
Snow flakes falling
Foggy weather
Winter wet . . . winter cold
winter cold
winter cold
winter cold
sitting near hot fires
Short days long nights,
Winter snow flakes falling . . . winter slippery
winter slippery
winter slippery
winter slippery

Jordan Walker (Age 9)

Dear Mum . . .

We're on our way to the dreadful battle,
Shooting as we go . . .
We'll try our best going through,
The destructive foe.

We're on our way to war,
Shooting as we go . . .
People coming more and more,
Shooting as they go . . .

More and more evil foe coming to help the enemy,
Even though some of them would die.
Soldiers screaming in the battle,
Falling on the ground.
But commanders back at base,
Looking for a week spot,
While soldiers,
Shouting and screaming are
SHOT . . .

James Wiseman (Age 10)

Easter

E aster eggs gorgeous chocolate
A mazing Easter eggs
S o much chocolate
T all Easter eggs arrive
E aster treats coming up
R ip rap here comes the Easter bunny!

Jacob Woodley-Edmondson (Age 9)

Gran Can You Rap?

She rapped to the market, she rapped to the beach
Then she screamed "I wanna peach".
She rapped to the donkey, she rapped to the pig
Then she shouted "I'm wearing a wig"
"I'm the best rappin' gran the world's ever seen
I'm a tip-top tick-tock rap rap queen

Liam Willis (Age 9)

The Ballad Of Old Lucy

She was now an old girl,
A hundred years or more.
She walked around old London town,
It was a struggle I'm sure.

She felt she had been happy,
Although she was quite poor.
She found her life unbearable,
She could take no more.

So there and then she said it,
"I'll find a way somehow,"
She looked at the bogs murky water,
"I'm going to do this now!"

So then she laid down her tired body,
Her life swept away like dust.
But what do you rich folk care,
Not even you my Lord.

Matthew Ward (Age 10)

The Forest

The vast and lonely forest, black with fear
The wind howling through the trees
Looking up, at the grey and cloudy sky.
The moon glistening like a crystal,
Huge owls sitting silently in the trees
Trying to get away
I am trying to get out of this chilly and damp place.
Wondering?
Will I ever get home . . .
I sit
Slowly fall asleep . . .

Suddenly . . .
A sparkling light what can it be?
Am I dreaming?
I follow in my mind
Wondering what will be at the end
Till finally
I reach the end
And awaken.

Sarah Wood (Age 10)

A Seasonal Poem

I like the winter because
You can make snowmen

I like the spring because
The trees are green
And the birds sing

I like the summer because
I can play in the pool
And I can eat ice-cream.

The autumn is also good
Because I can kick the leaves
And have conker fights

Joshua Worby (Age 6)

Cat

Soft
Cuddly
Cute
And
Drinks
Milk

Melissa Woodcock (Age 8)

My Best Friend

I like playing with my best friend,
Because when I do the fun won't end.

My best friend sticks up for me,
And lets me go to his house for tea.

He is a great defender,
He tackles like a food blender.

Although he supports Man U,
Me and him are like piglet and pooh.

He's always wearing a smiley face,
And walking around with an untied lace.

My best friend is very kind,
His kindness sticks in my mind.

My best friend likes playing jokes,
He takes the mick out of old folks.

My best friend is very funny,
He used to have a pet bunny.

My best friend is usually cool,
But sometimes he's rather a fool.

Joshua Wilks (Age 10)

Alone

When I'm getting ready for bed
I feel very lonely
I do as my mum said
"Quickly before I become horribly stony!"

I brush my teeth
There's a transparent ghost behind me
But to my relief
It's my pet budgie flying behind me "Silly Budgie"

Then I wash my face
Is that a howling werewolf behind me?
I keep up a quick pace
I hear the drop of a tear

Isabel Williams (Age 7)

Easter

E aster
A ll eat chocolate eggs
S tuffing your face with chocolate
T reats are toppling down your neck
E aster bunny bouncing up and down
R unny chocolate and dreamy chocolate

Matthew Winn (Age 8)

What Is Red

What is red
The poppy is red when the soldiers are dead

What is blue
The sky is blue with a midnight gloom

What is white
The clouds are white in the flight

What is green
The grass is green when they are seen

What is purple
The unicorn is purple with a fur ball

What is yellow
The sun is yellow when it is shining in the meadow

What is pink
The cup is pink with a drink

What is orange
Why an orange is orange

What is gold
The stars are gold in the midnight cold

Elise Walker (Age 6)

What Is The Sun?

The sun is a shining sequin
Sparkling in the sky
It is a golden bullet
Shot into the sky

The sun is a glittering disco ball
Twirling in the air
It is a golden frisbee
Thrown into space

The sun is a yellow doughnut
Circling the earth
It is a beautiful ball
Spinning in space

Victoria White (Age 8)

The Cool Countryside

In the countryside
I can see a golden shining tractor ploughing

In the countryside
I can hear a very smooth chicken clucking

In the countryside
I can smell a lovely beautiful flower garden

In the countryside
I can touch a black fluffy sheep

In the countryside
I feel happy

Jack Williams (Age 6)

Snow

When the wind blows and it snows
It knocks down my snowman, it tingles my nose
It's really, really cold
So mum tells me to come in and do as I'm told
But I'm staying out here in the freezing weather
Whilst me and my snowman stand together
And when we feel like there's a breeze
We shiver and shiver we wobble our knees
It's now freezing cold, so I'm going inside to be warm
Cos the weather man said there will be a storm
I'm inside and I'm going to have hot chocolate in my favourite cup
Shaped like a snowman and filled with luck
So maybe next week I <u>can</u> play in the snowy storm
But for now . . . I'm lovely and warm!

Rachel Ellen Ward (Age 10)

What Is The Sun?

The sun is a golden apple
Spinning in the sky
It is a golden gem
Glistening in the sky

The sun is a shining sequin
Dazzling in the sky
It is a yellow doughnut
Spinning through the clouds

The sun is a red balloon
Dancing in the sunset with the stars
It is bobbing up and down
In the wind and the breeze

The sun is a golden face
Speaking to God and Jesus
It is a toffee apple
Flying into space

Hannah Walker (Age 7)

Before The Show

Taxis driving
Children arriving

Coats hanging
Doors slamming

Tickets tearing
Sweeties sharing

Bells ringing
Seats filling

Excitement mounting
Conductor counting

Lights dimming
Show beginning

Beth Wilson (Age 9)

My Family

In my family there are five
I'm glad we're all still alive

Tat is the name of my dad's band
He plays guitar with a rapid hand

Mum looks after the family
She is as busy as she can be

Leo is at All Saint's School
He likes to laugh and play the fool

Then there's me, Cal's the name
I want to be involved in fame

Now there's my sister, her name is Elly
All she thinks about is the telly

Including our cats Sox and Tilly
All in all it is a great family

Callum Wrest (Age 10)

Winter Wonderland

Winter come,
Winter go,
Winter cold . . . winter wet,
Winter wet,
Winter wet,
Winter wet,

Warm fires,
Keep you warm,
Nice warm . . . hot chocolate,
Hot chocolate,
Hot chocolate,
Hot chocolate,

Birds fly,
Far away,
But not . . . the robin,
The robin,
The robin,
The robin,

Shelby Ward (Age 9)

Chick

C hicks chuckle cheekily chubby chick chats
H arvey hamster hums to chick humungously
I nteresting idiot is interested in igloos
C hubby china chills out cheekily
K ing Kong kicks cats and kills kings

James Wright (Age 9)

The Hedgehog

I am the prickly fat hedgehog
Who loves to munch on the leaves
And catch worms ready to eat tomorrow
I care for my babies and go in my lair
And sleep for the winter to get up later!

Courteney Williams (Age 8)

Six Ways Of Looking At Fireworks

The fear of the fireworks
Shake your body madly

The tension is coming to you
While you wait for it to blow

The colour is fantastic like a rainbow exploding
To you as you watch

The noise is terrifying to some people
It sounds like a window smashing

The shapes are cool like stars and moons
To lots of people

The brightness is very fierce
Especially to black cats

John Whitfield (Age 9)

Two Monkeys And Nanas

Monkey Blue is going to,
Climb to the top of the Banana tree.

Monkey Blue is going to,
Climb to the top of the Banana tree.

But Monkey Red wants to go instead,
To eat the bananas on the Banana tree.

That's the case, they'll both have a race,
To get to the top of the Banana tree.

They climb up high, into the sky,
To eat the bananas on the Banana tree.

One falls down, the other falls down,
No-one gets to the top of the Banana tree.

Claire Worthington (Age 12)

A Farm Poem

"Ribit Ribit" says the frog, in the muddy sticky bog.
"Tweet Tweet" says the sparrow, sitting on a wheelbarrow.
"Baa Baa" says the sheep, eating rudely half asleep.
"Maa Maa" says the goat, with his fluffy, woolly coat.
"Oink Oink" says the pig, dancing in a silly jig.
"Honk Honk" says the goose, "My best friend is a moose".
"Eek Eek" says the mouse, "I have been running round the house."
"Woof Woof" says the dog, running through the hollow log.
"Cluck Cluck" says the hen, "I can count up to ten".
"Scuttle Scuttle" says the spider, "I want to be a bike rider".
"Snuffle Snuffle" says the hedgehog, "Who's helping that poor old frog?"
"Ribit Ribit" says the frog, free at last from that sticky old bog!

Ciara Ward (Age 8)

Alone At Christmas

The wind is blowing harsh and cold
I look at my life and how it's unfolded
And how my face and features have moulded
And as I sit alone this Christmas
What I could have done could have seen could have said

Daniel Wills (Age 14)

Horse

Hay eater
Apple muncher
Carrot cruncher
High leaper
Polo sucker

Katrina Wilson (Age 8)

The Wonder Of The Rainforest

The wonders of the Rainforest, bright and beautiful.
The trees of the Rainforest, tall and proud.
The sound of the Rainforest, calm and peaceful.
Apart from the birds noisy and loud!

The insects of the Rainforest, crawly and wriggly.
The fish of the Rainforest, slippery and slimy.
The birds of the Rainforest, colourful and peckish.
The ants of the Rainforest, hard working and tiny!

Drew Woodhouse (Age 10)

Dinosaur

D inosaurs are scary
I am afraid of dinosaurs
N ever touch a dinosaur
O h no he is going to get me!
S ome dinosaurs have horns
A Diplodocus has a long neck
U p flies Pteranodon
R un away a T-Rex is coming to get you
S cary dinosaurs!

Harvey West (Age 6)

Lonely Street

There is a little road with no-one around.
The trees are slowly waving side to side.
The grey clouds look down on the road with their
Glazed eyes, it looks like they have been hypnotised.
The cat is running around trying to look for its owner.
The leaves fall down from the trees like dancing ballerinas.
The flowers haven't been watered for a long time
Because nobody bothers to come out.
The sky is as grey as a dirty old blanket.
Nobody will every come out,
The only day I will come out is on a Sunday.

Imogen Wellsbury (Age 11)

Standing High

An icy tower standing high
The sun rises
It starts to melt
Getting smaller and smaller
Creating an icy puddle
The flame grabs hold of the wick
When it's windy
The flame continues
Until it reaches the bottom
As the flame does the smoke swirls up

Nathan Wheeler (Age 11)

Cats Eating

Cats eating
Mice squeaking
Storks squawking
Horses walking
Fish popping
Kangaroos hopping
Giraffes peeping
People sleeping
Monkeys swinging
People singing
Dogs sleeping
People speaking
Cows mooing
People shouting

Charlotte Westwood (Age 6)

I Love The Countryside

In the countryside
I can see
A cute, snowy white bunny rabbit bouncing

In the countryside
I can hear
A black and white dog barking

In the countryside
I can smell
Lots of pretty golden buttercups smiling

In the countryside
I can taste
The juicy rosy red apples swaying

Kayla Woods (Age 7)

Riddle

My first is in mouth and also in thumb,
My second in octopus but not in fish,
My third's in berry but not in cherry,
My fourth is in ice and also in rice,
My fifth is in lip but not in chip,
My last is in elephant and also in echo.

What am I?

Katie Williams (Age 12)

Fear

Running, running for my life
Like an animal in pain
Breathing, breathing like thunder
Dry, dry, dry mouth like a piece of dry soil
Heart, heart beating like an Indian drum
Then I go and hide in their room
And then I climbed out of the window
Then suddenly . . .

Flora White (Age 9)

The Countryside

In the countryside
I can see
A fish

In the countryside
I can hear
The water splashing

In the countryside
I can smell
Grass growing

In the countryside
I can touch
A red apple growing

In the countryside
I can taste
The corn blowing

In the countryside
I feel happy

Jack Watson (Age 7)

The Storm

The storm came unexpected
Even the clouds were affected
As the waves came towering
The water started showering
Suddenly the waves were crashing
The water started smashing
The boats were sinking
But then . . . there was silence all were thinking
Will it ever come again?

The storm came unexpected
Smashing, crashing all in its path
Even the stars were affected
The waves came towering
The water came showering
Over the tiny boats
The people were frowning
Frowning with horror
But then . . . there was silence all were thinking
Will it ever come again?

James Wong (Age 11)

Fear

My lips went dry, dry like the Sahara Desert
When I was running, running for my life,
This twenty five foot high monster was chasing me,
Half dinosaur, half wolf,
But all evil,
I locked myself in a cupboard
But it crashed down the door,
I found a box made of cardboard,
I shoved it over his head,
I ran to find more of them,
Then . . .

Callum Wonnacott (Age 9)

Sweets

Sweets, sweets everywhere
In the shop window
I like to glare

Chocolate buttons, strawberry laces
I can't bear it
I've got to buy some.

Chocolate pennies, gobstoppers
Disappear out of sight
I fought with all my might
But still they disappear out of sight.

Theo Woodland-Hill (Age 12)

Chocolate!!!

Chocolate cake,
Chocolate bar,
Chocolate drink,
Chocolate milkshake,
Chocolate biscuit,
Chocolate sponge,
Chocolate finger,
Chocolate ice-cream
         and
     Easter's
Chocolate bunny

Ryan Woodland (Age 10)

Spring

Spring is the day
For flowers to grow
Daffodils pop at spring
Oh the joy spring brings
The sun shines
And flowers grow on vines
The sun gives power
To make a flower
Baby lambs are born
And crops are being planted in corn
The flowers pop out of their heads
And that is a sign of spring

Miles Yeomans (Age 8)

Sweet Shop

They wait they do, the sweets
They just sit there and wait
Waiting to be eaten as treats.

Lying on the counter
Chocolates, toffee and creams
Sitting on the counter,
Screaming at you it seems.

A child eating an apple
Walks right in,
Looks at all the sweeties,
The apples in the bin.

The sweets are at the check out
Being counted one by one,
The money's handed over
Now it's all been done.

Kayleigh Wright (Age 12)

Storm

I am the storm,
Thrashing and raging,
Gargantuan!
I'm like a hungry troll,
I am the storm.

I am the wind,
Howling and swirling,
Untamed!
I'm like a macho wrestler,
I am the wind.

I am the lightening
Jabbing and stabbing,
Jagged!
I light up the midnight sky,
I am the lightning.

Laura Wheeler (Age 10)

The Day I Fell Out Of The Sky

One day I got a funny feeling, all around me my friends, brothers, sisters, aunties and uncles were all dropping out of the sky, then, oh no! I fell too on to a hard mountain tip. I trickled down the mountainside; I was parted from my family as they had frozen solid. I met many new people as I flew farther and farther downthe river, racing and chasing with my new friend, the Kingfisher. Then he flew away . . . Suddenly, I'm trapped in a reservoir but the gulls were handling it nicely, flying overhead like free spirits and I thought to myself, "I wish I could fly". Then a sign of movement, the gates had opened and we were off yet again. In the distance I spy a fishing boat and set off in hot pursuit. "Finally" I thought "The sea at last", I was there. I had made it unscathed . . .

But wait, I'm being hoisted into the air ready to go round again.

Jordan Wilson (Age 10)

The Man We Will Wait For

As we lay in our beds all snuggled up tight
We imagine in our heads lots of houses with lights
And presents and food all good things they are
But St. Nicholas has come very far
To cause all this joy and laughter and fun
That very long journey all this way he has come

Ellena Wilson (Age 9)

Chocolate

Chocolate in the morning
Chocolate at night
Chocolate can be dark
Chocolate can be white
Chocolate in a wrapper
Chocolate by itself,
Chocolate wrapper blue and yellow too,
Yet the colour of the wrapper does not really matter
I love chocolate
Fills the hole
I love chocolate
Fills you up if you're in luck

Rebecca Wheeler (Age 11)

Environment

The fluffy white clouds walk on the air gracefully,
The sun recognises all of Earth passing by,
The star reads a story of a beautiful world below,
The rock listens to the magnificent sea as the waves splash,
And the shell speaks to me of the great flowing river,
The sea shell swims to the bottom of the ocean,
The moon lights up the sky above

Melissa Wood (Age 11)

Brazil

B ig beautiful costumes!
R ace you to the rainforest!
A lovely carnival!
Z og zog is a cute Brazilian monkey!
I love Brazil!
L ungs of our earth!

Poppy Wilson (Age 7)

Car Kenning

Puddle sprayer
Windscreen wiper
Horn beeper
Ride giver
Bug squasher
Light flasher
Road clogger
Shopping carrier
Tyre screecher
Traffic jammer
Smog maker
City noiser
Hedgehog flattener

Jamie Wassell (Age 9)

Tracy Beaker

Tracy Beaker is sometimes nice
She hates mice
She also hates Justine Littlewood
She lives in a care home
She loves the food
She has a mood
She is my favourite character
I wish to meet her

Laura Wingrove (Age 9)

Spring

Beautiful birds singing sweetly,
Flower buds emerging neatly,
Amazing animals being born,
Woolly hats no longer worn,
Foals cantering cheerfully,
Cows grazing merrily,
Magnificent warmth from the sun,
Spring time has begun.

Alyesha Wainwright (Age 11)

Autumn

In Autumn it is
Cold and the birds
Fly south squirrels are
Loading up for winter I
Can feel the crunchy leaves
Under my feet the leaves
Are turning red autumn
Leaves they lie on
The Autumn
Path

Mikala Williams (Age 9)

The Sea The Sea The Ocean Sea

The ocean sea is crashing and bashing
The sea the sea
The ocean sea is lovely as a blue butterfly
The sea the sea
The ocean sea
The ocean sea is aggressive and oppressive
The sea the sea
The ocean is splashing with the sun
The sea the sea
The ocean sea

Nicole White (Age 9)

Volcano

The panda is waking with powerful force,
The scarlet red lava is spraying in the air,
The panda kicks the rocks then the volcano erupts,
The panda
Goes to sleep
And settles in his
Flower bed.

Megan Whiting (Age 9)

Snow

I can see snow around me, everything's peaceful
All around me just birds and cars
The white sky around me
The birds, the trees, the wind.
I can taste the water, I can taste the snow
I can feel the cold snow on my back
I can feel the wind rushing through my hair
I can smell the clear outside smell of trees
This is what you get when it snows

Nicole Weston (Age 10)

Thunder!

A horse pounding its hooves on the rocky cliffs
An angry rhino rampaging into the city
A dark magician causing chaos
A giant stomping about
Hits the ground like a screeching baby
A teacher shouting at a student
Getting angrier as he walks the earth
Lurking, waiting, watching, laughing
Suddenly . . .
THUNDER!

Sa'ad Wajih-Ahmed (Age 11)

The Girl Who Never Brushed Her Teeth

There once was a girl who never brushed her teeth
And her breath smelt horrible
Her name was Sheila Robinson
She always got picked on in class
When she gets angry she always breaks the glass

When she talks they always covered their mouths and ran away
She got really mad and decided to tell the class
She needed to change her ways

She got right home and brushed her teeth and bit her lip
And brushed her teeth night and morning
Her bad breath went and she had friends
And they called her Sheila Robinson instead of mean names

Nicole Wenham (Age 10)

234

Four O'Clock Friday

On Monday everybody was making a party for me
On Tuesday I managed to get my spellings right
On Wednesday I got my maths right
On thursday I managed to keep the ball in the ring
On Friday I managed not to be late
On Saturday I went to the park to play with my friends
And we played tag, hide and seek, limbo, football, duck, duck goose.

Jasmin Walter (Age 9)

Summer Days

Flowers settle
Leaves grow
Butterflies flutter
Boats row

Sheep are shaved
Scorching sun
Sand boiling
Having fun

Chloe Williams (Age 9)

Dance Diva

Dancing around
Singing into your hairbrush
You're a total diva
Even though nobody knows it

Turn the stereo up
Take no notice of the next door neighbours
You're a total diva
Even though nobody knows it

Gemmie Williams (Age 13)

Gran Can You Rap?

She rapped to the boat she rapped to the car,
She rapped to the chicken "WOW" that's far,
She rapped past the town she rapped past the street
She said to little boy "Boy I'm neat",
"I'm the best rapping Gran this world's ever seen"
I'm a hip, hop, tip, tap, rap, rap Queen . . . YO YO YOO.

Curtis Whittle (Age 9)

Snakes

Snakes are fun,
Snakes are slimy,
Snakes are slithery,
Snakes are slippery
Snakes are scary

Harrison Washington (Age 6)

The Last Firework

Crashing and shimmering
the fireworks startle the crowd.
Sizzling and fizzing the long fuses are lit,
caboom! The fireworks dart into the air
and colours swell into the night sky.
Whistling and screaming
the minute white lights create a fountain of glory.
Thud, there's a silence
as the sound of the gigantic fireworks frantically spark towards you.
There's a massive clash in the air around you
that forces the crowd to clap and cheer.
It was the last firework, beautiful, exciting, amazing

Max Andrew Willis (Age 11)

Pony

Tail swisher
Apple muncher
Ground scratcher
Loud neigher
Foot stamper

Georgina Yallop (Age 8)

Breezy

Breezy, breezy it is so breezy
Rich and rare and winter cold
Ending now hooray, oh no it's coming back
Every creature wakes from its sleep
Zipping breeze of cold air
Yawning people in their cosy beds

Korin Zegze (Age 8)

Frogs

Frogs lay frogs spawn in spring
Baby tadpoles hatch out of the frogs spawn
Baby tadpoles grow legs and turn into frogs
They live in a pond
They jump in a pond
They jump in a shining pond

Jack White (Age 7)

The Night

The night train is chugging swiftly along
Tracks are singing a squeaky song
The smoke shoveling over her shoulder
Like a fairy dragon as it gets colder
Red and black shining in the night sky
Sparks are flying ever so high
The smoke shoveling over her shoulder
Like a fairy dragon as it gets colder

Emily-Jane Webb (Age 9)

People In Distress

Look at the man, sitting there on the street
Cup in hand, paper on feet

Look at that girl, lying there on her side
Never stirs, never cares for what she might find

Look at that boy, standing there in the queue
Mother died, father died, might die too

Look at those kids, running there on their own
Kicking large stones, why are they alone?

Look at that woman crying there in her grief
Daughter lying on the street, dead, a damaged leaf

Look at those bodies, lying there on the fire,
Burning, burning, on a funeral pyre

Look at that teacher, swimming there in her worries,
Kids have gone, school has finished, screaming bedtime stories

Look at that parent, collapsed on the cart,
Buy that, buy this! Life ends - a stopped heart

Look at that man, sitting there on the street
Cup in hand, paper on feet . . . . . .

Jamie Yates (Age 12)

Spring Means

Spring means Easter bunnies bouncing in the fields
Spring means sunshine, hot and bright
Spring means daisies popping out of the ground
Spring means baby chicks hatching and lambs squeezing to get out
Spring means wrapped up eggs in the garden
Spring means leaves growing on the trees

Katrina Woodbridge (Age 8)

Brazil

B rilliant scenes
R onaldinho scores
A mazon river flows!
Z illions of brilliant birds!
I nteresting place
L oads of trees!

Gregory Whyley (Age 8)

Silence

No sound, no noise.
I stand in the almost dead room
The silence is so thick I can almost feel it
What is silence?
Where has the power of language gone?
The air vibrates but still no sound
Echoes of past music
Play in my head
Silence almost deafens me
Tunes that once floated in the air
Have now vanished, like a snowflake melting.

Toby Young (Age 11)

Spring

Spring spring
Wonderful spring
When blossom and green leaves
Whish in the wind
And daffodils grow
And bumble bees wake up
And start making honey
Here comes the Easter bunny!!

Matthew Young (Age 8)

Music Of The Spheres

The peaceful music is calming me down,
It comes from the peaceful stars
The wars have stopped as wonderful as a victory

It comes from the spheres is so joyful
What a wonderful song
It is as musical as a violin

Arman Zand (Age 9)

Summer Time

Flowers growing
Birds singing happily
Children splashing in the water
Tweet tweet

Shawna Young (Age 9)

Animal Poem

Have you ever had a centipede wriggling in your bed?
I had one once and it reached my head.
Have you ever had a hippo swimming in your sink?
I had one once and it was dressed in pink.
Have you ever seen a turtle at the tip?
I did once and it was in the skip

Thomas Young (Age 7)

Easter

E ggs are laid
A lamb is born
S eeds are grown
T rees grow buds
E ggs are stuffed in mouths
R abbits run

Tom Whatmough (Age 7)

BIOGRAPHIES
OF
POETS

ADEY, CHARLIE: [b] 02/10/93; Redditch; [home] Worcester, Worcestershire; [p] Samantha & Howard; [brother] Lewis; [sister] I don't have a sister but my best friend Rosie is like a sister to me!; [school] Blessed Edward Oldcorne Catholic College; [fav sub] English; [hobbies] Running, Shopping, Listening to music, & Hanging out with friends; [ambition] To become an Archaeologist;

AHMED-SAKHI, RAYA-TUL-ISLAM: [b] 14/07/96 London; [home] Wimbledon; [p] Saghir Ahmed & Seham Kaid; [brothers] Ibrahim, Sulaiman, Yusif & Muhammad; [school] Burlington Junior; [hobbies] Football, Reading & Sports; [pets] Rabbit; [ambition] To become a Doctor;

ALDRED, SUMMER: [b] 14/07/95 Morden; [home] Morden, Surrey; [p] Suzanne & Mark; [sisters] Layla & Bonnie; [school] Abbotsbury Primary; [fav sub] Science; [hobbies] Music, Dancing & Cycling; [pets] Dog (Beau); [ambition] To be famous;

ALLAN, ELLIS: [b] 11/05/98 Barnet; [home] St Albans, Herts; [p] Phil & Mandi; [sister] Elodie; [school] Cuningham Hill; [fav sub] History; [hobbies] Football, Football, Football!; [ambition] To play football for England;

ALLEN, HOLLY: [b] 09/02/98 Salisbury; [home] Salisbury, Wiltshire; [p] Donna & Lee; [brother] Jake; [sister] Alice; [school] Sarum St Pauls; [fav sub] English; [hobbies] Dancing & Reading; [pets] Rat (Deliah) [ambition] To become a Dancer;

ALLISON MATTHEW: [b] 20/09/95 Stockport; [home] Whaley, High Peak; [p] Julie Bridge & Mark Allison; [school] Stockport Grammar; [fav sub] Art & Design Technology; [hobbies] Cricket, Cycling & DIY; [pets] 2 Cats (Tommy & Tilly); [ambition] To become a Car Designer;

ALPERN, JOANNA: [b] 11/01/92; [p] Diane Reyniers & Steve Alpern; [school] City of London School for Girls; [hobbies] Writing, climbing trees & seeing friends; [pets] Ted (a big rabbit);

ANTONIOU, JAMES: [b] 26/07/97 Redhill; [home] Merstham, Surrey; [p] Mother - Stephanie (deceased) Grandparents-Tony & Kate Antoniou; [school] Nutfield C of E; [fav sub] History; [hobbies] Acting; [pets] Cats (Herbie & Ruby); [ambition] To become a famous and successful Actor;

ARNOLD, CALLUM: [home] Hoddesdon, Herts; [school] Cranbourne Primary; [fav sub] Maths; [hobbies] Playing Guitar & Golf; [pets] Rabbit (Rocky); [ambitions] To be a Rock Star or a Firefighter;

ARTERTON, WILLIAM [b] 12/02/93 London; [home] Oxted, Surrey; [p] Lucy & Alex; [brothers] Benedict & Oliver; [school] Hazelwood School; [fav sub] English; [hobbies] Drawing & Painting; [pets] 1 Cat & 2 Guinea Pigs; [ambitions] To do something involving Art or to be an Author;

AULAKH, JAI-PUNEET: [b] 06/12/93 Amsterdam; [home] Walsall; [p] Sukhdev & Balbir; [brother] Joban; [sister] Tarran; [school] Joseph Leckie Community Technical College; [fav sub] English, Maths, Science & Art; [hobbies] Reading, Art, Travel & Computing; [ambition] To become a Visual Effects Supervisor;

BABAI, MATTHEW: [b] 24/12/93 Edgware; [home] Oxted, Surrey; [school] Hazelwood School; [fav sub] Maths; [hobbies] All Sports, especially Sailing; [pets] Goldfish (Fred); [ambition] To become a Doctor;

BACKHOUSE, DOMINIQUE: [b] 05/10/96 Hemel Hempstead; [home] Hemel Hempstead, Herts; [p] Paul & Deborah; [brothers] Paul, Jason & Ryan; [sisters] Nadine & Natalie; [school] Aycliffe Primary; [fav sub] P.E. or Art; [hobbies] Dancing & Swimming; [ambitions] To become an Actress, Girl Footballer, Dancer or Singer;

BAGGOTT, JORDAN: [b] 09/03/97 Plymouth; [home] Ivybridge, Devon; [p] Stephanie & Jamie; [sister] Angel; [school] Stowford Primary; [fav sub] Handwriting; [hobbies] Football & Skateboarding; [pets] Dog (Ellie); [ambitions] To be a professional Skateboarder or Footballer;

BAICHOO-HOSKINS, LAUREN: [b] 27/06/97 Tooting; [home] Colliers Wood, London; [p] Leah Baichoo & Gerald Hoskins; [sister] Alyssia; [school] Benedict School; [fav sub] Art; [hobbies] Arsenal F.C.; [pets] Fish (Kisha & Bart); [ambitions] To be an Artist and Poet;

BAILEY, BROOKE: [b] 03/01/99 Greenwich; [home] New Eltham, London; [p] Leigh Bailey & Robert Clarke; [brother] Ben; [school] Montbelle; [fav sub] Mathematics; [hobbies] Brownies & Drawing; [pets] Dog (Lillabelle) [ambition] To become a famous Pop Star;

BAINBRIDGE, REBECCA: [b] 10/04/06 St Albans; [home] St Albans, Herts; [p] Rachel & Phillip; [brother] Luke; [school] Cunningham Hill Junior; [fav sub] Art; [hobbies] Horse Riding, Music & Sport; [pets] None, but would love lots; [ambitions] To be a Poet, Musician, Artist, Dancer & Actor;

BAMFORTH, THOMAS: [b] 12/01/97 Huddersfield; [home] Huddersfield, W. Yorkshire; [p] Chris & Debbie; [school] St Patrick's Primary; [fav sub] Numeracy; [hobbies] Guitar, Cubs & Football; [pets] 3 Cats, 2 Rabbits & 2 Guinea Pigs; [ambition] To never be bullied again;

BANKS, PAIGE: [b] 28/06/96; [home] New Eltham, London; [p] Terry & Deborah; [brother] Scott; [sisters] Jessie & Poppy; [school] Montbelle Primary; [fav sub] Art; [hobbies] Gymnastics; [pets] 2 Cats, Dog & Hamster;

BARBER, JACK: [b] 17/08/96 Kingston upon Hull; [home] Beverley, E. Yorkshire; [p] David & Stephanie; [sisters] Rachael & Jennifer; [school] Molescroft Primary; [fav sub] Art; [hobbies] Basketball & Tennis; [pets] Cat (Lucky), 3 Degus; [ambition] To be a professional Tennis Player;

BARBER, TAMSIN ALEYSHA: [b] 03/08/93 Ascot; [home] Godstone, Surrey; [p] Liz & Jeff; [school] Hazelwood School; [fav sub] Sport; [hobbies] Dance, Swimming, Tennis, U13 England Rounders; [ambition] To compete in the 2012 London Olympics in the Heptahlon [footnote] Tamsin has dyslexic tendencies and English has not been an easy subject for her. She would like a special mention for Mr Nick Kibblewhite, Head of English at Hazelwood, for his expert tutelage which has greatly inspired her;

BARNES, NIKITA: [b] 04/09/96 Gorleston; [home] Corton, Lowestoft; [p] Vicky & Bob; [brother] James; [sisters] Kirsty & Kate; [school] Corton Primary; [hobbies] Dancing, Singing & Brownies; [pets] 2 Dogs, 1 Cat;

BEDFORD, KIERAN G: [b] 07/07/95 Bishop Auckland; [home] Coundon, Durham; [p] Michelle & Andrew; [sister] Yasmin; [school] Coundon Primary; [fav sub] P.E. & Science; [hobbies] Football & Cricket; [pets] 2 Dogs, 2 Goldfish; [ambition] To be a professional Footballer;

BEKOE, RAY: [b] 06/01/96 Newham; [home] Canning Town, Newham; [p] Linda Harris; [brother] Kevin; [school] St Andrew's Primary; [fav sub] Maths; [hobbies] Football & Basketball; [pets] Fish; [ambitions] To become a Judge, Doctor or Basketball player;

BENJAMIN, SOPHIE: [b] 15/02/95 Watford; [home] Abbots Langley, Herts; [p] Alison & Alan; [brother] Lewis; [school] Abbots Langley; [fav sub] Art; [hobbies] Reading & Swimming; [pets] 2 Guinea Pigs (Ben & Hunny); [ambition] To go on Safari in Africa;

BENTLEY, AMY: [b] 11/03/97 Dewsbury; [home] Gomersal, West Yorkshire; [p] Jadine & David; [sister] Charlotte; [school] Gomersal First School; [hobbies] Ballroom & Latin Dancing, Learning the Piano, Puzzle Books & Brownies; [pets] Cat (Tabatha);

BERESFORD, SOPHIE: [b] 07/05/98; [home] Huddersfield, W. Yorkshire; [p] Alison & Patrick; [sisters] Molly, Lucy & Amy (Triplets) [school] St Patrick's Catholic School; [fav sub] Reading; [hobbies] Karate, Riding my Motorbike; [pets] Charlie, Rosie, Spike, Chloe & Poppy; [ambition] To be Famous;

BERRYMAN, SAMUEL: [b] 01/04/99 Bradford; [home] Wrose, W. Yorkshire; [p] Joanne & Chris; [brothers] Oliver & Rhys; [school] Low Ash Primary; [fav sub] Numeracy; [hobbies] Football & Swimming; [pets] Fish; [ambition] To be a professional Footballer;

BITTU, JITHIN JEO: [b] 24/04/94 Calicut, India; [home] Thiruva Mbady; [p] Joseph Thayyil & Marina Bittu; [brother] Joel; [school] Blessed Edward Old Corn Catholic College; [fav sub] Mathematics; [hobbies] Cricket, Hockey & Reading; [pets] Dog; [ambition] To become a Scientist;

BLAKE, ANNA: [b] 03/05/99; [home] Beverley, East Yorks.; [p] James & Julie; [brother] Matthew; [school] Molescroft Primary; [fav sub] Art & Numeracy; [hobbies] Gymnastics, Swimming & Reading; [ambition] To be a Teacher like Miss Steel at Molescroft;

BLAKE, JOSHUA: [b] 15/07/93 Bury St Edmunds; [home] Kettlebaston, Suffolk; [p] Louise & James; [sister] Imogen; [school] St Louis R,C. Middle School; [fav sub] Design/Technology; [hobbies] Watching Ipswich Town F.C. & Playing Table Tennis; [pets] Dogs (Barney & Daisy); [ambition] To become a Marine Biologist;

BLAKE SAM: [b] 18/10/97 Salsbury; [home] Salisbury, Wiltshire; [p] Stu & Karen; [sisters] Lucy & Jodie; [school] Sarum St Pauls; [fav sub] Art; [hobbies] Football; [pets] Dog (Charlie); [ambition] To be a Footballer;

BLAYMIRE, HAILEY: [b] 24/10/96 Leeds; [p] Michelle; [brother] Ashley; [school] Newhall Park Primary; [fav sub] Art; [hobbies] Drawing, Making things & Reading; [pets] Fish; [ambition] To become a Doctor;

BOHANA, PHOEBE: [b] 07/01/00 Bath; [home] Westbury, Wiltshire; [p] Lynn & Anthony; [brother] Connor; [school] Westbury Leigh C of E School; [fav sub] English; [hobbies] Ballet, Swimming & French; [pets] Cat (Cuddles) & 3 Goldfish; [ambition] To be an Author and to be famous;

BONDATTI, DANIEL: [b] 15/02/96 St Margaret's Bay; [home] St Margaret's Bay, Kent; [p] Daniela & Paul; [brothers] Joseph & Max; [school] Northbourne Park School; [fav sub] Sport; [hobbies] Writing Stories & Sport; [pets] Yorkshire Terrier (Poppy); [ambition] To be a professional Tennis Player;

BOWDEN, JESSICA: [b] 19/12/96 Bury St Edmunds; [home] Thurston, Suffolk; [p] Andrew & Tracy; [sister] Emily; [school] Hardwick Primary; [fav sub] English; [hobbies] Gymnastics & Drama; [pets] Cats (Tom & Barbara); [ambition] To be in the Olympics;

BOWMAN, ABIGAIL: [b] 24/06/2000 Norwich; [home] Norwich, Norfolk; [p] Paula Ratcliffe & Stephen Bowman; [brother] Ryan Guild; [sister] Ellen Guild; [school] Nightingale First; [fav sub] Art & Crafts; [hobbies] Dogs & Drawing; [pets] All Sorts (17 in total); [ambition] To be a Vet;

BOWMAN, JAKE: [b] 29/04/97 Oxford; [home] Grove, Oxfordshire; [p] Mark & Jayne; [brother] Harry & Archie; [sister]

Phoebe; [school] Millbrook Primary; [fav sub] Art; [hobbies] Swimming & Running; [ambition] To become an Artist;

BRAMWELL, CHLOE: [b] 15/01/95 Leamington Spa; [home] Berkswell, West Mids; [p] Catherine & Martin; [brothers] Kieran, Charlie & Archie; [school] Abbotsford; [fav sub] English, Drama & History; [hobbies] Horse Riding, Acting & Singing; [pets] German Shepherd (Tex); [ambition] To become a best-selling Author;

BRENNAN, JAMES LEE: [b] 09/06/98 Beverley; [home] Molescroft, Humberside; [p] Andrea & Lee; [sister] Katy; [school] Molescroft Primary; [fav sub] Art; [hobbies] Caravanning; [pets] Dogs (Barney, Lucy & Ellie); [ambition] To be a Policeman;

BRIERLEY, ALEXANDRIA: [b] 05/06/98 Durham; [home] Stanley, Durham; [p] Joanne; [school] Tanfield Lea Juniors; [fav sub] Literacy; [hobbies] Writing Poetry & Art; [pets] Dog (Lucky); [ambition] To be a Writer;

BRIGGS, JOSHUA KEITH WAYNE: [b] 06/09/95 Bradford; [home] Bradford, W. Yorkshire; [p] Victoria Briggs & Andrew Rawson; [school] St Columbas; [fav sub] Maths, Literacy & Science; [hobbies] Growing Plants;

BRISTOW, LIAM: [b] 17/11/94 London; [home] South Nutfield, Surrey; [p] Jess & Pat; [brother] Robert; [sisters] Lucy & Maddy; [school] Nutfield Church Primary; [fav sub] Design & Technology; [hobbies] Cricket, Judo, Reading & Puzzles; [ambition] To travel the world and do 'Wheelies' on my bike;

BROOKES, SCOTT: [b] 13/10/98 Manchester; [home] Prestwich, Manchester; [p] Paul & Victoria; [brothers] Michael & (twin brother) David; [school] St Margaret's C.E. Primary; [fav sub] Maths; [hobbies] Playstation 2 & Computers; [ambition] To become a Teacher;

BROUWER, OLLIE: [b] 10/12/96 St Albans; [home] St Albans, Herts; [p] Lucy & Joop; [brother] Fabian; [sisters] Elsa & Freya; [school] Cunningham Hill Junior; [fav sub] Geography & Science; [hobbies] Playing the Piano & Celo, Singing & Playing Tennis; [ambitions] To become an Archeologist or Animal Conservationist;

BROWN, CONNOR TOM: [b] 09/07/96 Leeds; [home] Beverley, East Yorks; [p] Jane & Michael; [brother] Tim; [sister] Emma; [school] Molescroft; [fav sub] History; [hobbies] Football & Reading; [pets] Dogs, Cat, Rabbits & Guinea Pigs; [ambitions] To be a Master

Carpenter and explore the world;

BUCKINGHAM, ABIGAIL ROSE: [b] 23/12/94 Watford; [home] Abbots Langley; [p] Gill & Steve; [sisters] Imi & Ashleigh; [school] Abbots Langley; [fav sub] Design & Technology; [hobbies] Swimming & Netball; [pets] Cat (Snuggles); [ambition] To become a Vet;

BURKE, REBECCA ELAINE: [b] 14/04/96 Cardiff; [home] Porteskewett, Monmouthshire; [p] Paul & Andrea; [sister] Natalie; [school] Archbishop Rowan Williams Church in Wales Primary; [fav sub] Literacy, History & Art; [hobbies] Swimming, Cycling & Netball; [pets] Guinea Pig (Pippin), Goldfish (Nemo); [ambitions] To be an Author, Illustrator & Athlete;

BURRIDGE, TAYLOR: [b] 02/03/97 Marlborough; [home] Marlborough, Wiltshire; [p] Becky & Colin; [school] St Peters Junior; [fav sub] Science; [hobbies] Swimming & Playstation; [pets] Dog (Holly) & Cat (Millie); [ambition] To become a Policewoman;

BURTON, JASMINE: [b] 21/05/95 Bury; [home] Radcliffe, Bury; [p] Julie & Brian; [school] St Andrews; [fav sub] Maths; [hobbies] Football; [ambition] To be a Dancer;

BUTLER, SOPHIE: [b] 11/11/93 Ipswich; [home] Bressingham, Norfolk; [p] Dawn & Steven; [brother] Lee (10); [sister] Kelly (5); [school] Diss High School; [fav sub] P.E.; [hobbies] Playing Rugby & Dancing; [pets] Dog (Rosie) & Cat (Puss Puss);[ambition] To be a Policewoman or an Actor;

BYNON, NAOMI: [b] 09/02/2000 Bury; [home] Radcliffe, Manchester; [p] Andrew & Lynn; [brother] Joel; [school] St Andrew's C.E. Primary; [fav sub] Art; [hobbies] Painting; [pets] Rabbit (Snuggles); [ambition] To be a Singer or an Artist;

CAIN, NATALIE ROCHELLE: [b] 24/11/96 Aberdeen; [home] Hemel Hempstead, Herts; [p] Tracey & Sylvan; [brother] Daniel; [school] Aycliffe Drive Primary; [fav sub] English & Poetry; [hobbies] Majorettes, Netball & Writing poems; [pets] Rabbits (Emily & Deffy); [ambition] To be a Poet and Author;

CALDICOTT, DANIEL: [b] 10/09/96 Oxford; [home] Grove, Oxon; [p] Ian & Sheila; [school] Millbrook Primary; [fav sub] Art; [hobbies] Football; [ambitions] To be a professional Footballer or design Playstation games;

CALVER, MAXIM HARRY: [b] 22/12/99 Gt. Yarmouth; [home]

Gorleston, Norfolk; [p] Ian & Stella; [sister] Evie; [school] Corton Primary; [fav sub] Literacy; [hobbies] Football & Cello; [ambition] To play football for Norwich;

CANNON, SOPHIE: [b] 19/03/97; [home] Wantage, Oxfordshire; [p] Lee & Louise; [brother] Callum; [school] Millbrook Primary; [fav sub] Literacy; [hobbies] Horse Riding & Football; [pets] Birds, Cat, Fish & Hamster; [ambition] To do well at school so that I can get a good job;

CARLESS, TOBY: [b] 21/01/98 Worcester; [home] Worcester, Worcs; [p] Maurice & Sally; [brother] Jack; [school] Whittington C.E. Primary; [fav sub] History; [hobbies] Swimming & Tennis; [pets] Cats (Ronnie, Daphne & Rosie); [ambitions] To become a Vet or a Swimming Instructor;

CARPENTER, DAN: [b] 15/03/93 Basingstoke; [home] Basingstoke, Hampshire; [p] Richard & Susie; [brothers] Tom, Adam & Simon; [school] Brighton Hill Community College; [fav sub] English; [hobbies] Golf, Swimming & Football; [pets] Dog (Harry); [ambition] To be a Pilot;

CARTER, BILLY: [b] 05/08/98 Yeovil; [home] Crewkerne, Somerset; [p] Lisa & Danny; [brother] Mitchell; [sister] Kaitlyn; [school] West Coker Primary; [hobbies] All Sports & Keyboard; [pets] German Shepherds (Cori & Miss C); [ambition] To make lots of money;

CHANDLER, WILLIAM: [b] 19/02/96 Bath; [home] Stoney Stratton, Somerset; [p] Sally & Gerry; [brother] Jack; [sisters] Kate & Lucy; [school] Upton Noble C of E Primary; [fav sub] History; [hobbies] Playing Rugby & Cricket; [pets] 5 Guinea Pigs; [ambitions] To work on a Farm and play Rugby;

CHILDS, LAURENCE: [b] 29/12/96 Belfast; [home] Huddersfield, W. Yorkshire; [p] Roger & Alice; [sisters] Annie & Grace; [school] St Patrick's Primary; [fav sub] Writing Stories & Poetry; [hobbies] Reading and watching Wildlife; [pets] Not allowed; [ambitions] To protect animals and plants and make the world a better place;

CHIPPENDALE, CHARLOTTE: [b] 16/10/97 Bradford; [home] Bradford, West Yorks; [p] Carol & Darron; [school] St Columbas Primary; [fav sub] Numeracy; [hobbies] Reading, Writing & Swimming; [pets] Chickens, Dogs, Guinea Pigs, Fish & Pigeons; [ambitions] To become a Vet, Dog Groomer or Hairdresser;

CHRISTIAN, BRANDON ALEXANDER: [b] 16/04/97 Frimley; [home] Farnham, Surrey; [p] Julie & Graham; [brother] Kieran; [sisters] Lily & Lauren-Elissa; [school] Hale Primary; [fav sub] Maths; [hobbies] Football, Golf & Cubs; [pets] Cat (Pepsi); [ambition] To become a Football Referee;

CHU, ZOE: [b] 25/11/95 Bramhall; [brother] Daniel; [sister] Rachel; [school] Stockport Grammar Junior; [fav sub] P.E. [hobbies] Sport, Climbing & Helping animals; [pets] Rabbit (Patchey); [ambition] To teach climbing;

CLARK, REBECCA: [b] 28/10/96 Frimley; [home] Farnham, Surrey; [p] Lesley Blaker & Stewart Clark; [brothers] Daniel, Chris, Alex, Olly, Josh, Harry, Jamie, Jack; [sisters] Laura; [school] Hale School; [fav sub] Art; [hobbies] Dancing & Swimming; [pets] 2 Dogs, Rabbit, Chickens, Doves, Pigeons, Hamster & Fish; [ambitions] To be a conservationist and to write more poems;

CLARK, TROY: [b] 21/05/94 Stoke Mandeville; [home] High Wycombe, Bucks; [p] Helen Clark; [school] Lord Williams's School; [fav sub] P.E. [hobbies] Football, Cricket & other Sports; [pets] Hamster (Scampers); [ambition] To be a professional Footballer;

CLARKE, KATE: [b] 11/02/92 Fareham; [home] Fareham, Hampshire; [p] Karey & Dale' [brother] Mike; [school] Henry Cort Community College; [fav sub] Drama, P.E. & History; [hobbies] Swimming & Music; [pets] Dog (Max); [ambitions] Undecided;

CLARSON, TYNE-LEXY: [b] 02/02/97 Cannock; [home] Wedges Mills, Cannock; [p] T. Clarson; [school] St. Dominic's; [fav sub] Art, Drama & Maths; [hobbies] Drama, Dancing & Riding; [pets] Toy Poodle (Tilly); [ambition] To be an Artist;

COATES, MATTHEW: [b] 06/11/95 Chesterfield; [p] Sheena & Philip; [brother] Steven Lee; [school] Brimington Junior; [fav sub] P.E. [hobbies] Football, Table Tennis; [pets] Dogs (Suckie Mae & Braidy); [ambition] To run my own business;

CODD, OLIVIA: [b] 12/03/93; [home] Limpsfield, Surrey; [p] Anne & David; [brother] Nick; [school] Hazelwood; [fav sub] English; [hobbies] Dancing, Swimming, Shopping & Seeing my friends; [pets] Cat (Tilly); [ambition] To become an Actress;

COCHRANE, AMBER: [b] 07/06/96 Sidcup; [home] Sidcup, Kent; [p] Sharon

& Peter; [brother] Sonny; [sister] Sienna; [school] Montbelle; [fav sub] English; [hobbies] Swimming & Dancing; [pets] Dog (Scruffy); [ambition] To own a beach house in the sun!

COCKS, VICTORIA: [b] 21/05/97 Trowbridge; [home] Westbury, Wilts; [p] Andy & Alex; [brother] Sam; [school] Westbury Leigh Primary; [fav sub] Art; [hobbies] Gymnastics & Horse Riding; [pets] 4 Rabbits, 2 Hamsters, 1 Cat & Fish; [ambitions] To be a famous Jockey and Gymnast;

COLBOURNE, JAMES: [b] 09/10/95 Walsall; [brothers] Pace, Kai & William; [sister] Lizzy; [school] County Bridge Primary; [fav sub] Art; [hobbies] Wrestling & Rock'n'Roll; [ambition] To be a Spy - preferably in MI5/6!

COLE, PHOEBE: [b] 23/11/99; [home] Westbury, Wilts; [p] Shannon & Jason; [brother] Charlie; [school] Westbury Leigh C of E; [fav sub] D.T.; [hobbies] Writing & chatting; [ambition] To become a Vet;

COLLINS, BETHANY: [b] 26/06/98 Beverley; [home] Beverley, East Yorks.; [p] Angela & Ian; [brother] Ben; [sister] Rebecca; [school] Molescroft; [hobbies] Horse Riding, Running & Swimming; [pets] Cat (Sammy), Rabbit (Binky), Hamster (Rufus);

COLLINS, DANIEL: [b] 13/10/93; [home] Chinnor, Oxfordshire; [p] Debbie Lovell; [sister] Stacey; [school] Lord Williams's Lower School; [fav sub] P.E.; [hobbies] Football, Cricket; [pets] Hamster (Stan); [ambitions] To be a Rally Driver or Footballer;

COLLYER, DANIEL MARK: [b] 19/10/95 Salisbury; [home] Westbury, Wilts; [p] Andrew & Denise; [brothers] Justin & Christopher; [sisters] Lisa, Claire & Nicole; [school] Westbury Leigh; [fav sub] Maths; [hobbies] Football; [pets] Dog (Dexter); [ambition] To join the Police Force;

COOPER, FREYA: [b] 14/11/99 Huntingdon; [home] Dolton, Devon; [brothers] Zachary & Sabian; [school] Dolton Primary; [fav sub] Reading; [hobbies] Baton Twirling & Swimming; [pets] Dog (Murphy), Pony (Pepper); [ambitions] To become a Doctor or a Teacher;

COOPER, IMOGEN ROSE: [b] 29/06/99 Kingston-upon-Thames; [home] Thames Ditton, Surrey; [p] Clare & Antony; [sister] Felicity; [school] Maple Infants; [fav sub] Art & Literacy; [hobbies] Ballet, Dancing & Art; [pets] Not yet!; [ambitions] To become a Zoo

Keeper or a Dancer;

CORDING, NATALIE JADE: [b] 24/11/97 Cottingham; [home] Molescroft, East Yorkshire; [p] Samantha & Ross; [brothers] Jamie & Luke; [school] Molescroft Primary; [fav sub] Music; [hobbies] Dancing & Swimming; [pets] Dog (Jess), Fish (Burt & Bob); [ambition] To become a Teacher;

CORNELLY, TOMÁS: [b] 01/11/96 Huddersfield; [home] Huddersfield, West Yorkshire; [p] Kevin & Jo-Ann; [brother] Niall; [sisters] Domonique, Leoni, Niamh & Nuala; [school] St Patrick's Catholic School; [fav sub] P.E.; [hobbies] Drawing & Colouring; [ambitions] To be an Artist or a Teacher;

CORRY-MEAD, GABRIELLE: [b] 21/02/96 London; [home] New Malden, Surrey; [p] Judy Corry & Geoff Mead; [school] Burlington Junior; [fav sub] English; [hobbies] Reading, Writing Stories; [pets] Cat (Tom), Donkey (Chocolate); [ambition] To be a Writer or an RSPCA Officer;

COTTRELL, LUCY: [b] 20/09/95 Bury; [home] Radcliffe, Lancashire; [p] Deborah & Paul; [brother] Thomas; [school] St Andrews C of E Primary; [fav sub] Art; [hobbies] Singing, Dancing & Acting; [pets] Dog (Tilly); [ambition] To be a famous Singer;

DALE, ASHLEY: [b] 06/02/92 Gosport; [home] Gosport, Hampshire; [p] Tracey & Colin; [sisters] Samantha & Danielle; [school] Henry Cort Community College; [fav sub] Drama; [hobbies] Kickboxing & Rugby; [pets] Dog (Dexter), Rabbit (Snowball); [ambition] To fight for my Country;

DAVIES, LEWIS: [b] 14/12/95 Welwyn; [home] Stanstead Abbotts, Herts; [p] Michele & Owen; [brother] Rhys; [sister] Bethan; [school] Cranbourne Primary; [fav sub] Maths; [hobbies] Football; [pets] Rabbit; [ambitions] To play football;

DAVIS, ALEXANDRA: [b] 14/05/97; [p] Jacqueline & Tim; [sisters] Joanne & Elizabeth; [school] St. Dominic's School; [fav sub] Literacy; [hobbies] Horse Riding; [pets] Dogs & Horses; [ambitions] To become a Geologist of rocks, shells and stones;

DAW OLIVER: [b] 11/08/93 Plymouth; [home] Exmouth, Devon; [p] Steve & Debbie; [sister] Emily; [school] Exmouth Community College; [fav sub] PE & English; [hobbies] Football, Swimming & Computer Games; [ambition] To run a Marathon;

DESSER, JAMES: [b] 20/04/95

Manchester; [home] Ainsworth, Lancs; [p] Sarah & Simon; [sister] Phoebe; [school] King David Junior; [fav sub] Science; [hobbies] Playstation & Guitar; [pets] Cat (Vienna); [ambition] To be in a Rock Band;

DILLON-BOYLAN, MILLIE: [b] 21/08/96 Bristol; [home] Westbury, Wiltshire; [p] Mark & Michelle; [brother] Troy; [sister] Jemma; [school] Westbury Leigh; [fav sub] DT; [hobbies] First Aid & Computer; [ambition] To become an Archaeologist;

DIXON, HOLLY: [b] 15/12/96 Beverley; [home] Newport, East Yorks.; [p] Helen; [brother] Michael; [sisters] Bryonie & Tanicha; [school] Newport C/P; [fav sub] Maths; [hobbies] Swimming & Music; [pets] Dog & Cat; [ambitions] Undecided;

DIXON, TOBY: [b] 19/01/95 Stoke; [home] Andover, Hants; [p] Francis & Sue; [brother] Jake; [school] St. Mary Bourne; [fav sub] Maths & Rugby; [hobbies] Rugby, Cricket & Motorbiking; [pets] Dog (Milo); [ambition] To become a Pilot;

DOBSON, ALASTAIR: [b] 26/10/93 Shrewsbury; [home] High Offley, Staffs; [p] Sheila & Scott; [sister] Lorna; [school] Stafford Grammar; [fav sub] Science; [hobbies] Football & Cricket; [ambition] To become a Pilot;

DOBSON, BRADLEY: [b] 14/09/95 Sunderland; [home] Peterlee, Durham; [p] Jacqueline & Keith; [sister] Kirsty; [school] Howletch Primary; [fav sub] PE; [hobbies] Swimming; [pets] Dog (Sally); [ambition] To swim in the 2012 Olympics;

DUCKWORTH, GEORGIA: [b] 23/04/96 Beverley; [home] Newport, E. Yorkshire; [p] Gill & Jez; [brother] Joshua; [sister] Frankie; [school] Newport; [fav sub] English; [hobbies] Brownies & Trampolining; [pets] Cat (Cher), Dogs (Charlie & Roxy), Guinea Pig (Jason); [ambition] To become a Vet;

EDEN, JACK: [b] 06/09/94 Roehampton; [home] Morden, Surrey; [p] Ashley & Lisa; [brother] Harry; [school] Abbotsbury Primary; [fav sub] P.E.; [hobbies] Football; [pets] Dogs (Rosie & Taz), Cats (Honey & Goodie); [ambitions] To play football for Chelsea FC and to be rich;

EDWARDS, ABIGAIL GEORGIA: [b] 02/05/95 Bury; [home] Manchester, Lancs; [p] Francine & Andrew; [sisters] Ellie (9), Allana (6) & Orli (3); [school] King David Junior; [fav sub] Art; [hobbies] Netball & Swimming; [ambition] To do something with Art;

EDWARDS, ELLIE: [b] 26/11/99 Norwich; [home] Taverham, Norfolk; [p] Julie & Martin; [brothers] Jack & Archie; [school] Nightingale First; [fav sub] Reading; [hobbies] Swimming & Gym; [ambition] To become a Teacher;

EDWARDS, KYE: [b] 23/04/96 Welwyn Garden City; [home] Hoddesdon, Herts; [p] Bryan & Sandra; [sister] Tayla; [school] The Cranbourne School; [fav sub] Maths; [hobbies] Playstation & Karate; [pets] Dog (Zack), Cat (Kayfer), Snakes (Spot & Daisy); [ambition] To be Happy;

ELEY, CHARLEIGH: [b] 25/09/94 Goodmayes; [home] Harpley, Norfolk; [p] Kelly & Steve; [brothers] Zachary, Ashley, Austin, Arron & Aiden; [school] Harpley V.C; [fav sub] Art & DT; [hobbies] PC, Drawing and making things; [pets] Snakes (Ozzie & Phantom), Dog (Bubbles), Mouse (Nibbles); [ambitions] To be a Poet, Novelist and PC Game maker;

ELEY, ZACHARY: [b] 26/04/96 Goodmayes; [home] Harpley, Norfolk; [p] Kelly & Steve; [brothers] Ashley, Austin, Aaron & Aiden; [sister] Charleigh; [school] Harpley V.C.; [fav sub] Maths; [hobbies] Exercise, Sports, PS2 Games & Computer Games; [pets] Snakes (Ozzie & Phantom); [ambition] To be an Animatronic Technician;

ELLIS, KATE: [b]18/0-8/95 Hemel Hempstead; [home] Hemel Hempstead, Herts; [p] Ian & Caroline; [brother] Jake; [sister] Vicky; [school] Aycliffe Drive Primary; [fav sub] English; [hobbies] Swimming & Scuba Diving; [pets] Cats (Access & Visa) & Goldfish (Martin); [ambitions] To become a Police Driver & to go to Australia;

ELLWOOD, NICOLA: [b] 31/08/96 Stockport; [home] Woodley, Cheshire; [p] Tim & Sue; [brother] Adam; [sister] Lynsey; [school] Stockport Grammar Junior; [fav sub] English; [hobbies] Art & Playing Piano; [pets] Cat (Domino) Cocker Spaniel (Honey);

ESTEVES, LAURA: [b] 17/06/98 Huddersfield; [home] Huddersfield, West Yorkshire; [p] Steven & Phillippa; [brother] Nathan; [sister] Rebecca; [school] St Patrick's RC School; [fav sub] Art; [hobbies] Brownies & Sport; [pets] Dog & 2 Hamsters; [ambitions] To become either a Poet or a Designer;

EVANS, LEVI [b] 27.01.97 Hemel Hempstead; [p] Martin Evans & Michaela Jennings; [brothers] Ben, Joe & Joshua; [sisters] Samantha, Chloe, Leah & Jade; [school] Aycliffe Drive Primary; [fav sub] Maths; [hobbies] Football, Writing

Poetry; [ambition] To be a Professional Footballer;

FAITHORN, MATTHEW: [b] 31/07/95 Sidcup; [home] Sidcup, Kent; [p] Robin & Julie; [brother] William; [school] Montbelle Primary; [fav sub] History; [hobbies] Football, Cricket , Table Tennis, Rugby & Hockey; [ambition] To be in the 2012 Olympics;

FEAVIOUR, KATHERINE: [b] 10/04/98 Plymouth; [home] Ivybridge, Devon; [p] Rachel & Kevin; [Grandparents] David & Christine Stokes; [school] Stowford Primary; [fav sub] English; [hobbies] Horse Riding & Cycling; [pets] Horse, Ducks, Chicken, Dog, Pigs & Sheep; [ambition] To become an Architect;

FERGUSON, HOLLYBETH: [b] 12/10/96 Redhill; [home] South Nutfield, Surrey; [p] Joleen & Dean; [sister] Millie; [school] Nutfield Church Primary; [fav sub] P.E. & Maths; [hobbies] Swimming, Skating & Cycling; [pets] Cat & Hamster; [ambition] To work with animals;

FILBY, JASMINE: [b] 14/10/99 Norwich; [home] Taverham, Norfolk; [p] Lisa & Matthew; [brother] Euan; [school] Nightingale First; [fav sub] Reading; [hobbies] Swimming & Dancing; [pets] Hamster (Peachey); [ambition] To be a Nurse;

FITZPATRICK, HOLLY: [b] 06/10/96 Huddersfield; [home] Huddersfield, W. Yorkshire; [p] Catherine & Matt; [sister] Lucy; [school] St Patrick's; [fav sub] Literacy; [hobbies] Gymnastics & Dance; [pets] Dog, Fish & Guinea Pig; [ambitions] To be a Vet, Dogs Trust;

FLATMAN, NICOLE: [b] 17/11/93 Norwich; [home] Shelfanger, Norfolk; [p] Maurice & Maryann; [sister] Anrika; [school] Diss High; [fav sub] Art; [hobbies] Netball & First Aid; [pets] Rabbits; [ambitions] To be a Doctor or a Paramedic;

FOLLOWS, LUCY: [b] 14/04/95 Stafford; [home] Cannock, Staffs; [p] Robert & Jane; [school] St. Dominic's; [fav sub] Music; [hobbies] Trampolining & Netball; [pets] Labrador (Elle); [ambitions] To be a Singer or Presenter;

FORDRED, OLIVER: [b] 02/06/95 Plymouth; [home] Westbury, Wiltshire; [p] Pippa & Russell; [brother] Harry; [sisters] Jessica & Hattie; [school] Westbury Leigh Primary; [fav sub] Science; [hobbies] Reading & Guitar; [pets] Cat (Toby), Guinea Pigs (Rhubarb & Custard); [ambition] To be a Chemist;

FOSTER, STEPH: [b] 08/10/92 Redhill;

[home] Caterham, Surrey; [p] Chrissie & Paul; [brother] Ollie; [school] Hazelwood; [fav sub] Games; [hobbies] Tennis & Swimming; [pets] Cat (Sam); [ambitions] To be on television and to travel the world;

FORWARD, LUKE JACK: [b] 30/08/98 Bristol; [home] Ivybridge, Devon; [p] Helen & Christopher; [brother] Robert; [school] Stowford Primary; [fav sub] P.E.; [hobbies] Football & Cricket; [pets] Guinea Pig, Dog, Cat, Rabbit & Hamster; [ambitions] To play Football/Cricket for England;

FRANCE, MOLLY: [b] 14/09/97 Sheffield, [home] Sheffield, S. Yorks.; [p] Ian France & Helen Kay; [brothers] Johnny & Geo; [school] Carterknowle Juniors; [fav sub] Art; [hobbies] Reading Poetry; [pets] Cat, 2 Guinea Pigs, & 3 Chickens; [ambitions] To work in a Corner Shop all by myself and to swim with Dolphins;

FREEMAN, ALEX: [b] 04/08/94 Pembury; [home] Westerham, Kent; [p] Nick & Kate; [brother] Andrew; [sister] Catherine; [school] Hazelwood School; [fav sub] Sports; [hobbies] Cricket & Football; [pets] Cat (Cookie); [ambitions] To be a Cricketer and to own a Worldwide Shop;

FREEMAN, JESSICA: [b] 29/11/96 Bury St Edmunds, Suffolk; [p] Mark & Rachael; [brothers] Kieran & Oliver; [sisters] Carla, Lara & Rebecca; [school] Hardwick Primary; [fav sub] Art; [hobbies] Horse Riding & Gym Club; [pets] Dog, Cat, Rabbits, Guinea Pigs & Fish; [ambition] To be a Singer;

FURNIVAL-JONES, HANNAH: [b] 03/06/97 Sheffield; [home] Sheffield, S. Yorks.; [p] April & Graham; [school] Carterknowle Junior; [fav sub] Art; [hobbies] Drawing & Playing; [pets] Cat (Buster); [ambitions] To be an Artist or Writer;

GADSBY, VICTORIA: [b] 05/04/94 Stafford; [home] Stafford, Staffordshire; [p] Steve & Leela; [school] Stafford Grammar School; [fav sub] History, Drama & English; [hobbies] Dancing, Martial Art, Craftwork: [ambition] To work with animals;

GALLAGHER, SHANNON: [b] 28/11/96 New Cross; [home] Wolverhampton; [p] Lusia Gallagher & Roy Hancher; [school] St. Dominic's; [fav sub] Literacy, P.E. & Maths; [hobbies] Day dreaming, Wrting poems & Sports; [pets] 2 Rabbits (Snowy & Fluffy), Dog (Pippa); [ambitions] To be an Actress, famous Writer, famous Singer, Vet, or anything to do with animals or acting;

GARBUTT, HONOR LOIS: [b] 28/01/97 Coventry; [home] Codsall, Staffordshire; [p] Philip & Charlotte; [school] St Dominic's; [fav sub] History; [hobbies] Drawing + Writing stories & poems; [ambitions] To be a famous Author & Poet and work at a dog's trust;

GARDINER, ROXANNE: [b] 26/12/91 Basingstoke; [home] Basingstoke, Hampshire; [p] Pennie & Tony; [school] Brighton Hill Community College; [fav sub] Spanish & History; [hobbies] Trampolining; [pets] Cats (Lillie & Daisie); [ambition] To be a Crime Scene Investigator;

GARDNER, MATTHEW: [b] 06/11/96 Sidcup; [home] Eltham, London; [p] David & Deborah; [brothers] Michael, Stephen, John & Alfie; [sister] Tiffany; [school] Montbelle Primary; [fav sub] Maths; [hobbies] Hockey & Football; [pets] Cat (Kitty), Rotwieller (Zoe); [ambition] To be a Pilot or Mechanic;

GARDNER, TIFFANY: [b] 04/12/94 Greenwich; [home] Eltham, London; [p] David & Deborah; [brothers] Michael, Stephen, John, Alfie & Matthew; [school] Montbelle Primary; [fav sub] Art & English; [hobbies] Hockey & Football; [pets] Cat (Kitty), Rotwieller (Zoe); [ambition] To be successful at whatever I do;

GEORGE, RYAN: [b] 15/12/98 Norwich; [home] Thorpe Marriott, Norfolk; [p] Chris & Julie; [sister] Emily; [school] Nightingale First ; [fav sub] P.E.; [hobbies] Watching Dr. Who & Trampolining; [pets] Dog (Holly); [ambitions] To become a Policeman;

GILDING, CAITLIN: [b] 13/07/98 Norwich; [home] Taverham, Norfolk; [p] Cheri; [brother] Liam; [sister] Kara; [school] Nightingale First ; [fav sub] English; [hobbies] Swimming; [pets] goldfish; [ambition] To become a Hairdresser;

GILMOUR, KIRI A.: [b] 12/10/94 Morden; [home] Morden, Surrey; [p] Androulla Adamou & Paul Gilmour; [sister] Mia; [school] Abbotsbury Primary; [fav sub] Design & Technology & P.E.; [hobbies] Skateboarding, Football & PS2; [pets] Cat (Yogi); [ambition] To be a Millionaire;

GOODERSON, ETHAN: [b] 26/11/99; [home] Westbury, Wiltshire; [p] Lisa & Dean; [brothers] Kayleb, Jared & Corbin; [school] Westbury Leigh; [fav sub] Reading; [hobbies] Swimming, Karate & Golf; [pets] Dog (Dexter);

GORDON-SMALLEY, CONNOR: [b] 25/11/95 Kingston-upon-Thames; [home] New Malden, Surrey; [p] Adam Smalley & Lee Gordon-Smalley; [sisters] Siobhan & Niamh; [school]Burlington Junior; [fav sub] Maths; [hobbies] Swimming; [pets] Tortoise; [ambition] To be a Data Tester;

GRAINGER, CHARLOTTE: [b] 17/05/95 Wolverhampton; [home] Coven, Staffordshire; [p] Jo & Rod; [brother] Thomas; [school] St. Dominic's; [fav sub] Art; [hobbies] Shopping & Rollerblading; [ambition] To be an Interior Designer;

GRAY, ABIGAIL LAUREN: [b] 28/01/06 Salisbury; [home] Westbury, Wiltshire; [p] Lianne Symms-Fahey; [brothers] Jake & Keon; [sister] Mayghan; [school] Westbury Leigh; [fav sub] I.C.T [hobbies] Football; [pets] Dog (Rolo); [ambition] To be successful;

GRAY, LOGAN: [b] 09/09/95 Bishop Auckland; [home] Leeholme, Durham; [p] Linda & Peter; [sister] Rayann; [school] Coundon Primary; [fav sub] Maths; [hobbies] Fishing & Reading; [pets] Dog (Cindy), Cat (Ziggy); [ambitions] To become a Rugby Player and to learn to drive;

GREEN, PAIGE ALYSSA: [b] 18/03/96 Newton Abbot; [home] Newton Abbot, S. Devon; [p] Annabelle Green & Benjamin Perkins; [brother] Elliott; [school] Highweek Community; [fav sub] Science; [hobbies] Swimming & Football; [pets] Rabbits (BB & Tamba); [ambitions] To work with animals, either as a Vet or Zoo Keeper;

GREENFIELD, EMILY: [b] 19/08/98 Ipswich; [home] Elmsett, Suffolk; [p] Phillip & Mandy; [school] Elmsett; [fav sub] Literacy; [hobbies] Horse Riding; [pets] Dog & Pony; [ambition] To work with animals;

GREENSTEIN, ROMY: [b]29/08/95 Johannesburg, S. Africa; [home] Manchester, Lancs; [p] Heidi & Mark; [brothers] Jonathan & Alan; [school] King David Junior; [fav sub] Art; [hobbies] Writing Stories & Drawing; [pets] Fish & Hamster; [ambitions] To become an Actress, to write books & poems and become a Make up Artist;

GRILIOPOULOS, IONA: [b] 27/04/96 Stockport, Cheshire; [p] Karen & Dimitri; [brothers] Sam, Dan, David & Corrie; [school] Stockport Grammar; [fav sub] Art & Science; [hobbies] Swimming, Dancing & playing the Piano; [pets] Chinchillas (Nuno & Freddie); [ambitions] To travel the world and do well in my exams;

GULOWSEN EKEBERG, REBECCA: [b] 05/02/98 Basildon; [home] Danbury, Essex; [p] Helle Gulowsen & Rolf Ekeberg; [brother] Thomas; [school] Danbury Park School; [fav sub] P.E.; [hobbies] Tae-Kwon-Do; [pets] Cat (Billy); [ambitions] To become a Black Belt in Tae-Kwon-Do;

GUTTERIDGE, SOFIE: [b] 17/02/93 Leicester; [home] Leicester; [school] Leicester High School; [fav sub] P.E.; [hobbies] Tennis, Gymnastics & Hockey; [pets] 2 Rabbits & 2 Guinea-Pigs; [ambitions] To drive a pink Bentley and compete as a Gymnast in the Olympics;

HALL, AIMEE: [b] 20/02/99 Bury; [home] Prestwich, Manchester; [p] Jonathan & Deana; [brother] Alfie; [sister] Amelia; [school] St Margerets C.E; [fav sub] Spanish; [hobbies] Horse Riding & Brownies; [pets] Dog (Rosie); [ambition] To become a Teacher;

HAMBURGER, LAURA IVANA: [b] 13/03/95 Bury; [home] Prestwich, Manchester; [p] Richard & Gillian; [brother] Jason; [school] King David Junior; [fav sub] Mathematcis; [hobbies] Acting & Netball; [pets] Goldfish; [ambition] To be happy in whatever I choose to do;

HANLEY, BRONAGH: [b] 17/12/96 Weybridge; [home] Walton, Surrey; [p] Geraldine & Paul; [sister] Toiréasa; [school] St Charles Borromeo; [fav sub] Art & History; [hobbies] Drawing, Reading, Piano & Athletics; [ambition] To be an Artist;

HARDS, ABBI: [b] 11/8/95 Greenwich; [home] Eltham, London; [p] Richard & Janice; [brothers] Billy & Jamie; [school] Montbelle Primary; [fav sub] Art; [hobbies] Cooking & Drawing; [pets] Black Cat (Bubbles); [ambitions] To be an Artist and Poet;

HARDWICK, KAYLEIGH: [b] 24/05/96 Kingston-upon Thames; [home] New Malden, Surrey; [p] Amanda Vallis & Darran Hardwick; [brother] Matthew; [school] Burlington Junior; [fav sub] Science, History, Writing, Physics & Art; [hobbies] Making up stories; [pets] Cat (Jess), Dog (Hubble); [ambitions] To be an Author /Movie Maker/Pop Singer/Song Writer/Banker/Study animals;

HARDY, AMI L.: [b] 12/10/95 Torquay; [home] Kingskerswell, Devon; [p] Nicola Hardy & Paul Hutchings; [sister] Chloe A. Knowles; [school] Highweek Primary; [fav sub] Art, Design Technology, Drawing; [hobbies] Gymnastics, Canoeing, Reading & Writing Poems; [pets] Gerbils (Sonny & Caramel); [ambitions] To write poems as good as Ted Hughes & write famous stories;

HARRISON, JAMIE: [b] 24/09/95

Winchester; [home] Woolwich, London; [p] Sara & Simon; [brother] Ben; [sister] Sophie; [school] Montbelle Primary;[fav sub] Art; [hobbies] Football; [pets] Dog (Barney); [ambitions] To own a Racing Car and be a Footballer;

HARRISON, PIPPA: [b] 07/05/95 Kingston-upon-Thames; [p] Andrew & Carolyn; [sisters] Izzy & Evie; [school] Northbourne Park; [fav sub] Art; [hobbies] Horse Riding; [pets] Goldfish (Fairy); [ambitions] To become an International Three Day Eventer;

HARVEY, SAMANTHA LOUISE: [b] 06/02/93 Basingstoke, Hants; [p] Teresa & Brian; [brother] Scott; [sister] Stacy; [school] B.H.C.C.; [fav sub[Drama; [hobbies] Dancing; [pets] 2 Rabbits; [ambitions] To become an Infant Teacher or a Beautician;

HATHAWAY, ISABELLA: [b] 14/08/97 Farnham; [home] Farnham, Surrey; [p] David & Elaine; [sister] Ellen; [school] Hale; [fav sub] [hobbies] Dancing, Skiing & Golf; [pets] 2 Cats, 2 Guinea-Pigs & Fish; [ambition] To be a top Golfer;

HAWORTH, JORDAN: [b] 07/09/94 Bury; [p] Debbie & Gary; [sister] Amber; [school] St Andrews; [fav sub] Physical Education; [hobbies] Football & Drawing; [pets] Dog (Sponsor-Zak); [ambitions] To be an animator for Disney;

HAYNES, AARON MARK: [b] 22/03/96 Bury; [home] Radcliffe, Lancashire; [p] Joanne & Mark; [brother] Ryan; [sister] Lauren; [school] St Andrews C of E Primary; [fav sub] Maths; [hobbies] Football & PS2; [ambition] To become a Professional Footballer;

HEAVENS, JAMIE: [b] 09/05/94 Maidstone, [home] Exmouth, Devon; [p] Carol & Mark; [sister] Ella; [school] Exmouth Community College; [fav sub] Mathematics; [hobbies] Sports & Computer Games; [pets] Tropical Fish;

HENDRY, JOSHUA JAMES: [b] 08/06/97 Bury St Edmunds, Suffolk; [p] Mark & Tanya; [sister] Stephanie; [school] Hardwick Primary; [fav sub] Mathematics; [hobbies] Football, Rugby & Basketball; [ambition] To become a Millionaire through writing;

HIBBERT, LAUREN: [b] 14/02/95 Ashton-Under-Lyne; [home] Radcliffe, Manchester; [p] Andrea & Ian; [brother] Ross; [school] St Andrews; [fav sub] Art; [hobbies] Skating, Swimming & Gym; [pets] Cat (Jarvis);

HICKEY, FINLEY BECK: [b] 08/04/99; [home] Hoddesdon, Herts; [p] Chloe & Steven; [brothers] Stanley &

Buster; [school] The Cranbourne Primary; [fav sub] Literacy; [hobbies] Reading & Riding my Bike; [pets] Dog (Georgie); [ambitions] To become a Vet and a Millionaire;

HICKINBOTTOM, KAYLEIGH: [b] 03/08/94 Walsall; [home] Walsall, West Mids; [p] Nigel; [brother] Liam; [sisters] Lauren & Brodie; [school] Joseph Leckie C.T.C; [fav sub] P.E.; [hobbies] Cinema & Iceskating; [pets] Dog & 2 Fish; [ambition] To become a Child Carer;

HIGGINS, CONNIE MABEL: [b] 20/03/97 Frome; [home] Witham Friary, Somerset; [school] Upton Noble; [fav sub] Art; [hobbies] Dance, Horse Riding, Reading & Violin; [pets] 2 Guinea-Pigs & a Puppy; [ambition] To become a Vet;

HILLERY, LAUREN: [b] 21/07/98 Rotherham; [home] Oakworth, West Yorkshire; [p] Martin & Deborah; [sister] Amy; [school] Lees Primary; [fav sub] Art; [hobbies] P.E. & Dancing; [ambition] To become a Teacher;

HINCHLIFFE, JODY: [b] 02/12/94 Sunderland; [home] Stanley, Durham; [p] Christopher & Julie Anne; [school] Tanfield Lea Juniors; [fav sub] Mathematics; [hobbies] Piano, Horse Riding, Karate & Swimming; [pets] 2 Horses, 2 Cats, 1 Dog & 1 Goldfish; [ambitions] To work with horses and become a Vet;

HINKS, JOLLY: [b] 07/07/95 Watford; [home] Abbots Langley, Herts; [p] Janie & Adrian; [older brothers] Lee, Benn & Oliver; [sister] Lisa; [school] Abbots Langley; [fav sub] Design Technology; [hobbies] Gardening & Pets; [pets] Chocolate Labradors (Kai & Zak); [ambition] To become a Vet;

HIVES, JOSH MITCHEL: [b] 30/05/99; [home] Norwich, Norfolk; [p] Mandy & Steve; [brothers] Robbie & Daniel; [sisters] Skye & Xanthe; [school] Nightingale First School; [fav sub] P.E.; [hobbies] Going to the cinema; [pets] Dogs (Jack & Sadie); [ambition] To be a Sports Allstar;

HIVES, ROBBIE BRANDON: [b] 30/05/99; [home] Norwich, Norfolk; [p] Mandy & Steve; [brothers] Josh & Daniel; [sisters] Skye & Xanthe; [school] Nightingale First School; [fav sub] Mathematics; [hobbies] Swimming; [pets] Dogs (Jack & Sadie); [ambition] To become a Teacher;

HOLLINSHEAD, CHARLOTTE: [b] 24/03/95 Stourbridge; [home] Bridgnorth, Shropshire; [p] Diane & Lyndon; [brother] Alex; [school] St. Dominic's; [fav sub] Art, DT & PE; [hobbies] Ice

Skating & Tennis; [pets] 2 Dogs & 3 Cats; [ambitions] To become a Fashion Designer or Interior Designer;

HUNT, STEPHANIE: [b] 07/02/96 Kingston Upon Thames; [home] New Malden, Surrey; [brother] William; [sister] Natasha; [school] Burlington Junior; [fav sub] Art; [pets] Cats (Lucy & Romulus);

HUNTER, KIMBERLY LEAH: [b] 12/04/97; [home] Westbury, Wiltshire; [p] Robert & Jackie; [brother] Stephen; [school] Westbury Leigh CE Primary; [fav sub] Literacy; [hobbies] Reading; [pets] Dog & 4 Gerbils; [ambitions] To become a Make Up Artist;

HYMAN, ANNIE: [b] 11/02/98; [home] Manchester, Lancashire; [p] Robert & Karen; [sisters] Ellie & Milly; [school] King David Junior; [fav sub] Art & Sport; [hobbies] Swimming; [pets] Cats; [ambition] To swim the channel;

HYSON, MOLLY: [b] 01/01/95 Shropshire; [home] Shifnal, Shropshire; [p] Virpi & Glen; [sister] Hannele; [school] St. Dominics; [fav sub] English; [hobbies] Badminton; [ambition] To be a Firewoman;

IGLESIAS, JAVIER GONZALES: [b] 31/07/94 Exeter; [home] Exmouth, Devon; [p] Debbie & Pedro; [brothers] David, Adam & Dominic; [sisters] Bianca & Eloise; [school] Exmouth Community College; [fav sub] Drama; [hobbies] Football & Riding my Bike;

ILLSLEY, BEN: [b] 30/01/93 Kingston Upon Thames; [home] Kingston Upon Thames, Surrey; [p] Ann Dixon & John Illsley; [sister] Abbie; [school] The Tiffin School; [fav sub] Art; [hobbies] Art; [pets] 2 Cats; [ambitions] To be a Graphic Designer and Animator;

INGLES, NICOLA: [b] 17/03/98 Maldon; [home] Danbury, Essex; [p] Marion & Barry; [sister] Rebecca; [school] Danbury Park; [fav sub] Literacy; [hobbies] Football, Netball, Tennis, Swimming & Choir; [ambition] To become a professional Footballer;

INWOOD, CHRISTOPHER: [b] 12/10/95 Swindon; [home] Little Massingham, Norfolk; [p] Tony & Annette; [brother] Michael; [sister] Chrystal Rose; [school] Harpley; [fav sub] Maths, D.T. & Art; [hobbies] Army, Biking & Swimming; [pets] Chicken & Geese; [ambition] To be a Policeman;

ISLAM, SYED NAZMUL: [b] 22/09/97 Hemel Hempstead; [home] St. Albans, Herts; [p] Halima & Shahed; [brother] Mohinul; [sister] Tahmina; [school]

Cunningham Hill Junior; [fav sub] Art & Science; [hobbies] Drawing & Writing; [pets] Not yet, but would like a Parrot; [ambition] To own a Speedboat;

JIVRAJ, ABBAS: [b] 25/03/92 Carshalton; [home] Ewell, Surrey; [p] Mehboob & Yasmin; [brother] Muntazir; [sister] Nazneen; [school] Tiffin Boys; [fav sub] Biology; [hobbies] Reading; [pets] 3 Goldfish; [ambition] To study Dentistry;

JOHNSON, BETH: [b] 18/12/96 Stanley; [home] Stanley, Durham; [p] Marie & Ian; [brother] Tom; [school] Tanfield Lea Junior; [fav sub] English & History; [hobbies] Swimming & Piano; [pets] Rabbit (Toffee); [ambition] To travel the world;

JOHNSON, CRAIG: [b] 09/01/97; [home] Tantobie, Durham; [p] Stephen & Susan; [sister] Rebecca; [school] Tanfield Lea Junior; [fav sub] Maths; [hobbies] Football & Playstation; [pets] Dog (Scamp); [ambition] To make lots of money;

JOHNSON, DECLAN: [b] 08/02/99 Torquay, S. Devon; [p] Nikki & Ian; [brother] Ayrton; [school] Hennock Primary; [fav sub] Mathematics; [hobbies] Horse Riding, Football & Cycling; [pets] Bulldog, Rabbit, Fish & Cat; [ambition] To be a F1 Driver, preferably for Ferrari;

JONES, HANNAH: [b] 30/05/93 Walsall; [home] Walsall, W. Mids; [p] Colleen & Anthony; [brother] Matthew; [sister] Alice; [school] Joesph Lockie CTC; [fav sub] Enjoy them all; [hobbies] Judo & Music; [pets] Dog (Jet); [ambitions] To play the Keyboard, Violin & Drums;

JONES, TOBY: [b] 03/09/94 Stockport; [home] Stockport, Cheshire; [p] Val & Richard; [brothers] William & Louis; [school] Stockport Grammar Junior; [fav sub] Games; [hobbies] Reading, Classical Guitar, Football & Badminton; [pets] Tropical Fish, Hamster & Rabbit; [ambitions] To be a Poet/Novelist;

JONES, WILLIAM: [b] 31/01/97 Stockport; [home] Stockport, Cheshire; [p] Val & Richard; [brothers] Toby & Louis; [school] Stockport Grammar; [fav sub] English; [hobbies] Making things & Sport; [pets] Hamsters, Rabbit & Fish; [ambition] To become a Civil Engineer;

JOY, JADENE: [b] 16/03/95 Salisbury, Wiltshire; [p] Steve & Maria; [brothers] Curtis & Danny; [school] Sarum St Pauls; [fav sub] History & Games; [hobbies] Singing, Dancing & Computers; [ambitions] To be a Teacher, Hairdresser

or Model;

KAHRAMAN, DEVIN: [b] 1997 Brisbane, Australia; [p] Nesli & Hakan; [sister] Ilayda; [school] Molescroft Primary; [fav sub] Science; [hobbies] Drawing; [pets] Had 2 dogs in Australia; [ambition] To be an Earth Scientist;

KAPOOR, KESHAV: [b] 11/03/94 Stevenage; [home] Heston, Middlesex; [p] Rik, Poonam; [brother] Gaurav; [school] Tiffin Boys; [fav sub] Maths & French; [hobbies] Badminton & Home Computing; [ambitions] To become a Doctor and to play for Arsenal F.C.

KAPONDORO, JAMES: [b] 15/03/95 Mutoko, Zimbabwe; [home] Abbots Langley, Herts; [p] Ian / Rudi Gray; [sister] Naomi; [school] Abbots Langley; [fav sub] Literacy; [hobbies] Sports; [ambitions] Art, Footballer, Sports etc.

KEARNEY, LUKE: [b] 28/05/97 Bury St Edmunds; [home] Bury St Edmunds, Suffolk; [p] Jan & Jack; [brother] Alex; [school] Hardwick Primary; [fav sub] P.E. [hobbies] Football, Wrestling & Art; [pets] Cat (Iggy), Rabbit & Goldfish; [ambitions] To own a Lamborghini Murchilago and be a famous Runner;

KEIRLE, NICK: [b] 11/02/91 Kingston Upon Thames; [home] Kingston Upon Thames; [p] David & Lesley; [brother] Matthew & Simon; [school] Tiffin School; [fav sub] History; [hobbies] Playing guitar & writing; [pets] Cat (Tigger); [ambition] To become a successful Musician;

KEMSLEY, KIERAN: [b] 05/09/95 Birkenhead; [home] Prenton, Merseyside; [p] Anita & Jason; [sister] Amber; [school] Lyndale; [fav sub] Numeracy; [hobbies] Football (playing & watching); [pets] Springer Dog (Megan), Cat (Aiesha), Hamster (Toffee); [ambition] To be a Policeman;

KINGSCOTT, OLIVIA: [b] 04/11/97 Gloucester; [home] Ivybridge, Devon; [p] Karen & Paul; [brothers] Sam & Jacob; [sister] Mia; [school] Stowford Primary; [fav sub] Art; [hobbies] Swimming; [pets] Fish; [ambition] To become a Hairdresser;

KNIGHT, ANNABEL: [b] 14/05/98 Chelmsford; [home] Gt. Baddow, Essex; [p] Lynne Cunningham & John Knight; [brothers] Barry & Bryan; [sister] Sarah; [school] Danbury Park Primary; [fav sub] Art; [hobbies] Scrap booking & Horse Riding; [pets] Fish; [ambitions] To be a Pop Star and Horse Rider;

LAMBLE, ALISHA: [b] 01/07/98 Plymouth; [home] Ivybridge, Devon; [p] Karen & Phil; [brother] Austen; [school] Stowford Primary; [fav sub] Art;

[hobbies] Singing & Dancing; [pets] Birds & Fish; [ambition] To be a Popstar;

LAMPEN, EDWARD: [b] 14/06/96 Greenwich; [home] Eltham, London; [brother] Frederick; [sister] Georgina; [school] Montbelle Primary; [fav sub] I.C.T.; [hobbies] Guitar & Rugby; [pets] Cat (Toby), Hamster; [ambitions] To design and build houses;

LAMPEN, FREDERICK: [b] 21/09/94 Greenwich; [home] Eltham, London; [brother] Edward; [sister] Georgina; [school] Montbelle Primary; [fav sub] Maths; [hobbies] Building & Puzzles; [pets] Cat (Toby); [ambitions] To fly a Plane, go into Space and become a Policeman;

LARARD, SOPHIE JANE: [b] 31/12/97 Beverley; [home] Beverley, E. Yorkshire; [p] Jason & Kate; [school] Molescroft Primary; [fav sub] Science; [hobbies] Swimming & Dancing; [ambition] To look after animals;

LAYTON BULLOCK, HAYDEN: [b] 25/04/99 Lowestoft; [home] Corton, Suffolk; [p] Ang & Bob; [sisters] Georgia & Daisy; [school] Corton Primary; [fav sub] P.E. & Art; [hobbies] Collecting Dr. Who & Drawing; [pets] Dog (Spider), 2 Guinea-Pigs; [ambitions] To be an Actor and act in Dr Who;

LEADER, COURTNEY: [b] 31/10/96 Huddersfield; [home] Lindley, Yorkshire; [p] Carole & Tim; [brothers] Joe & Mikey; [school] St Patrick's R.C.; [fav sub] English; [hobbies] Dancing; [pets] Rabbit; [ambition] To be an Actress;

LEES, THOMAS RICHARD: [b] 08/12/95; [home] Ramsgate, Kent; [p] Amy; [brother] Joey; [school] Northbourne Park; [fav sub] Art; [hobbies] Cricket, Swimming & Computer games; [pets] Rabbit; [ambitions] To be Happy & Successful;

LESTER, HANNAH: Age 10. Hannah bo danner tiddlyanna fi fanna! Lively, sunny, cuddly, messy, fun loving budding Artist and Rollerblader who loves singing and playing the drums very loud (sorry Mum & Dad) Oh and annoying my big brother Rory X; ps. We have 3 Cats (Sparky, Kipper & Tabby) plus Pepper the Dog;

LEWIS, KAILEEN: [b] 06/09/96 Bethnal Green; [home] Enfield, Middlesex; [p] Steven & Donna Lewis; [brother] Kaide Lewis; [sister] Cher-Amour Defreitas, Cheyenne Lewis; [school] Capel Manor; [fav sub] Art; [hobbies] Watching films; [pets] Cat; [ambition] To become an Actor;

LISTER, HELEN: [b] 09/01/96; [home] Saxlingham, Norfolk; [p] Caroline; [brother] Matthew; [school] Greshams Prep; [fav sub] English; [hobbies] Art & Mosaic; [pets] None; [ambition] To have a Dog;

LOVELOCK, LUCY SAMANTHA: [b] 30/07/93 Basingstoke; [home] Basingstoke, Hampshire; [p] Dawn & Keith; [brother] Sam; [school] Brighton Hill Comm. College; [fav sub] Art & Drama; [hobbies] Gym, Swimming & looking after cats; [pets] Cat (Prissy); [ambition] Undecided at present;

LOWTHER, OLIVIA: [b] 12/05/96 Hartlepool; [home] High Hesleden, Co. Durham; [p] Jane & Tom; [sister] Helena; [school] Howletch Primary; [fav sub] English & Art; [hobbies] Swimming & Gymnastics; [pets] Chocolate Labrador (Coco); [ambition] To become an Actress;

MACKINTOSH, JAMIE-LEIGH: [b] 07/09/95 Bury; [home] Thetford, Norfolk; [p] Lorna Mackintosh & Anthony Crighton; [sister] Shannon; [school] Queensway Junior; [fav sub] Art; [hobbies] Swimming; [pets] Dog, Cat, Fish, Hamster; [ambitions] To be a Poet, Artist or Vet;

MAHMOOD, SOHAIL: [b] 24/06/96 Bradford; [home] Heaton, W. Yorkshire; [p] Khalid & Farzana; [brother] Khawar; [sisters] Saiqa & Faaria; [school] Heaton Primary; [fav sub] Art; [hobbies] Playing & Reading; [ambition] To be an Artist;

MALINIC, TINA: [b] 01/05/96 London; [home] New Malden, Surrey; [p] Durdica & Loran; [brother] Luka; [school] Burlington Junior; [fav sub] PE; [hobbies] Playing Sports; [pets] Hamster (Beny) & Bird (Ozzy); [ambitions] To be an Athlete or Songwriter;

MALLETT, ZOË: [b] 17/02/98 Harlow, Essex; [p] Steven & Penny; [brothers] Daniel & Toby; [school] St Andrew's Primary; [fav sub] D.T. & Art; [hobbies] Gymnastics & Brownies; [pets] Dog (Shy); [ambition] To work in a Pet Shop;

MANNING, RHYS: [b] 27/05/94; [home] Oxford, Oxfordshire; [p] Penny Manning & Brian Cutler; [sisters] Stephanie, Chlöe, Katie & Shannon; [school] Mabel Pritchard; [fav sub] Science; [hobbies] Computer Games & Swimming; [pets] 3 Cats; [ambition] To work with Computers;

MARCEL, JEROME: [b] 10/10/97 Swindon; [home] Marlborough, Wiltshire; [p] Lynne & Rosario; [brother] Alex; [school] St Peter's School; [fav sub] P.E.; [hobbies] Football & Guitar; [pets] 2 Cats, 2 Fish, 1 Rabbit; [ambition] To be a

Detective and to travel the world;

MARGOLIS, JACK: [b] 28/04/96 Manchester; [home] Whitefield, Manchester; [p] Suzanne & Simon; [brothers] Dan & Harry; [sister] Sadie; [school] King David Junior; [fav sub] History; [hobbies] Reading, Football, Swimming & Cricket; [ambitions] To be Happy & Successful;

MARSHALL, HANNAH JANE: [b] 26/01/96 Plymouth; [home] Ivybridge, Devon; [p] Darah & Jon; [sister] Millie; [school] Stowford Primary; [fav sub] Art; [hobbies] Swimming & Cycling; [pets] Guinea-Pigs (Simba & Chocolate Fudge), Cat (Red); [ambition] To become a Dentist;

MASON, ELLIOTT: [b] 04/03/94 Stafford; [home] Calf Heath, Staffordshire; [p] Vanessa & Darrel; [sisters] Emily & Jessica; [school] Stafford Grammar; [fav sub] Geography; [hobbies] Swimming, Rugby & Piano; [pets] Dogs, Cats, Horses, Ducks, Birds & a Tortoise; [ambitions] To become a Pilot, Journalist or Policeman;

MASON, SOPHIE: [b] 14/06/96; [home] Peterlee, Durham; [p] Joanne & David; [sisters] Becky & Gabrielle; [school] Howletch Primary; [fav sub] English; [hobbies] Dancing & Reading; [pets] Dog (Ruby); [ambitions] To be a School Teacher and a Dance Teacher;

MATHER, ALISHA: [b] 16/12/99 Bury; [home] Radcliffe, Manchester; [p] Steven & Paula; [brother] Jacob; [school] St Andrew's; [fav sub] History; [hobbies] Dancing, Swimming & Reading; [pets] Dog (Fudge), Fish (Belle); [ambition] To become a Pop Star!

MATTHEWSON, JESSICA: [b] 09/11/97 Norwich; [home] Beetley, Norfolk; [p] Karen Moore & Dean Matthewson; [schhol] When poem was written Nightingale First School, now Beetley Primary; [fav sub] English & Science; [hobbies] Riding my Bike; [pets] Dog (Sally), Cats (Poppy, Pixie & Bara); [ambitions] To become a Hairdresser and own my own Horse;

McCLURE, CHLOE: [b] 26/06/94 Norwich; [home] Diss, Norfolk; [p] Vicki & William; [sisters] Ellen & Katie; [school] Diss High; [fav sub] Art; [hobbies] Violin; [pets] Milly, Jake, Speckles & Brandy;

McKEOWN, ALEX: [b] 29/02/96 Peterborough; [home] Stockport, Cheshire; [p] Vivienne & Barry; [brother] James; [sister] Isabel; [school] Stockport Grammar Junior; [fav sub] English; [hobbies] Swimming & Cycling;

[ambitions] To own my own business and become an Actor & Singer;

McLAREN-STERLING, SHARI: [b] 02/06/93 West Bromwich; [home] Birmingham, West Midlands; [p] Maxine McLaren & Martin Sterling-Haig; [brother] Trehan Sterling-Haig; [sisters] Rochelle Sterling & Kailen Sterling-Haig; [school] Joseph Leckie CTC; [fav sub] Music; [hobbies] Singing & Dancing; [ambitions] To be an Accountant, Singer or Dancer;

McMAHON, CHARLOTTE: [b] 10/11/92 Taunton; [home] Evesham, Worcestershire; [p] Liz; [brother] Jake; [sister] Anna; [school] St Edwins; [fav sub] English & Maths; [hobbies] Cooking & Swimming; [pets] Goldfish (Jasmin); [ambition] To run my own business;

McNAIR, AIMÉE: [b] 16/07/95 Winchester; [home] Whitchurch, Hampshire; [brother] Ethan; [school] St Mary Bourne Primary; [fav sub] Drama; [hobbies] Ice Skating & Trampolining; [pets] 2 Dogs; [ambtition] To work in Performing Arts;

MERCER, NAOMI: [b] 24/11/95 Prestwich, [home] Manchester; [p] Peter & Vikki; [brothers] Adam, Sam & Leo; [sisters] Sarah & Rosie (twin); [school] King David Junior; [fav sub] Art & Music; [hobbies] Playing my Clarinet, Rambling, Gardening & Baking; [pets] Cat, 2 Fish & 8 Stick Insects; [ambitions] To learn to play the Bassoon well;

MERCER, ROSIE: [b] 24/11/95 Prestwich, [home] Manchester; [p] Peter & Vikki; [brothers] Adam, Sam & Leo; [sisters] Sarah & Naomi (twin); [school] King David Junior; [fav sub] Art; [hobbies] Playing French Horn, Drawing, Swimming; [pets] Cat, Stick Insects & Fish; [ambitions] To be an Illustrator and Horn player;

MILES, HOLLY: [b] 03/12/96 Woking; [home] Dolton, Devon; [p] Helen; [brother] Robert; [school] Dolton C of E Primary; [fav sub] Literacy; [hobbies] Horse Riding & Drawing; [pets] Cats; [ambition] To become a Vet;

MILLAR, CHRISTOPHER: [b] 26/01/97 Bath; [home] Westbury, Wiltshire; [p] Robert & Toni; [sisters] Gemma & Kirsty; [school] Westbury Leigh C.E. Primary; [fav sub] Maths; [hobbies] Football & Making Models; [ambitions] To be a Pilot or Footballer;

MILLAR, HOPE: [b] 01/02/97 Shrewsbury; [home] Newport, Shropshire; [p] Katy & Glenn; [sisters] India (10) & Scarlett (1); [school] St Dominic's; [fav sub] Art; [hobbies]

Cooking; [pets] Would like a dog; [ambition] To open my own Restaurant;

MISTRETTA, LAUREN: [b] 09/07/99 Trowbridge; [home] Westbury, Wiltshire; [p] Ellie & Peter; [sister] Sofia; [school] Westbury Leigh C of E Primary; [fav sub] Literacy; [hobbies] Reading, Swimming & Writing; [pets] Fish (Lola), Cat (Nellie); [ambitions] To become a Poet or a Pop Star!

MITCHELL, LUCY ANTONIA: [b] 25/03/96 Romiley, Cheshire; [p] Tony & Yvonne; [sisters] Faye & Millie; [school] Stockport Grammar; [fav sub] Art; [hobbies] Singing & Netball; [pets] 2 Dogs; [ambitions] To help disadvantaged animals;

MONTGOMERY, ELLIE: [b] 11/01/95 Harlow; [home] Hoddesdon, Herts; [p] Jacqui & John; [brother] Ben; [school] The Cranbourne School; [fav sub] Maths & PE; [hobbies] Karate, Swimming, Netball & Trampolining; [pets] Cats (Simba, Kizzy & Bilee), Rabbit (Toffee); [ambition] To be a Vet;

MOORE, REBECCA JAYNE: [b] 07/12/95 Huddersfield; [home] Huddersfield, W. Yorks.; [p] Stephen & Jayne; [sister] Rachel (older); [school] St Patrick's Catholic Junior; [fav sub] Games; [hobbies] Football, Running & Music; [pets] Border Collie (Ben) & Gerbil (Blackie); [ambition] To become a Musician;

MOORE, ZOE: [b] 26/07/98 Durham; [home] Tanfield Lea, Durham; [p] Debbie & Stephen; [brother] Michael; [school] Tanfield Lea Junior; [fav sub] History; [hobbies] Swimming, Computer & Playing; [pets] Dog (Poppy), Cat (Chloe), Rabbits (Bessie & Bugsey); [ambitions] To be a Singer & Guitarist;

MORGAN, REBECCA: [b] 29/05/93 Basingstoke; [home] Basingstoke, Hampshire; [p] Carol & Idris; [school] Brighton Hill Community College; [fav sub] Science; [hobbies] Horse Riding, Reading & Animals; [pets] Border Terrier (Barney); [ambitions] To be a Vet or an Author;

MORRIS, CATHY EMMA: [b] 29/03/94 Salisbury; [home] Thame, Oxon; [p] Robert & Emma; [brothers] Colin, Calvin, Callum, Connor, Cameron & Craig; [sisters] Christine, Charlotte, Chloe, Casey; [school] Lord Williams's; [fav sub] English; [hobbies] Reading, Writing, Dancing & Singing; [pets] Dogs, Cats, Rabbit, Hamster, Fish; [ambitions] To become a Fashion Designer & Writer;

MORRIS, DANIEL: [b] 05/06/96 Bath; [home] Westbury, Wiltshire; [p] Gareth &

Tracy; [sisters] Jessica & Molly; [school] Westbury Leigh C.E. Primary; [fav sub] History; [hobbies] Scouts, Guitar & Tree Climbing; [pets] Cats (Smudge & Smokey); [ambition] To become a Pilot

MORRISH, CAMERON: [b] 09/01/94 Exeter; [home] Exmouth, Devon; [p] Christopher & Clare; [school] Exmouth Community College; [fav sub] History; [hobbies] Snooker, Speedway & Football; [pets] Cats (Daisy & Lottie); [ambition] To become a Chef;

MORROW, MATTHEW JACK: [b] 30/09/95 Bury; [home] Radcliffe, Manchester; [p] David & Michelle; [brothers] Alex & Sam; [school] St Andrew's C of E Primary; [fav sub] Art; [hobbies] Football & Games Consoles; [ambitions] To play professional football for any team except Man. Utd!

MUMFORD, REBEKAH L.: [b] 10/01/95 Epsom; [home] Westbury, Wiltshire; [p] Anthony & Angela; [brothers] Samuel & Jonathan; [school] Westbury Leigh C of E Primary; [fav sub] History; [hobbies] Playing Violin & Orchestra; [pets] Hamster (Sunshine), Dog (Keisha); [ambition] To become a Music Teacher;

MUNRO, JEMMA: [b] 22/10/94 Reading; [home] Edington, Wiltshire; [p] Kirsti Munro & Keith Cowell; [brother] Matt; [sister] Jackie; [school] Westbury Leigh; [fav sub] Art & Literature; [hobbies] Writing Poetry & Drawing; [pets] Rabbit, Hamster, Great African Land Snail; [ambition] To be an Actress;

MURPHY, ALICE: [b] 27/09/95 Weybridge; [home] Weybridge, Surrey; [p] Sophie & Phil; [brother] Mark; [school] St Charles Borromeo; [fav sub] Maths; [hobbies] Basketball & Electric Keyboard; [pets] Cat (Amber); [ambition] To become a Dentist;

MURRAY, LAURA JO: [b] 06/12/91; [home] Whitefield, Grt Manchester; [p] John & Sandra; [brother] Andrew Paul; [school] St Monic's R.C.; [fav sub] Science; [hobbies] Sports-Hockey, Football etc; [pets] Cats (Minky & Mog), Hamster (Midge); [ambition] To become a Zoologist;

MUSSELWHITE, THOREN: [b] 12/02/98 Salisbury; [home] Salisbury, Wiltshire; [p] Aly & Toby; [brothers] Shane & Ethan; [sister] Brooke; [school] Sarum St Pauls; [fav sub] English; [hobbies] Fishing & Motox; [pets] Hamster & Rabbit; [ambition] To become an Architect;

MYERS, LAYLA: [b] 11/02/96 London; [home] Holt, Norfolk; [p] Mary & Justin;

[brothers] Will & Fred; [school] Gresham's Prep; [fav sub] Drama, English & Art; [hobbies] Playing the Piano, Drawing, Tennis & looking after my pets; [pets] 2 Dogs, 2 Cats, 1 Gerbil, 3 Chickens, 1 Duck, 2 Pigs, 6 Sheep & lots of Fish; [ambition] To become an Actress;

NEWBERRY, ROXY: [b] 21/01/94 Exeter; [home] Exmouth, Devon; [p] Lucy & Peter; [school] Exmouth Community College; [fav sub] Drama & Maths; [hobbies] Swimming & Trampolining; [pets] Dog, 2 Rats & 3 Rabbits; [ambitions] To travel the world and become a Teacher;

NEWELL, BETHANY: [b] 24/12/95 Salisbury; [home] Westbury, Wiltshire; [sister] Charlotte; [school] Westbury Leigh CE Primary; [hobbies] Swimming, Recorder & Dancing;

NEWMAN, JORJA: [b] 02/05/97 Marlborough; [home] Marlborough, Wilts; [p] Wayne & Tracey; [brothers] Cameron & Harry; [sisters] Roxann & Kacey; [school] St Peter's Junior; [fav sub] English; [hobbies] Reading & playing Kerby;[pets] Cat (Cfer) & Dog (Peggy); [ambition] To be a Teacher;

NEWMAN, MADDIE: [b] 17/06/96 New Malden; [home] New Malden, Surrey; [p] Dorte & Vince; [brother] Luke; [school] Burlington Junior; [fav sub] English; [hobbies] Skating, Gymnastics & Flute; [pets] Hamster, Lizard & a Bird; [ambition] To be a Puppeteer:

NOKE, RHIANNON: [b] 01/11/93 Bath; [home] Westbury, Wiltshire; [p] Caroline & Martin; [brother] Tom; [school] Westbury Leigh; [fav sub] Art; [hobbies] Drawing & Reading; [pets] Dog (Jake) Cats (Ben & Otis); [ambition] To become a Vet;

NORTH, JOHANNA: [home] Hoddesdon, Herts; [p] Nicola; [brothers] Martyn (18) & Michael (12); [school] The Cranbourne School; [fav sub] History; [hobbies] Swimming, Trampolining & All Sports; [pets] Jack Russell (Sammy) Cat (Poppy); [ambitions] To become an RSPCA Inspector or a Bailiff!!

OATES, ALYSSA NADINE: [b] 18/12/97 Plymouth; [home] Buckfastleigh, Devon; [p] Louise & Paul; [sisters] Leah Justine Kelley; [school] Stowford Primary; [fav sub] Art; [hobbies] Watching TV & Playing Sport; [pets] Cat (Tessa); [ambition] To become an Athlete;

OLIVEIRA, DANIELA: [b] 03/12/94; [home] Cantunbela, Angola; [p] Madalena & Goncalves; [brothers] Dennis & Dario

Oliveira; [sisters] Shamim & Swalha Mohamed; [school] Abbotsbury Primary; [fav sub] English, Music & PE; [hobbies] Swimming, Rounders & Basketball; [ambition] To become a Doctor;

OLIVER, PAIGE: [b] 11/09/96 Shotley Bridge; [home] Stanley, Durham; [p] Raymond & Jayne; [brother] Shane; [school] Tanfield Lea Junior; [fav sub] Maths; [hobbies] Football; [pets] Fish & Hamster; [ambition] To play football on TV for England Girls Team;

ORR, LAURA ASTRYD: [b] 30/09/97 Worcester; [home] Worcester, Worcs; [p] Malcolm & Debra; [brother] John; [school] Whittington CE Primary; [fav sub] Art; [hobbies] Swimming, Horse Riding, Dancing & Singing; [pets] Hamster; [ambitions] To be a Pop Star or Model;

OTARU, TITI: [b]09/02/95; [home] London; [p] Carlene McEwan; [brother] Darren; [sisters] Francesca & Phillippa; [school] Montbelle Primary; [fav sub] P.E., ICT & Literacy; [hobbies] Reading & Sports; [pets] Cats; [ambitions] To become a Teacher or an Actress;

PANTON, BEN: [b] 09/08/93 Hull; [home] Patrington, East Yorkshire; [p] Nick & Lesley; [brother] Sam; [sister] Rosie; [school] St Annes Special School; [fav sub] Art & Drawing; [hobbies] Sport-Football, Swimming & Cycling; [pets] Pony (Smokey), Dog (Shifty); Cat (Tango);

PARKER, JAKE: [b] 26/03/98 West Coker; [home] Yeovil, Somerset; [p] Mel & Rob Heaton; [brother] Joe Heaton; [sister] Georgie Parker; [school] West Coker School; [fav sub] English & Art; [hobbies] Reading, Colouring & Computers; [pets] Cat (Titchy); [ambitions] To perform on stage and to join the RNLI;

PARTON, MADISON: [b] 21/05/96 Bury; [home] Radcliffe, Manchester; [p] Jayne & Craig; [brother] Benjamin; [school] St Andrew's C/E; [fav sub] Art; [hobbies] Swimming; [pets] Dog (Daisy); [ambition] To become a Vet;

PATEL, RAJESH: [b] 19/07/93 Crawley; [home] Copthorne, W. Sussex; [p] Anil & Anita; [sister] Aneesha; [school] Copthorne Prep; [fav sub] Maths, Science; [hobbies] Football, Tennis & PSP;

PATEL, REESHA: [b] 18/08/99 Kingston; [home[Kingston, Surrey; [p] Kamlesh & Darshana; [sister] Heenal; [school] Maple Infant; [fav sub] Art; [hobbies] Swimming; [pets] Fish; [ambition] To become a Teacher;

PATTON, VICTORIA RUTH: [b] 24/06/96 Hartlepool; [home] Peterlee,

Durham; [sister] Amanda Jane; [school] Howletch Primary; [fav sub] Art; [hobbies] Football, Swimming & Drama; [pets] Cat (Dixie); [ambitions] To be a Pop Star / Singer;

PAYNE, FINLAY: [b] 29/03 99 Norwich, Norfolk; [p] Gavin & Viktoria; [sister] Trinity; [school] Nightingale First; [fav sub] Maths; [hobbies] Motocross; [pets] Dog (Jonah), Cat (Domino);

PEARCE, TOM: [b] 24/05/97 Aylesbury; [home] Dolton, Devon; [p] Jill & Phillip; [sister] Amy; [school] Dolton Primary; [fav sub] Drawing; [hobbies] Drawing; [pets] Dogs (Heidi & Jessie); [ambition] To be a Cartoon Artist;

PEARD, KATIE: [b] 01/03/98 Ivybridge; [home] Ivybridge, Devon; [p] Julie & Gary; [brother] Ryan; [school] Stowford Primary; [fav sub] English; [hobbies] Horse Riding; [pets] Cat, Horse;

PEARSON, GEMMA: [b] 04/03/95 Watford; [home] Abbots Langley, Herts; [p] Karen & Steve; [brother] Sam; [sisters] Zoe & Claire; [school] Abbots Langley; [fav sub] P.E.; [hobbies] Playing Football, Netball & Reading; [pets] Dogs (Tank & Alfred), Cat (Fluffy); [ambition] To play for the England Ladies Football Team;

PELL, EMI: [b] 12/11/96 Epsom; [home] Weybridge, Surrey; [p] Debbie & Chris; [brother] Jamie + another baby on the way; [school] St Charles Borromeo; [fav sub] Writing poetry & Singing; [hobbies] Football, Rugby, Singing & Poetry; [pets] Rabbit (Lucky); [ambitions] To achieve in a poetry contest and a singing contest;

PERRY, SOPHIE: [b] 21/11/92 Portsmouth; [home] Worle, Somerset; [p] Shaun Perry & Sian Howells; [brothers] Michael & Marc; [school] Queen's College; [fav sub] Art; [hobbies] Art, Music, Sport & Travel; [pets] Hamster; [ambitions] To get good GCSE's and A level results;

PHILLIPS, HARRIET: [b] 16/08/91 Stafford; [home] Colton, Staffs; [p] Vicky & Guy; [brother] Tom; [school] Stafford Grammar; [fav sub] English; [hobbies] Singing & Shopping; [pets] Rabbit; [ambitions] To do well in my exams and go to University;

POWELL, LUCY: [b] 01/11/89 Eccleshall; [home] Eccleshall, Satffordshire; [p] Emma & Alan (Step Dad-Michael); [sister] Kate; [school] Stafford Grammar; [fav sub] English & German; [hobbies] Listening to music and watching football; [pets] 10 altogether including Cat (Ellie); [ambitions] To be a Journalist and to live with a family in Eccleshall- like my Mum does;

POWER, CONNIE ROSE: [b] 16/01/95

Watford; [home] Abbots Langely, Herts; [p] Emma Power & Mark Ash; [brothers] Tommy & Rooney Ash; [school] Abbots Langley JMI; [fav sub] Art; [hobbies] Dancing; [pets] Would love a Dog; [ambition] To be Famous;

PRICE, CHRISTOPHER: [b] 18/10/85 Trowbridge; [home] Melksham, Wiltshire; [p] Barry & Pat; [brother] Dean; [sister] Sheri-Anne; [school] Forest & Sandridge CE School; [fav sub] Maths; [hobbies] Football; [pets] Cat; [ambitions] To race Motor Bikes or be a Footballer;

RALPH, HANNAH: [b] 14/12/96 Farnborough, Hants; [home] Westbury, Wilts; [p] Brian & Clare; [brother] Thomas; [school] Westbury Leigh; [fav sub] Art; [hobbies] Swimming, Trampolining & First Aid Club; [pets] Cat (Gem) & 2 Guinea-Pigs; [ambition] To become a Primary School Teacher;

RALPH, SHAY: [b] 08/07/98 Hemel Hempstead; [home] St Albans, Herts; [p] Marion King & Derek Ralph; [brother] Callum; [sister] Ellie; [school] Cunningham Hill Junior; [fav sub] Art; [hobbies] Animals & Football; [pets] Hamster (Harry); [ambitions] To go on Safari and become either a Professional Footballer or a Vet;

RANDHAWA, SHANNON: [b] 10/10/96 Ealing; [home] Langley, Berkshire; [p] Jas & Suky; [brother[Arun (12); [school] Ryvers School; [fav sub] Science; [hobbies] Playing Tennis, Singing & Drawing; [ambitions] To go to University, do well, get a good job and make everyone proud;

RAVEENDRANATHAN, LAVANGAN: [b] 30/04/95 London; [home] Morden; [p] Mr & Mrs K Ravenndranathan; [brother] Preyangan; [school] Abbotsbury Primary; [fav sub] Maths; [hobbies] Reading books & playing games; [pets] Parrots & Fish; [ambition] To become a Doctor;

RAWLINGS, DANIEL: [b] 13/09/96 Oxford; [home] Grove, Oxon; [p] Hayley & Mark; [sister] Holly; [school] Millbrook School; [fav sub] Maths & Sports; [hobbies] Football-Man Utd; [ambition] To play professional Football;

REVILL, LEWIS: [b] 15/01/95 Chesterfield; [home] Brimington, Derbyshire; [p] Lisa & Kev; [brothers[Dominic & Oliver; [school] Brimington Junior; [fav sub] P.E.; [hobbies] Animals; [pets] Hamsters, Chickens, Cockrel, Dog, Hedgehog, Gerbils & Fish; [ambition] To help at the RSPCA;

REVILL, OLIVER: [b] 31/12/97 Chesterfield; [home] Brimington, Derbyshire; [p] Lisa & Kev; [brothers]

Dominic & Lewis; [school] Brimington Junior; [fav sub] I.T.C; [hobbies] Computers & playing games; [pets] Hamsters, Chickens, Cockrel, Dog, Hedgehog, Gerbils & Fish; [ambition] To be Prime Minister of England;

REYNOLDS, ELLIE BETHAN: [b] 09/10/98 Bury; [home] Prestwich, Manchester; [p] Catherine & Kieron; [sisters] Mica & Faye; [school] St Margaret's C.E; [fav sub] History; [hobbies] Swimming & Jujitsu; [ambitions] To become a History Teacher or a Singer;

RICHARDSON, JAMES: [b] 15/07/98 Plymouth, [home] Lee Moor, Devon; [p] Kurt & Sarah; [brother] Luke; [sister] Laura; [school] Stowford Primary; [fav sub] Art; [hobbies] Football, Cricket & Running; [pets] Dog (Mopsy), Rabbit (Zoe), Chickens (Lightbulb & Archie Two); [ambition] To become a professional Footballer;

RICHARDSON, MEGAN: [b] 02/06/95 Watford; [home] Hurworth, Co. Durham; [p] Elaine & Steve; [brother] Jake; [sister] Bethany; [school] At time of writing Abbots Langley, now Hurworth Comp.; [fav sub] PE, Design & Technology, ICT; [hobbies] Horse Riding, Running & Swimming; [ambitions] To go to University and become a famous horse rider;

RICHARDSON, NATHAN A.J.: [b] 06/12/95 Roehampton, London; [p] Michele Richardson & Michael Judson; [sister] Natasha; [school] Robin Hood Primary; [fav sub] Science, Sport & Design & Technology; [hobbies] Swimming, Martial Arts, Cycling; [pets] Snakes (Bonsai Tree & Cactus); [ambitions] To go to China, do deep sea diving looking for Sharks & be Famous;

RING, GEORGIA NEA: [b] 25/03/97 Bury St Edmunds; [home] Bury St Edmunds, Suffolk; [p] James & Paula; [sister] Jessica; [school] Hardwick Primary; [fav sub] Art; [hobbies] Brownies & Wednesday Gang; [pets] Hamsters (Holly, Polly & Molly), Cat (Fizzs); [ambitions] To be rich and to work in a Beauty Shop;

RING, SAMANTHA: [b] 17/02/97 Trowbridge; [home] Westbury, Wilts; [p] Allan & Tracy; [brothers] Paul & Tony; [sister] Lisa; [school] Westbury Leigh C of E; [fav sub] Maths & Art; [hobbies] Karate & Clarinet; [pets] Dog (Spuddy), Rabbit (Snowy); [ambition] To be a Karate Teacher;

RIPPON, MEGAN: [b] 03/05/94 Oxford; [home] Ickford, Bucks; [p] Matt & Valerie; [brothers] Tom & Olly;

[school] Lord Williams's; [fav sub] P.E.; [hobbies] Horse Riding & Swimming; [pets] 2 Dogs, 2 Cats, 1 Pony & 9 Chickens; [ambition] To be a Horse Rider;

RIST, KATE: [b] 15/02/95 Winchester; [home] St Mary Bourne, Hampshire; [p] Christopher & Jane; [sisters] Cassie & Eliza; [school] St Mary Bourne Primary; [fav sub] English; [hobbies] Swimming, Reading & Painting Pottery; [pets] Cat (Belky) & Rabbit (Cookie); [ambitions] To design pottery pictures or be a Writer;

ROBERTS, CHARLOTTE LUCY: [b] 04/07/97 Chesterfield; [home] Brimington, Derbyshire; [p] Darren & Melanie; [sister] Victoria Kate; [school] Brimington Junior; [fav sub] Art; [hobbies] Karate & Dancing; [pets] Labrador & Snake; [ambitions] To become an Actress or a Dancer;

ROBERTS, OLLIE: [b] 14/08/94; [home] Haddenham, Bucks; [p] Darryl & Steve; [brother] Matthew; [sister] Amy; [school] Lord Williams's; [fav sub] Science; [hobbies] Computer Games, Reading & Warhammer 40,000; [pets] Rabbit, 3 Fish, Hamster; [ambitions] To design computer games, or be an Author or an Advertising Executive;

ROBERTS, WILLIAM: [b] 14/01/96 Canterbury; [home] Lyminge, Kent; [p] Sara & Charles; [brothers] Henry & James; [school] Northbourne Park; [fav sub] English; [hobbies] Cricket; [pets] Dog (Moppy); [ambitions] To be a Lawyer or an Author;

ROBERTS-POPHAM, RICHARD: [b] 16/05/97 Huddersfield; [home] Huddersfield, West Yorkshire; [p] John & Portia; [sisters] Naomi & Rachael; [school] St Patrick's; [fav sub] Science; [hobbies] Football & Reading; [pets] Cats (Boris & Harry); [ambition] To become a professional Footballer;

ROBERTSON-STEEL, CHLOE EMMA FREYA: [b] 27/09/96 Shrewsbury; [home] Telford, Shropshire; [p] Iain & Lesley; [brother] Douglas; [sisters] Fiona & Hannah; [school] St Dominic's; [fav sub] Science; [hobbies] Riding, Sailing, Music & Painting; [pets] Dog; [ambitions] To be a Doctor, to travel and to fly in a balloon;

ROBERTSON-STEEL, HANNAH LOUISE: [b] 07/10/94 Shrewsbury; [home] Telford, Shropshire; [p] Iain & Lesley; [brother] Douglas; [sisters] Fiona & Chloe; [school] St Dominic's; [fav sub] Science; [hobbies] Kayaking, Sailing & Music; [pets] Dog; [ambitions] To be a Teacher & gain a Science Degree;

ROND-ALLISTON, SACHA: [b]

08/04/94 Little Milton; [home] Little Milton, Oxon; [p] Laurelle & Richard; [sisters] Natasha & Melinda; [school] Lord Williams's; [fav sub] Music; [hobbies] Lord of the Rings & Warhammer; [pets] Old English Sheepdog & Degu; [ambitions] To be a Doctor, or Scientist, or Cosmologist, or Geologist;

ROSEBLADE, MATTHEW: [b] 16/10/90 Walsall; [home] Walsall, W. Mids; [p] Alison & Lee; [brothers] Macaulee & Levi; [sister] Keilee; [school] Joseph Leckie C.T.C.; [fav sub] Music; [hobbies] Playing Guitar; [pets] Rottweiller; [ambition] To become a Music Teacher;

ROYAL, KELSEY: [b] 06/06/97 Sidcup; [home] New Eltham, London; [p] Kelly & Mark; [brothers] Lewis & Oliver; [sister] Olivia; [school] Montbelle Primary; [fav sub] English-writing poems and stories; [hobbies] Collecting Pocket Dragons; [pets] Dog, Bichion Frisè (Pippin); [ambition] To be an ICT Teacher like my Mum;

RUANE, CONOR PATRICK: [b] 06/11/96 Huddersfield; [home] Oakes, West Yorkshire; [p] Michael & Sandra; [sister] Niamh Mairead; [school] St Patrick's R.C.; [fav sub] English & History; [hobbies] Story writing & Football; [pets] Cats (Lucy, Penny & Lilley); [ambition] To be a published Author;

RUDDOCK, LINDSAY: [b] 13/01/96 Hartlepool; [home] Peterlee, Durham; [p] Muriel & Ernie; [brother] Carl; [school] Howletch Primary; [fav sub] Music; [hobbies] Gymnastics; [pets] Budgie; [ambition] To be a Gymnastics Teacher;

RUTTER, PATRICK GERARD: [b] 30/01/95 Coventry; [home] Coventry, W. Midlands; [p] Marie & Gerry; [school] Abbotsford; [fav sub] I.T.; [hobbies] Reading, Football & Computer Games; [pets] Cats (Miggy & Marmy); [ambition] To become an Actor;

SAANTHAKUMAR, SHANKAR: [b] 08/12/93 Greenwich; [home] Tolworth, Surrey; [p] Mr & Mrs Saanthakumar; [school] Tiffin Boys; [fav sub] D.T.; [hobbies] Swimming, Violin & Electric Guitar; [pets] Rabbit (Winchy); [ambition] To work for Microsoft or Apple;

SAEED, NAZISH: [b] 27/07/96 Manchester; [home[Stockport, Grt Manchester; [p] Naveed & Saimah; [brother] Zain; [school] Stockport Grammar Junior; [fav sub] English; [hobbies] Reading & Swimming; [ambition] To become a Doctor;

SANDERS, JO: [b] 17/12/93 Aylesbury; [home] Cuddington, Bucks; [p] Jill & Dave; [brother] Ben; [sister] Lauren; [school] Lord Williams's; [fav sub] P.E.; [hobbies] Horse Riding; [pets] Dog & Rabbit; [ambition] To be a Show Jumper;

SANDIFORD, JACK: [b] 08/09/94 Redhill; [home] Nutfield, Surrey; [p] Jane & Kent; [sister] Sarah; [school] Nutfield Church C of E Primary; [fav sub] Art; [hobbies] Reading; [pets] Dog (Billy); [ambitions] To become a Graphic Designer or an Artist;

SANDHU, SIMRAN: [b] 21/03/94 Leicester; [home] Leicester, Leics; [p] Ravinder & Kashmir; [brother] Gubi; [sisters] Davina & Harmeew; [school] Leicester High School for Girls; [fav sub] Drama; [hobbies] Taikwondo, Gymnastics & Writing; [pets] Used to have 2 Guinea-Pigs; [ambition] To be Sir Alan Sugar's future Apprentice;

SANSOM, DANIEL: [b] 18/02/98 Ivybridge; [home] Ivybridge, Devon; [p] Adrian & Carolyn; [brother] Thomas; [school] Stowford Primary; [fav sub] Literacy; [hobbies] Football, Reading & Cubs; [pets] Fish (Oliver, Fagin, & The Artful Dodger) & Cat (Sam); [ambitions] To be a Fireman like my Dad or a Footballer;

SARGESON, DANIEL: [b] 10/01/97 Plymouth; [home] Ivybridge, Devon; [school] Stowford Primary; [fav sub] P.E.; [hobbies] Tennis; [pets] Dog (Alfie & Cats (Micky & Lester);

SARSON, ROBERTA: [b] 05/03/95 Crewe; [home] St Mary Bourne, Hampshire; [p] Lesley & Ian; [sister] Eleanor; [school] St Mary Bourne Primary; [fav sub] P.E.; [hobbies] Gymnastics & Trampolining; [pets] Cat (Mowzer); [ambition] To become a Fashion Designer;

SAUNDERS, CHARLIE: [b] 29/01/96 Oxford; [home] Higher Poynton, Cheshire; [p] Jocelyn & Mark; [sister] Abigail; [school] Stockport Grammar Junior; [fav sub] Science; [hobbies] Football; [pets] Dog & 3 Cats; [ambition] To be a Surgeon who flies in a helicopter to accidents;

SAVERY, GINA: [b] 21/09/98 Cottingham; [home] Beverley, E. Yorks; [p] Catherine & John; [brothers] Luke & Jay; [sister] Lucy; [school] Molescroft Primary; [fav sub] Maths; [hobbies] Ballet & Football; [ambitions] To be a Pop Star/Singer;

SCOTT, CARTER: [b] 25/02/97 London; [home] Eltham, London; [p] Peter & Wendy; [brothers] Riley & Tyler; [school] Montbelle Primary; [fav sub] Playtime; [hobbies] Music & PSP;

[ambitions] To be a Rap Artist & Wrestler;

SCOTT, SAMANTHA JEAN: [b] 31/05/97 Bradford, West Yorkshire; [p] Trevor & Lynne, [school] Newhall Park Primary; [fav sub] Art & DT; [hobbies] Drawing & Painting; [pets] Rabbit; [ambition] To become an Artist;

SEABROOK, HARRIET: [b] 12/11/98 Kingston; [home] Surbiton, Surrey; [p] Debbie & Mark; [brother] Joe; [sister] Alice; [school] Maple Infants; [fav sub] Maths; [hobbies] Dancing; [pets] 2 Cats, 3 Fish, 1 Tortoise; [ambition] To become a Make Up Artist;

SHAH, KARAN: [b] 01/02/96 Chertsey; [home] New Malden, Surrey; [p] Harish (Dad) & Sonal (Mum); [sister] Bhagyashree; [school] Burlington Junior; [fav sub] Maths; [hobbies] Riding Bike; [ambition] To invent a car that flies:

SHEFIK, TALIA: [b] 24/12/99 Sidcup; [home] Eltham, London; [p] Jaime & Charla; [brother] Rashid; [school] Montbelle Primary; [fav sub] Writing; [hobbies] Swimming; [ambition] To be an Accountant;

SHERBERSKY, MAIA: [b] 29/06/99 Exeter; [home] Hennock, Devon; [p] Hannah & Simon; [brother] Leo; [school] Hennock County Primary; [fav sub] Literacy; [hobbies] Reading, Playing & Ballet; [pets] Mr Small; [ambitions] To be a Ballerina, an Explorer or a Teacher;

SHERRIN, GEORGE: [b] 01/05/97 Farnborough; [home] Orpington, Kent; [p] Julia & Dean; [brother] Jack; [school] Montbelle Primary; [fav sub] P.E.; [hobbies] Football; [pets] Hamster (Bow); [ambition] To be the next Ronaldinho;

SHERRIN, JACK: [b] 05/06/95 Farnborough; [home] Orpington, Kent; [p] Julia & Dean; [brother] George; [school] Montbelle Primary; [fav sub] P.E.; [hobbies] Football, Cricket etc.; [pets] Hamster (Hagrid); [ambition] To be a good builder;

SHINER, SOPHIE VICTORIA: [b] Nunsthorpe, Grimsby; [home] Goole, E. Yorks; [p] Angela Cole & Terry Shiner; [brother] David; [sister] Rebekah; [school] Kingsway Primary; [fav sub] Art; [hobbies] Amateur Dramatics; [pets] Cat; [ambition] To design clothes for a famous person;

SINGH, SUKHI: [b] 03/06/98; [home] Sheffield, S. Yorkshire; [p] Rebecca Mountain & Ranjit Singh; [brother] Moses (Tay); [sister] Maisie (Tay), Twins to be born; [school] Carterknowle; [fav sub] Literacy; [hobbies] Reading & Writing; [pets] Hamster (Goldie); [ambitions] To be a Writer/Poet;

SLINEY, NICOLE: [b] [home] Grove, Oxfordshire; [p] Michelle & Mark;

[brother] Lewis; [school] Millbrook; [fav sub] Maths; [hobbies] Reading & Swimming; [pets] Gerbil (Starsky);

SMITH, CHARLOTTE: [b] 01/05/95 Bury; [home] Radcliffe, Manchester; [p] Gill & Barry; [sister] Rebekah; [school] St Andrew's C of E; [fav sub] P.E.; [hobbies] Hockey, Football & Swimming; [ambition] To play Hockey for England as Goalkeeper;

SMITH, CHLOE: [b] 08/09/98 Bomin, London; [home] North Weald, Essex; [p] Kay & Chris; [brother] Andrew; [school] St Andrew's Primary; [fav sub] History & Art; [hobbies] Singing & Dancing; [ambitions] To be a Model or an Artist;

SMITH, EMMA: [b] 06/12/94 Chesterfield; [home] Chesterfield, Derbyshire; [p] Sally-Ann & Richard; [brother] Daniel; [sister] Rachel; [school] Brimington Junior; [fav sub] Art; [hobbies] Netball, Rounders, Water Polo & Dancing; [pets] Goldfish; [ambition] To become a Fashion Designer;

SMITH, HANNAH: [b] 03/07/98; [home] North Weald, Essex; [p] Laurence & Elizabeth; [brother] Joseph; [sister] Rebecca; [school] St Andrew's Primary; [fav sub] History; [hobbies] Gymnastics; [pets] Cats (Phoebe & Scatty); [ambitions] To be a famous Horse Rider or Gymnast;

SMITH, JAMIE: [b] 21/05/95 Basingstoke; [home] St Mary Bourne, Hants; [p] Maggie; [school] St Mary Bourne Primary; [fav sub] Science; [hobbies] Football & Guitar; [pets] Dog (Lilly), Cat (Zippy); [ambitions] To be a Footballer or Musician;

SMITH, PHILIP: [b] 25/11/92 Fareham; [home] Fareham, Hampshire; [p] Adrian & Jane; [sisters] Francesca & Ilona; [school] Henry Cort Community College; [fav sub] Science; [hobbies] Hockey, Karate, Computer Games & Books; [pets] Dogs (Grommit & Pippin);

SMITH, RACHEL: [b] 11/01/98 Chesterfield; [home] Chesterfield, Derbyshire; [p] Sally-Ann & Richard; [brother] Daniel; [sister] Emma; [school] Brimington Junior; [fav sub] Art; [hobbies] Dancing, Bench Ball & Brownies; [pets] Goldfish; [ambition] To be a Nursery Teacher and to buy a Villa in Spain;

SPILLER, NATASHA L.: [b] 27/10/91 Fareham; [home] Titchfield, Hampshire; [p] Keith & Terri; [brother] Christopher K; [school] Henry Cort Community College; [fav sub] English; [hobbies] Karate, Reading, Cooking, Playing Video Games; [pets] Golden Retriever (Jasmine), Black Labrador (Bess); [ambition] To be a Forensic Scientist;

STELLING, PHOEBE: [b] 15/01/00 Sidcup; [home] New Eltham; [p] Joanne

251

& Leslie; [brother] Elliot; [school] Montbelle Primary; [fav sub] Maths & English; [hobbies] Dancing, Gymnastics, Drawing & Reading; [pets] Boxer (Smudge); [ambitions] To be a Vet, Dancer or Ballet Teacher;

STEVENS,NATHAN: [b] 11/07/98 Basildon; [home] Danbury, Essex; [p] Dean & Karen; [sister] Robyn; [school] Danbury Park; [fav sub] History & Art; [hobbies] Football & Pokemon; [pets] Dog (Scooby Doo); [ambitions] To be a Firefighter or a Footballer;

STEVENS, RACHEL: [home] Peterlee, Durham; [school] Howletch Lane Primary; [fav sub] Art; [hobbies] Clarinet, Guitar & Netball; [pets] Mog the Cat;

STEVENSON, JACK: [b] 28/07/95 Nottingham; [home] Worcester, Worcs; [p] John & Debbie; [brother] Ben; [school] St Barnabas C.E. Primary; [fav sub] Geography; [hobbies] Football; [pets] Guinea-Pigs; [ambition] To become a Journalist;

STOCK, AMY: [b] 27/11/96 Hoddesdon; [home] Hoddesdon, Herts; [p] Sue & Jeff; [brothers] Richard & Jonathan; [school] The Cranbourne School; [fav sub] English; [hobbies] Writing, Art & Singing; [ambitions] To be a Writer or Singer;

STRAIN, DANIEL: [b] 05/09/96 Oxford; [home] Grove, Oxon; [p] Tracy & Arthur; [sister] Lisa; [school] Millbrook; [fav sub] Geography; [hobbies] Collecting Teddies; [pets] Dog (Diesel); [ambition] To work and care for animals;

STUDDERT-KENNEDY, MEGAN: [b] 17/06/98 London; [home] Marlborough, Wiltshire; [p] Anne & Andrew; [brother] Jamie; [sisters] Phoebe & Alice (my twin); [school] St Peter's Junior; [fav sub] ICT; [hobbies] Art & Craft, Writing stories, Riding my bike; [pets] Hamster; [ambitions] To be a Writer and to own a Chocolate Factory;

STUPPLE, TOBY: [b] 24/09/96 Bath; [home] Witham Friary, Somerset; [p] Joy & Colin; [brother] Kevin; [sisters] Kelly, Roxanne & Megan; [school] Upton Noble; [fav sub] Maths; [hobbies] Football & Playstation; [pets] Tropical Fish; [ambition] To be a Premiership Footballer;

STURGES, MOLLIE LOUISE: [b] 21/01/96 Hemel Hempstead; [home] Hemel Hempstead, Herts; [p] Maria & Jason; [brothers] Shaun & Jack; [school] Aycliffe Drive Primary; [fav sub] English; [hobbies] Dancing, Reading, Football; [pets] Lakeland Terrier (Dylan); [ambition] To be a famous Writer;

STURMAN, GRACE: [b] 03/07/99 Norwich; [home] Taverham, Norfolk; [p] Louise & Chriss; [brother] Julian; [sisters]

Harriett, Tazmynn, Sophie & Kira; [school] Nightingale First; [fav sub] Maths; [hobbies] Baton Twirling; [pets] Cats (Oscar & Twinkle); [ambition] To be a Hairdresser;

SUTHERLAND, KIRSTEN: [b] 04/02/96 Canterbury; [home] Sandwich; [p] Simon & Fiona; [school] Northbourne Park; [fav sub] Drama; [hobbies] Reading & Running; [pets] Cat (Louis); [ambitions] To be an Actress or Author;

SWINNERTON, LOIS: [b] 20/07/92 Stafford; [home] Adbaston, Staffs; [p] Ken & Bridget; [brother] Lee; [school] Stafford Grammar; [fav sub] English, Drama & P.E.; [hobbies] Horse Riding & Hockey; [pets] Horse (Cookie) & Dog (Alfie); [ambition] Not sure at present;

SYMES, JOSHUA: [b] 14/03/97 Trowbridge; [home] Dilton Marsh, Wiltshire; [p] Mark & Tania; [sisters] Zoe & Alexis; [school] Westbury Leigh Primary; [fav sub] P.E.; [hobbies] Football; [pets] Gypsy & Purdie; [ambition] To play football for England;

TAJAMMAL, SYEDA ZOYA: [b] 7/10/96 Pakistan; [home] Mitcham, Surrey; [p] Syed Abrar Tajammal & Ghazal Abrar; [brothers] Arfin Ahmad & Anwar Ahmad; [sister] Syeda Afir; [fav sub] Art, Story Writing, Relogous Education; [hobbies] Swimming, Wali-Ball & Skipping; [pets] Birds; [ambition] To be a Teacher and a good human being;

TAYLOR, JAMES: [b] 05/04/95 London; [home] Morden, Surrey; [p] Sara & Bill; [sister] Holly; [school] Abbotsbury Primary; [fav sub] Maths; [hobbies] Football; [pets] 2 Cats; [ambition] To be rich;

TEATHER, BILLY: [b] 13/05/99 Harlow; [home] Epping, Essex; [p] Debbie & Stacy; [sister] Codie; [school] St Andrew's; [fav sub] Maths; [hobbies] Football & Swimming; [pets] Dogs, Guinea-Pigs, Chickens, Ducks & Budgies; [ambitons] To be a Fireman or a Policeman;

TELLETSON, LUCY: [b] 11/07/96; [home] Bradford, West Yorkshire; [p] Dawn & Ian Mathers; [brother] Lewis; [school] Low Ash Primary; [hobbies] Running & Football; [pets] Dogs; [ambitions] To be a famous runner or woman footballer;

THEWLIS, DOMINIC: [b] 27/06/97 Huddersfield; [home] Huddersfield, West Yorkshire; [p] Brian & Therasa; [brothers] Jonathan & Luke; [school] St Patrick's Primary; [fav sub] Art & Numeracy; [hobbies] Reading, Football & Rugby; [pets] Dog (Mollie), Cats (Tom & Tabby);

THIBAULT, LION: [b] 30/11/94 Paris; [home] Coventry, Warwickshire; [p] Isabelle & Oliver; [brothers] Clement,

Hadrien & Gauthier; [school] Abbotsford; [fav sub] Sport & Music; [hobbies] Nature & Animals; [pets] Cat & Fish; [ambition] To protect Wildlife;

THOMPSON, REMY D.A.: [b] 03/12/93 Princeton, NJ USA; [home] Canterbury, Kent; [p] Dan Thompson & Susan Griffin; [sister] Leah; [school] Northbourne Park; [fav sub] Reading; [pets] Cat (Skye); [ambition] To become an Actor;

THORNE, ALEXANDRA: [b] 10/04/95 Hull; [home] Beverley, East Yorkshire; [p] Justin & Sarah; [brother] Sophie; [school] Molescroft Primary; [fav sub] Maths; [hobbies] Art, Playing Guitar; [pets] Dog (Rosie); [ambition] To become a Cartoon Animator;

THURSTON, ALEX: [b] 01/06/98; [home] Beverley, East Yorkshire; [p] Dawn & Anthony; [brother] Jack; [school] Molescroft Primary; [fav sub] Numeracy; [hobbies] Football & Karate; [pets] Cats (Buster & Tyson); [ambitions] To be a Footballer, Pop Star or Teacher;

TIDMAN, NATHAN: [b] 10/08/95 London; [home] Morden, Surrey; [p] Kevin & Caroline; [sister] Maia; [school] Abbotsbury Primary; [fav sub] Science; [hobbies] Football, Rounders & Cooking; [ambitions] To be a Footballer and a Chef;

TIPPER, HELENA: [b] 03/03/95 Hillingdon; [home] Wokingham, Berkshire; [p] Jane & Jonothan; [brothers] Jamie & Christopher; [school] Westende Jnr (formerly Abbots Langley); [fav sub] Maths; [hobbies] Art, Scouts, Football, Playing Orchestral Percussion & Trumpet; [pets] Cat (Ollie); [ambitions] To be a Computer Animator or to join the Transport Police;

TRIGWELL, CHLOE: [b] 11/03/98 Salisbury; [home] Salisbury, Wilts; [p] Jo & Wes; [brother] Ethan; [sisters] Lucy & Ellie; [school] Sarum St Pauls; [fav sub] Literacy; [hobbies] Squash & Tennis; [pets] Mac, Bernie, Poppy, Cheeky, Annie; [ambitions] To be a Writer and Singer;

TRINDER, JACK: [b] 25/06/97 Oxford; [home] Grove, Oxfordshire; [p] Nick & Sally; [brothers] Harry & Alfie; [school] Millbrook Primary; [fav sub] Literacy; [hobbies] Football; [ambition] To be a Footballer;

TURNER, GEORGE S.K.: [b] 04/03/98 Bury St Edmunds; [home] Thurston, Suffolk; [p] Lily & Adrian; [sister] Olivia; [school] Thurston Primary; [fav sub] Science; [hobbies] Golf, Swimming & Building Lego Bioicles; [ambition] To be a Scientist;

TURNER, KYLE: [b] 16/12/06 Ivybridge; [p] Jenny; [brother] Nate; [school] Stowford Primary; [fav sub] Games; [hobbies] Stagecoach; [pets] Dog;

TYLER, SAMUEL: [b] 02/09/97

Edinburgh; [home] Stanstead Abbots, Herts; [p] Alison & Ian; [sister] Abigail; [school] The Cranbourne Primary; [fav sub] Literacy & P.E.; [hobbies] Cricket & Computer Games; [ambitions] To be a Writer or a Banker!;

VINCENT, STACEY: [b]01/02/95 Salisbury; [home] Salisbury, Wilts; [p] Carolyn & Paul; [sister] Phoebe; [school] Sarum St Pauls; [fav sub] Maths; [hobbies] Sport & Music; [pets] Budgie & Rabbit; [ambition] To be an Actress;

WAIN-WILLIAMS, HARVEY: [b] 09/06/94 Wolverhampton; [home] Penkridge, Stafford; [p] Paul & Carol; [sisters] Holly & Georgina; [school] Stafford Grammar; [fav sub] Art & English; [hobbies] Horse Riding, Music & Poetry; [pets] Cat (Alley) & Rabbit (Snowy); [ambitions] To be a Poet, or write childrens stories;

WAINWRIGHT, ALYESHA: [b] 27/03/95 Chesterfield; [home] Brimington, Derbyshire; [p] Richard & Angela; [brother] Daniel; [school] Brimington Junior; [fav sub] Physical Education; [hobbies] Horse Riding & Netball; [pets] 2 Cats, 2 Dogs, 1 Pony; [ambition] To be a professional Showjumper;

WALKER, JORDAN: [b] 04/02/97 Norfolk; [home] Eltham, London; [p] Joanne & Paul; [sister] Danielle; [school] Montbelle Primary; [fav sub] Maths; [hobbies] Football; [pets] Fish; [ambition] To be a professional Footballer;

WALLACE, THOMAS: [b] 09/09/93; [home] Hersham, Surrey; [p] John Wallace & Eileen Woodward; [school] Tiffin; [fav sub] English & Drama; [hobbies] Magic, Writing & Painting; [ambitions] To be a famous Writer & Magician;

WALTER, JASMIN: [b] 12/03/97 Bath; [home] Westbury Leigh, Wiltshire; [p] Colin & Charmaine; [sister] Alysha; [school] Westbury Leigh C of E Primary; [fav sub] Art; [hobbies] Swimming, Karate & Bike Riding; [pets] Fish; [ambitions] To be a Police Officer, Nurse, Lifeguard or Fire Person;

WARBURTON, XAVIER: [b] Cheshire; [p] JM & Julie; [sisters] Pia & Tao; [school] Stockport Grammar; [fav sub] Science; [hobbies] Go Karting & Boating; [pets] Dog (Harvey); [ambitions] To do well and try hard;

WARD, MATTHEW: [b] 21/01/95 Preston; [home] Huddersfield, Yorkshire; [p] Tom & Irene; [school] St Patrick's; [fav sub] P.E.; [hobbies] Sport, Modelling & Music; [pets] Fish; [ambitions] To be opening batsman for Yorkshire and England+ British No 1 for Tennis;

WATERS, MATTHEW: [b] 04/07/98 Hemel Hemstead; [home] St Albans, Herts; [p] Trisha; [school] Cunningham Hill Juniors; [fav sub] Literacy; [hobbies] Pokemon & Swimming; [pets] Cat (Tiddles); [ambition] To be a Policeman;

WATSON, JACK: [b] 07/11/98 Norwich; [home] Taverham, Norfolk; [p] Carolyn & David; [sister] Bryony-May; [school] Nightingale First; [fav sub] Painting & Drawing; [hobbies] Playing on

Trampoline; [ambition] Not sure yet;

WEBB, EMILY-JANE: [school] Westbury Leigh CE Primary; [fav sub] Art & Drawing; [hobbies] Drawing; [pets] 4 Cats; [ambition] To be a Singer;

WEBSDALE, REBECCA: [b]19/01/99 Cottingham; [home] Walkington, Yorkshire; [p] Joanne & Anthony; [sister] Georgina; [school] Molescroft Primary; [fav sub] PE; [hobbies] Swimming; [pets] Dog (Ben); [ambitions] To be an Artist or Teacher;

WELLSBURY, IMOGEN: [b] 21/10/94 Shrewsbury; [home] Wightwick, W. Midlands; [p] Mr E James & Jane Wellsbury; [brothers] Rupert & Miles; [school] St Dominic's; [fav sub] Drama; [hobbies] Singing, Drama, Dancing & Horse Riding; [pets] Dog (Zara), Cat (Edward); [ambitions] To be on stage all the time as a Singer!;

WENHAM, NICOLE: [b] 10/11/95 Bradford; [home] Wrose, West Yorks; [p] Tony & Lorna; [brother] Theo; [school] Low Ash Primary; [fav sub] I.C.T. & P.E.; [hobbies] Dancing, Cheer Leading & Swimming; [pets] Fish; [ambition] To own a Beauty Salon;

WEST, HARVEY: [b] 30/09/99 Sidcup; [home] New Eltham, London; [p] Nicki & Mark; [brother] Mason; [sister] Chelsey; [school] Montbelle Primary; [fav sub] Maths; [hobbies] Sport & Maths; [ambition] To become a professional Footballer;

WESTON, NICOLE: [b] 28/04/95 Basingstoke; [home] Whitchurch, Hants; [p] Sue & Paul; [brother] Tyler; [sister] Alisha; [school] St Mary Bourne; [fav sub] Art; [hobbies] Poetry & Singing on Singstar; [pets] 2 Guinea-Pigs & 5 Cats; [ambitions] To be an Actress or a Singer;

WESTWOOD, CHARLOTTE: [b] 28/01/00; Tewkesbury; [home] Westbury, Wiltshire; [p] Ian Smith & Denise Westwood; [school] Westbury Leigh C of E; [fav sub] Art; [hobbies] Horse Riding; [pets] Rabbit; [ambitions] To become a Musician, Show Jumper, Vet or Actress;

WHATLEY, CATHERINE: [b] 15/06/96 Bramhall, Cheshire; [p] Sue & Greg; [sister] Rachel; [school] Stockport Grammar Junior; [fav sub] Art & DT; [hobbies] Cooking & Sports; [ambitions] To become a Chef and Artist;

WHEELER, LAURA: [b] 01/06/95 Watford; [home] Abbots Langley, Herts; [p] John & Rachel; [brother] Hayden; [school] Abbots Langley; [fav sub] P.E.; [hobbies] Netball, Swimming & Rollerblading;

WHEELER, NATHAN: [b] 03/09/94 Trowbridge; [home] Westbury, Wiltshire; [p] Robert & Phillippa; [brother] Thomas; [school] Westbury Leigh Primary; [fav sub] Science; [hobbies] Football & Swimming; [pets] Cat (Tigger); [ambition] To study Archaeology;

WHITE, BETHANY: [b] 30/09/91 Basingstoke; [home] North Waltham, Hampshire; [p] Roy & Elizabeth; [sisters] Clemency & Madeleine; [school] Brighton Hill Community College; [fav sub] History; [hobbies] Dance; [pets] Cat

& Guinea-Pig; [ambition] To travel;

WHITE, NICOLE PAIGE: [b] 17/09/96 Enfield; [home] Enfield; [p] Karen, Mick (Step dad) & Martin (Dad); [brothers] Bradley, Ashley & Ethan; [school] Capel Manor; [fav sub] Literacy; [hobbies] Judo & Football; [pets] Dog & Rabbit; [ambitions] To be a Singer and a Teacher;

WHITTLE, CURTIS: [b] 23/05/96 Sunderland; [home] Peterlee, Co. Durham; [p] Tony & Jean; [sisters] Ashleigh (11) & Kira (6); [school] Howletch Primary; [fav sub] Art; [hobbies] Football & Swimming; [pets] Poodles (Jack & Boot), Rabbit (Jingles); [ambitions] To be an Archaeologist and to play football for Sunderland;

WHYLEY, GREGORY: [b] 08/12/97 Beverley; [home] Beverley, East Yorkshire; [school] Molescroft Primary; [fav sub] History; [hobbies] Football; [pets] Black Labrador (Maddie); [ambitions] To be an Inventor or Footballer;

WICKS, HANNAH: [b] 27/08/00 Norwich; [home] Taverham, Norfolk; [p] Cate & Robert; [brother] Billy; [school] Nightingale First; [fav sub] Maths; [hobbies] Playing with my brother; [pets] Rabbit (Carrots); [ambitions] To be famous or a Princess;

WILLIAMS, COURTENEY: [b] 14/06/97 Shrewsbury; [home] Telford, Shropshire; [p] Wayne & Kie; [sister] Megan; [school] St Dominic's; [fav sub] Maths; [hobbies] Gymnastics & Trampolining; [pets] Giant Schnauzers (Summer & Moe); [ambition] To become a British Gymnast for the Olympics;

WILLIS, GEORGINA: [b] 18/05/93 Redhill; [home] Oxted, Surrey; [p] Lorraine & Keith; [sister] Sophie; [school] Hazelwood; [fav sub] Sport & Science; [hobbies] Sport, Art & Music; [pets] 2 Guinea-Pigs, 2 Rabbits & 1 Fish; [ambition] To travel and see the world;

WILLIS, MAX: [b] 29/07/94 Exmouth; [home] Exmouth, Devon; [p] Kathryn & Garon;[sister] Anna; [school] Exmouth Community College; [fav sub] Wood Technology; [hobbies] BMX'ing & Archery; [pets] Hamster (Nuffler); [ambition] To become a good BMX'er;

WILLS, DANIEL: [b] 31/01/92 Hillingdon; [home] Basingstoke, Hampshire; [p] Angela & Brian; [brother] Christopher; [sister] Kelly; [school] Brighton Hill CC; [fav sub] Drama; [hobbies] Golf; [pets] Dog & 2 Cats; [ambition] To be rich;

WILLS, VICKY: [b] 21/09/94 Bishop Auckland; [home] Coundon, Durham; [p] Sharon & Steven; [brother] Tyler Jay; [sister] Leah; [school] Coundon Primary; [fav sub] Art & Writing; [hobbies] Horse Riding & Running; [pets] Rabbit; [ambition] To be a Chef in a famous restaurant;;

WILSON, POPPY: [b] 22/07/98 London; [home] Beverley, E. Yorks; [p] Sara Wilson & Tom Baxter; [sister] Jessica; [school] Molescroft Primary; [fav sub] Literacy; [hobbies] Ballet; [pets] Dog, Hamster & Guinea Pig; [ambition] To be a Ballerina;

WINGROVE, LAURA: [b] 06/12/96 Sidcup; [home] New Eltham, London; [p] Julie & Martin; [brother] Adam; [school] Montbelle Primary; [fav sub] Maths; [hobbies] Tenpin Bowling & Karate; [pets] Dog (Holly) & Goldfish; [ambitions] To be a Teacher or a Nurse;

WITCHELL, JOSEPH: [b] 28/06/98 Chelmsford; [home] Danbury, Essex; [p] Mandy & Jon; [brother] Daniel; [school] Danbury Park Primary; [fav sub] Art; [hobbies] Simpsons Games; [pets] Dog (Charlie); [ambition] To be a Pilot with Easy Jet;

WOODLEY-EDMONSON, JACOB: [b] 27/03/97 Bradford; [home] Bradford, West Yorkshire; [p] Annmarie Woodley & Simon Edmonson; [school] New Hall Park Primary; [fav sub] Art; [hobbies] Climbing; [pets] Dogs; [ambition] To be a Rock Climber;

WORBY, JOSHUA: [b] 18/09/98 Harlow; [home] North Weald, Essex; [p] Annabelle & John; [sister] Megan; [school] St Andrews; [fav sub] Art & P.E.; [hobbies] Football; [pets] Rabbit (Jess); [ambition] To play football for Chelsea;

WORLEY, RACHAEL: [b] 30/09/97 Bury St Edmunds; [home] Thurston, Suffolk; [p] Robin & Lesley; [school] Thurston CEVC Primary; [fav sub] Science; [hobbies] Disco Dancing & Brownies; [pets] Rabbit & 2 Guinea-Pigs; [ambitions] To play Guitar and become a Hairdresser;

WORTON, LYDIA: [b] 19/01/98; [home] Corton, Suffolk; [school] Corton V.C. Primary; [fav sub] Art & History; [hobbies] Dancing & Crafts; [pets] Fish; [ambition] To become a Teacher;

WRIGHT, EVIE: [b] 29/08/97 King's Lynn; [home] Heacham, Norfolk; [p] Andrew & Tracey; [brother] Charlie; [school] Ingoldisthorpe Primary; [fav sub] Art; [hobbies] Tennis, Swimming & Football; [pets] Cat (Oscar) & Goldfish (Speedy); [ambition] To be a famous Tennis player;

YEOMANS, MILES BENJAMIN: [b] 29/01/98 Keighley; [home] Keighley, West Yorkshire; [p] Nicola & Mark; [school] Lees Primary; [hobbies] Swimming & Running; [pets] Cat (Mugli); [ambition] To be an Olympic Swimmer;

YOUNG, MATTHEW: [b] 16/01/98; [home] Ashburton, Devon; [school] Ilsington C of E Primary; [fav sub] Science; [hobbies] Cycling, Football & Rugby; [ambition] To be a Rally Driver;

INDEX
OF
POETS